CREATING THE BIG EASY

CREATING

THE BIG EASY

New Orleans and the Emergence of
Modern Tourism, 1918–1945

Anthony J. Stanonis

THE UNIVERSITY OF GEORGIA PRESS

Athens & London

Designed by Erin Kirk New
Set in Sabon by BookComp, Inc.
Printed and bound by Thomson-Shore

The paper in this book meets the guidelines for
permanence and durability of the Committee on
Production Guidelines for Book Longevity of the
Council on Library Resources.

Printed in the United States of America

10 09 08 07 06 C 5 4 3 2 1

10 09 08 07 06 P 5 4 3 2 1

Library of Congress Cataloging-in-Publication Data

Stanonis, Anthony J. (Anthony Joseph)
    Creating the Big Easy : New Orleans and the emergence
of modern tourism, 1918–1945 / Anthony J. Stanonis.
        p. cm.
    Includes bibliographical references and index.
    ISBN-13: 978-0-8203-2817-1 (cloth : alk. paper)
    ISBN-10: 0-8203-2817-0 (cloth : alk. paper)
    ISBN-13: 978-0-8203-2822-5 (pbk. : alk. paper)
    ISBN-10: 0-8203-2822-7 (pbk. : alk. paper)
    1. Tourism—Louisiana—New Orleans—History.
2. New Orleans (La.)—Description and travel.   I. Title.
G155.U6S645 2006
338.4'79176335—dc22

                                        2005029469

British Library Cataloging-in-Publication Data available

TO *David J. Stanonis*

CONTENTS

ACKNOWLEDGMENTS

In many ways, my family helped fulfill New Orleans businessmen's dreams—tourists who fell in love with the city so thoroughly that they moved there. Uncle David drove to New Orleans in the late 1940s and was charmed by the French Quarter, by the broad boulevards lined with stately homes, by the people. A decade later, he leapt at the chance to return to New Orleans—this time to accept a job as a chemist at a federal research facility. My paternal grandparents began to visit him, usually in the winter months to escape the Kentucky cold. They eventually decided to stay permanently in New Orleans, renting a second-floor apartment carved out of a house near the intersection of Canal Street and Jefferson Davis Boulevard. My parents followed in the 1970s. I was born in an old military hospital a few blocks from Audubon Park.

Although I was raised in the suburbs, I spent a lot of time visiting my grandparents, accumulating memories that have kept alive my passion to write about my hometown. As a child, I played in the shadow of the Jefferson Davis statue, a monument regularly defaced by spray paint—acts of protest against the racial regime represented by the former Confederate president. From the Canal Street neutral ground ("median" for those not familiar with the city), I stared at the distant skyscrapers downtown. Glowing red letters spelled *Marriott* near the top of the tallest building in view. Family drives carried me past Bayou St. John to the Fairgrounds—my grandfather loved "betting on the ponies," as we called it. From the upstairs window of my grandparents' apartment, I watched in excitement the passing Mardi Gras parades: Endymion, Mid-City, Pegasus, Carrollton, Truckers. I remember the chiropractor who rented an office on the first floor of the apartment building. "Doc" liked to wear women's footwear. He said the shoes were more comfortable and better for the feet. Years later, in my teen years, I saw him dressed in full drag on Mardi Gras. I also recall the day drops of dried blood appeared on the front porch. The previous night a wounded burglar had attempted to escape pursuing police officers by hiding in the shadows.

As I aged, I went to a Catholic elementary school, a Catholic high school, and a Catholic university. I realized two things in high school. First, my high school history teachers, particularly Brian Altobello and Tom Rice, instilled in me a deep curiosity about the past. I knew that I wanted to become a historian. Second, I began to recognize the powerful role of race—even more than religion—in shaping New Orleans culture. Religion courses were sparse on theology. Instead, the curriculum substituted messages about social justice, an odd emphasis in a school that could best be described as a segregation academy, a suburban institution founded during the heat of the school desegregation battle in the city proper. Little had changed by the time I attended high school in the early 1990s. Only 3 of the 214 students in my graduating class were black. My university experience finally exposed me to the diversity that is New Orleans, a place that has long defied neat categorizations that attempt to separate white from black.

Racial identity nevertheless remains a force in New Orleans and, as the pages ahead show, the tourism industry. One day, during my graduate studies at Vanderbilt University, fellow student Cheryl Hudson asked me to explain a peculiarity about New Orleanians. In New York, strangers will ask each other how much each pays in rent. In Los Angeles, strangers will ask each other about involvement in "the business," meaning Hollywood. But New Orleanians pose a very different question when they make an acquaintance. They'll ask, "What high school did you go to?" Cheryl wondered why residents of the Crescent City were so preoccupied with their secondary schools. I had never noticed that I too carried this cultural baggage. In many ways, high schools in metropolitan New Orleans continue to be markers of class and race. Legacies are important. In 2000, I drove with a colleague, Rob Lawson, to a conference in Charleston, South Carolina. One evening, we had dinner with another graduate student. She was a native New Orleanian. We talked about tourism, about the blues, and about race. She asserted that she was not "black." Everyone in her family was "Creole."

As I entered adulthood, I began to realize the impact of tourism on New Orleans. Relatives from Germany regularly visited my parents' house. I've done the "must-see" attractions so many times I've lost count: a cruise on the steamboat *Natchez*, a trip to Marie Laveau's tomb, a tour through St. Louis Cathedral, a jazz concert at Preservation Hall, a quick stop to order beignets at Café du Monde or Hurricanes in a souvenir glass from Pat O'Brien's. Everywhere on these jaunts I spotted tourists carrying a shopping bag in one hand and a cup of booze in the other. My journeys downtown during high school and college more often landed me in the company of transplants and vacationers than in the company of locals. Their images of the city were so different from my own encounters with New Orleans. Outsiders saw decadence and foreignness, but, to me, the "foreign" was commonplace. And the city's "decadence" didn't stand out—that is, until my first trip to a dry county in a state that faithfully kept blue laws. Here, in the relationship of New Orleans to the national culture, was a story to tell.

Although I did not know it at the time, I began this book my junior year at Loyola University. Students considered David Estes a tough English professor, but he taught such darn interesting classes that I decided to take a chance on a course entitled "New Orleans in Literature." The syllabus included a rather obscure William Faulkner novel, *Pylon*, which I chose to analyze for my term paper. The novel, set in the 1930s, addressed Mardi Gras, the French Quarter, new transportation systems, tourism, economics, and vice in the Crescent City. But as I began my research, I found little written about the social or cultural history of New Orleans during the interwar years. I followed my analysis of *Pylon* with an honors thesis written under the direction of history professor Mark Fernandez. The thesis studied the New Orleans encountered by Tennessee Williams during his visit in the late 1930s. Through these projects, my mentors taught me valuable lessons about the historian's craft and exposed me to the fertility of New Orleans as a possible dissertation topic. I thank David and Mark for encouraging me ever since. I also thank David Moore, Bernard Cook, and Mike Ross of the Loyola University History Department for always making me feel welcome.

No one contributed more directly to the completion of this project than Don Doyle. I could not have had a better adviser during my graduate studies at Vanderbilt University. Always available, amazingly prompt with feedback, and (thankfully) patient, he gave me the freedom to develop my argument. I continue to value his guidance and expertise.

I must also thank the other members of Vanderbilt's history department. David Carlton proved a valuable asset as I worked my way through the dissertation process. His keen ability to uncover weaknesses in my argument helped me avoid a number of mistakes. The other members of the dissertation committee, including Thadious Davis, Dennis Dickerson, and Jim Epstein, broadened my perspective and encouraged me to continue working on the project. Equally valuable were the comments of Helmut Smith and Michael Kreyling. Thanks as well to Joyce Chaplin, Paul Conkin, Sam McSeveney, Rowena Olegario, and Don Winters for making my graduate school experience enjoyable.

The graduate students I befriended in Nashville not only contributed to my understanding of New Orleans and urban society but provided the camaraderie that kept me from becoming a hermit hidden away in the library. I thank Carole Bucy, Mike Crane, Tycho deBoer, Chris Everett, Ed Harcourt, Cheryl Hudson, David Karr, Rob Lawson, Steve McNutt, Josh Roberts, Emily Story, and Jim Terrell. I owe each of you a beer. And, of course, without the late Jim Lengel, my time in Nashville would not have been nearly as much fun.

I offer general thanks to the history department at Vanderbilt University. Without the department's financial support, I could never have written this book. A pair of Blanche and Henry Weaver Fellowships allowed me to devote two entire summers to research. A 2002–3 J. León Helguera Fellowship gave me the time to complete the first draft.

Over the past several years, I have had the pleasure of sharing ideas and chapters with a number of scholars, many of whom helped refine my argument and save me from some errors. First and foremost, I thank Fitz Brundage and Ted Ownby for their comments. Despite their busy schedules, they took the time to slog through an early—and very rough—draft. I have also benefited from conversations with Emily Epstein, Georgina Hickey, Karen Leathem, Alecia Long, Hal Rothman, and Mark Souther.

I send a big thanks to the Watson-Brown Foundation and the Institute for Southern Studies at the University of South Carolina. A Watson-Brown Foundation Postdoctoral Fellowship for 2004–5 allowed me to transform the dissertation into a book. I thank Tad Brown for giving me the opportunity to concentrate on the revision process. Furthermore, my colleagues in Columbia provided me with stimulating conversation as well as a great place to work. Many thanks to Tom Brown, Walter Edgar, and Bob Ellis. I would also like to thank Valinda Littlefield, Patrick Maney, Kenneth Perkins, Lauren Sklaroff, Mark Smith, Marjorie Spruill, Patricia Sullivan, and the rest of the history department. And, once again, Don Doyle.

I would have been lost without the help of dedicated librarians and archivists. For months on end, I depended on the staff at the Louisiana Division of the New Orleans Public Library. I am particularly grateful for the assistance of archivists Wayne Everard and Irene Wainwright. The staff at the Special Collections at Tulane University assisted in the long weeks spent combing the manuscript collections and *New Orleans Association of Commerce News Bulletin*. I especially thank Kenneth Owen for pointing out several items within the archives. Siva Blake guided me through the materials held by the Williams Research Center at the Historic New Orleans Collection. At the University of New Orleans's Louisiana and Special Collections, the staff always proved helpful. Without the assistance of Florence Jumonville and John Kelly, I never would have known about the Grandon-Telling Family scrapbook and other relevant holdings. I also thank Greg Lambousy and Michelle Fontenot at the Louisiana State Museum for arranging my access to the institution's biennial reports. Mary Linn Wernet at the Cammie G. Henry Research Center at Northwestern State University in Natchitoches, Louisiana, helped me to explore the Federal Writers' Project materials and the writings of Lyle Saxon. Mattie Sink at the Mitchell Memorial Library, Mississippi State University, facilitated my examination of Elizebeth Werlein by granting me access to the recently received Hodding and Betty Werlein Carter Papers. I also thank Hodding Carter III for permission to use these materials.

A special thanks goes to the University of Georgia Press. It has been a pleasure to work with Nancy Grayson, Andrew Berzanskis, and the rest of the staff. I also thank the anonymous readers for their comments.

Writing a book means that everyone from family to friends must endure the author's complaints and frustrations, and I know that my redundant conversations about my work certainly did not help matters. For their constant support, I thank my family. My father, Benedict, and mother, Michaela, tolerated my frequent trips back home—and the boxes of photocopies and books that followed me. I am very grateful to my late Uncle David, Uncle Frank, and Aunt Marilyn for their encouragement. My close friends Ronald Scalise and Peter Talluto provided me much-needed time away from the computer. I also thank Tracy Buccino for placating me by proofreading the seemingly endless number of drafts and for tolerating my academic tantrums. I officially nominate you for sainthood.

To everyone, thank you again.

CREATING THE BIG EASY

INTRODUCTION

The City of Myths

> New Orleans existed, like only a few other American cities, in a realm
> of mythology and fantasy and history and romance that made it more
> than a mere city. . . . Like New York City, it is a center against which
> America defines itself; and, perhaps more than New York, New Orleans
> is our most foreign city. There the loose, drunken, partying society
> we've come to think of as French and Catholic contrasts with the
> Protestant and the straitlaced and the early-to-bed/early-to-rise English.
> It is all myth. But in New Orleans's romantic decay, it is possible to
> project, and isolate, those antidotes to rectitude Americans want to
> have. —Randall Kenan, *Walking on Water*

Randall Kenan's observations at the end of the twentieth century suggest the power of New Orleans's mythology. The myths identified by
Kenan accentuate local uniqueness in a nation of homogenizing mass
consumerism. Stories about the past, touched with fictitious embellishments, have defined New Orleans's relationship to the modern world.
An intertwined set of images and assumptions about New Orleans
has penetrated the national consciousness. But how and when did the
mythology emerge? For what purposes was it propagated? Why has it
seeped so deeply into the American mind?

An examination of the years between the First and Second World Wars, when persistent tourism boosters and prolific popular writers crafted urban images with a mass appeal, offers insight into the mythology. Several writers from the period—most notably Grace King, Lyle Saxon, and Robert Tallant—forged careers by writing books about New Orleans that have remained in print and well read since the interwar period. In addition, literary figures Sherwood Anderson, William Faulkner, and Tennessee Williams provided descriptions of New Orleans that both captivated readers and turned mundane built environments into alluring tourist attractions, a process that also occurred in Charleston, South Carolina, which capitalized on DuBose Heyward's *Porgy*, and Monterey, California, which exploited John Steinbeck's *Cannery Row*.[1] Nevertheless, despite the importance of literary figures in crafting popular perceptions of New Orleans, their pens alone did not create the Big Easy. A wider assortment of residents either knowingly or unwittingly shaped the tourist city. The works of writers merged with the efforts of tourism boosters to enhance the images associated with New Orleans: the elegance of Creoles, the skill of jazzmen, the seductiveness of courtesans, the joy of Mardi Gras maskers, the romance and exoticism of the French Quarter. Although such legends had existed prior to 1920, the ensuing flood of writing about the city along with the determination of promoters popularized and reshaped Americans' view of New Orleans. As Michael Kammen has argued in his study of national memory, many Americans during the interwar period sought to "democratize tradition" through "meaningful, purposive myths that could explain and justify how their 'world' had come to be the way it was."[2] The appearance of more and more travelers gave impetus to this trend. In New Orleans, the need to create and propagate an urban mythology intensified as the mass tourism industry penetrated the local culture.

A Dangerous City

The tourism industry that emerged in New Orleans between the world wars evolved from the images and sites popular since the previous century. The past provided tourism boosters with a rich ore from which to fashion tales about the ethnically diverse city that prospered from river commerce. Until the 1920s, however, the ore possessed impurities that prevented urban leaders from successfully casting New Orleans as a mass tourism destination. Negative perceptions of the American urban environment persisted from the age of Thomas Jefferson through the era of muckraking journalism in the early twentieth century.[3] The American aversion to cities as tourist destinations, coupled with specific negative associations with New Orleans, revealed the limitations faced by tourism advocates before the First World War.

In 1802, resident James Pitot recorded his observations of life in New Orleans. His commentary attempted to persuade French officials to reclaim the colony, which had been languishing both culturally and economically since it was ceded to the Spanish in 1763. Spain had little interest in developing Louisiana, conceiving it primarily as a buffer to protect Central American colonies against encroachment by the British and, after 1783, by the United States. Because Spain exerted little cultural influence over Louisiana, Pitot identified a population that was "still generally French in its tastes, customs, habits, religion, and language." He also maintained faith in New Orleans's future prosperity, situated as it was on the Mississippi River. Defending his optimism, Pitot noted that his opinions countered "many opposing views, especially among those who, misled by the information they have received regarding this part of the New World upon visiting it, have experienced only boredom, privation, and misfortune." He criticized shortsighted "visitors . . . frightened by the unhealthiness of a land whose disadvantages have been aggravated and perpetuated by the government's indifference and neglect." Pitot made a special point of championing New Orleans as a place worthy of investment. However, his argument called attention to the general disinterest in the city. Many observers and locals, according to Pitot, failed "to ascertain the real origins of its mediocrity."[4]

Neither the transfer of Louisiana into the hands of U.S. officials in 1803 nor the subsequent boom in cotton and slave trading altered perceptions of the mediocrity—and dangers—that plagued New Orleans.

Death haunted the city. In October 1807, Christian Schultz, a traveler curious about the newly acquired territory, wisely delayed his voyage down the Mississippi River after receiving a "report brought up by a barge just arrived from New Orleans, that the inhabitants were dying there so much faster than they could be buried, that the negroes were provided with long poles and hooks, with which they dragged the bodies of the dead to the Mississippi, and there committed them to the flood." Stunned by the "melancholy news," he decided to journey upriver until the epidemic passed. Mosquitoes, a constant annoyance, facilitated the spread of disease. Recording his experiences in 1819, architect Benjamin Latrobe complained, "As soon as the sun sets the muskitoes appear in clouds & fill every room in the house, as well as the open air. Their noise is so loud as to startle a stranger to its daily recurrence. It fills the air, & there is a character of occasional depression & elevation in it, like that of a concert of frogs in a marsh." Theodore Clapp, a clergyman who established residence in New Orleans to assist the sick during the recurrent yellow fever and cholera outbreaks, offered similar accounts: "Not unfrequently the alternations of health and sickness, joy and sorrow, commercial prosperity and misfortune, sweep over the Crescent City with the suddenness and fury of those autumnal hurricanes which occasionally visit it, by which in a few moments of time the strongest edifices are leveled with the dust, the majestic live oaks and cypresses prostrated, and the vessels along the levee overwhelmed in the flood." In the worst years, the odors, sights, and sounds of the dying overpowered even longtime veterans of the city. The yellow fever epidemic of 1853 was so severe that Clapp could "smell the offensive effluvium that filled the atmosphere for miles around, resembling that which arises from putrefying animal or vegetable matter." Not surprisingly, Clapp "was seized with fainting and vomiting" as he made his way through the streets. Conditions barely improved after the Civil War. The death of noted Confederate General John Bell Hood, his wife, and eldest child during an 1879 yellow fever outbreak underscored the persistent dangers of life in New Orleans.[5]

During much of the nineteenth century, tourists found little to distinguish New Orleans's culture and architecture from that of other cities.

According to a perceptive study by Sandra Frink, travelers regularly made sense of New Orleans by drawing comparisons with New York, Boston, Charleston, Savannah, and even London and Paris. In 1853, Fredrika Bremer described the New Orleans she encountered on her tour of the United States without a hint of romanticism or exoticism: "The crescent-formed site of the city on the Mississippi is beautiful, and it has some handsome streets and markets, and splendid houses surrounded with trees and shrubs, like other American cities." Even in the French Quarter, the oldest section of the city, Bremer saw plainness: "The French and older portions of the city have a more bald and business-like character; but New Orleans is beyond everything else a business and trading city." Bremer was not alone. Writing for the *New York Times* in December 1884, a northerner identified as A.K.F. sneered, "Visitors who expect to find New-Orleans greatly different from other American cities will be disappointed. It has its peculiarities, not all of which are interesting." The traveler reported, "The first thing a stranger looks for to gratify his expectations of novelty is the old French town below Canal-street. If he is enthusiastic, he may find it very quaint and picturesque. It is unquestionably pretty old; on the whole, extremely shabby, and indubitably it is dirty. Perhaps there are elements of the picturesque, but those old French builders of houses had no notion of appealing to the aesthetic." A.K.F. concluded that "New Orleans is beginning to be enterprising and very ambitious, but its general aspect is that of a rather staid, quiet, slipshod community, with peculiarities that give it a very thin foreign-like veneering, which is chipping off rapidly."[6]

Commercial prosperity, enjoyed throughout the nation during the antebellum years, added decadence to the list of negative associations suffered by ports such as New Orleans. Prosperity aided the creation of a conformist middle class while reinforcing the popularity of vices, including gambling and prostitution. With piety the cornerstone of many middle-class homes, the severity of the evil lurking within cities was magnified. Whereas twentieth-century guide writers such as Eleanor Early made light of morality by declaring cities a "sin and shame" to miss, their nineteenth-century ancestors believed sin and shame to be serious matters. The *New York Daily Times* captured Americans' anxiety: "In the advancing career of civilisation, it is much to be regretted, that the necessities of men and women should urge them into so many expedients to obtain a livelihood, and that there should be such a universal desire and ambition to live showingly and ostentatiously. Considerations of vice and pleasure predominate over those of virtue and sobriety, and the love of display is the ruling passion of the times." Worse, members of the middle and upper classes, particularly men, often privately supported the carnality condemned by popular culture. Urban centers such as New Orleans appeared to be immoral cesspools as well as dull, business-dominated communities.[7]

The association of hedonism with New Orleans possesses deep historical roots. In an 1826 travel account, *Recollections of the Last Ten Years*, Timothy Flint wrote, "Much has been said about the profligacy of manners, and morals [in New Orleans]; and this place has more than once been called the modern Sodom." However, Flint also generally equated New Orleans with other major urban centers in such matters, commenting that "amidst such a multitude, composed in a great measure of the low people of all nations, there must of course be much debauchery, and low vice." "On the whole," Flint continued, "I judge from an observation at different times, of thirty weeks, that this city, as it respects people who have any self-estimation, is about on a footing with the other cities of the Union in point of morals."[8]

The presence of a large black population reinforced New Orleans's reputation for sexual depravity. In antebellum New Orleans, sex across the color line and the brutality of human bondage became a dominant theme in abolitionist tracts and novels, most famously Harriet Beecher Stowe's *Uncle Tom's Cabin*. The Crescent City was an easy target because it possessed the largest slave markets in the South—markets that kept Louisiana's sweltering cotton and sugar plantations stocked with laborers. Auction houses with their human chattel drew many travelers curious about the region's peculiar institution. Furthermore, the years under the control of Spain, which had relatively liberal manumission laws, had led to the creation of a large population of free persons of color. *Plaçage*, a custom of formalized mistress keeping often involving light-skinned free blacks, soon emerged and persisted into the antebellum period. Some white husbands lived double lives, with a white wife at home and a black woman at another residence. Conversely, white entrepreneurs unable to afford a wife and house regularly chose a black helpmate until becoming wealthy enough to establish a more reputable lifestyle. The fruits of these mixed-race relationships encouraged the popular fascination with New Orleans's decadence. Unlike most communities in the United States, the city did not just recognize a difference between blacks and whites but also harbored a complex social system based on multiple racial categories, each with a strong sense of identity. According to Frederick Law Olmsted, who visited during the 1850s, New Orleans was populated by whites, negroes, mulattoes, quadroons, *metifs, meameloucs, sang-meles, marabons, griffes,* and *sacatras.* "And all of these, with the sub-varieties of them, French, Spanish, English, and Indian, and the sub-sub-varieties, such as Anglo-Indian-mulatto, I believe experts pretend to be able to distinguish," chuckled Olmsted.[9]

In postemancipation New Orleans, whites expressed even greater anxiety over the presence of blacks of varying hues and their effect on white supremacy and morality. J. W. Buel included five cities in his 1883 urban exposé, *Mysteries and Miseries of America's Great Cities.* New York City supplied lessons on how affluence led to vices such as alcohol and extramarital sex. Washington, D.C., revealed how political power corrupted the morals of elected officials. Buel then turned his attention to the brothels and opium dens of San Francisco's Chinatown, the polygamy practiced by Mormons in Salt Lake City, and finally the voodoo and other "superstitions" associated with blacks in New Orleans. "New Orleans of to-day is far removed from the sensuality that distinguished her twenty years ago," explained Buel as he took note of emancipation, "yet like all cities, aye, towns and hamlets, she gives shelter to depraved objects, and is no exception to the adage: 'Vice, like talent, thrives best in large cities.' " Buel's claim, not uncommon in the nineteenth century, that the Louisiana heat served to "develop and sensualize women" likely convinced curious American families to rethink a trip to New Orleans, especially during seasons other than winter. But the heat also had another effect, according to Buel. It attracted blacks from across the South to what was believed to be the hottest spot in the region. This was assumed natural for a freed people seeking a climate closest to that of tropical Africa. Buel argued, "New Orleans has always been reckoned the negro Mecca, for those who have never visited that city are hoping to do so before they die." The city may have possessed beauty, but the link between travel to New Orleans and race likely gave whites pause. Buel continued, "And this wish is quite a natural one, for where can be found so many things pleasing to the colored man's tastes and ambitions; rich planters, liveried servants, fine people, high stakes and everybody a gambler, steamboats lining the landing, with negroes covering the levee, while fun and frolic invite them at every corner; where the sun perpetually kisses an atmosphere of sensuous delight, and where all nature has formed a combination with industry to make a darkey paradise." Scattered among the Creoles, identified as a "mongrel hodge-podge of humanity . . . repulsive in feature and without grace of form" as a result of miscegenation, the author discovered a few of the "handsomest women in the world." These "very Cleopatras with nut-brown and half-transparent complexions . . . emit flames of infectious passion." Like yellow fever, young Creole women left death and broken homes in their wake. Buel complained that "these women have been as a bane to Southern life, for they have been the inciting cause to many duels, and inspired illicit amours that have disrupted thousands of once happy families." Storyville, the city's vice district established in the 1890s, perpetuated sex across the color line as a titillating adventure for white men who wanted to verify for themselves the beauty of the city's mixed-race women.[10]

The perception of New Orleans as decadent was buttressed by its Latin-Catholic heritage, which tinted the lens through which Americans viewed the Louisiana port. Settled by the French in 1718 and populated by significant numbers of migrating Frenchmen into the 1850s, New Orleans suffered from Anglo characterizations of French laziness. Even Creoles, the native-born of French or Spanish descent, received sharp criticism. That many such New Orleanians were Catholic only darkened the city's reputation in the eyes of the predominantly Protestant citizens of the United States. Eleanor Parke Lewis, the adopted daughter of George Washington and briefly a resident of New Orleans during the 1830s, wrote, "The Creoles are indolent & dirty, & places which will produce with scarcely any trouble, flower & everything beautiful are really disgusting under their management." The pious Lewis, like many fellow Americans, considered Catholicism morally dangerous because the faith seemed to encourage indolence and to erode Protestant stoutness. Lewis penned to a friend, "Sunday among the French & Creoles & indeed among the Americans too is like any other day. Pedlars go about, cake sellers, & they really appear to have no idea beyond this world & its enjoyments. We do not visit or receive visits on Sunday, but it is a gala day here generally."[11]

The flood of immigrants, many of them Catholic Irish, into port cities from the 1830s through the 1850s heightened American animosity against foreigners and popery. Even a literary genre alleging immoral sexual escapades in monasteries and nunneries gained popularity. In New Orleans, the presence of a large ethnic population stereotyped as morally lax reinforced Anglo-Protestant biases. The Crescent City grew from a population of less than 18,000 in 1810 to more than 168,000 by 1860. During that period, approximately 550,000 immigrants passed through New Orleans, including more than 350,000 after 1847. Observers cringed at the number of strangers who packed the streets. Describing conditions in 1858, the *New York Times* lamented that "New Orleans is, unquestionably, the most un-American city in our whole Confederacy." The result was moral weakness. Protestant Americans fell short of reforming the city because "emigrants from the Northern States are mostly absorbed by their business pursuits, and take but little interest in local politics." Arrivals from Ireland and other lands therefore conformed "to the French rather than to the American habits of the people, and thus the original elements of society are preserved, and the traditions of the first settlers of the colony are kept up." A political movement soon culminated in the short-lived nativist Know-Nothing Party. Although in New Orleans the Know-Nothings briefly united Anglo-Americans with established French families in opposition to the immigrant newcomers, the movement's anti-Catholic sentiment quickly eroded the alliance and heightened Anglo-American fears of a papist cancer within the republic. Street violence erupted, vaulting New Orleans into national attention. The *New York Times* summarized popular opinion: "It is in New-Orleans . . . that we should naturally look for a *coup d'etat*, a revolution after the manner of Paris, Madrid, and Mexico."[12]

The linkage of post–Civil War racial violence to Catholicism further damaged New Orleans's reputation. An 1875 article from *Harper's Weekly* described life in the city as its citizens grappled with political and racial issues: "Since 1868 the fear of its dangerous class and the constant insecurity of life and property have made New Orleans no attractive place for merchants and mechanics. Its shops and houses are untenanted, or let for only a meagre return; its streets have been the scene of frequent conflicts between the [white supremacist militia known as the] White Leaguers and their opponents." Caught up in the heated presidential politics of 1877, the partisan *Harper's Weekly* identified a source of the continued violence in New Orleans and elsewhere in the former Confederacy: "And to the various acts of cruelty and violence which have marked the lawless classes of the country for ten years past, the Roman Catholic priesthood have given an open approval." Silence from Catholic officials was interpreted as giving active support for vigilantism in the South. The editorial went on to imply that the lives of well-to-do white northerners—those most likely to afford a trip below the Mason-Dixon Line—were not safe in the region: "It is true, the victims whose fate [the Catholic Church] would hide or condone are only poor white and colored Republicans—Protestants, perhaps—who have perished far away, at Hamburg, South Carolina, in the recesses of Georgia and Florida, or the savage riots of Mississippi and Louisiana; but their murderers are just as guilty as if they had stricken down opulent citizens of New York or Boston." The editors of *Harper's Weekly* proposed that neither wealth nor status could protect an individual from the extralegal violence rampant across the South.[13]

Anti-Catholic sentiment poisoned national discourse through the 1920s but then began to dissipate. Fears that Catholic allegiance to the Vatican undermined loyalty to the United States often dominated political discourse, as occurred during the 1884 presidential election.

Waves of Catholic immigrants from Italy and other European nations washed ashore in the 1890s and 1900s, strengthening the relationship between xenophobia and suspicion of Catholicism. Near the turn of the century, a mob of New Orleanians created an international incident when they lynched eleven Italians wrongly accused in the murder of the city sheriff. By the mid-1910s, the Ku Klux Klan reemerged, with anti-Catholicism joining anti-Semitism and racism in a trinity of hate. During the mid-1920s, however, the Klan collapsed under the weight of scandal. Despite the tensions raised by the 1928 presidential race between Herbert Hoover and Catholic candidate Al Smith, anti-Catholic sentiments waned by the end of the decade as Americans grew disgruntled with Prohibition and the economic crisis brought on by the Great Depression.[14]

Opposition to the conservatism of American society—whether manifested in support for the KKK, Prohibition, or religious Fundamentalism—further eased the stigma against New Orleans by fostering admiration for French liberality. New Orleans's French heritage reinforced the city's image as a place to indulge in carnal pleasures. In the late nineteenth century and early twentieth century, for example, American prostitutes marketed their oral skills as "French" sex. Urban residents, particularly men, enjoyed dances known as French balls. These popular masquerades, often held as political fund-raisers or to attract customers to theaters or saloons, offered salacious activities that brought men together with prostitutes in an elaborate setting. Moreover, the most expensive prostitutes in the United States tended to be French women. The image of France and of New Orleans, for that matter, was one of sexual and alcoholic indulgence. And the social liberality of both attracted expatriates from the conservative popular culture dominating the United States during the 1920s, including most notably Ernest Hemingway, William Faulkner, and Sherwood Anderson.[15]

Though some travelers had celebrated the city long before the First World War, understanding the image of New Orleans at that time requires making a fine distinction. On one hand, as already discussed, New Orleans was not exceptional. All major cities shared, in varying degrees, heterogeneous populations, customs, and religious practices.

In their diversity, urban centers were the same. Cities generally contained Anglo-Protestants, ethnic Catholics, immigrants, free and enslaved blacks, the working and middle classes, and so on.[16] On the other hand, compared to life on farms, on which most Americans earned a living until the 1920s, cities were unusual, even exotic sites. The perceived immorality and chaos of cities was both alluring and threatening. Observers may have seen New Orleans as exceptional, but it did not differ substantially from other urban centers. Consequently, New Orleans was not necessarily unique for being New Orleans per se but for being a large city in a predominantly rural republic.

A Carnival Town

The emergence of tourism in the Western world coincided with the rise of romanticism and the Industrial Revolution. Travelers sought encounters with awe-inspiring picturesque scenes of natural wonders or ancient ruins—sites distant from the noisy bustle of growing cities and factory towns. As Colin Campbell has argued, "Romanticism provided that philosophy of 'recreation' necessary for a dynamic consumerism." Romanticism's emphasis on "self-expression and self-realization" fostered the desire to experience the sublimity of nature. To the literate elite—those few who possessed the resources to vacation during the nineteenth century—communion with nature provided escape from the modern world of urban clutter and industrial waste. Rural journeys also acquainted travelers with the natural resources that permitted the economic growth of urban centers, the places where many tourists of the period earned their livelihoods. For these reasons, the splendor of certain rural scenes stoked nationalist sentiments. Popular tourist sites such as Niagara Falls, Mammoth Cave, and the Hudson River Valley reinforced patriotism. Americans believed that their nation had received divine sanction, apparent in the rich resources and abundant natural wonders within the United States. The construction of the Erie Canal through the landscape of New York revealed the young republic's ingenious ability to harness the continent's resources. In her study of the waterway, Carol Sheriff has argued that American tourists saw the countryside as "something to be conquered rather than preserved" even as they also recognized that nature provided a "healthy escape, a place enticing precisely because it remained untouched by 'civilized' human beings and progress." Though the reasons for visiting rural America rested on seemingly conflicted viewpoints, tourists generally found the countryside more appealing than urban centers.[17]

The alleged physical and spiritual benefits of beaches and highlands attracted a growing number of travelers. In the decades after the Revolutionary War, isolated resorts—most famously at White Sulphur Springs, Virginia, and Martha's Vineyard, Massachusetts—catered to the needs of the American elite. The mid-nineteenth-century emergence of railroad travel brought a proliferation of hotels near hot springs and mountain air. Companies laid track through rocky terrain and dense forests to give travelers better access to formerly remote areas. Railroad barons also connected urban centers in the Northeast to the Atlantic coast. By the end of the century, entrepreneurs had converted once isolated sea resorts for the wealthy into sites for the urban masses. The relatively low cost of rail travel and the close proximity of the beach allowed even the working class to escape the grime and heat of urban living, at least for a day. For members of the upper classes, railroad companies also pioneered the tourism industry in the American West, offering long-distance trips to such trendy destinations as Yellowstone, Yosemite, and the Grand Canyon.[18]

Although the American penchant for mountain or seaside vacations made tourism untenable for New Orleans and other urban centers, Americans remained fascinated with their cities' size and activity. Tourism had factored into the urban economy in some form since the first settlers surveyed locations with a freshwater supply and adequate transportation routes. Cities were born as adventurous undertakings and remained exhilarating places, especially in a country—and world—predominantly populated by rural dwellers. The excitement stirred by the seeming chaos of urban centers made cities mysterious but also dangerous. William Drysdale, a New Yorker who visited New Orleans in 1884, described the thrill of exploration: "Mr. Columbus, I think, when he landed at San Salvador, must have felt very much as I did on landing in New-Orleans; for he had an unknown country before him, and so had I." Having just returned from a lengthy journey through the Southwest, Drysdale felt and looked more like a country bumpkin than a sophisticated urbanite. He mused, "Three months in the South-west, followed by a week on a Red River steamer, make a man forget that he ever was familiar with city ways, and perhaps this was why a dozen street cars seemed to make a dead set at me every time I crossed the street." City folk were equally threatening: "There was something extremely funny to an old New-Yorker in walking up this strange street in a strange city, sachel [*sic*] in hand, and having all the bootblacks, hackmen, idle porters, sidewalk merchants, and seedy sharps mark him for their own. My homely but very serviceable stick, my muddy boots, my general mountaineer appearance, marked me at once in their eyes for an easy victim." Accounts of such victimization—and worse—fascinated the nation. The bustle of the city thrilled as well as intimidated tourists. Americans eagerly read the tales of murder and sexual license associated with the urban scene. To many pious Americans, the sinfulness of cities reflected the depravity of human beings needful of salvation.[19]

Restoring nature to the city or even casting the city as rural made urban centers such as New Orleans more palatable. Landscape architect Frederick Law Olmsted, who built his reputation by restoring rural enclaves to the built environment, expressed an opinion shared by many Americans. Olmsted saw in his journey to antebellum New Orleans a city tainted by licentiousness. Only one place supplied a reservoir of virtue. The creator of New York City's Central Park declared that "in rural life the advantage of the North . . . is incomparable." Vast spaces dotted by family farms formed an ideal (white) America. Because cities lacked rural spaces, Olmsted plugged parks between skyscrapers and residential neighborhoods. Olmsted's nephew would bring this vision to New Orleans near the turn of the century by developing Audubon Park. Given the perceived superiority of rural expanses, Charles Dudley Warner, a writer who crafted a favorable account of New Orleans for an 1887 issue of *Harper's New Monthly Magazine*, paused to assess whether something was wrong with his psyche. He joked, "I suppose we are all wrongly made up and have a fallen nature; else why is it that while the most thrifty and neat and orderly city only wins our approval, and perhaps gratifies us intellectually, such a thriftless, battered and stained, and lazy old place as the French quarter of New Orleans takes our hearts?" But, to hear Warner tell it, New Orleans was less a city than a lush jungle. Streets were "shabby"; open gutters were "green with slime"; "tumble-down picturesque" buildings were engulfed in roses that "overrun the porches," "climb the sides of houses," and generally "take possession" of everything. Accompanying illustrations depicted buildings covered in vegetation. To complete the transformation of New Orleans from bustling metropolis to languid tropical haven, Warner populated the port with blacks. "The African pervades all parts of the town, except the new residence portion of the American quarter," claimed Warner. Sketches again reinforced the written description. Various street scenes showed blacks either working or loafing. Whereas Olmsted reintroduced the rural environment to cities through parks, Warner did much the same through his literary imagination. In a culture that associated blacks with the jungles of the Dark Continent or the cotton fields of Dixie, Warner brought nature to New Orleans—indeed, he enveloped the city in greenery and blackness.[20]

Beginning in the 1870s, urban businessmen such as those in Louisiana attempted to offset the negative imagery associated with the built environment by hosting expositions highlighting the emergence of urban centers as tourist destinations. Lasting several months and garnering national press, the most noteworthy of these events included the Centennial Exposition of 1876 in Philadelphia, the World's Industrial and Cotton Centennial Exposition hosted by New Orleans in 1884, and the Chicago World's Columbian Exposition of 1893. Such celebrations allowed boosters to market their city without placing the city itself at the center of attention. As historian James Gilbert has argued, exposition organizers attempted to create "perfect cities" within the fairgrounds, free of the slum conditions and social tensions that marred the surrounding urban environment.[21]

New Orleans and other cities also attempted to attract visitors by developing annual festivals. Mardi Gras appeared in New Orleans during the antebellum period, but the 1870s brought an elaboration of the festival as krewes, the name parading organizations adopted for themselves, granted regal titles and constructed extravagant floats. Although other efforts to promote Carnival appeared throughout the urban South, very few lasted longer than a handful of years. As *Harper's Weekly* reported in 1873, "The attempt to inaugurate similar festivities in Washington two years ago was a wretched failure, and the experience has wisely been avoided in our Northern cities." A decade later, Mark Twain noted in *Life on the Mississippi* that Carnival celebrations had "spread to Memphis and St. Louis and Baltimore." The search for continuity with the antebellum past of plantations and slaves—a past increasingly romanticized as halcyon days—fostered the creation of royal courts that suggested the stability and racial purity of regional bloodlines. Carnival provided a symbolic means of reempowering a region devastated by war. Twain observed, "Take away the romantic mysteries, the kings and knights and big-sounding titles, and Mardi Gras would die, down there in the South. The very feature that keeps it alive in the South—girl-girly romance—would kill it in the North or in London." In New Orleans, the effort to enhance Mardi Gras stemmed from the political pressures of Reconstruction. Krewes became notorious for creating float designs that lambasted Republican officials. Carnival became a way to usurp, however briefly, Republican political dominance. In doing so, the local elite reasserted its strength.[22]

The persistence of the festival in New Orleans reflected more than just the political power exhibited by the krewes. Mardi Gras attracted tourists, albeit only for a few days each year. Ernst von Hesse-Wartegg, a German who traveled the Mississippi River Valley in 1879–80, recognized that Carnival allowed New Orleans to proclaim cultural, economic, and political hegemony over the nation: "Weeks before Carnival the king's proclamations flood the United States. Big, bright-colored posters, decorated with all sorts of coats of arms and other designs, carry a kind of speech from the throne, announcing *Mardi Gras in New Orleans* and requesting *come one, come all*." Despite the national publicity, local organizers emphasized New Orleans's regional importance. Rex, the self-proclaimed King of Carnival, ruled "as absolute monarch of this and every other city of the South." The arrival of tourists reinforced the city's regional influence. "From every city in the country—St. Louis, Memphis, Louisville, Galveston; yes even New York, 1,500 miles away—the grand pleasure steamers have departed for New Orleans."[23]

The development of Carnival reflected a shift in the nation's cultural interests. In the handful of decades after the Civil War, Americans embraced the idiosyncrasies of local cultures, even those found in urban neighborhoods, largely as a result of advances in technology. Ironically, the increasing homogeneity of national culture spurred efforts to uncover communities and traditions untainted by the forces of modernity. The railroad in the late nineteenth century not only linked cities but reached into the hinterlands. Urban culture started to heavily influence rural America. Baseball leagues, vaudeville troupes, mail-order catalogs, name-brand goods, and other developments gave greater uniformity to the entertainment and consumer products encountered throughout the nation. During the early twentieth century, silver screens and phonographs brought Americans the sights and sounds of urban living, enticing country people to the exciting life offered by urban centers. Telephone and electrical lines slowly stretched outward from cities into the countryside, a process largely completed under the Rural Electrification Administration, a New Deal agency. A web of improved roads and a rise in automobile ownership further shrank the cultural distance between urban and rural America.[24]

Attitudes toward New Orleans exemplified the curiosity about indigenous urban culture. Touring the city just prior to the World's Industrial and Cotton Centennial Exposition in 1883, Mark Twain strolled through the French Quarter with George Washington Cable, a nationally noted writer whose stories dealt with New Orleans's Creole population, and saw a neighborhood that differed markedly from the dull structures described some decades earlier by Fredrika Bremer. Cable's knowledge of the district's history and his literary embellishments recreated the French Quarter, giving Twain "a vivid *sense* as of unseen or dimly seen things—vivid, and yet fitful and darkling; you glimpse salient features, but lose the fine shades or catch them imperfectly through the vision of imagination: a case, as it were, of ignorant near-sighted stranger traversing the rim of wide vague horizons of Alps with an inspired and enlightened long-sighted native." Cable's writings brought these visions to American readers. "In truth," explained Twain, "I find by experience, that the untrained eye and vacant mind can inspect [the French Quarter] and learn of it and judge it more clearly and profitably in [Cable's] books than by personal contact with it." Cable, along with another popular author, Lafcadio Hearn, thus crafted the first romantic, exotic images of New Orleans.[25]

A business-driven, dangerous city slowly became enticing, more accessible, and safer—at least in literary accounts. The creation of romanticized images had more to do with rescuing for posterity traces of a rapidly acculturating French population and selling stories at a time when local color reached the height of popularity than with attracting visitors to the Crescent City. Few Americans at the time could afford to walk through the streets of New Orleans in the footsteps of Cable and Hearn. But those who did often interpreted what they saw in terms of what they had read. In a fictionalized travel narrative published in 1887, Rebecca Harding Davis recounts the experiences of several northern tourists who journey to New Orleans for the exposition. A well-read wife, Mrs. Ely, scours the city in search of all the sites and characters she had encountered in books. Davis elaborates, "Mrs. Ely, like the majority of Northerners at the Exposition, was perpetually in search of something 'typically Southern.'" Each pursuit proved fruitless. The cosmopolitan setting intruded on literary fantasy: "She went to the French Market on Sunday morning with the mob of tourists, and fell a victim to the Jew peddlers who had orange-wood canes for sale manufactured of pine in New York. She promenaded the Boulevard Esplanade, looking out for Mr. Cable's creoles, and regarding every old man with white hair and black eyes with awe as a possible Grandissime." Mrs. Ely persisted, but each effort met with frustration: "She made vain pretences of asking her way from people whom she fancied were Legrees, or Madame Delphines, or Texan cow-boys; but they all turned out to be from Duluth or Chicago. She had heard all her life of the wickedness of New Orleans, and she took a fearful joy in venturing into quarters which were said to be its worst haunts; but they now turned gay, decent faces to the passing stranger." Albert Phelps, writing for *Atlantic Monthly* in 1901, also used literature as a guide, depicting the French Quarter as "quaint and foreign to the American visitor." What he saw, however, was filtered through the pages that he had read. Unlike Mrs. Ely, who perused stories directly related to New Orleans, Phelps was influenced by literary accounts of French towns. Phelps concluded, "In fact, there is only one way to describe the impression exactly: to live in this quarter, to know its houses, its streets, its people, its stories, is like reading Balzac."[26]

Spurred in part by these literary accounts, a fledgling urban tourism industry emerged. In a brief study of New York City, Neil Harris has shown that the economic growth of American cities made the 1890s in particular "the take-off decade" for urban tourism. Railroads lowered fares, and postcards emerged to spread images of cities nationwide. Urban environments opened to tourists as railroads, hotels, and local business boosters tapped the market in travelers. Considerable friction developed, however, between wealthy tourists spending freely on leisure and locals who labored out of need or out of a still-strong ethic that prized work over pleasure. Travel remained expensive for most of the American public. The upper classes continued to dominate the tourist trade, limiting its economic and cultural impact on the urban scene. Few Americans could afford to take weeks off from work, much less purchase hotel rooms or long-distance train fare simply for leisure. Concerns with social propriety based on class and gender conventions restricted individuals' freedom to sightsee. The ability of women to walk city streets, even when they traveled as part of a family unit, was circumscribed by lingering cultural taboos about entering the public space. As historian Catherine Cocks has demonstrated, the organized tour companies of the first two decades of the twentieth century offered a means by which wealthy travelers could avoid "socially heterogeneous crowds."[27]

Between the 1890s and 1910s, tourism in New Orleans rested largely on revelers eager to partake in Mardi Gras and male travelers drawn to Storyville, the city's vice district. As Alecia Long has argued in her study of sexuality in New Orleans prior to the First World War, the city's attractions catered to a primarily male clientele. Middle- and upper-class women as well as pious men trod with care through city streets for fear of being associated with either persons of questionable morals or members of the working class. An annual influx of northern families also ventured to New Orleans each winter to escape the cold. Yet these were closer to being residents than tourists. Rather than merely visit the city for a few days or weeks, they remained for months and usually made the pilgrimage to New Orleans each year. Businessmen also traveled to New Orleans, but their interest in coming to the city involved economics rather than leisure.[28]

A 1903 scrapbook reveals the limits of New Orleans tourism during the Progressive Era. The album records the activities of the members of the Telling and Grandon families of Illinois, who arrived by railroad on the Friday before Mardi Gras. Train travel, just like travel by ship, restricted the families to areas within walking distance of the downtown terminal. Immediately after arriving, members of the family went "bumming"—that is, they walked. A stroll through the streets represented a step down in class. This was part of the alluring urban experience. Like typical well-off tourists of the time, the families mixed highbrow and lowbrow activities. They shopped along Royal Street and the French Market. They watched parades, had their fortunes told, attended performances at the French Opera House, visited the federal mint, and observed vessels along the riverfront.

But several incidents recorded by the two families exposed an urban society not yet open to tourism, whether in New Orleans or elsewhere in the United States. Despite the various activities and sites available in the city, the families made sure to visit their "favorite resort; the home of the films." Movies competed against the city for the attention of the tourists. Reality could not hold their interest for long, especially since businessmen had yet to exploit emergent technologies and marketing strategies to captivate visitors with a wide array of fantastic tales. Furthermore, the Telling and Grandon families were threatened with rebuff when they arrived at the Rex ball. Their wealth was affirmed by their ability to procure entrance to the ball, an exclusive celebration hosted by the Carnival krewe. But their habit of bumming almost hid their social standing too well. As they dressed for the masquerade, the family members found themselves short on time, "but fortunately by running hard" they arrived before the event began. When they attempted to enter, however, a "slight delay" occurred when "the gentleman at the stairs . . . doesn't like Ma's looks and won't let her up. After pacifying the animals we all assemble in the ball room amid a throng of youth and beauty composed of little heenies and sheenies." The hesitancy of the doorman reflected a culture suspicious of the virtue of women, especially when classes and genders mixed in the streets. Concern with morality and preoccupation with womanly virtue restricted respectable womanhood to the domestic sphere. Women thus encountered an urban space that automatically questioned their character when they ventured out in public. Gender conventions limited women's role as tourists.[29]

Mardi Gras, not the city, had attracted the Telling and Grandon families, and without persistent marketing that wrapped urban poverty and decay in the cosmetic glow of nostalgia and exoticism, tourists regularly confronted upsetting scenes in urban spaces. Encounters with residents from the social margins imperiled tourists' enjoyment of New Orleans. The Telling and Grandon children were shocked to find on the door of a liveryman's carriage "the appalling statement—'No tramps allowed. . . .' Terror siezes [sic] upon their souls and their tender hearts beat a furious-trip hammer duet." Worse, without a municipal waterworks or sewer system, the city was unsanitary, and yellow fever remained a threat until as late as 1905, when the last major outbreak occurred. "New Orleans is a dangerous city in which to spend the night in the open air," remarked the scrapbook's author. Thus, prior to Progressive Era reforms, public fears imposed limits on the urban tourism industry.[30]

New Orleans Mass Tourism

A look at the 1920s and 1930s reveals a period when Americans had more in common than ever before. Most prostitution districts in major cities had been closed as a result of military orders during the First World War. Prohibition had become national law. Across the country, women forced a reconsideration of gender roles. Racial issues such as segregation grew slowly into a national question as southern blacks continued to flee the hardships of sharecropping and tenancy for the dream of a better life in northern urban centers. The Great Depression subsequently afflicted the entire population and led to a strengthened federal government capable of protecting the general welfare and the national economy. All of these trends and events shaped tourism and the manner in which civic leaders, including those in New Orleans, marketed their city and molded the urban space to accommodate tourists.

The social changes that occurred between the First and Second World Wars gave rise to what I label modern, or mass, tourism—a tourist trade inclusive of the middle- and lower-class members of both sexes in which urban communities facilitated public access to promoted sites. Though the American electorate sought a return to normalcy during the 1920s, direct contact with European cultures during the Great War had kindled curiosity about the nation's British, French, and Spanish ancestors, and interest in the past extended to Native American and immigrant cultures. Inspired by wartime patriotism, Americans sought contact with their national heritage. After the First World War, automobiles and road construction projects facilitated travel even over hundreds of miles, with cars both serving as a means of transportation and, if necessary, providing a place to sleep. Drivers possessed the freedom not only to travel but also to avoid the high prices of downtown hotels and restaurants, on which railroad travelers depended. Historian Warren Belasco has shown the powerful, liberating impact of automobiles as well as the erosive effect of automobile-oriented tourism on the compact downtown districts. The car unleashed American wanderlust. Yet too often, the automobile is seen as the generator of change rather than just part of numerous cultural shifts that altered the way Americans experienced the urban space.[31]

The forces of technology, mass production, demographic shifts, and national law led to significant change within cities. Aymar Embury II, an architect writing in 1911, noted the impact on New Orleans, explaining that the national fascination with the French Quarter, for example, had grown in direct relation to the appearance of "tall, modern buildings" a few blocks upriver. The "fact that New Orleans is at present interesting to the architects has arisen from the development of the business district, not in its former position, but in a new one."[32] Skyscrapers accentuated the perceived charm of old, crumbling buildings. New Orleanians capitalized on such nostalgia by reinventing the urban past, developing mass tourism, and converting negative associations involving foreigners and vice into positive attributes that stirred out-of-towners' curiosity about the mysterious city near the mouth of the Mississippi River. By the 1920s, Americans not only embraced new technologies such as radios and automobiles but also adjusted to demographic changes. The United States became increasingly urbanized in the interwar years. The 1920 census announced that for the first time more Americans lived in urban communities of at least twenty-five hundred people than in rural areas. National culture and urban life had become increasingly intertwined.

The story told in the following pages is one of a mass tourism industry constructed by whites for whites. New Orleans tourism was grounded on the interests and assumptions of white city business leaders. Despite the city's complex web of racial mixtures, white leaders affirmed white supremacy. The image making associated with tourism served as a vehicle that enabled whites to popularize racial stereotypes while exaggerating the division between the races. The myth of white supremacy aided Progressive reformers who attempted to separate the races as a means of creating racial order out of a perceived urban chaos signified by racially mixed neighborhoods. Tourism boosters thus projected the contemporary ideal of racial division and black submission.

A study of tourism, furthermore, is an examination of the relationship between local boosters and travelers. Urban tourism did not emerge in a vacuum. Rather, the industry developed as city leaders responded to vacationers' interests. Tourists' voices are difficult to uncover, a problem faced by all scholars who have addressed the industry. Although the opinions of famous authors and social commentators are readily available, the historical record offers less evidence from the thousands of ordinary vacationers who traveled alone or with their families. This study attempts to break the silence by gathering material from newspaper editorial pages, letters uncovered within municipal papers, correspondence with local residents, and the records of the New Orleans Association of Commerce, which encouraged tourists to contact the organization. Though the voices are not a chorus, the available evidence reinforces the ample material concerning local efforts to craft the industry. Boosters were astute businessmen well in tune with the desires of vacationers. Through mailed surveys, information-gathering tours, and conversations with visitors, tourism organizers responded to visitors' interests as much as to local concerns.

The story of tourism in New Orleans during the interwar years involves local leaders recognizing the industry's potential. In some respects, post–World War I tourism resembled that of previous decades, focusing on conventions and Mardi Gras. Nevertheless, the appearance of the automobile as a means of travel galvanized local leaders. Statistical evidence on the number of vacationing motorists who came to New Orleans was and remains imprecise. Tracking the size of the New Orleans tourism industry during the interwar years has thus proved difficult. The inability to quantify the data on motorists spurred near paranoia within the business community at the time. As John Urry has argued, the era of "post-Fordist consumption" ushered in by the automobile created a "disorganized capitalism." The irony of the car industry, which benefited from the horizontal and vertical integration of manufacturing enterprises, was that fuel-powered vehicles unleashed human desires for consumption, tempting businesses to offer a wider variety of goods and services. Motorists were less bound by time and distance than earlier travelers had been. Drivers gained the ability to seek out diverse shopping opportunities and recreational spaces. Ordered modernity collapsed under the pressure. Businessmen who easily tabulated travelers at conventions and railway terminals faced a conundrum with motoring tourists freed from the calculable payment of dues or ticket purchases. In a society increasingly dominated by consumerism, the profits promised by tourism were too high for local leaders to ignore even if the increase in automobile travel largely rested on perception rather than hard figures. Urban centers diffused outward along highways, and the desires of the masses, less than the will of the elite, became increasingly apparent within the cityscape.

Mass tourism emerged during the interwar years, but the industry did not mature until the 1940s. After the Second World War, city leaders gained a firmer grasp on the number of tourists visiting the city and the economic impact of those visitors, but the figures still told little about levels of consumption and profit. In a telling development, local leaders in the late twentieth century measured the success of Mardi Gras not simply by hotel occupancy rates or tax revenues but by the amount of garbage gathered by sanitation crews. Trash—the residue of consumption—provided the best, if still imprecise, means of estimating the success of the tourism industry.[33]

In August 2005, Americans watched large sections of New Orleans disappear under the floodwaters unleashed by Hurricane Katrina. A levee breach turned back the clock to 1718. Some television networks and newspaper editors could barely see beyond the French Quarter, as if the city remained a colonial outpost precariously perched on the banks of the Mississippi River. A reporter for the Associated Press offered an assessment of damage to New Orleans's "iconic locations," including nightspots (Bourbon Street, Preservation Hall), restaurants (Café du Monde, Galatoire's, Acme Oyster House, Commander's Palace), and popular sites (author Anne Rice's home, Fair Grounds racetrack, the Garden District, the St. Charles streetcar line).[34] Other reporters presented a citywide bacchanalia of looting and violence. Only after several days did the nation awaken to the extent of the crisis. Cameras captured the Louisiana Superdome and Ernest N. Morial Convention Center devolving from tourist sites to emergency shelters to death traps. Perhaps the delayed reaction was the cost of being too dependent on tourism. How could anything serious happen in New Orleans? How important, after all, is a tourist town?

What most Americans did not see—maybe even refused to see— was the modern New Orleans. The city had trusted in technology. Sophisticated levees and pumps had converted muck into valuable property. Electricity powered communication systems, air-conditioning, and lighting. Waterworks purified drinking water and filtered sewage. Gasoline fueled buses and police vehicles. The inventions that permitted the expansion of the metropolis failed. The city gambled on nature and lost. But New Orleans has lost before—when fires consumed the city in 1788 and 1794, when yellow fever regularly shredded the social fabric during the nineteenth century, when the Mississippi River inundated much of Louisiana in 1927. Each crisis and its resolution reshaped the city both in physical form and in the way residents lived their daily lives.

The tragedy of Katrina has roots in the interwar period, when boosters began massive levee projects not only to tame the Mississippi but also to claim a recreational waterfront on par with those promoted in Florida and southern California. For this, New Orleanians looked to the development of the lakeshore. Rather than promote their city as an exemplar of modernity, however, business and political leaders opted for an urban image that cast the city as a relic, a leftover still mired in French Catholic traditions. The gimmick worked. Tourists began to flock to the city. New Orleanians had created the "Big Easy," although the nickname itself would not drift from the local vernacular into national culture until the 1980s.

By examining New Orleans, this volume delves into questions about urbanism, culture, and tourism to shed light on the dramatic changes affecting American society between the First and Second World Wars. The book has two aims. First, the following chapters examine the construction of images within the New Orleans tourism industry to better understand their purpose. Second, the study explores the social factors that shaped the images. The first chapter turns to businessmen and how they reconceptualized the economic importance of tourism and the image of New Orleans as a product of a romantic, foreign past rather than a symbol of efficient, American modernity. Though still committed to the development of industrial and commercial enterprises, businessmen focused increasing attention on the tourism industry, especially given Americans' love affair with the automobile and the economic downturn caused by the Great Depression. The second chapter explores how the Great Depression impacted the finances of the municipal government. Taxes linked to tourism-related enterprises solidified officials' support of the tourism industry. The third chapter then examines how Prohibition and the end of sanctioned prostitution, combined with the suffrage movement and increased appearance of women on city streets, altered urban attractions and city spaces. Bars and brothels had served a male clientele; by the 1920s, however, urban public spaces, once deemed a masculine domain, became hospitable to women concerned with propriety. The activism of women directly engaging themselves with life in the streets quickly manifested itself in the preservation of the French Quarter, the topic covered by the fourth chapter. Preservationists, dominated by women, altered the cityscape in gendered ways that gave rise to the neighborhood as a tourist attraction. How tourism boosters reshaped urban culture for the benefit of tourists is the subject of the fifth chapter, which closely follows the emergence of Mardi Gras as a hallmark tourist event designed with the pleasure of visitors in mind. In the final chapter, white New Orleanians' efforts to "whiten" jazz and French Creole culture reveal the extent to which New Orleans boosters designed tourism as a whites-only activity.

CHAPTER 1

A CITY OF DESTINY

New Orleans Businessmen and Modern Tourism

Members of the Convention and Tourist Bureau (C & T Bureau), a department of the New Orleans Association of Commerce, proudly unveiled a new slogan in 1922: "New Orleans—America's Most Interesting City." Through the distribution of one hundred thousand stickers bearing the phrase, to be used on packages mailed throughout the United States and the world, local businesses hoped to relegate to the scrap heap the familiar descriptions of New Orleans as the "City That Care Forgot" and the "Paris of America." These old slogans needed correction if not erasure from the public mind. References to Paris or carefree attitudes expressed "naught but frivolity and gaiety," making life in New Orleans seem little more than "a series of parades and Bacchanalian debaucheries." Such a public perception damaged the city's ability to attract investors. The new slogan shifted attention to New Orleans's "tremendous strides" in commercial and industrial development while permitting association with the "city's antiquity." Although the French Quarter received recognition as a "tourist attraction that is equalled nowhere in the United States," the promotion of tourism lay far from many businessmen's minds. The focus remained on New Orleans's position as the "second port of the country" and the South's "leading city." The Crescent City, according to the ad campaign organizers, was an economic powerhouse devoted to prosperity, not frivolity. Industrial and commercial interests were paramount.[1]

During the early interwar years, New Orleans businessmen espoused an understanding of capitalism that favored production over consumption, work over leisure. Historian David Harvey's insight into the link between urbanization and capitalism suggests why businessmen initially shied away from tourism: leisure sites form "relatively permanent strictures of social and physical spaces both within and between urban centers," whereas the growth of cities during the Industrial Revolution was marked by the streamlining of the productive process through the concentration of capital and the means of production. As industries and even agriculture became vertically and horizontally integrated, investors eager to capitalize modes of production sought locations that held economic advantage and allowed the maximum use of labor over time. Openness to change, whether in response to technology or geography, was vital to profitability. In contrast, areas devoted to consumption attempted to halt time and spatial changes. The proliferation of city parks and national parks, the preservation of landmarks, and the emergence of entertainment districts within restored historic neighborhoods (for example, New Orleans's French Quarter or later Memphis's Beale Street and Dallas's Deep Ellum) reflected the tendency of spaces devoted to "vacation, leisure, and entertainment" to become fixtures on the urban landscape during the twentieth century. New Orleans businessmen desirous of industrial and commercial growth hesitated to encourage tourism because the public perception of a city as consumer or leisure oriented undermined efforts to foster industrial and commercial enterprises by making the city appear physically stagnant rather than dynamic.[2]

During the interwar years, businessmen pursued a fully efficient and prosperous urban environment based on a morality defined by white middle- to upper-class Americans. Efficiency meant fostering a downtown, a space increasingly known as the central business district, home to retail stores, financial institutions, and other large companies. As Robert Fogelson has shown, downtown areas across the country were "extremely concentrated, even more so in the 1920s than in the 1890s."[3] Efficiency and urban development also meant upgrading dock facilities and constructing better roads, which formed the paths that linked downtown to markets in the hinterland and around the world. To contemporaries, the stronger the tentacles of business stretching outward from the central business district, the more empowered and enriched the city would become. Booster rhetoric and civic concerns focused on two economic enterprises, commerce and industry, with the ideal of creating a metropolis, a symbol of progressive modernity since the late nineteenth century.[4] Such were the goals of the New Orleans Association of Commerce, the umbrella organization under which businessmen promoted their vision. The organization exercised tremendous influence within the city, both as an independent entity and behind the doors of City Hall. Circumstances magnified this influence. Divisions that had long sapped the association's energies dissipated as the closure of Storyville and the onset of Prohibition severely weakened the influence of concert-hall owners, restaurant operators, slumlords, brewers, and other businesses linked to nightlife—groups with a history of contesting the vision of New Orleans championed by commercial and industrial interests. As political scientist Douglas Rae has demonstrated in regard to New Haven, Connecticut, municipal governments from the 1900s through the 1920s were "business regimes" closely aligned with if not dominated by business organizations that actively shared in the governance of the urban environment. New Orleans fit the pattern.[5]

New Orleans businessmen's commitment to commerce and industry wilted, however, in the face of increased automotive travel and the onset of the Great Depression. Automobiles liberated growing numbers of Americans from train schedules and iron rails. As travel became decentralized, New Orleanians could no longer rely on railroad companies to promote the city as a destination. Gasoline-powered vehicles allowed families and adventurous souls to seek encounters with the exotic, which, in New Orleans, encouraged the packaging of urban life to meet tourists' desires for both service and the unusual. Cars permitted Americans to explore formerly isolated corners of a nation bound ever tighter by ribbons of paved roadways. In addition, the Great Depression shattered the hopes of local industrialists and commercial men. New Orleanians lost faith in traditional economic enterprises. Industry did not supply relief from economic collapse. Commerce along the riverfront withered as Americans' pocketbooks thinned. Labor unrest further tarnished the pursuits businessmen had so cherished. The optimism born from the defeat of strikes during the early 1920s faded as unions regained strength in the 1930s. Rising unemployment and growing bankruptcy rolls led desperate New Orleanians to rethink tourism. Although well-ordered, tightly scheduled conventions remained important, the desire to attract vacationing families and individuals—tourists eager for distractions from the hard times and the harsh business climate—soon captivated business leaders. Tourism no longer served merely to accentuate the industrial strengths or commercial capacity of New Orleans. Tourism meant creating a service-oriented economy. Within the Association of Commerce, businessmen, tempted by tourist dollars, redefined their role as urban boosters. Talk of the romantic, leisurely past replaced the rhetoric of businesslike, progressive modernity. Tourism became increasingly likened to the previous economic pillars of manufacturing and agriculture. By 1939, James Thomson, publisher of the *New Orleans Item*, could boast that the "surest crop that Louisiana can plant is the tourist crop."[6]

Voice of the Community

The first person invited to speak to the Members Council of the New Orleans Association of Commerce in 1919 was George Creel, a prominent muckraking journalist. Creel had augmented his reputation during the First World War by accepting President Woodrow Wilson's offer to chair the U.S. Committee on Public Information (CPI), an agency that directed government efforts to mobilize the American people. Creel's CPI initially limited itself to compiling information on the daily operation of government offices, to distributing pamphlets that explicated U.S. involvement in the European conflict, and to organizing the "Four-Minute Men," individuals who addressed audiences about the importance of the war effort in a restrained, fact-laden manner. As months passed, however, Creel broadened the CPI's efforts. Ads appeared in popular magazines, expanding the agency's audience. The reporting of facts soon gave way to accounts of German brutality as Creel increasingly instructed filmmakers and public speakers to litter their fact giving with atrocity tales and other sensational images. The CPI became a "crude propaganda mill," in the words of one historian. Creel's efforts revealed to American businessmen the power of persuasion through advertising, and Creel proudly carried this message into the postwar period. In New Orleans as elsewhere, he convinced businessmen within the Association of Commerce to invest in publicity campaigns, promising access to American wallets and purses.[7]

The war pressed businessmen to use their expertise and learn new methods for mobilizing the citizenry—methods invaluable to the eventual promotion of tourism as the industry slowly took form over the next two decades. The U.S. government had relied on business organizations to promote war aims, such as Victory Garden and Liberty Bond campaigns, and prominent business leaders, including members of the Association of Commerce, had joined government agencies. To use the business community's own words, the "national and civic work" in which businessmen engaged during the First World War taught them that their organizations should not simply pursue industry, commerce, or urban improvement but also serve as a "general source of information." Wartime mobilization awakened urban businessmen to the advantages of an even greater centralization of their efforts and financial resources. Unity provided for more successful booster campaigns. An editorial written a year after the armistice summarized the new vision heralded by the directors of the Association of Commerce: "The ideal of the organization of 1915 has passed, the new ideal is one of service and education—service for the Government, for its city, and for its people—and education, that the people of the community may learn that through its Chamber of Commerce, its organization, and its machinery, every man has the opportunity of taking his place and doing his share in such work for his community as befits his duty as loyal citizen." To fulfill the newly identified educational function, the association directed greater attention to mass media campaigns. Success, as the businessmen understood, depended on staying in tune with public desires and exploiting New Orleans's position as a trade center near the mouth of the Mississippi River.[8]

The New Orleans Association of Commerce was typical of thousands of business-related and reform-minded organizations that began to appear around the turn of the twentieth century. Born from concerns about keeping the city economically competitive, the association formed in 1913 after a restructuring of its predecessor, the New Orleans Progressive Union, which had been founded in 1898. The centralization of industries and the development of new technologies created anxieties that could in turn be soothed by membership in business organizations capable of voicing concerns and lobbying for reforms. Originally established to protect the interests of small businessmen who felt threatened by the formation of trusts and holding companies, chambers and associations of commerce soon competed against each other. New Orleans businessmen, emphasizing industrial development, proved their worth through "factory grabbing"—that is, snatching manufacturers away from other cities. The creation of factory- and commerce-friendly urban environments pressed the association to call for physical improvements to the city. By the 1910s, business associations nationwide took on the burdens of their respective urban centers. Businessmen such as those in the Crescent City considered it "their right and duty" to involve themselves in community affairs, seeing organizations such as the Association of Commerce as the "voice of the community" (by which they meant white men). As in other cities, the New Orleans Association of Commerce provided a unity of vision that, by the early 1920s, championed a modern, progressive city.[9]

The Association of Commerce represented a broad array of local business interests but focused on promoting industry and commerce. In 1920, the organization counted more than five thousand members. Although membership fluctuated with the economic tide, the Association of Commerce remained between four and five thousand strong until the onset of the Great Depression cut the ranks to under three thousand. The members split into two major factions. Retailers, shippers, cotton brokers, bankers, and manufacturers formed the most powerful group, with interests closely tied to the productivity of factories and the flow of materials along the Mississippi River. Hotel operators, restaurant owners, theater owners, and other service-oriented businesses occupied a less prominent position. At one time a strong alliance capable of challenging promoters of modernization along with the requisite tax increases, many of the businesses tied to the alcohol and sex markets faced extinction during the 1920s. Confronted with the successful moral reform campaigns of the Progressive Era, the service sector struggled to survive, much less force its views on the association. Most members thus saw the push to develop the city's industrial and commercial capabilities as the most viable means of economic growth. [10]

Well into the 1920s, the focus of boosterism in New Orleans and other cities remained on creating the optimal business environment for industry and commerce, not on promoting tourism. Progressive Era reforms to the cityscape received renewed and vigorous support. Association President B. C. Casanas succinctly reported on the change in society as the organization entered the 1920s: "The war has forced the world to turn its attention to the science of efficiency." Businessmen sought lower death rates, fewer urban fires, and urban beautification, among other improvements that determined a city's regional and national reputation. Population growth received particular attention, since it implied a healthy, expanding economy. As a 1924 editorial in the association's *News Bulletin* announced, "Men will not bring their families to live in cities which can not promise . . . the average comforts of life. . . . The man who does not strive to improve his condition in life is dead indeed. In the same sense, a city which does not try to improve living conditions for its inhabitants is dead." The number of goods produced in New Orleans and the amount of trade passing through the city were the most important and obvious indicators of local economic conditions, the "major part of the foundation and super-structure" of a city. New Orleans businessmen harped on the port facilities, trade routes, and products moving through local terminals. [11]

In the Association of Commerce's ideal business climate, only a thin conceptual line separated leisure from laziness. Recreation received sharp criticism, and tourism gained only scant attention. When fewer than forty individuals appeared at an August 1919 general membership meeting of the association, the editors of the *News Bulletin* expressed outrage. Many businessmen who could afford to escape the summer heat had left town, resulting in dismal attendance rates at business meetings. Chastising members for their lack of interest, association leaders sarcastically concluded, "You can't get anybody out to a meeting in New Orleans during the summer unless you have a parade and refreshments."[12] A couple of years later, the *News Bulletin* reprinted a story from *Collier's* expressing the need for civic work rather than leisure, hammering home the lesson by emphasizing that wartime mobilization had taught the need for "myriad non-political groups, to fight waste, crime, injustice, and ignorance." Efficiency demanded personal sacrifices, though not drastic ones—civic activities were deemed "pretty good fun besides." In addition, volunteerism saved money. Public service by private citizens kept the cost of government low by providing an alternative to the hiring of "hordes of public officials and salaried busybodies." The editorial ended by boasting, "Pulling an oar yourself might raise a blister, but its [*sic*] mighty good for the waistline."[13]

Californians' enthusiasm for boosterism served as a model for New Orleans business leaders. A 1921 visit by a group of San Franciscans to a local convention awed the New Orleans business community. The conventioneers exuded "optimism" and talked of "California until you couldn't hear anything else." That Californians and boosterism were firmly connected in the "public mind" impressed New Orleans businessmen, who reported on the westerners' tactics in the *News Bulletin*. The San Franciscans explained that their success stemmed from the fact that "everyone is 'sold' on California before he gets there." Once settled in the state, the person is urged "to talk it up and continues to do so until he begins to believe what he's saying." The end result was that boosterism became an incurable "disease." New Orleans businessmen sought to spread a similar "epidemic of 'boostitis,'" infecting "every mother's son" with the desire to "'buy' a big hunk of New Orleans" and to "'sell' it" whenever traveling beyond the city limits.[14]

New Orleans businessmen also studied their competitors to the southeast. Floridians marketed their state as a healthy destination and

an excellent real estate investment. Following the example set by Californians, Floridians adopted well-financed promotional campaigns,
and a postwar land boom brought substantial urban growth. Despite
the collapse of the Florida real estate market by the late 1920s, the
development of Florida swamps suggested to New Orleanians the profitability of expanding their city's borders.

Unlike New Orleans boosters, however, Californians and Floridians focused their promotional campaigns on year-round, leisure-based
tourism. Promoters in both states emphasized that the warm climate allowed uninterrupted access to beaches, golf courses, and other outdoor
sites increasingly popular within American culture. One ad published in
the national magazine *Outlook* by the All-Year Club of Southern California proclaimed the state an "ideal summerland" where "the wonders
and the beauties and the fun of three continents combined." With "*no
rain* to mar a single hour" of "outdoor play," Californians, especially
those in Los Angeles, openly marketed the state for leisure purposes.
Promotional materials, street names, and architecture reinforced the
message of year-round recreation with references to the stable, warm
climate of the Mediterranean, particularly Spain and Italy. In their
study of Florida, for example, Alejandro Portes and Alex Stepick have
declared that St. Augustine "became far more Spanish under [Henry
Flagler] than it had ever been during three centuries of Spanish domi-
nation."[15]

As early as 1919, members of the C & T Bureau began to see the
importance of tourism for New Orleans's growth, pointing out that
Florida and California devoted millions of dollars to advertising while
New Orleans "spent nothing." According to the C & T Bureau, the
time had "come when we must be on the job in the matter of civic
development in order to hold the interest of the tourist travel of the
United States." The city lay on a major train route to the Pacific, and
railroads offered a ten-day stopover for riders interested in visiting the
city on their way west. New Orleans could thus benefit from the Californians' promotional efforts. Visitors to Florida, however, bypassed
New Orleans.[16]

Nevertheless, New Orleans businessmen hesitated to jump on the tourism bandwagon. Rather than foster an image of year-round leisure, New Orleans businessmen looked to the Mississippi Gulf Coast as a means of spatially segregating leisure areas from the business-oriented urban core. Residents of Mississippi's three coastal counties, as the *Biloxi News* reported, had long considered themselves ‑"more of an integral part of Louisiana, and of New Orleans in particular," than of Mississippi. New Orleans reciprocated by promoting the area's economic potential and touting the Mississippi strand as the city's playground. Development of the coast eased the pressure of housing the seasonal influx of winter visitors to New Orleans and offered opportunities for visitors to bathe, fish, golf, and enjoy other outdoor activities. The distance between New Orleans and Mississippi, however, allowed the Association of Commerce to safeguard the city's image as a serious business center separated from the constant frivolity found on the Gulf Coast. Businessmen, as the Association of Commerce boasted, saw the "climatic advantages proclaimed and capitalized" by Florida "right at our doors." With "New Orleans in convenient distance, the Gulf Coast resorts could offer any degree of rest, relaxation or entertainment desired by the most cosmopolitan incomparably superior to anything in the United States." All the Mississippi resorts needed was the "magic hand of a [Henry] Plant or a Flagler to advertise them and prepare adequate accommodations."[17]

City leaders' only concession to the leisure culture of California and Florida within city limits manifested itself along Lake Pontchartrain. The early 1920s brought a major development project meant to enhance the lakeshore. Politicians and businessmen proposed the construction of a seawall, a shoreline drive, and even large islands to harbor yachts and homes. Although the push for an island chain failed, the other projects improved access to the water. The shoreline was eventually lined with concrete steps to accommodate spectators for possible water sports events. An extensive levee system allowed the city to drain the nearby marshes and open the land to prospective homeowners. L. C. Spencer, a native of New Orleans and a professor at Spencer Business College, captured the copycat thinking of civic leaders when he declared, "Atlantic City, Miami, and Los Angeles bask in the sunshine of world renown because of their superb water fronts." But Spencer recognized the dichotomy between business-oriented urban spaces, which in New Orleans included the downtown riverfront, and leisure-oriented spaces: "Down to the sparkling, rippling waves, come millions of pleasure seekers from the quiet inland farm and from the bustling activity of the great American cities." The *Times-Picayune* simply described the proposed renovation of the lakefront, with the requisite demolition of historic fishing camps, dance halls, and restaurants at West End and Milneburg, as the creation of the "playground of a metropolis." The development of the lakefront coincided with interest in making a resort of the so-called Ozone Belt on the northern shore of Lake Pontchartrain. Some civic leaders even advocated the construction of a causeway to connect New Orleans to Mandeville, a distance of more than twenty miles. Although the proposal, with some alteration, would not be realized until after the Second World War, the call for a bridge highlighted the importance of maintaining separate spaces for business and leisure.[18]

Key to promotion of any city for purposes of factory grabbing, commercial expansion, or—eventually—tourism, was image creation. Before crafting New Orleans as the exotic, old-time French city designed for vacations, businessmen gained experience packaging the Crescent City for potential investors. Several municipal identities informed local marketing campaigns and in time allowed the creation of illusions central to developing a profitable mass tourist trade. Based on the rhetoric of the Association of Commerce, New Orleans businessmen, like their colleagues in other large cities, masked their role as self-interested boosters and instead packaged themselves as patriotic Americans. Their economic pursuits offered to the nation a grand metropolis with economic ties to foreign ports around the globe. Trade made New Orleans internationally prominent, especially in regard to Latin and South America. Domestically, the city's businessmen concentrated on the Mississippi River Valley, which gave New Orleans a claim to the American heartland. New Orleanians also presented themselves as southerners and advocated projects that provided supposed proof that southerners formed part of the American mainstream. New Orleans boosters were progressive regional leaders who honored the plantation past and the Lost Cause—but not to the point of distraction from economic development. The vision of a New South attracted fervid believers in the Louisiana port. Finally, businessmen thought of themselves as loyal, cosmopolitan New Orleanians. Pride in the locality reinforced the city's reputation and provided a springboard for the launch of municipal improvements. High civic morale permitted effective mobilization of resources, bolstering the city's regional and national standing. Businessmen therefore cloaked their interests in language that appealed to a larger audience that sympathized with American, southern, or more local concerns.[19]

The successful manipulation of these personas kept businessmen tuned to national and regional trends. Highly competitive economic struggles among cities required vigilance. Missed opportunities translated into lost profits. New Orleans businessmen prided themselves on their city and viewed their pursuit of global trade and the development of modern port facilities as evidence of economic greatness. Urban improvements, according to local business leaders, supplied proof that New Orleans belonged to the American pantheon of trade capitals, including Chicago and New York. In an early 1920s editorial entitled "Let 'Em Holler," the association boasted of New Orleans's rank as the country's second-busiest port and ridiculed other cities for their attempts to overtake New Orleans.[20] When Galveston replaced Philadelphia as the third-busiest port in 1921, members of the Association of Commerce responded with a gleeful jibe, "pitying" their northern competitors' fate even though "prone to believe . . . that while Philadelphia was third port, she spent more time in trying to prove that she was second port than she did in trying to retain that rank."[21] Yet a serious challenge from such a nearby rival as Galveston also brought a swift response, as association members raged against the Galvestonians for exaggerating their city's importance by including figures for Houston and Texas City in their calculations.[22]

Advertising and boosterism represented city leaders' weapons of choice in a variety of battles, including the fight to influence national opinion in the wake of the Mississippi River flood of 1927. The Association of Commerce attacked a Chicago reporter's story on the damage as "Flood Lies . . . about the South."[23] To deflect attention from the disaster, the association launched a twenty-thousand-dollar national publicity campaign, further expanding the organization's role and giving the members experience in manipulating public opinion through direct advertising. The ads, published in trade journals such as the *Furniture Manufacturer* as well as in such mass newspapers as the *New York Times* and *Chicago Tribune*, emphasized New Orleans's industrial and commercial strengths. In previous ad campaigns, Crescent City businessmen either purchased space in business publications or mailed prepared articles to mass audience newspapers and magazines in hopes that the editors would print the stories for free because of a need to fill space or because readers might find the material of interest. A follow-up campaign in 1928 continued the theme and the fresh approach to marketing, and the resulting public pressure brought a federal commitment to construct and maintain levees, spillways, and other measures to prevent future floods. This success convinced association leaders of the value of reaching the general public, and mass media campaigns became part of their marketing arsenal.[24]

Although civic leaders' attempts to mobilize public support for industrial and commercial improvements led to the accentuation of New Orleans's unique history, progress trumped preservation. During the 1910s and 1920s, for example, numerous cities began constructing municipal flags, part of a movement fueled by the desire for municipal reform as well as the patriotism stirred by the First World War. According to the *American City*, a national journal that reported on urban trends, the creation of flags expressed "civic spirit," while the selection of colors and figures permitted the symbolic ordering of the urban environment. The banner would then provide "appropriate and uniform decorations of streets and buildings on public ceremonial occasions," stirring "dormant energies" and "new ambitions" for civic improvement by highlighting the uniqueness of the local community. In 1918, New Orleans's municipal government adopted a flag depicting three gold fleurs-de-lis on a red, white, and blue striped background. When city official Andre Lafarge presented the flag to the mayor of

Orleans, France, in a 1922 ceremony, he proclaimed, "Strewn with golden lilies, the red, the white and the blue of our flag will forever stand as the perpetuation of the founding, growth and development of our city. Your colors are ours, your ideals and traditions are likewise ours. We are proud of our flag, because it reminds us of old France and of young America." Past and modern mores competed. Yet the emphasis remained on development out of French ways. A youthful America promised growth and prosperity.[25]

The attempt to forge a progressive, modern image of the city clashed with the desire to preserve the past. Some association members in 1929 complained about the city seal, which depicted two figures in Indian dress standing on either side of a river, beneath which sat a yawning alligator. New Orleans businessmen sarcastically declared the seal "undesirable unless someone can discover some beautiful historic significance that no one seems to know anything definitely about but some are willing to guess at." The business community argued for an "up-to-date" seal. Although a municipal seal was expected to express the historical roots of a community, the promotion of the community's progressive drive was deemed of greater value. Faced with opposition from local historical societies as well as several others who saw the seal as part of the city's heritage, the Association of Commerce leadership compromised. A coat of arms would now appear on letterheads, medals, engravings, and other municipal material. Members of the association happily reported that the seal remained in use only "for the formal purpose of legalized documents."[26]

Author Sherwood Anderson sparked particular anger among Association of Commerce members when he criticized the local assault on historic neighborhoods and customs deemed a hindrance to progress, including calls to demolish the French Quarter and replace it with a skyscraper-filled business district, thus further completing the vision of the city as a business center with tourist attractions pushed to the outskirts of the metropolis. Written in the mode of a fragmentary conversation spoken over some glasses of illegal beer, Anderson's "New Orleans," which appeared in the August 1926 issue of *Vanity Fair*, presented nameless characters spurting their observations: "The end of

New Orleans—the old town, the sweet town, is already in sight," declared one drinker. Another erupted, "Them millionaires run in packs." Los Angeles, Miami, and Coral Gables beckoned wealthy Americans in Anderson's brief tale, but his characters announced that New Orleans "aint never been boomed none." The city still possessed character. "Corrupt politics," "smells," "dirt," and "shiftlessness" made New Orleans vibrant. Life was "pretty wide-open" in the city. Anderson's characters lamented the modernization efforts pressed by local businessmen. One character mimicked the cry of local boosters: "I'm going to tell you [the relaxed pace of life] won't last long. New Orleans is a swell town. It can be put on the map and it will be too. Its [sic] in the air now. Better invest some money down here." The carefree, leisurely lifestyle "stuff," Anderson wrote, did not sit well with the Association of Commerce members. They wanted people "worried." Businessmen rejected the community of artists and writers gathered in the deteriorating French Quarter. "Such a lot don't do a town no good," observed one drinker, describing the businessmen's attitude. Anderson attacked businessmen's blind pursuit of "northern money" in the form of commercial trade and industrial investment. One character voiced the common attitude of civic leaders: "A lot of us down here need money. We'll like you better if you bring it down."[27]

Editors for the Association of Commerce *News Bulletin* retorted with an aptly titled editorial, "Anderson's Sneer." They saw Anderson as little more than "the eminent dispenser of luscious morsels for the literati" and dismissed his attacks as "only kidding." At the same time, the businessmen classified Anderson and his fellow writers as "purely literary and purely impractical" figures. Although on some occasions "it is good to be able to forget cares," no man "with ordinary common sense . . . will contend that it is good for New Orleans to advertise itself upon all occasions as the city that has forgotten to care—a city devoted to carelessness." New Orleans had suffered too long under such a perception. The "unfortunate and erroneous reputation" praised by Anderson had led countless investors "seeking progress and aggressiveness" to place their money in "competing cities." As for preserving historic buildings in the French Quarter, the businessmen hedged only slightly. Association members "appreciate fully with Mr. Anderson the value to New Orleans of the distinctiveness of the old quarter." Neither New Orleans nor any other city, however, could "live and prosper on scenic and romantic distinctiveness alone." The ability to "maintain for posterity the architectural heirlooms of the Vieux Carre is directly dependent upon the prosperity of New Orleans." The Association of Commerce proudly claimed its role as guardian of the city's economic well-being. Progress, born from the development of industry and commerce, could not be sacrificed.[28]

Conventions of the Better Sort

Given civic leaders' commitment to traditional economic pursuits during the 1920s, interest in tourism was limited to the attraction of conventions of business organizations. After losing the mayoral election in 1920, Martin Behrman, the longtime boss of the city's political machine, known as the Old Regulars, became chairman of the C & T Bureau and began championing conventions as valuable contributors to the New Orleans economy. Appealing to local businessmen's competitive spirit, Behrman emphasized that "every large city in the United States of any consequence" pursued "as many state, district and regional conventions as possible" and cleverly argued that conventions benefited the industrial and commercial enterprises vigorously pursued by the Association of Commerce. In Behrman's words, conventions brought "prospective buyers" and potentially expanded the city's "trade territory." The common view of a convention delegate as "a man or woman decorated with a badge of some bright color, making a lot of noise, with nothing to do but play and plenty of money to spend" was erroneous. As Behrman explained, a conventioneer was a "high grade business man, or woman, who has affiliated himself with his trade organization for the purpose of gaining the benefit of others' experience in his line for the improvement of his business." "Intelligent, prosperous, successful and progressive" conventioneers—including bankers, manufacturers, educators, lawyers, doctors, and other professionals—made for a "desirable type of citizen for any city." Conventions thus provided publicity for a city, and an attractive urban environment had the potential to convince conventioneers to invest in local businesses or even establish residences. Moreover, profits did not just impact restaurants or hotels but trickled through the local economy. According to the Bureau of Statistics in Washington, D.C., conventions formed a billion-dollar industry, and Behrman wanted New Orleans to join the "few cities" that annually plundered the convention treasure trove.[29]

The late nineteenth and early twentieth centuries saw a proliferation of organizations as businessmen and professionals sought to share information and foster camaraderie within their respective fields. Increased specialization and the importance of expertise encouraged such fraternity. Advances in transportation and communication technologies facilitated these organizational efforts, and local, regional, and national societies ranging from the massive American Legion to more job-specific organizations such as the Louisiana Optometrists Association came into existence. Many such organizations arranged annual gatherings of their members, spurring the convention-hosting industry in urban centers.[30] In 1920, the editors of the New Orleans Association of Commerce *News Bulletin* argued that an emerging and "accepted method of advertising, profitably used by all the larger and more alert American cities, is the securing and entertaining of conventions of the better sort." The article emphasized that the "visual impression carried away by the convention delegate is generally recognized as the most potent form of community advertising."[31]

The First World War contributed to New Orleans's development as a convention city. According to the C & T Bureau, the conflict made "over seas travel impossible." Furthermore, federal restrictions on travel hampered individual tourists more than conventions, which federal officials believed allowed for the most efficient use of trains, fuel, and time. By holding such highly visible meetings, businessmen could adjust their policies to government needs and publicly declare support for the American cause. Moreover, in the superpatriotic wartime social climate in which Americans suspected the presence of saboteurs and spies, conventions served to screen out-of-towners, giving legitimacy to the presence of visitors in a city.[32]

Economic conditions encouraged the Association of Commerce to court conventions. A postwar recession resulted in high travel costs, reducing railroad travel by 25 to 40 percent. Therefore, rather than organize broad publicity campaigns aimed at the general population, the association committed its financial resources to convention hunting, and from the late 1910s into the 1920s, the C & T Bureau functioned "solely as a convention securing bureau." Conventions provided calculable returns on funds spent, while tabulating the number of individual vacationers was an imprecise science and deciphering how much money those tourists spent was even more difficult. Organizations, however, kept membership rolls and registered participants. Even fiscally conservative New Orleans businessmen could recognize the profitability of hosting conventions.[33]

Furthermore, the promotion of industrial and commercial strengths over recreational attractions resonated with an audience of businessmen spread across America. In her study of vacationing in the United States, Cindy Aron has argued that tourists in the early twentieth century struggled with a paradox. According to Aron, "Industriousness and discipline helped to make people middle class and thus entitled them to vacations, but vacations embodied the very opposite of what the middle class most valued." Travelers therefore regularly combined leisure with self-improvement by attending religious revivals, lectures, expositions, or other events that excused time away from work. Business conventions served a similar purpose. Earl McGowin, the son of an Alabama lumber mill operator, recalled that his father "didn't do traveling just for pleasure's sake." Although occasional business trips took the elder McGowin to Louisville, Mobile, Pensacola, and New York, the annual Southern Pine Association convention in New Orleans was different: he took along his wife and children. The trip "was a great pleasure for all of us." The message of economic development fueled the tourist trade. Family members typically explored the streets while husbands attended meetings and cut deals, thus melding business and tourism.[34]

Local boosters likewise mixed business with pleasure when they put the port on display. Rarely did a convention pass without local leaders providing conventioneers a cruise on the Mississippi River, highlighting improvements to port facilities and the presence of major plants. The role of the river as a source of transportation was central to the message supplied by New Orleans boosters. Reporting on preparations for the arrival of the Young Business Clubs of America in 1916, George Merkel declared that "entertainment, consisting chiefly of showing the facilities of the Port of New Orleans, has been planned, with the idea in view of securing more trade for the Port of New Orleans."[35] On occasions, the river cruise included elegant banquets and dancing. Wholesale merchants attending the New Orleans Fall Buyers Convention in 1920, for example, enjoyed an excursion on the steamer *Sidney*.[36] The romance of the river, however, took a secondary position to the probusiness message. When a convention of secretaries arrived in the Crescent City in 1938, the business community arranged a harbor trip on the "palatial river steamer President." The vessel carried the out-of-towners on a "route up river in sight of the thirteen million dollar Huey P. Long Mississippi River Bridge, the interesting riverfront panorama of docks, oceangoing steamers, river boats, grain elevators, cotton warehouses, etc."[37] The dinner and dance cruises usually occurred on steamboats, reminding conventioneers of New Orleans's antebellum prosperity and of river transportation's long, profitable history.

Dramatic social reforms contributed to the focus on conventions. Conventioneers provided a substitute for the male travelers who no longer came to a city cleansed of brothels and bars. The implementation of Prohibition and other reform legislation stunned operators of hotels, restaurants, retail stores, and transportation companies, who formed a significant segment of the membership of the C & T Bureau. Voicing the complaints of its constituents, the bureau protested "the desire of the people of New Orleans to so closely regulate the lives of her citizens and visitors as to reduce their pleasurable occupations to a minimum." The closure of New Orleans's breweries, which contributed more than 10 percent of the C & T Bureau's average nine thousand dollar annual budget, severely weakened efforts to promote New Orleans as a destination. The C & T Bureau's funding came from payments from the Association of Commerce general fund, and the rise of blue laws,

Prohibition, and restrictions on prostitution caused businesses dependent on travelers to fear that the C & T Bureau would receive inadequate financial support. In 1923, association members reached a compromise under which hotel operators and their allies were allowed to divert membership fees into a special C & T Bureau fund independent of the general fund. Hotel and restaurant owners nevertheless remained uneasy and sought to guarantee that funds earmarked for tourism promotion remained beyond the reach of the association leadership, which was less enthusiastic about fostering tourism. By the end of 1924, a faction of these businessmen formed the New Orleans Hotel and Restaurant Association to protect their tourism-related interests as well as to supplement C & T Bureau activities.[38]

The hotel and restaurant owners rallied around Behrman, who called on the entire business community to invest in the growing convention trade. A highly successful year brought a wide variety of conventions and tantalizing profits, a point Behrman and his supporters hammered home at every opportunity. In 1922, New Orleans hosted meetings of forty-eight organizations—twelve national associations, twenty state-oriented groups, and sixteen regional bodies. The conventions brought a total of 58,900 visitors to New Orleans, nearly 90 percent of them as part of the national gatherings, which included that of the American Legion. Estimating daily spending at $15 per attendee, the Association of Commerce calculated an influx of approximately $2,340,000 from national conventions, with an additional $190,000 earned from state and regional gatherings. Although 1922 was exceptional as a result of the American Legion convention, even more typical years brought impressive crowds. In 1929, for example, seventy-six conventions with a total attendance of more than 22,000 came to the city. In addition to the occasional convention with more than 1,000 delegates, such as the meeting of the Society of American Florists and Ornamental Horticulture, New Orleans hosted numerous meetings of smaller organizations with as many as 500 delegates, including such groups as the Coca Cola Bottlers Association, the American Food Manufacturers Association, the Associated Ad Clubs of the World, and McGowin's Southern Pine Association. The impressive figures made even businessmen in industrial and commercial enterprises take note of tourism and its economic impact.[39]

Despite its success, the 1922 American Legion convention revealed the city's limited capacity to host conventions. That the legion's members were not governed by the etiquette of modern business only made matters worse. The large numbers of raucous veterans overwhelmed the city's hotel rooms and spilled into tent camps, facilities on a nearby army base, and Pullman train cars. Furthermore, although New Orleanians were accustomed to the annual flock of con men and street vendors who followed vacationing northerners to warmer climes during the winter months, the arrival of opportunists seeking to exploit the Legionnaires' convention threatened the civic leaders' ability to showcase the city. Future New Orleans mayor T. Semmes Walmsley, chair of the American Legion's National Convention Committee, faced a logistical nightmare as the convention date neared and the Ringling-Barnum Circus announced plans to descend on the city. Walmsley complained that "this enormous circus of one hundred or more cars, with more than a thousand people, and hundreds of animals arriving in New Orleans simultaneously with thousands of Legionnaires will, undoubtedly, greatly congest the railroad traffic and delay a great number of New Orleans Legionnaire guests' arrival." Not only would the delays cost the city revenue, but the circus would siphon money away from area attractions. To grow as a convention city and eventually as a mass tourism destination, New Orleans needed to develop its tourism infrastructure and become less dependent on railways.[40]

The drive to attract conventions encouraged the Association of Commerce to develop its role as community educator so that every citizen could serve as a knowledgeable tour guide. Business leaders harped on the need for all locals to know the city's strengths. A 1919 editorial in the *News Bulletin* asked readers, "When a stranger comes to town and wants to know what New Orleans has and what New Orleans has done, what do you tell them?" That someone, especially a businessman, might pause to think about a response or even fail to provide an answer became a major concern. Accuracy was especially important "because the spreading of truthful information" about local strengths provided "the best advertising available." The association thus became a clearinghouse for information. Leisure sites, such as historic structures or noteworthy restaurants, did not figure into the organization's thinking. Instead, the Association of Commerce offered to inform locals about "facts and figures" and "about the principal points in favor of this city as a manufacturing center, the Port of the Valley to the World and metropolis of the South."[41]

The education of local businessmen also benefited the city by converting personal vacations into public relations trips. The Association of Commerce announced that it was "glad to arm its members with valuable information any time they go away." Traveling businessmen thus became traveling salesmen, prepared to converse about the city as much as possible—and even to excess.[42] Urban boosters, as association leaders explained, reacted to the "queer twist of human nature" that showed that some New Orleanians knew "more about Chicago than a resident of the Western Metropolis." The realization that residents of a city often possessed greater knowledge about urban centers other than their own both disturbed and invigorated local businessmen. Curiosity about locations away from home helped convince association members that mass promotional campaigns could bear fruit despite the difficulty of gauging public response. Conversely, local disinterest about area sites suggested weak civic pride. In response, the Association of Commerce stressed the need for residents to learn "how to talk about their city when they go away" as well as to visitors in New Orleans streets.[43]

The emphasis of the municipal government and local business community on promoting traditional enterprises through conventions emerged most clearly with the construction of the Municipal Auditorium. Members of the Association of Commerce recognized that the city sorely needed a large civic hall open to visiting organizations, as was the case in cities such as San Francisco and New York, that would enable New Orleans to "compete for great conventions such as Knights of Columbus, Shriners, and other fraternal assemblies and great political and business rallies." Plans for New Orleans's convention center rose from the ashes of the French Opera House, a famous French Quarter hall gutted by fire in 1919. The disappearance of the landmark created an urgent need for a large assembly center near downtown. Business-men showed only halfhearted interest in restoring a once vital piece of the historic Vieux Carré. Instead, New Orleans economic leaders pur-sued a modern facility with an edifice not harking to an archaic French past but to a bountiful American future. The Association of Commerce campaigned for a building that would serve as a centerpiece for fur-ther development of other municipal structures "located as centrally as possible with reference to the business district . . . so as to encourage a greater use." Although advocates sought to place the structure in an "attractive and pleasing neighborhood," very few considered construct-ing the auditorium on the French Opera House site. The Vieux Carré was still a slum on the periphery of Canal Street retail shops and the banking houses, cotton brokerages, and other businesses located on the upriver side of the thoroughfare. Local resident Frank Farrell lamented in 1921, "There seems to be a disposition on the part of some to set at naught things of a historical nature belonging to old New Orleans, and the desecration of the spot where the French Opera House stood seems to be in line with the new progress New Orleans is making in the downtown section of the city."[44]

For much of the 1920s, civic leaders hotly debated the purpose of an auditorium within New Orleans. The issue of segregating leisure activities from economic endeavors underlay the controversy. A vo-cal minority within the Association of Commerce argued for a new French Opera House to be placed in the French Quarter and funded by the public. Most members favored a more utilitarian structure. The size, placement, and intended use of any new hall stirred antagonism among businessmen and politicians. Proposals to make the auditorium a memorial for veterans of the Great War met with considerable ap-proval, although some people, among them a Tulane University pro-fessor, argued that a "memorial to the soldiers should not be shared by commercial interests." Arthur Parker, president of the Association of Commerce, discarded suggestions to use the hall for conventions and local arts events like operas and "ventured the opinion that opera has a value of its own, which would be destroyed if combined with any other venture." Conversely, A. S. Amer, manager of the St. Charles Hotel, voiced the opinion that "opera would never pay in New Orleans, and therefore the artistic should be somewhat sacrificed in the architecture of the building, so as to combine with it business features" appropriate for conventions. Suggestions that any such building be turned over to the city government to ensure a tax-exempt status increased opposition to the proposed project. Businessman Charles Claiborne complained that "the giving over of another public building to be administered by the city would mean one more dirty, badly kept building in the city of New Orleans." With businessmen and politicians divided, New Orleanians refused to foot the bill for a proposed auditorium, voting down such a measure in 1922.[45]

After years of debate, city leaders in 1926 finally won public support for a bond issue to fund the construction of an auditorium, and a commission soon began making arrangements for construction. Public outrage blocked the use of Beauregard Square, a site that honored New Orleans's highest-ranking Confederate general, P. G. T. Beauregard. Instead, the municipal government acquired land adjacent to the famed park. The location, wedged between the French Quarter and the Union Terminal, was within easy walking distance of downtown. When the new Municipal Auditorium opened its doors to great fanfare in 1930, the building stood as a monument to the business community. The location served the interests of progressive-minded businessmen who saw urban advancement in new, gleaming white buildings.[46]

A Product for Tourist Consumption

Despite businessmen's efforts to foreground industry and commerce, outside observers continued to admire the city's cultural and architectural uniqueness. Guest speakers at two Association of Commerce gatherings in 1923 expressed dismay at the organization's campaign to rid the city of its leisurely image. James Schermerhorn, publisher of the *Detroit Times*, called New Orleans an "all soul city, because it is a city which hasn't forgotten how to play." Mardi Gras parades such as Rex, Comus, Momus, and Proteus provided evidence of the city's lighter side. Schermerhorn explained, "Unfortunate is the city which looks only to the material side of things, the city which can talk and think only in terms of bank clearings, report and export figures, post-office receipts." In Schermerhorn's view, American cities, including New Orleans, had "too much" interest in business. The consequence was unnecessary rivalry and too "many petty jealousies."[47] Edgar O. Lovett of Houston's Rice Institute expressed a similar opinion. In his eyes, New Orleans, along with Boston, Washington, San Francisco, and Cleveland, stood apart from other American cities. New Orleans differed "because of its delightful Southern charm, distilled from the Spanish, French and Anglo-Saxon civilizations; its five-fingered railroad system; and its shipping to the seven seas to the world." The city, a product of its transportation network and diverse heritage, was worth visiting: "No American city . . . is quite so romantic as New Orleans."[48]

By the late 1920s, New Orleans businessmen had begun to listen to these arguments, embracing mass tourism as well as the romantic imagery they had previously criticized as detrimental to the city's economic well-being. Rising automobile ownership allowed tourists greater freedom to travel where and when they wanted. Road construction programs, originally intended to boost trade, grew into efforts to satisfy motorists' hunger for adventure. Furthermore, the automobile required a physical restructuring of the city. Cars congested the urban space, requiring parking facilities, traffic regulations, stoplights, and improved roadways. Although conventions appealed to businessmen's sense of order and efficiency, the automobile introduced reasons for crafting a broader promotional program aimed at a national audience.

In the years immediately following the First World War, road conditions remained poor, and efforts to designate interstate highways fell short of expectations. Local boosters facilitated the creation of a well-maintained road, promoted as the Old Spanish Trail, connecting Florida and California. Such roads, however, rarely provided optimal driving conditions until well into the interwar years. The "Pine-to-Palm" route between Winnipeg and New Orleans was introduced in 1915 but remained incomplete until the mid-1920s. A 1919 inspection tour by a group of association businessmen had "to use oxen and mules to pull [cars] out of mud holes," causing the embarrassed boosters to run a day behind. Shortly before Mardi Gras 1925, Louisiana author Lyle Saxon was driving to pick wildflowers on the outskirts of New Orleans when the car "went into a ditch and had to be pulled out." A month later, while visiting a friend in northern Louisiana, he almost met his death when the car in which he was riding "ran over a hog and all of us were thrown down the banks of Cane River."[49] Only the very adventurous risked touring the state when faced with driving conditions so bad that lives were endangered.

Communities throughout the nation eventually rallied against deplorable road conditions, resulting in an explosion of road construction in the two decades after the First World War. Shortly after the armistice, the federal government gave surplus military trucks and tractors to state highway departments, and Congress subsequently passed the Federal Highway Act of 1921, which provided matching federal funds for state road construction projects, thereby not only encouraging states to build quality roads but also linking the various intrastate systems. Within a few years, a numbering system was instituted for the newly constructed interstate highways, better orienting motorists along thousands of miles of paved roadways. For Louisiana, massive construction efforts under Governor Huey Long and later New Deal programs further linked New Orleans to the rest of the nation.[50]

The Association of Commerce initially advocated road construction programs as a means of boosting the influx of goods from surrounding areas and increasing sales in downtown stores. Lengthy, well-maintained roads designed for automotive traffic achieved an importance reminiscent of that of railways during the late nineteenth century. The association spearheaded efforts to lobby nearby states and municipal governments, urging them to finance sections of highway that would link New Orleans with other major population centers. In the early 1920s, the organization stressed that the "more closely a city is connected by GOOD ROADS with the territory surrounding it, the greater is the TRIBUTE OF TRADE that city draws from the territory." Prominent New Orleanians conducted regular motorcades and "Know New Orleans" tours through surrounding towns to publicize the excellent road network as well as New Orleans businesses. By 1935, the association's *News Bulletin* could boast that New Orleans was a "terminus of more named or nationally numbered highways than any other city in the country." [51]

With an interstate road system in development and the mass production of automobiles giving free rein to American desires for travel, New Orleans civic leaders faced a national culture being radically altered by the horseless carriage. As early as 1926, the Association of Commerce recognized that Americans had become "a people who live on rubber tires." This "Motor Age" brought new concerns for New Orleans businessmen. In their classic 1929 sociological study, *Middletown*, Robert and Helen Lynd revealed that cars affected every aspect of daily life but especially "revolutionized its leisure." The Lynds' work focused on Muncie, Indiana, part of a region New Orleans boosters would target in their earliest tourism marketing campaigns. The Lynds found that, prior to the automobile, train excursions to towns as close as fifteen miles away were considered "great events." Travel by car revolutionized conceptions of leisure, making recreation "a regularly expected part of every day and week rather than an occasional event." By 1927, more than half of the nation's 27.5 million families owned automobiles, and two years later, an unprecedented 5.3 million motor vehicles rolled off assembly lines. The Lynds' follow-up work in the 1930s discovered that automobile ownership was "one of the most depression-proof" aspects of Americans' lives. Americans embraced the automobile and continued to travel extensively despite the onset of the Great Depression. Contemporary observer Frederick Lewis Allen explained that American society had become bogged down in the "routine and smoke and congestion and twentieth-century standardization of living." From Allen's perspective, trains symbolized modernity, whereas automobiles recalled a pioneer spirit. Americans used their automobiles to "escape . . . into the free sunshine of the remembered countryside, into the easy-going life and beauty of the European past, into some never-never land which combined American sport and comfort with Latin glamour." [52]

Businessmen could ill afford to ignore automobiles' powerful new influence on U.S. cultural life. Although mass production led to the saturation of the American automobile market by the time of the Great

Depression, Americans' desire for travel intensified during the 1930s. Money expended on car-related products such as gasoline inched upward from $1.04 billion in 1929 to $1.102 billion in 1933 despite the depression. Americans in the 1930s spent more on travel than on movie tickets, radios, and other recreational activities combined. Whereas rail travel required food purchases and rental of hotel rooms downtown, cars permitted Americans to stretch their financial resources by transporting their own food or by staying at cheaper roadside motels. Motorists also comparison-shopped by scouting local eateries and boarding places, thereby avoiding high prices.[53]

Businessmen in New Orleans documented a steady increase in the number of automobiles entering the city from out of state. In 1926, the police department's Foreign Motor Vehicle Registration Bureau reported that 4,122 automobiles from outside Louisiana visited New Orleans, and Association of Commerce officials equated those figures to around 10,000 tourists. The numbers grew steadily over the next few years despite the Great Depression. A two-week survey taken in the summer of 1931 revealed an approximately 25 percent increase in the number of motorists visiting the city compared to figures for 1930.[54]

At the same time Americans became fixated on automobiles, a sharp national decline occurred in passenger railroad service, with railroad companies' income plummeting from $201 million in 1929 to $80 million in 1933. As long as trains served as the preferred method of long-distance travel, businessmen could rely on railroad companies to promote destinations along their routes and to facilitate convention hosting by granting discounted rates. The decline of train travel meant the end of such inducements. Moreover, the depression also severely weakened business organizations, as businessmen terminated memberships as a means of saving money. Whereas in 1928 and 1929 New Orleans hosted 41 and 76 conventions, respectively, with more than 22,000 in attendance each year, the 1934 convention season brought fewer than 16,600 conventioneers—and that for 144 conventions.[55]

A July 1936 survey conducted by *Fortune* magazine captured the evolving American attitude toward automobiles, railroads, and travel.

Of those interviewed, almost half declared that they expected to take between one and sixteen days of vacation. Although an equal proportion stated that they would have no vacation, the surveyors at *Fortune* qualified the evidence by revealing how "more than half are farmers and their wives who have seasonal leisure during which they do a good deal of driving around without calling it vacation." More significantly, the poll reported that "Americans not only like to spend their vacations away from home, but they want to get as far away as they have time to go, preferably to another part of the country." Less than a quarter expected to travel fewer than a hundred miles, while 39.5 percent planned to travel between one hundred and five hundred miles and 26.3 percent planned to travel more than five hundred miles. A meager 1.9 percent of the respondents expressed a desire to remain at home. Furthermore, as *Fortune* declared, "The automobile, of course, is the principal means of going on vacation: 75 per cent of the vacationers travel in it, only 13.6 by train, and 5.6 by bus." Even a proposed reduction in train fares from the standard 3.5 cents a mile to 2 cents a mile would not pry Americans away from their steering wheels, as more than 80 percent of respondents indicated that they would still prefer to drive. Although regional variations in travel patterns existed, the Midwest, the primary target of New Orleans publicity campaigns, stood as the bastion of motoring. Said *Fortune*, "The Middle Westerner . . . is a restless soul who favors just plain driving his car above any other objective."[56]

Data collected by the Association of Commerce revealed the prominence of midwesterners within the New Orleans tourism industry. In January and February 1934, the association received 1,042 inquiries about the upcoming Mardi Gras season. Six of the top sixteen states represented were from the Midwest, including Illinois, Missouri, and Ohio. The South, led by Alabama, Texas, and Florida, was represented by seven states. The three other states that sent a significant number of inquiries were New York, Pennsylvania, and California. (See figure 1.) The New Orleans tourist market consisted largely of travelers from nearby southern and midwestern states that had been economically tied to the city since the days when antebellum farmers sent their crops through the port. Data on vacationers in New Orleans confirms the strong presence of midwesterners. In February 1938, 3,328 people registered at the association's Mardi Gras information desk: 596 of the visitors (nearly 18 percent) were from Illinois, and seven of the other top ten states represented were also in the Midwest.[57] (See figure 2.)

As automobiles shrank distances and enticed Americans to travel, urban tour companies discovered the profitability of year-round, regularly scheduled tours. Consequently, private guide companies began to pressure Association of Commerce leaders to adjust their policies on tourism. Beginning in 1927, tour-company owners George Toye and Louis Higgins argued that out-of-towners preferred seemingly unbiased descriptions offered by professional guide companies to the more booster-oriented association-sponsored tours frequently arranged for conventioneers. Toye reassured the association that his guides remained focused on "selling New Orleans to its prospects who are on the ground" by impressing visitors in the "most effective manner" through detailed, highly polished lectures given at the tour stops. Tour companies served as information clearinghouses, repeating association-approved lectures in a more informal manner. Specialized, professional guides also reduced the spread of misinformation. J. E. Fitzwilson, one of six association representatives to evaluate the effectiveness of professional tours, warned fellow members not to disregard the value of services provided by men such as Toye and Higgins. "Show your guests points of interest and of advantage in New Orleans by taking them on one of the sightseeing bus tours, instead of displaying your own ignorance by trying to take them in your own car," argued Fitzwilson.[58]

In the face of these arguments, the C & T Bureau in 1928 reevaluated its positions on tourism. Procedures designed to host conventions of businessmen in a railroad-centered age were not suited for maximizing profits in a car culture. As a result, attitudes toward conventions changed. New Orleans tourism boosters argued that they were "slipping behind other communities for the tendency is away from this overdoing of hospitality, even in other Southern cities." The previous policy of meticulously planning conventioneers' visits became outmoded, replaced by a tourism infrastructure consisting of carriage

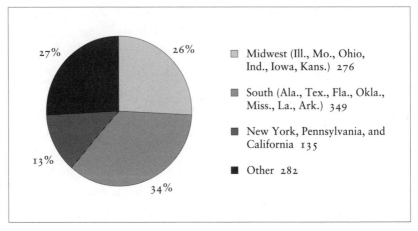

During the 1934 Mardi Gras season, the Association of Commerce received 1,042
inquiries from potential tourists. The top sixteen states represented were Illinois (94),
Alabama (73), Texas (66), Florida (65), New York (62), Missouri (52), Oklahoma
(43), Pennsylvania (42), Mississippi (37), Louisiana (36), Ohio (34), Indiana (33),
Iowa (33), California (31), Kansas (30), Arkansas (29).

Source: "Universal," *Association of Commerce News Bulletin*, 27 February 1934.

rides, bus tours, and riverboat cruises operated by private companies.
Association-organized tours became not only unnecessary but also economically unwise. No longer would the association arrange "complimentary land and river sight-seeing excursions." A luncheon and a
short harbor trip were considered "sufficient courtesy."[59]

Advocates for change in the association's convention-hosting policy
sought to squeeze more profits from conventioneers. First, scripted programs failed to grant enough leisure time. Conventioneers were "kept
very busy at the sessions of the convention" without "much time to
themselves." The lack of free time for conventioneers to wander the city
translated into reduced income for area entertainment venues, restaurants, and other popular tourist spots. Reformers declared that conventioneers lacked "an opportunity to spend their money." Furthermore,
the new agenda called on businesses to halt the reduction of fares or

FIGURE 2   Registrants at Help Desk of the Association of Commerce,
Mardi Gras 1938

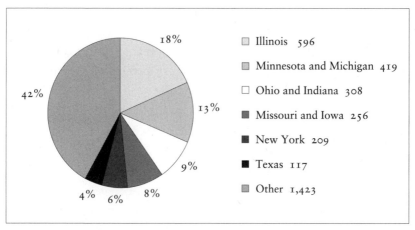

18%	☐ Illinois 596
42%	▨ Minnesota and Michigan 419
13%	☐ Ohio and Indiana 308
9%	■ Missouri and Iowa 256
8%	■ New York 209
6%	■ Texas 117
4%	▨ Other 1,423

During the 1938 Mardi Gras, the Association of Commerce registered 3,328 visitors at
the organization's help desk. The top ten states represented were Illinois (596),
Minnesota (214), New York (209), Michigan (205), Wisconsin (192), Ohio (166),
Indiana (142), Missouri (138), Iowa (118), Texas (117).

Source: "Mardi Gras Visitors Set Records at Association Information Desk," *Association of
Commerce News Bulletin*, 8 March 1938.

rates for local amusements. The distribution of free tickets received
sharp criticism. A new age in the treatment of conventions had arrived.
The city's reputation as a convention city had become secure enough
not to require extensive inducements. As an editorial in the *News Bulletin* explained, "Visitors come prepared to spend their money and are
willing to pay standard sums for their pleasure just so there is no 'sky-
rocketing' of charges." The association thus firmly rejected the "traditional Southern hospitality idea." Courtesy to visitors need not require
granting guests freebies.[60]

As Toye and Higgins had probably hoped, the association's new policy depended on the development of companies capable of catering
to motor-age tourists. Tour companies, along with restaurants, hotels,
and souvenir shops, began to form a network through which tourists
passed. Guide buses or carriages regularly stopped at hotels to pick up

customers. Routes often featured local stores or eateries. As the tourism infrastructure solidified, visitors faced not a confusing cityscape but an urban environment where numerous businesses facilitated tourists' enjoyment of New Orleans.[61]

The new infrastructure and rise of automobile tourism required New Orleans businessmen to develop new ways of advertising the city. In October 1928, the association successfully petitioned the Louisiana Motor Vehicle Bureau in Baton Rouge to change the state license plate to feature the full state name rather than the abbreviated "LA," providing "the state more obvious publicity and distinction." Since cars at the time often carried a mounted spare tire in the rear, tire covers offered another means for promoting the city. The association issued covers that juxtaposed an image of the St. Louis Cathedral with the words "New Orleans Second Port." The popular tourist site thus joined a commercial slogan, thereby reflecting the growing acceptance of the city's antiquity as a valuable asset. Starting in 1930, the Association of Commerce distributed bumper stickers that proclaimed in large letters, "I HAVE BEEN TO NEW ORLEANS—IT'S AMERICA'S MOST INTERESTING CITY." To ensure that stickers were attached to bumpers, agencies such as the Automobile Club of Louisiana offered prizes to clerks who "personally" supervised the placement of the signs on vehicles.[62] Billboards also sprouted along roadsides to welcome motorists.

In 1929, the Association of Commerce launched an innovative mailing campaign. The first wave of mailings, announced in the *News Bulletin*, carried invitations to "prominent persons, who are in the habit of traveling regularly, in 105 communities in 15 states from Montana to Pennsylvania and from the Gulf to Canada, the names of whom were obtained through the co-operation of correspondents at these places." Association President Al Danziger signed the invitations, stressing "climate, cuisine, recreation, history" and other points about the city. The promotional material included a colorful folder heralding the city's main attractions as well as its industrial and commercial strengths. A courtesy card, also tucked in the envelopes, offered potential visitors maps and other materials available at the Association of Commerce headquarters. Mayor Arthur O'Keefe signed follow-up invitations mailed six weeks later. A third wave of mailings containing another multicolor folder about New Orleans soon followed. By the end of the campaign, nearly 100,000 pieces of literature had been distributed around the country.[63]

The mailing campaign marked a significant change in the association's attitude. The focus on individuals rather than conventions served to popularize the city to the general public even though the promotional literature targeted only wealthy individuals widely known in their communities. According to the association, courting socially prominent persons would produce a trickle-down effect as other citizens mimicked the travels of the elite. Thus, even as the directors of the mailing effort aimed their rhetoric and images at a particular class, they hoped to reach a broad audience. The ultimate goal was to penetrate the grassroots of society and develop New Orleans tourism by word of mouth. Although the results of the campaign "could never be definitely known," the association assured members that "compensating benefits" would follow. Furthermore, the promotional literature downplayed industry and commerce for a more historical, romantic depiction of the Crescent City. An editorial in the *News Bulletin* explained, "Each year finds a multitude of habitual travelers yearning for a change of scenery, of climate and of custom. Many are in a quandary as to where to go and will psychologically absorb the suggestion to come to New Orleans, especially because of the tempting forces behind it."[64]

In 1930, the C & T Bureau became the Convention and Visitors Bureau (C & V Bureau). The rationale for the name change clearly revealed the evolution of the association's perspective on tourism. "Tourist," the association leadership believed, implied "a special class of persons," usually the professionals associated with conventions or well-to-do groups of travelers. "Visitors," however, meant anyone passing through the city. Over the next decade, the Association of Commerce increasingly came to view tourism as a two-faceted enterprise directed on one hand at conventioneers and on the other hand at vacationers. Sam Fowlkes, who served as the bureau's secretary in 1936, argued that individual travelers formed the "retail" side of the tourist trade, while conventioneers formed the "wholesale" portion.

Tourism had become a serious business, worthy of comparison to long-established enterprises. Past conceptions of tourism and boosterism withered among businessmen who welcomed the promise of profits drawn from the automobile caravans of twentieth-century American nomads.[65]

With the Great Depression intensifying American desires for cheap but captivating getaways, New Orleans businessmen fully committed themselves to promoting the city as a leisurely oasis from hard times. Whereas depressed conditions worked against furthering industrial development or commercial enterprises, mass tourism offered a salve to both New Orleans businessmen and ordinary Americans. A. M. Lockett, Association of Commerce president in 1931, announced that the "business depression" made "visitors with new money to pour into our channels of trade" all the more important to the city's economic survival. In November 1931, with the depression worsening, the association proposed a massive five-phase program to bolster the local economy, primarily by attracting more visitors. In a reversal of earlier attempts to bolster the image of New Orleans as a business-minded metropolis, national advertisements stressed the "city's exotic charm" as well as "its health and recreational assets." Commercial development and the attraction of industry ranked second and third, respectively. Although the fourth point emphasized exploitation of the surrounding trade territory, the fifth aspect of the program returned to the question of tourism by urging urban improvements to make the city "more attractive to outsiders." A referendum voted on by all members of the association solidified local businessmen's general support of tourism development. No longer were the concerns voiced by hotel or restaurant owners isolated from those of the rest of the business community.[66]

Despite stressing the city's advances as a port and industrial center during the 1920s, association leaders could not escape New Orleans's past, nor did they want to. Local history, such as the city's French origins, provided an opportunity to magnify the obstacles overcome in the creation of a modern, American city. As Blaine Brownell has argued in his study of the urban South, businessmen during the 1920s used local history as a means of justifying "an 'evolutionary' or 'progressive' interpretation of the urban past."[67] Past events created the present, but the present created the future. The depression, combined with the heightened interest in attracting tourists, altered this view of history. Businessmen sought reassurance that the economic disaster could be overcome. Furthermore, New Orleans boosters worked to exploit public fascination with the exotic and the past by emphasizing the antique, Latin heritage of modern, American New Orleans. Late in 1930, the *News Bulletin* ran an ad published by New Orleans Public Service that depicts two individuals looking at a blueprint of a future New Orleans. One figure is a Mercury-like man symbolizing the future; the other man, symbolizing the past, looks much like Jean Lafitte, the famed local hero (and pirate) who aided Andrew Jackson at the Battle of New Orleans. Lafitte reassuringly points at the blueprint and places a firm, guiding hand on the shoulder of the futuristic Mercury, thereby blurring distinctions between the city's past, present, and future.[68] Similarly, the Association of Commerce ran an advertisement in *Time, Forbes, Fortune,* the *New York Times,* and several other national publications that showed the French minister Talleyrand at the time of Louisiana's 1803 sale to the United States. The heading quoted Talleyrand, "Without New Orleans All Western Land Is Valueless."[69]

Travelers' desires for unusual places pushed businessmen to embrace the foreign, romantic images of New Orleans that many local leaders had previously attempted to erase. In 1930, the association began offering photograph sessions for conventioneers and other visitors, with background imagery depicting "typical New Orleans scenes." The Chalmette Monument, located on the battlefield where Andrew Jackson defeated the British in the War of 1812, and the Absinthe House, a famous French Quarter bar, joined symbols of commercial and industrial strength, like the impressive new Hibernia Bank skyscraper, as photographic settings. The historic past emerged as a profitable inheritance rather than a costly hindrance. In 1933, the president of the Association of Commerce, speaking about the need for the organization to tighten its "financial belt," noted the importance of tourism. He argued that although the port remained the centerpiece of the local economy, "it is by no means the only factor" contributing to the city's well-being.

"Our mild climate, our recreational possibilities, our Mardi Gras and the Old Quarter and our Creole traditions all combine to give our city a reputation of being the most interesting in America." The alchemy of marketing promised to transform such traits into riches extracted from tourists' wallets.[70]

An informal survey of public opinion undertaken by the association between 1931 and 1932 revealed both the intensifying local commitment to mass tourism and the importance of popular sentiment in determining how to market the city as a tourist attraction. A representative of the C & V Bureau, Wilson Callender, traveled the Mississippi River Valley to gather opinions about New Orleans. After two hundred interviews in twenty-eight cities across ten states, Callender reported that "New Orleans, as a product for tourist consumption is already more than half sold." A variety of reasons accounted for the city's popularity, including food, scenic attractions, golfing facilities, fishing and hunting opportunities, cruises, and the proximity of the Mississippi beaches. However, Callender also met two men, "a bit confused," who "suggested we advertise more our famous 'Italian quarter.' " Callender's report comforted businessmen with the knowledge that the city was a popular destination, although the variety of responses, especially the mislabeling of the French Quarter, caused some unease. With this effort, the Association of Commerce began systematically to attempt to gain insight into the general public's perceptions of New Orleans and thereby better satisfy expectations.[71]

The Association of Commerce renewed its efforts to make locals more courteous to visitors and knowledgeable about popular sites. Promoters in 1932 urged the formation of a committee capable of arranging "a model talk, pointing out some of the attractions to bring people here, and then organize a large group of excellent speakers so that one could appear before each organization of every kind and nature in this city." Businessmen strove to enlist the "citizenship in helping to enable our visitors, whether they come as tourists or convention delegates, to better enjoy their stay—having the citizens speak to them whenever an opportunity is afforded and learn if they are getting to see the things that they would like to see and if they are not have them referred to the

Association of Commerce for information." Having identified tourists as a potentially rich tax resource for a cash-strapped city treasury, Commissioner of Public Finance A. Miles Pratt explained in a WSMB radio broadcast "how important the visitor is in sustaining the city's economic well-being." By awakening New Orleanians to the economic value of tourism, businessmen and politicians attempted to spark a word-of-mouth promotional juggernaut. Said Pratt, "We must arouse in these visitors a permanent interest in New Orleans, so that they will become so enthusiastic about our city that they will want to come back again, will urge their friends to come and so that they may ultimately come back to stay or invest." To further ensure the friendly reception of tourists, the Association of Commerce arranged several meetings with the "entire police force, calling their attention to important facts and to what a great impression courtesy makes on strangers in our city." The goal was to convert New Orleanians into gracious hosts.[72]

Publicity campaigns launched during the 1930s revealed the extent to which Association of Commerce members embraced romantic images of New Orleans to cater better to the interests of vacationers. In a 1932 campaign, the organization attempted to thwart competition from the Washington Bicentennial celebration and the Chicago Century of Progress Exposition, buying space in *National Geographic* as well as in Chicago, St. Louis, Kansas City, Cincinnati, Cleveland, and Detroit newspapers. One ad pictured the St. Louis Cathedral framed by the floral gardens in Jackson Square. A small article underneath proclaimed, "The charm of the Vieux Carre (French Quarter) is undimmed by mortal worries or the modern city's haste. This is your thrifty trip abroad." Another ad depicted the French Quarter and declared, "Romance of France just a day away." The campaign also stressed area golf courses and Mardi Gras. In 1934, an advertising campaign run in the newspapers of Houston, Dallas, Tulsa, Memphis, Birmingham, and Atlanta attempted to develop regional interest in visiting New Orleans, proclaiming, "The 'Old World' City So Close to You." Readers were reassured that the "quaint City is so worth seeing. Broad paved highways lead to New Orleans." By 1939, the Association of Commerce went so far as to provide illustrations for inclusion in the financial reports of area businesses, especially those institutions that sent reports to out-of-towners. One illustration showed the French Quarter, while another depicted the city's various recreational opportunities and listed five of its most important qualities: "History," "Romance," "Glamour," "Scenic Beauty," and (in smaller print) "Modern Progress."[73]

The new approach to encouraging tourism met with dramatic success. The most useful gauge of tourist flow through New Orleans comes from the attendance figures posted by the state-funded Louisiana State Museum, which operated one of the city's central attractions, the Cabildo. Seat of the colonial government and site of the signing of the Louisiana Purchase, the Cabildo was filled with historical displays open to the public at no charge. In 1920 and 1921, respectively, 141,000 and 133,700 people visited the Cabildo, with the largest crowds (more than 20,000 a month) between December and April and fewer than 7,000 per month from June through August. The number of visitors grew to 179,500 in 1928 and 169,200 in 1929 before dipping in the early years of the Great Depression and then rising sharply, reaching 240,100 in 1937, 278,377 in 1938, 302,423 in 1939, 338,727 in 1940, and 430,906 in 1941. With the Second World War crowding the city with military personnel and war industry workers, the Cabildo welcomed more than 470,000 individuals in 1943 and 1944. (See figure 3.) Furthermore, the museum reported little seasonal variation during the late 1930s, a sign that New Orleans boosters had successfully converted the city into a year-round tourist destination.[74]

But who were these visitors? In 1934, the Association of Commerce reported that roughly 75 percent of the Cabildo's more than 200,000 visitors that year came from outside New Orleans. Given that fewer than 17,000 conventioneers had come to the city and that the association believed that many people in town for conventions did not have time to visit a museum such as the Cabildo, more than 125,000 vacationers can be estimated to have visited New Orleans. Furthermore, analysts recognized the significance of motor vehicles in bolstering the figures posted by the Louisiana State Museum. Economist Walter Parker expressed amazement at the Cabildo's continued success during the Second World War "when the use of automobiles is restricted by the

FIGURE 3   Annual Visitors to the Cabildo

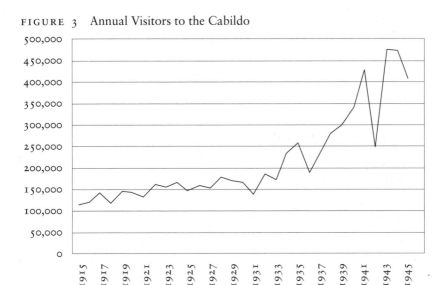

Cabildo visitation climbed dramatically during the Great Depression.

Source: Biennial Reports of the Board of Curators, 1918–46, Louisiana State Museum.

Note: Schoolchildren no longer included after 1936

inability to purchase new tires." Parker assumed the obvious: travelers used automobiles, not trains or public transportation.[75]

Hotel capacity expanded to meet the influx of visitors to New Orleans. A 1935 report found that the city had added approximately 2,000 "first-class hotel rooms" since the First World War. Four years later, a more detailed analysis revealed that the city could accommodate between 12,000 and 14,000 overnight visitors in 3,154 first-class hotel rooms, 559 rooms in small hotels, 250 rooms in tourist camps (later known as motels), 200 rooms in boardinghouses, and 1,901 rooms in private homes registered with the Association of Commerce for use by tourists. Though generally satisfied with the city's ability to house travelers, the report emphasized the continued need to placate the "$8-per-day automobile tourist" by providing more motels and parking facilities within New Orleans.[76]

In 1939, the C & V Bureau printed a pamphlet with the striking title "New Orleans' Largest Industry Has No Smoke Stack." The publication outlined the rapid expansion of tourism and the reemergence of the convention trade during the late 1930s. The bureau rejoiced that in "the past five years the 'payroll' of this (convention) industry has grown from $651,805.00 in 1934 to $6,841485.00 for 1938." The figure represented "an increase of over 1000% with a total of *over 18 million dollars* for the five year period." From the meager 16,571 conventioneers in 1934, the number of conventioneers had boomed to nearly 150,000 in 1937 and to more than 152,000 in 1938. More than six thousand New Orleanians were employed by the convention industry. The figures—impressive given the depressed condition of the national economy—excluded the money left by vacationers not directly associated with conventions. Although tabulating the amount of money spent by individual tourists was more difficult, the C & V Bureau reported that it maintained direct correspondence with more than seven hundred travel agencies and automobile clubs and shipped information about the Crescent City in response to more than ten thousand inquiries each year. New Orleans businessmen had come to accept tourism on equal terms with traditional economic pursuits.[77]

The Game of Tag

In 1930, the New Orleans Association of Commerce published an ad in fourteen national publications, including *Time*, *Forbes*, *Atlantic Monthly*, *Harper's*, and the *Wall Street Journal*. The ad depicted an expanding business district. One photograph showed New Orleans's unimpressive 1920 skyline. Beneath it was a larger photograph from 1930 captioned, "In enduring stone the city graphs its growth—the skyline of today." An even larger picture anticipated the more crowded cityscape of 1950 and the promise of economic prosperity implied by multiple skyscrapers. Over these illustrations appeared President Herbert Hoover's statement that New Orleans was "a city of destiny." According to Hoover, flood-control efforts on the Mississippi River promised safety for both the population and trade. The potential for economic development, argued Hoover, produced "industrial and economic influences" for New Orleans that "must be taken into account nationally."[78] Even as Hoover spoke, however, social and economic forces began to push New Orleans into tourism rather than commercial or industrial enterprises. Ironically, the ad's photographs of the business district were taken from the historic French Quarter. They were snapshots from the developing heart of the New Orleans tourism industry.

New Orleans had laid the foundation for a tourism industry supported by all local economic leaders. Businessmen were ready to push for mass tourism and images that associated the city with its foreign past. Members of the Association of Commerce eagerly engaged in national competition, snatching tourist dollars away from competitors in Miami, Los Angeles, and other urban centers. As a 1924 *News Bulletin* editorial had boasted, "THE MEN OF NEW ORLEANS are playing the game—the game of TAG with other American cities."[79] Tourism emerged as a new event in American businessmen's economic Olympics. The more romantic and exotic a city, the more profits gained from an increasingly motorized American population. New Orleans excelled in this competition.

CHAPTER 2

NEW ERA NEW ORLEANS

The Great Depression, Taxation, and Robert Maestri

In late 1932, New Orleans Mayor T. Semmes Walmsley addressed an appreciative crowd of welfare workers, who honored him for his efforts to boost employment through municipal projects. Walmsley expressed gratitude at their thankfulness, but his tone reflected the gloom Americans felt as the depression reached new depths. He pondered, "While, of course, I feel that prospects are not very bright and there isn't much hope at present for us all, I am not going to say, as it has been said in the past that the depression will be over in the next thirty days and that prosperity is Hoovering around the corner." No matter the harsh economic conditions, Walmsley and his fellow New Orleanians maintained their sense of humor. The election of Franklin Roosevelt to the presidency offered hope: said Walmsley, "The letter 'R' is the greatest letter in the alphabet, it is in the beginning of Roosevelt and the end of Hoover." President-elect Roosevelt promised a more active assault on the stagnant national economy. Americans would receive a new deal in which the federal government stepped up relief efforts as well as primed the nation's economic pump. Walmsley declared that as long as New Orleanians believed that a "new era" loomed, the citizenry would persevere.[1]

Walmsley's joking remarks about the letter *R* could well be extended because the leadership of New Orleans also embraced an enterprise—

recreation—that formed a bulwark potentially capable of sustaining an otherwise severely fractured economy. Politicians, like the members of the New Orleans Association of Commerce, sought to mitigate the effects of economic depression through mass tourism. Municipal officials harnessed New Orleans's financial well-being to the promise of the tourism industry. Traditional forms of taxation such as property assessments failed to pay municipal bills during the depression, and other possible revenue sources such as industrial and commercial enterprises were too weak to shoulder a greater share of taxes. Consequently, the city's cash-strapped politicians restructured the tax system, compensating for budgetary shortfalls with levies on urban amusements and tourist attractions, thereby shifting the tax burden as much as possible away from New Orleanians. Taxes on entertainment-related enterprises supplied a means of sustaining city services while passing costs to nonresidents and locals capable of affording leisure activities.

New Orleanians, particularly Walmsley's successor, Robert Maestri, also used Roosevelt's New Deal programs to change the physical appearance of the cityscape as well as to preserve the city's history, often with tourists in mind. Corporations interpreted the success of populist politician Huey Long as an attack on them, and the more tyrannically Long exercised power in the state and the more vehemently he assaulted the city's Old Regular political machine, the more tourism became an economic and political lifeline for Long's opponents hunkered down in City Hall. Efforts to promote the city brought positive publicity in the face of an increasingly ugly political row between Long and the New Orleans–based machine. The political war strengthened Roosevelt's commitment to his allies in Louisiana as he attempted to weaken Long's base of operations going into the 1936 presidential election. New Deal programs permitted New Orleans politicians to bolster the tourism industry by adding new attractions and enhancing old ones. Maestri's ascendance to the mayor's office in 1936 solidified the political commitment to tourism. Though a devoted Longite, Maestri agreed to a deal with Roosevelt shortly after the assassination of the troublesome Long. While the president neutralized the powerful political network left by the slain U.S. senator, the new mayor received the benefits of federal largesse and made a long-term commitment to tourism.[2]

The Whole Tax Structure Has Broken Down

As the depression approached its nadir in late 1932, New Orleans Finance Commissioner A. Miles Pratt, in consultation with Mayor Walmsley, demanded a thorough overhaul of the municipal tax structure. The city budget for 1933 was 18 percent smaller than it had been prior to the economic crash a few years earlier, but even more drastic cuts were needed. More than 64 percent of the city's total revenue came from real estate taxes, a burden of taxation that Pratt "emphatically" argued remained "wholly out of balance" despite the fact that tax rates had already been reduced. Under such a system, "virtually all of the eggs of the city government [lay] in one basket," and the collapse in real estate values combined with New Orleanians' ability to pay their taxes had exposed the system's precarious nature. Without further tax relief, Pratt argued, "the breaking point is not far off." To assist families and businesses struggling to survive in the harsh economic climate, he proposed eliminating "every possible cent" levied against homes and other property. The news was bittersweet for municipal employees. Pratt also instituted "drastic and sweeping" reductions in salaries and personnel. Walmsley concurred, arguing to the Commission Council that the "whole tax structure has broken down." Pratt and Walmsley instead advocated the pursuit of substitute tax sources that promised to spread the financial burden more evenly among New Orleanians and, even better, to out-of-towners. With no end to the depression in sight, the Commission Council responded favorably to Pratt and Walmsley's pleas by quickly organizing a tax revision committee.[3]

In New Orleans, the prosperity of the 1920s left the city government ill prepared for the financial crunch of the 1930s, even though the economic boom had allowed for key improvements that enhanced the cityscape. Population growth and calls for reform exacerbated the demand for sewerage, street paving, street lighting, and sundry other projects. In the five years prior to 1930, city officials had constructed the Municipal Auditorium as well as begun work on a new criminal court. They had ordered the paving of more than a hundred miles of roadway, established a comprehensive zoning plan, built an incinerator, doubled the drainage capacity of the city's pumping stations, and added significant acreage to City Park. In one of the most costly projects, Canal Street underwent a thorough renovation. Elaborate lampposts lined the thoroughfare; terrazzo tiling beautified widened sidewalks; streetcar rails were rearranged to accommodate automobile traffic. The brightly illuminated street symbolized the opulence enjoyed by urban America in the 1920s. Tourists and locals alike found in New Orleans one of the most modernized urban centers in the country. Yet the recent completion of thirty-five million dollars worth of improvements left debt in its wake. The municipal government ran a deficit during the later part of the decade. New Orleans politicians worked financial wonders in the boom times of the 1920s but struggled to find any silver in the dark financial clouds gathering over the Crescent City in 1930.[4]

The depression shattered not only the New Orleans economy but the American economy as well. In the words of President Herbert Hoover, the "orgy of speculation" that occurred in the 1920s eroded the country's financial base. Production overran the expected enlargement of the consumer market, especially among automobile manufacturers. The economy further suffered from an increased concentration of wealth, a poor corporate structure, and a weak banking system. Whereas rapid growth exacerbated economic weaknesses within the United States, some sections of the national economy, such as agriculture, languished throughout the 1920s. Good times met an ugly reality when the 1929 stock market crash burst Americans' optimism. Throughout the nation, Hoover's name translated into a synonym for poverty. Hoovervilles, areas where the unemployed and their families gathered in makeshift shelters, sprouted in every major city. By 1933, even Hoover recognized that the United States had descended "to the bottom of the depression pit." The gross national product stood at one-third of the 1929 level. Unemployment among Americans of working age hovered at 25 percent.[5] The reversal of fortunes financially crippled a large number of Americans, overwhelming private relief agencies.

As was the case throughout the country, New Orleans's economy wilted. George Doyle found himself jobless in the first months of the depression, but as he told the *Times-Picayune*, he could at least take comfort in the fact that he was only one of a "great army."[6] Bank clearings (the total funds passing through local banks) dropped nearly 50 percent between 1928 and 1932. The city's foreign trade declined by 45 percent over the same period and by 1940 stood at just two-thirds of the 1928 level. Although a revival in domestic trade along the river occurred with the introduction of diesel barges and the construction of the Intracoastal Waterway, commerce through the city failed to rebound to predepression levels. To make matters worse, what little industry New Orleans possessed suffered as well. In 1939, the city claimed 142 fewer manufacturing establishments and 3,000 fewer industrial jobs than before the depression. The repeal of Prohibition, which allowed breweries to become the city's second-largest industry according to value of product, failed to offset plant closings. The depression hit New Orleans, the nation's fifteenth-largest financial center, harder than many other places in the country: bank clearings dropped more sharply there than in other southern urban centers, foreign trade declined at a higher rate than it did nationwide, and unemployment rates were more than 40 percent higher than the national average for much of the 1930s.[7]

Prior to the Great Depression, the city had funded improvement projects and day-to-day operations through annual loans from local banks secured by projected tax revenues for the upcoming year. The dangers of such a practice—which one historian has compared to sharecropping—were obvious, yet mortgaging the city's future did not seem foolish during the economic upturn of the 1920s, and city officials argued that the increased wealth derived from upgrades to the urban infrastructure would offset the mounting debt. Popular resentment of higher taxes made the procedure even more appealing. Preparing to give the oath of office to Walmsley and several other machine politicians in 1930, Louisiana Supreme Court Chief Justice Charles O'Neill boasted that the Old Regulars' improvement program during the 1920s had been accomplished "without the addition of a penny to the tax bills of the people." The development of the Intracoastal Waterway, improvements in port facilities, and the taming of the Mississippi River in the aftermath of the 1927 flood promised a larger, more efficient flow of commerce, which in turn meant prosperity. Such golden dreams paid little heed to a possible economic crunch.[8]

Then came the depression. New Orleans politicians typically allowed substantial amounts of property taxes to remain uncollected for up to two years, thereby accruing interest on the delinquent taxes at a higher rate than the city paid on its loans. In late May 1930, however, six cash-strapped local banks jointly called more than five hundred thousand dollars in loans secured by delinquent 1928 taxes. The decision publicized the instability of the local government as well as the local economy and potentially lowered real estate values by flooding the market with property seized by the city. Moreover, pressuring municipal leaders to collect delinquent property taxes threatened to increase homelessness, thereby shrinking the number of taxpayers who might at least offer some meager payments as well as increasing the number of citizens in need of relief. Despite the risks, the banks pressed the municipal government to liquidate some of its debt, deflecting criticism by pointing to pressure from the state government's banking department, which was spurred by Governor Huey Long in an effort to embarrass the Old Regulars. The municipal government's fiscal condition deteriorated over the next several years. Between 1930 and 1935, officials reduced the city's budget by nearly a third, from $8,732,745 to $5,914,436, reflecting the drop in property tax revenue, the city's primary source of income, which reached its depression-era low of $3,751,412 in 1936.[9]

Walmsley, who had cut his teeth as the commissioner of public finance before stepping into the mayor's office in 1930, struggled to keep the city financially afloat. He instituted a much-needed auditing system early in his administration, allowing him to boast that the municipal government was "collecting personal taxes on a scale never before approached." In spite of the mayor's efforts, the city continued to find it necessary to draw loans against projected tax revenues.

To make matters worse, by early 1932, deflation forced the municipal government to accept reduced property assessments. A major bond issue offered a temporary salve, in Walmsley's words "safely" supplying $750,000 for relief programs "without increasing the taxpayers burdens at this time, and without an increase of one penny in taxes." [10]

In October 1932, a fiscal bombshell exploded over the men in City Hall. The Louisiana Taxing Commission reported a sharper reduction in New Orleans property values than the Old Regulars had anticipated. Facing this "monumental" crisis, city officials cut deeper into municipal expenditures. Supply purchases nearly halted. All employees received orders to take a total of two weeks off without pay over the rest of the year. Recognizing that the loss of revenue promised to carry over into 1933, Walmsley announced that the next budget planned by Finance Commissioner Pratt and the Commission Council would adopt a policy of "strict economy" as well as a flat 10 percent reduction in salaries, which occurred on top of earlier pay cuts of as much as 20 percent. The only good news for city employees came when official policy no longer mandated that they contribute 5 percent of their salaries to welfare relief, a practice begun in the previous year. Officials were running out of options. In a meeting with the Association of Commerce, Finance Commissioner Pratt desperately urged area businessmen to join him in asking each citizen "to pay his taxes if it is humanly possible." [11]

Stopgap measures failed to compensate for the decline in property tax revenue, creating the need for a more permanent solution that avoided passing the buck to cash-strapped New Orleanians. The 1933 failure of three banks on which the city relied for credit exacerbated the financial crisis. As Commissioner Pratt reported, "out of the ashes of the old banks came two new institutions" opposed to extending the same credit amounts based on projected tax returns that the previous banks furnished. The reduced loans given by the new financial establishments, along with the continued "slowness" in tax payments by New Orleanians, amounted, in Pratt's words, to "a small drop in the bucket" compared to city needs. A desperate Pratt traveled to New York City and Washington, where some of America's leading financial institutions "cast even darker clouds" over New Orleans by refusing to grant loans to the city. Although Walmsley soothed public fears by announcing the limited extension of credit by a number of local businessmen, he and Pratt knew that the fiscal future appeared bleak. [12]

The Road to Well-Being

Walmsley and Pratt went to work uncovering any source of income that might keep the city financially afloat. In a city pressed for cash, the service sector supplied vital, fresh financial resources. Financial officers looked to levies on gasoline, amusements, gambling, and alcohol. Such taxes exploited the tourism industry and money-spending outsiders as well as the entertainment outlets New Orleanians chose to enjoy despite conditions. In time, even sales taxes, previously considered off limits since such measures stirred the wrath of the business community, became acceptable. Mounting debt, shrinking relief funds, and deteriorating city services pressed municipal leaders to tie the municipal government to the success of the tourist trade.

Even before the depression, Louisiana and New Orleans had already collected one of the highest per-gallon taxes on gasoline in the United States. In Louisiana, money raised from gasoline taxes was earmarked for road construction, a process that often required costly dredging and bridges over the state's rivers and marshland. The importance of highways to the progressive image promoted by politicians and businessmen justified the gasoline tax as a revenue source dedicated to the development and maintenance of roads.

With the financial crunch caused by the depression, however, states and municipalities, many cash strapped like New Orleans, siphoned revenue from gasoline taxes into depleted coffers. A 1930 New Orleans newspaper editorial pointed out that a quarter of all state legislatures "planned to go hot-foot" after higher gasoline taxes with the intention of diverting "more and more" of the money to fund schools, waterway construction, state government, and a myriad of other projects and services. With local governments desperate for money, "tax-eaters and tax-makers pretty much the country over" ignored the protests of conservative politicians and businessmen as well as the members of organizations such as the United States Good Roads Association, who feared that the new trend would undermine highway construction.[13]

By 1934, the Louisiana legislature authorized the New Orleans Commission Council to increase the tax on gasoline sold within city limits, with the funds raised reserved for municipal welfare programs in general and for the elderly, the handicapped, and needy mothers in particular. Municipal revenue from the gasoline tax increased from $335,298 to $821,304 between 1935 and 1937, and by 1938, the city's Department of Public Welfare was receiving between $75,000 and $90,000 a month from a tax of two cents per gallon.[14]

Exploitation of the budding tourism industry extended to controversial New Orleans attractions such as horse racing. A vocal campaign against gambling dated at least as far back as the 1870s. To opponents, the racetrack, known as the Fairgrounds, and the bookie system it fostered eclipsed the "illegal gambling evil" of slot machines and lotteries. As late as the 1920s, the business community had given serious consideration to reformers such as Herbert Homes, who headed an antigambling organization determined to eliminate horse racing, "the parent vice of all gambling in and about this city." For many civic leaders, gambling in its various manifestations was a wasteful, immoral cancer on the urban environment.[15]

During the 1930s, however, city leaders decided to harness gambling for the public good. In 1932, Fairgrounds operators held a day of Welfare Races at which the gate receipts from the record crowd of twenty-five thousand went to the Welfare Committee, a quasi-governmental organization responsible for coordinating New Orleans relief efforts. During the next racing season, Mayor Walmsley announced to an amazed public that the city no longer barred horse betting at the Fairgrounds on Sundays, with 50 percent of the Sabbath gate receipts and 10 percent of betting profits earmarked for the Welfare Committee. Violating the sanctity of the Sabbath shocked pious New Orleanians, but Walmsley told the Crescent City Jockey Club that the decision was in "no way . . . a precedent for permanent racing on Sundays"; rather, it "simply" served as an "emergency" effort designed to aid the Welfare Committee. Despite Walmsley's dictates, New Orleans politicians subsequently looked to the Fairgrounds for additional sources of funding for municipal programs, urging the state legislature to permit night races and even off-track betting parlors in addition to Sunday races. While not all New Orleanians felt comfortable with the municipal government's embrace of horse racing, many recognized the necessity of cultivating any new source of revenue. City resident Frank Smidtt flatly declared his support for such actions: "I do not believe it will hurt as an emergency measure, like the Liberty Bonds, the necessity and good will of[f]set the hurt." Opponents, according to Smidtt, were simply out of touch: "Let the reformers, sky pilots, and blue law states rave and howl." The increased dependency on track revenues in turn encouraged the municipal government to crack down on illegal off-track betting halls.[16]

Like the reversal of attitudes toward horse racing, the repeal of Prohibition sparked the resurgence of New Orleans nightlife and provided a valuable new source of revenue in the form of liquor licenses. Franklin Roosevelt's landslide 1932 presidential victory served as a national mandate to carry out his pledge to end Prohibition. Repeal not only supplied an economically hard-pressed population with alcoholic diversions but also returned to states and municipalities a valuable commodity for taxation. A New Orleans newspaper ran a cartoon that showed a steamroller labeled "Tax on Good Old Beer" crushing a roadbed obstructed by rocks tagged "Deficit" and "Debt," with a sign pointing the way down the "Rocky Road to National Well-Being." What was good for the nation was especially good for New Orleans, with its long history of alcohol-fueled recreations.[17]

Even before repeal took effect, public officials prepared for a wet—and lucrative—future. In 1933, Governor O. K. Allen, Long's submissive lieutenant, proposed a state tax of five dollars per barrel, a rate loudly condemned by New Orleans administrators and the local press as "prohibitive," particularly since the U.S. Congress had already levied a hefty tax on alcohol production in the face of the national budgetary shortfall. In the face of opposition from New Orleans civic leaders, the state government backed down and the legislature enacted a tax of two dollars per barrel, a rate fairly typical of other states throughout the country. City leaders wanted the levies on alcohol to remain low enough to permit the return of nickel beer. Affordable beer translated into high sales volume, thereby bolstering government revenues. According to the *Times-Picayune*, "this new source" of taxation would ease the monetary difficulties faced by the municipal government and dramatically improve society: "Thus fairly and reasonably priced, the tax yield will be very substantial, the bootlegging evil and the rackets and abuses going therewith can be abated and we shall have fulfillment in good faith of Democracy's promise to the people: Restoration of wholesome beer to be sold at a price within the reach of all lovers of that most universally popular of age-old beverages."[18]

Dollars quickly flowed into municipal coffers as New Orleans officials issued liquor licenses. Permit requests flooded City Hall. In April 1933, the Commission Council unanimously passed a measure permitting the licensing of businesses serving beer, wine, and drinks less than 6 percent alcohol. Immediately after the vote, Mayor Walmsley barked, "Give it here and I'll sign it right now." By late 1933, the municipal government prepared for the return of hard liquor as well, voting unanimously to create a licensing system for all establishments serving concoctions more potent than beer as well as importers and manufacturers. The newly created Beverage Department was responsible for setting appropriate fees and enforcing regulations. In 1935, the department collected more than $582,000, and two years later the revenue rose to more than $1.07 million, where it remained through the beginning of the Second World War. In addition to funding the Beverage Department, these monies went straight into the city's depleted general fund.[19]

Federal and city officials strictly regulated the alcohol trade to safeguard government revenue. Federal agents cracked down on bootlegging, and in sharp contrast to the Prohibition years, municipalities proved avid supporters of federal alcohol policy after local permits began sending money into city coffers. In April 1933, Walmsley ordered Police Superintendent George Reyer to instruct all his precinct commanders that no speakeasy was to remain open. Any police captain who turned a blind eye to an illegal establishment would find himself "immediately tried and dismissed from the service." His message to Reyer hinted at a reversal of official policy, which had secretly endorsed the operation of speakeasies during Prohibition.[20]

As part of its shift to tourism as a revenue source, the city also enacted an amusement tax. Although the state legislature had passed a measure in 1932 permitting the city to tax urban amusements, Walmsley and the Commission Council initially opposed such a levy. New taxes, an unpopular idea at any time, amounted to political suicide during a depression, even if the proceeds of the tax were supposed to be used to support people unable to work. The Commission Council refrained from enacting the new tax until 1934, when the city teetered on the brink of financial collapse.[21]

The city government finally acted on the amusement tax issue not simply to gain revenue at a time when repeal promised to enliven the increasingly tourism-oriented city but also to make political hay. Huey Long understood the political costs of an amusement tax and had orchestrated the passage of the state measure with the hope that Walmsley might take the bait and thus compromise his political standing. Although Walmsley understood the hazards of enacting an amusement tax, he also recognized the growing tension between Long, now serving in the U.S. Senate and contemplating a bid for the White House, and President Roosevelt. The New Orleans mayor couched his decision to back the tax in terms of his support of Roosevelt's New Deal: "Providing for these helpless unemployable people will be in accordance with the president's program and will prove our cooperation with him in an effort to provide not only for these needy, but will permit the city of New Orleans to co-operate in the face of the refusal by the governor and the state Legislature."[22] Roosevelt, in turn, appreciated allies in Louisiana, where Long had tightened his control over the state government to the point of claiming near dictatorial power.

The amusement tax affected the entertainment venues popular with tourists and leisure-pursuing locals. The measure placed a 2 percent levy on every ticket sold at a theater or movie house. Despite the depression,

Americans continued to flock to movie theaters, seeking escape from day-to-day hardships. The amusement tax also placed a 5 percent levy on other, more tourist-oriented attractions, including athletic contests, concerts, minstrels, nightclubs, cabarets, and dance halls. Excursion steamers, "aviation pleasure rides," carousels, scenic railways, merry-go-rounds, shooting galleries, and "all games of skill and chance," including "mechanical devices operated for pleasure or skill," fell under the ordinance. Such a sweeping tax risked raising the ire of the business community, especially restaurateurs, whose establishments were classified as nightclubs if they provided entertainment. But, with another depression winter quickly approaching, the outlook appeared bleak without the tax. The benefits of passing the levy on amusements had come to outweigh potential political consequences. By charging a tax to individuals who could afford leisure activities, city officials avoided loud mass protests. More importantly, taxing entertainment sites popular with tourists raised money without placing the burden solely on New Orleanians. Funds gained by the amusement tax were subsequently earmarked for the Department of Public Welfare, which in 1938 received between $7,500 and $9,500 per month from the levy.[23]

In 1936, the state legislature passed a "luxury" tax of 2 percent statewide with another 2 percent in New Orleans. Although politicians presented the levy as a luxury tax to avoid a public outcry, opponents recognized that the measure was just a cleverly named retail sales tax. Besides impacting New Orleanians, the tax tapped the wallets of out-of-towners, especially rural residents who regularly traveled to the city to shop. Despite grumbling from the citizenry, Robert Maestri, who had become mayor of New Orleans earlier that year, announced that the revenues formed an "important part in our public improvement program." In 1937, the measure provided more than $875,000 for the city, raising around $60,000 per month during the summer and nearly $100,000 per month between December and March, the peak tourist season.[24]

The creation of a more tourism-oriented economy and tax structure did not proceed without protest, especially among poorer New Orleanians. A local flier headed *The Anti-Taxer* decried the growing dependence on sales taxes, which further ate away at locals' spending power. Asked the sharp-tongued newsletter, "Most Unholy Property Hogs, why not tax the kids? What a source of revenue you are overlooking here. Why not petition The City Fathers to put a sales tax on snow-balls, all-day-suckers, baby-nipples, po-boi sandwiches, three-cent eatoriums and two-bit flop houses?" The economic evidence analyzed by historian Glenn Martin Runyan shows that New Orleans varied markedly from other urban centers across the United States. Early in the depression, the city's retail sales dipped more rapidly than was the case elsewhere; by the mid-1930s, however, retail sales in New Orleans rebounded. For the decade as a whole, the Crescent City's decline in retail sales was less than that experienced by comparable southern cities such as Atlanta, Birmingham, Houston, and Memphis. In fact, retail sales in New Orleans on the eve of the Second World War stood 9.2 percent higher than the 1928 level, whereas the national average showed a 13 percent drop over that time. Retail prices also remained higher in New Orleans than in other urban centers in the United States. Runyan has found that spendable income among New Orleanians dropped beyond the levels suffered elsewhere—57 percent in New Orleans compared to 54 percent nationwide. An explanation for New Orleans's deviation from regional and national norms can be found in the increased flow of tourists to the city. Tourists bolstered retail prices, and jobs in the industry offered low pay. Cost of living remained higher than the national average, thereby worsening living standards more severely than was the case in Memphis, Houston, Atlanta, or Birmingham.[25]

Local businessmen and city officials carefully analyzed the distribution of tourist dollars. According to data presented by the Association of Commerce in 1930, tourist spending fell into one of eight categories: of each dollar, retail merchants received 26 cents, restaurants gained 23.5 cents, and hotels earned 20 cents, while smaller amounts went to garages and gasoline stations (11.5 cents), transportation (7 cents), taxis (5 cents), theaters and other amusements (2.5 cents), and miscellaneous spending (4.5 cents). By 1939, the breakdown of the tourist dollar had changed in telling ways. Retail stores now gained 31 cents of every tourist dollar, while hotels earned 23 cents, restaurants received 18 cents, and garages took 10 cents. Theaters and other urban amusements earned 8 cents, while 10 cents went to miscellaneous expenditures. The sharp rise in tourism over the course of the decade, combined with visitors' increased spending on retail goods, likely sustained higher prices within New Orleans stores. Furthermore, tourists' spending patterns encouraged city officials to consider retail shops and amusements vital new sources of tax revenue.[26]

Businessmen embraced the correlation between tourism and municipal tax revenue in an effort to garner the support of the city government in passing measures beneficial to area enterprises. In 1937, for example, the New Orleans Restaurant Men's Association issued a "strong protest" to Commissioner of Public Finance Jesse Cave for permitting street vendors, particularly on Canal Street, during Mardi Gras. Association members decried the "serious encroachment upon the regular business operations of established restaurant and food serving places of business in New Orleans who are large annual tax payers and who depend a great deal upon increased opportunities of business offered by Mardi Gras and similar public celebrations."[27]

Subsequent revisions to state statutes and city ordinances altered the types of activities initially deemed taxable under the various measures passed in the mid-1930s, but the revenue gained from tourism remained vital to the municipal government. Because homeowners continued to struggle to make payments on their assessments, the gasoline tax, liquor licenses, gambling levies, luxury tax, and amusement tax offered various means of spreading the burden of taxation throughout the population. This did not mean that assessments on property were no longer important. However, taxes on gasoline, alcohol, and amusements added considerable, desperately needed sums to city coffers. By the late 1960s, less than 25 percent of municipal revenue came from property assessments, and sales taxes accounted for 40 percent of the city's operating budget. In contrast, sales taxes typically provided 5 percent of the budget for other major U.S. urban centers. Most importantly, nearly a fifth of the sales tax funds collected within New Orleans came from the pockets of visitors.[28]

The Tourist Is Always Right

As New Orleans financial advisers divined fresh financial wells, Mayor Walmsley supplied a face to the economic crisis in urban America. Walmsley's dexterity with urban finances enabled him to become chair of the U.S. Conference of Mayors during his first term. In 1933, he worked closely with federal authorities to push through Congress emergency relief funding. Walmsley also led city heads in advocating better-organized welfare programs. Near the end of 1934, the New Orleans mayor pointed to years of fruitless struggle against unemployment. "We have passed the stage of investigation," declared Walmsley, "the period of surveys, the time for study. There must be no more delays in providing proper, adequate and permanent solutions." New Orleans, like most major American cities, struggled to make ends meet, much less address the "acute" unemployment problem. According to Walmsley, the "new social era" demanded centralized relief efforts. But with a state government opposed to Walmsley and his fellow Old Regulars, federal grants to aid Louisiana's poor failed to trickle into the city. Unless the city found ways to provide relief through such means as new forms of taxation, "thousands of people" would discover themselves "in the cold, pining with hunger this winter in the City of New Orleans, who have no other place to turn and look to, as the United States government has declared its policy of turning the unemployables back to the states, and the state in turn, having refused to pass adequate legislation to care for them, thus leaves the burden to fall entirely upon the municipality and parishes wherein the people reside to care for and maintain them in their hour of need." Walmsley laid particular blame on rural voters, who denied assistance to urban communities. From podiums around the nation, Walmsley attacked the role of " 'cow' counties"—rural areas with disproportional representation in state legislatures—in limiting the power of urban America.[29]

Within Louisiana, those rural counties united behind Huey Long. The political rift between the Old Regular–controlled New Orleans government and the Long-dominated state government, an animosity muffled by an uneasy truce during the early 1930s, verged on open conflict by the middle part of the decade. The struggle placed New Orleans in the national spotlight. Furthermore, the political contest spurred actions that both enhanced the cityscape and enriched the municipal treasury by expanding the city's capacity to handle tourists.

The harder Long pushed to damage the city's political machine by curtailing finances, the more city administrators turned to tourism for income. Long's ascent worsened the economic turmoil and tarnished the city's national image as a business-friendly community as his heavy-handed tactics made headlines throughout the country. In addition, Long's populist antics disheartened local businessmen attempting to market New Orleans as an ideal location for investment in industry and commerce. Although Long primarily sought the accumulation of power, his attempts to cripple the Old Regulars—as in the case of the amusement tax—occasionally suggested a desire to encourage municipal commitments to the tourist trade. Long had a good reason for undertaking such ploys. His chief financial backers in Louisiana, Seymour Weiss and Robert Maestri, had built their fortunes from New Orleans tourism. Weiss operated the famed Roosevelt Hotel, while Maestri allegedly profited from ties to gambling and prostitution.

The 1934 municipal election brought the conflict between Long and the Old Regulars to the brink of open warfare. New Orleans businessmen shuddered as Long ordered National Guardsmen to the downtown voter registration office in an effort to intimidate his opponents. Walmsley in turn deputized five hundred additional policemen to guard City Hall, located across the street from where the Guard bivouacked. Members of the Association of Commerce shook their heads in disbelief as newsreels carried the "impression that New Orleans is an armed camp" to viewers throughout the country. On another occasion in 1935, Long traded words with Hugo Black of Alabama on the floor of the Senate. Businessmen were stunned when Long declared that the city did not need federal aid: "We would not care a rap or a snap of a finger if they should move the Federal Land Bank and anything else the Roosevelt administration has down there," barked Long. "Take it all and get out of there and stay out of there."[30]

Long's designs pressed municipal leaders to close ranks with Franklin

Roosevelt. Despite Long's strong opposition, a victorious but politically battered Walmsley emerged from the 1934 mayoral campaign eager to solidify his alliance with the president. Walmsley used his inaugural address to call on his fellow citizens to "cooperate to the fullest extent" with the federal government and its relief programs. He made little mention of Long and his regime in Baton Rouge other than to criticize legislative opposition to a plan to place some New Orleans taxes on an installment plan.[31]

In February 1935, Walmsley issued a defiant, pro-Roosevelt message that intensified Long's anger. Long had, according to the mayor, "repeatedly threatened to bankrupt" New Orleans, only to be thwarted. Walmsley used his influence in the U.S. Conference of Mayors to help persuade Congress to pass a law that protected municipalities from "harassment by persons trying to do unwarranted and unjustified harm to a City's credit." The U.S. Supreme Court upheld the law as well as a petition by the Walmsley administration asking for a readjustment of the city's open accounts and bank liquidations in view of Long's "tyrannical designs and crushing desires." The mayor enumerated the methods used to hinder the municipal government. Evidence showed that Long, working with a submissive state legislature, had blocked seven hundred thousand dollars earmarked for street maintenance in New Orleans. Long had also ordered the revision of an amendment to the state constitution that would have permitted the Commission Council to tax alcohol by volume and pressured the Louisiana Tax Commission to lower real estate assessments in New Orleans beyond levels sought by city officials. Municipal administrators refused to recognize the excessive reductions, but to little effect. Walmsley even accused members of the "Long coterie" of circulating through the city arranging kickbacks in return for lower assessments. Long balanced his efforts to slash city revenue with state laws restricting the usage of funds still trickling into the municipal treasury. The U.S. Supreme Court mandate loosened Long's financial stranglehold on New Orleans; nevertheless, Walmsley understood that the war was not yet over and remained defiant, awaiting "new raids" that would attempt to "cripple the operation of the government of the City of New Orleans."[32]

Walmsley and city administrators depended heavily on federal programs to sustain city functions. The Federal Emergency Relief Administration (FERA) and later Works Progress Administration (WPA) lightened the burden of caring for the unemployed and thereby sustained the makeshift financial structure so diligently crafted by Pratt and Walmsley. President Roosevelt carefully channeled funds and appointments to Long opponents in Louisiana while rekindling an investigation of Long and his lieutenants for evading income taxes. Although the FERA stipulated that every dollar of federal money was to be matched with three from the state, the refusal of the Long-controlled legislature to contribute to the program forced FERA officials to carry on the agency's work without the matching funds. In October 1933, more than eighty thousand New Orleanians—roughly 25 percent of all Louisianans receiving FERA aid and nearly 18 percent of the city's population—depended on the federal agency for survival. The complete federalization of FERA and WPA programs circumvented Long's attempts to prevent the Roosevelt administration from becoming involved in the state and protected the president's Louisiana allies. Funds to some areas were trimmed as a punitive though unsuccessful measure to shame the Longites into submission. Although congressional cutbacks subsequently shortened the employment rolls of New Deal work-relief programs, federal aid remained important in New Orleans, and in February 1935, FERA still employed some twenty thousand workers in the city.[33]

New Deal agencies offered not only employment and an infusion of cash vital to the local economy but also improvement projects beneficial to the tourism industry. New Orleans was not atypical. Historian Char Miller has shown how federal funds during the 1930s allowed boosters in San Antonio to construct pathways and stairways along the San Antonio River, creating a fertile site for tourism development. Similarly, federal relief agencies, guided by local politicians, put the unemployed into projects that dramatically improved the tourist value of the New Orleans cityscape. Programs beautified the shore of Lake Pontchartrain, restored historic buildings, constructed playgrounds, and cleared overgrown areas of City Park. Work gangs paved streets and installed drainage systems. Equally significant was the Louisiana branch of the

Federal Writers Project, under the direction of Lyle Saxon. With a deep admiration for New Orleans and the state, Saxon threw himself into his work and eventually produced two notable tour books, one on New Orleans and one on the state. Although Saxon's efforts, like most of the construction projects, came to fruition late in the decade, the programs pumped vital money into the New Orleans economy beginning in the mid-1930s.[34]

But federal programs failed to guarantee the survival of the anti-Long regime in New Orleans. By July 1935, a formerly unanimous Commission Council split on the issue of making peace with Baton Rouge, beginning a chain of events with dramatic consequences for the city's tourism industry. On a three-to-two vote, the council passed a resolution stating its "confidence and faith" in the Old Regular machine. The statement of loyalty disguised a mutiny against the mayor, however: the resolution also affirmed the published statement of commission members Pratt, Joseph Skelly, and Frank Gomila demanding the "absolute need that peace be effected with the state authorities so that the people of New Orleans may not suffer further and so that the employees of the city may be paid." No amount of patchwork financing, federal aid, and new taxes could keep the municipal government from collapse. For the majority on the council, the war of attrition waged by the Longites had taken too large a toll. Surrender was inevitable. Fred Earhart, Walmsley's lone remaining ally, attacked the resolution, declaring, "It is not the mayor who has caused this trouble; it is the state administration which has taken the food from the mouths of our people." He could not "make peace at any price." The Longites' program of taxing large corporations "diverted" manufacturers from New Orleans. Worse, Long's antics negatively affected the convention-hosting industry: "We can't ask conventions to come to New Orleans because of the conditions in the state of Louisiana. We can't honestly and conscientiously ask anybody to put a dollar into the state of Louisiana as an investment because of the conditions prevalent in the state." Walmsley vehemently opposed the resolution, making resistance a question of integrity: "You wouldn't deal with Al Capone. You can't deal with men who have been called thieves and crooks by each and every one of you and then uphold your honor." Calls for his resignation galled Walmsley, especially when they came from within the Old Regulars: "I will not compromise with principle at any time," he protested. "There is nothing that I will do that will bring back Banquo's ghost to haunt me and make the members of my family hang their heads in shame. Peace. I want peace; I love peace but never peace on the terms that have been offered."[35]

In late 1935, Longites in Baton Rouge decided to grant limited aid to the city in an effort to widen the emerging split in the Old Regulars. State officials agreed to give the city one million dollars, thereby winning the allegiance of Pratt, the commissioner of public finance. However, New Orleans did not receive control of the funds, as Walmsley had demanded. The mayor pointed out that the money "still remains in the hands of the State Civil Service Commission, and it is optional with them what they will do with the money. It can be spent for the Dock Board, or any Board, Commission, or agency of the State of Louisiana." Pratt nevertheless proceeded to negotiate with the state, arranging a municipal budget in which Longite legislators funded various city agencies, particularly the Fire and Police Departments. Walmsley, angry that Pratt had introduced his proposal while the mayor was out of town, countered with a budget that avoided a truce with the state government. For the mayor, capitulation amounted to the elimination of home rule for New Orleans.[36]

The animosity over the competing budgets spilled into the upcoming gubernatorial campaign, a watershed not only in the political history of New Orleans but for the future of the tourism industry. Walmsley's dwindling loyalists devoted all their energy into exploiting the power vacuum created in the Longite machine after a gunman assassinated Long in September 1935. The gubernatorial election held early the next year was Walmsley's last chance to break the Longite stranglehold on New Orleans. Although Long was no longer alive to press the war against New Orleans, the political machine he had organized remained powerful. The men at the helm may have lacked Huey Long's astuteness, but they were not foolish enough to allow a staunch opponent to regain strength. Walmsley backed candidates who promised to restore money and power to the New Orleans government, but Richard Leche, whom Walmsley distrusted and ardently campaigned against, never-theless won the gubernatorial race, assuring that the city-state animos-ity would continue. On 9 March 1936, Walmsley finally conceded. He asked for the return of "real local self government" in the Crescent City, publicly declaring that he would resign his office if Leche and the state legislature provided the necessary funds and power for the municipal government to again function effectively.[37]

At a Longite conference in Hot Springs, Arkansas, members of the state political machine decided to replace Walmsley with Robert Maestri. The defeated Old Regulars allowed Maestri to run unopposed in the special election held to fill Walmsley's unexpired term, thereby avoiding the turmoil of a campaign at a still politically volatile time. A Longite in the bastion of anti-Longism, Maestri occupied a tenuous position, but he and his administration worked vigorously to improve conditions in New Orleans, courting widespread support among the city's residents.[38]

Reporters from newspapers around the country recognized Maestri's special interest in developing the tourist trade. Jack Williams from the *Kansas City Journal Post* saw Maestri as Louisiana's "new dictator" and cited the new mayor's personal business history to explain his com-mitment to attracting out-of-towners: "He runs New Orleans and Lou-isiana. He is the city's largest tax payer. He owns the ball park and the race track. He formerly was in the real estate business and it is said he made a good profit from that real estate leasing it to cash in on tourist interest in New Orleans night life." Maestri possessed firsthand knowledge of tourists' value to the city. A reporter for the *Chicago Times* concurred. Whereas Long had "laugh[ed] at Mardi Gras as a 'silk stocking' affair" for the upper classes, Maestri sought to make the holiday bigger and better: "New Orleans is plotting to take over Dixie's winter tourist trade and leave neighboring Florida out in the bitter cold it has been capitalizing these many years." The descendant of Italian immigrants pushed New Orleans into the vanguard of cities pursuing tourist dollars.[39]

Immediately after taking office, Maestri worked to secure the city's fi-nancial structure. Possessing a reputation for frugality matched only by his shrewd business acumen, the new mayor resuscitated the city government by restructuring the tax-collection process into a more efficient system. Maestri also used his strong ties to the Longites to obtain low-interest loans from the state. With the Old Regulars out of the picture, legislators restored funds cut earlier in the decade. Under Maestri, municipal government expenditures increased from roughly $5,914,000 in 1935 to $10,289,000 in 1941.[40]

Increased federal funds were also forthcoming. Still fearing the Longites' power in the 1936 presidential election, President Roosevelt cut a deal with Leche. The governor and his allies pledged to turn down their anti–New Deal rhetoric, and in exchange Roosevelt agreed to curtail the federal income tax investigations of Long lieutenants, some of whom had already been indicted. The president also restored funds for Louisiana relief programs that had been cut in an attempt to curb the Longites' power: by the end of 1936, only 22 percent of funds authorized for the Public Works Administration and WPA in Louisiana were spent, far short of the more than 65 percent registered for the United States as a whole. A meager 18.5 percent of federal funds earmarked for New Orleans had been spent. Of the $465 million in federal grants and $290 million in federal loans to Louisiana between 1933 and 1939, about 60 percent came after Maestri and Leche compromised with Roosevelt.[41]

Mayor Maestri maintained an active and visible presence. During his first six years in office, he took daily tours of the city, monitoring the actions of workers and overseeing such minutiae as the laying of sidewalk, the paving of streets, and the painting of signs. Two Association of Commerce members sent to observe the projects remarked, "It is an obsession with our Mayor to see that every man on City payroll gives value received in the way of labor for money paid." The authors found particularly "amazing" the mayor's effective use of WPA labor: "The opinion prevails with some that our W.P.A. workers loaf on their jobs. Only wish they could see the gang of 150 or 200 W.P.A. workers busy paving Tchoupitoulas Street. Never did we see a lot of men working for general contractor or on piece work basis working harder and more efficiently than the men are working on this paving job."[42]

The New Deal projects proved particularly important since Maestri inherited a city government literally crumbling into ruins and incapable of presenting a clean cityscape to visitors. Edward Rapier, chair of the Civic Affairs Committee, profiled the equipment owned by the Department of Public Works in September 1938. Dump trucks were in "poor condition"; wagons were in "very poor physical condition." Nearly a third of the hundreds of mules still used to collect garbage needed replacement. The harnesses owned by the municipal government had been "mended so many times it is hard to see how they continue in operation." Of the city's seven inspection cars, only one functioned. Under Walmsley, equipment purchases had become a costly luxury the city simply could not afford. The shabby conditions identified within the Department of Public Works reflected the status of other municipal departments as well as conditions throughout New Orleans, where streets and parks had deteriorated.[43]

Undeterred by such handicaps, Maestri endeavored to enhance the cityscape. Beautification programs abounded. Workmen, many of them from the WPA, planted live oaks, azaleas, and flowering plants on the medians of almost every major thoroughfare within city limits. Maestri dedicated the "Floral Trail," a fifty-five-mile route "through the heart of New Orleans" marked with street signs bearing an azalea blossom. Residents along the boulevards were encouraged to provide "a dazzling array of multi-colored blossoms" for motorists to enjoy. City officials under Maestri also assisted the Association of Commerce in creating the "Visitor's Route." Marked by signs bearing a gold fleur-de-lis on a white background, the tour meandered for fifty miles past various historic sites and prominent landmarks. The "Keep New Orleans Clean" campaign further improved the cityscape. Although public clean-up campaigns had been common after the First World War, the Great Depression left people too concerned with survival to worry about trash in the streets. Under Maestri, more than seventy-six thousand families and businesses signed a pledge to gather garbage from the streets, while a modernized Department of Public Works efficiently collected the refuse. On Maestri's watch, the city added 150 trash receptacles to the business district and improved conditions at the garbage dumps, notorious for emitting foul odors that wafted into the French Quarter and the central business district. Edwin Heaton, president of the Carrollton Business Men's Association, congratulated the mayor on "the fact that every effort is being made by you, and by others to cooperate with you, in beautifying the city, not only for our own pleasure and benefit but to create a good impression on visitors to our City."[44]

Maestri bestowed particular attention on Canal Street, a thoroughfare lined with department stores that the municipal government had neglected since an expensive improvement project completed nearly a decade earlier. The street's filth angered many proud New Orleanians, including former finance commissioner A. Miles Pratt, who wrote to Maestri in early 1938, "I have a number of times heard severe criticism by strangers for the condition of our sidewalks and neutral ground due, almost entirely, to the unsightly 'chewing gum' spots." Maestri quickly responded to Pratt's concerns, and by the late 1930s the street was receiving a total of five cleanings a day: twice each day, two men, one carrying a broom and shovel while the other pushed a metal cart bearing garbage receptacles, patrolled the street, and water trucks sprayed the street at night, supplemented as needed by another patrol. Finally, a crew of ten men worked six hours each night cleaning the terrazzo sidewalks—rubbing away gum with straight-end hoes or hand scrapers, applying soap, and scrubbing the tiles with steel wool. Tourists who witnessed the late-night activities expressed amazement, testifying to the success of Maestri's city-beautification efforts.[45]

Maestri proved so committed to bolstering tourism that he spent his own money on preservation projects. He purchased the condemned Dufilho Pharmacy, a major French Quarter landmark celebrated in the guidebooks, destruction of which threatened the character of the historic neighborhood. Maestri donated the building to the city, garnering effusive praise from Louisiana State Museum curator James Fortier: "Museums, aside from their educational value, are great commercial assets, for visitors stay longer in our midst in proportion to the interest and entertainment which our Museums afford them." Businessmen also praised Maestri's foresight. As a high-ranking New Orleans Association of Commerce official wrote, the French Quarter was the "greatest asset" in attracting tourists, since nearly "everyone wants to go down there and they all rave about it."[46]

The Spring Fiesta, a festival created in 1935 to popularize the French Quarter, also benefited from Maestri's willingness to assist ventures that improved New Orleans's touristic value. Not only did Maestri provide organizers with space for a headquarters, but he also acted promptly on requests for funding, squeezing three hundred dollars from the cash-strapped municipal treasury for the 1938 celebration. "One never has to be embarrassed by a second request to our City Father who acts with immediacy and sympathy," wrote Helen Schertz in thanks.[47]

Maestri's proactive, tourism-oriented boosterism extended to sporting events. The business community encouraged the development of a golf championship in the early 1930s. Spokesmen for the Association of Commerce believed that the event would "prove instrumental in attracting many visitors to New Orleans, as well as prolonging the stay of many of those who will come to our city for Mardi Gras." Event coordinators nevertheless struggled to make the contest a major affair. Shortly after taking the reins of the municipal government, Maestri donated five thousand dollars of his own money to increase the cash prize awarded to competitors. When the first Crescent City Open Golf Tournament was held at City Park in early 1938, the event attracted numerous golfers from the Professional Golf Association as well as more than ten thousand spectators, bringing the city national publicity. Fred Corcoran, the association's tournament bureau manager, called it "one of the most successful events" on the tour. The popularity of golf among businessmen and other professionals meant that Maestri cultivated a crop of well-off tourists ripe for annual harvests.[48]

In 1934, city officials and businessmen inaugurated the Sugar Bowl series of college athletic contests, hoping to emulate the success of the Rose Bowl in Pasadena, California. The first such event, a football game between nationally prominent teams, served as a means of advertising one of Louisiana's most important crops and drew thousands of spectators to the city despite the Great Depression. In 1935, President Warren Miller of the New Orleans Mid-Winter Sports Association, the organization responsible for the football Sugar Bowl, proposed the addition of a basketball contest, which would "bring visitors to New Orleans for the benefit of our City and its hotels, merchants, etc., and since at that season of the year [Christmas] it seems as if the logical visitor to our City comes from the Mid-West, it would appear to be desirable to give them the sports that they most particularly like." Although basketball in New Orleans was an "untried proposition," Warren stressed that such a tournament supplied a means for the "upbuilding of the tourist trade to our City and for the advertising of our City." By the late 1930s, the program included not only a major football game and basketball tournament but a track meet and a tennis competition as well. Maestri wholeheartedly supported the expansion of the Sugar Bowl series of collegiate contests, especially after the sold-out 1937 football contest set a New Orleans record for attendance at a sporting event by attracting forty-two thousand fans. In 1938, Joseph Cousins, Miller's successor, called Maestri's tireless efforts a "life saver." Within a couple of years, attendance at the football game alone nearly doubled, climbing to more than seventy thousand.[49]

In addition to French Quarter preservation and the creation of nationally popular events, politicians and businessmen mobilized to have the site of the 1815 Battle of New Orleans declared a national memorial park. A variety of festivities were inaugurated in 1936 to celebrate the anniversary of the battle as well as gain publicity for the movement to preserve the battlefield. The Louisiana State Museum and Young Men's Christian Association sponsored a footrace commemorating the "double quick time run of the 'Brave Creoles' of General J. B. Plauché," who rushed his men from Spanish Fort on Lake Pontchartrain to assist General Andrew Jackson in defending the city. Museum officials also joined local politicians and businessmen to publicize an annual flag-burning ceremony by the Boy Scouts in Jackson Square. The event allowed New Orleanians to respectfully dispose of their worn banners. Support for such festivities had less to do with memorializing war heroes than with broadening the array of area attractions. A. Sidney Nunez, a leader of the movement to preserve the battlefield, explained to the mayor that the park promised to "attract to New Orleans thousands of visitors who probably would not otherwise come here." The story of the battle appealed to military buffs and neatly complemented the oft-told romantic tales of New Orleans life.[50]

The timing of the movement to preserve the battlefield revealed the marketing savvy of local politicians and businessmen. In January 1938, Cecil B. DeMille released *The Buccaneer*, a movie adaptation of Lyle Saxon's biography of Jean Lafitte, a pirate who assisted Andrew Jackson in fending off the British invaders. Premiering to great fanfare in New Orleans on the anniversary of the battle, the film attracted national media coverage. City officials worked to ensure that the reality of New Orleans mirrored the alluring city seen on film. In 1938, elaborate festivities honored DeMille as well as the actors from the movie. Men and women in period costume joined brass bands as part of the annual ceremonies. The winners of the Brave Creoles Run received the Cecil B. DeMille trophy, with actor Hugh Sothern, in full Andrew Jackson garb, bestowing the awards. Fact and fiction blended together. So did past and present. In a radio conversation with Saxon, DeMille commented, "More than a hundred years have passed since Jean Lafitte held the future of America in the palm of his hand, yet here in New Orleans, steeped in tradition and romance, it almost seems as if he were still alive." As an epic about the city's past, *The Buccaneer* was part entertainment, part history lesson, and part travelogue. Local boosters considered the last aspect particularly important. The film, in the words of Louisiana State Museum officials, "advertised New Orleans throughout the world." The actual battlefield thus became a stage on which tourists could walk in the footsteps of both historical figures and their favorite onscreen personalities. In 1939, in time for the 125th anniversary of the battle, the federal government agreed to make the site a national park.[51]

Maestri likewise courted federal aid to foster international tourism. The proposed construction of an International Goodwill Center near Lake Pontchartrain garnered strong support from the mayor. Maestri relentlessly courted White House funding for the project, arguing that the "Temple of Good Will" would put into physical form the Roosevelt administration's Good Neighbor policy by supplying a gathering place for Latin American and U.S. officials. Proponents emphasized the facility's potential as an attraction capable of drawing an otherwise untapped market of foreign tourists. One advocate envisioned a political, commercial, and cultural center capable of making New Orleans the "key city of Hispane [sic] America." Despite Maestri's persistence, federal monies were not forthcoming, and the project never left the drawing board. Nevertheless, the proposal revealed Maestri's eagerness to expand New Orleans tourism, even if doing so meant inventing landmarks to attract visitors.[52]

By the late 1930s, New Orleanians required little encouragement to foster tourism. The Benevolent and Protective Order of Elks proposed a citywide contest to encourage homeowners, businessmen, and municipal leaders to use lights and other decorations during the Christmas season. Newspapers and radio stations offered wholehearted support for the idea, which reflected civic pride at a time when decorating houses for Christmas was far from commonplace. More important, the light display would likely appeal to tourists, a further inducement to visitors drawn to New Orleans by the Sugar Bowl. Explained a flier distributed by the Elks, "We can assure [that tourists leave] New Orleans with a good word for us if we beautify with the Xmas spirit."[53]

Maestri also understood that a cash-strapped city eager for tourists needed not just to beautify the cityscape but also to control offensive public behavior. In addition to his cleanup campaign, the mayor ordered stringent enforcement of traffic regulations and antispitting ordinances. Providing tourists a safe, orderly urban space only partially explained Maestri's efforts. As members of the Association of Commerce Civic Affairs Committee pointed out in November 1936, fining violators of such measures resulted in funds for bare municipal coffers. Municipal finances and the cultivation of New Orleans as a tourist center merged in civic leaders' thinking.[54]

One of the most significant threats to the hospitable image of New Orleans and the tourism trade was the irresponsible use of fireworks. Rampant, often violent, use of fireworks plagued New Year's Eve celebrations. Prior to Maestri's rise to power, city administrators found curtailing the practice difficult. The *Times-Picayune* reported in 1935,

"There was, of course, the usual official warning, and the city was about as thoroughly policed for the holidays as was possible. However, a force of 10 times the size could not have coped with that barrage laid down on Canal street and near-by thoroughfares, nor have curbed it without an emphatic warrant from public opinion, which was not given." The dangers caused by the lighting of fireworks on Canal Street, where large crowds of revelers gathered, troubled civic leaders, and the presence of Sugar Bowl fans heightened concerns. Boosters feared that tourists would return home with a negative impression of the city. Curtailing the firework menace, as the *Times-Picayune* suggested, required a civic leader capable of stretching municipal resources as well as rallying public opinion.[55]

The fireworks issue came to a head between Christmas and New Year's Eve 1937. Tourist J. W. Hanson was one of many people who reported having a "large fire cracker" thrown into his car on Christmas Eve. Another tourist complained that he left the city with a "ruined pair of shoes" and "two burns on [my] hand when a firecracker fell on my hat & hand on Carondelet St." Conditions worsened on New Year's Eve, which local attorney Edward Estalote branded a "day of blood by which innocent victims were offered upon the sacrificial altar of drunken reckless [*sic*] frivolity." Two parents and their child went to a downtown movie theater, attending an early show to avoid the notorious explosions that increased as midnight approached. When they emerged from the theater, they were stunned by the chaos they encountered, which reminded the concerned mother of stories about the "war in Japan & China." Moreover, according to one longtime citizen of New Orleans, "grown, moronic men" had as much to do with the disturbances as unruly teenagers. Unless stopped, some New Orleanians feared the rampant, malicious use of fireworks might spread to other festivities, particularly Mardi Gras.[56]

Flooded with mail after the *New Orleans Item* urged citizens to express their support for a ban on fireworks, the mayor moved quickly to bring peace to the streets. Maestri immediately ordered Superintendent of Police George Reyer to provide a complete accounting of each injury caused by fireworks and where each incident occurred. Within days, the mayor and the Commission Council issued an ordinance outlawing the use of fireworks by private individuals inside city limits. A year later, the *Item* reported a dramatic decline in holiday injuries due to firecrackers.[57]

Maestri's concern with regulating public behavior coincided with the solidification of the tourism infrastructure. Whereas carriage rides, taxi tours, and bus guides aided tourists in identifying important sites, the growth of the tourism business spread concern among members of the business community about the quality of the stories told. The key word was *authenticity*, but businessmen were less concerned with establishing truths than with ensuring that everyone told similar tales. They feared that variations in the information recited by tour guides would lead tourists to discount the veracity of the claims made about the city.

Professional tour companies and the municipal government worked closely to regulate the stories told about New Orleans. The actions of a company formed in 1936, Louisianians Inc., exemplified the new arrangement. The agency's president, A. M. Billie Wilhelm, made sure that the mayor was the "first to know" of its existence and emphasized the importance of making certain that "guests" of the city "be apprised of an intelligent, dignified, and authentic service thru which they will be made acquainted with the true historical and romantic charm of our French Quarter." Maintaining the mirage of the "authentic" and "true" revealed the degree to which Wilhelm recognized the link between the myth of New Orleans and the economic impact of out-of-towners. He explained his "appreciation of [tourists'] stimulating effect upon our business life" and wrote of how he and his associates considered tourists' "real value as an active invaluable advertising medium." The officers of the company were "born and reared in the traditions" of the city, thereby wrapping Louisianians Inc. in the cloak of authenticity while bolstering the agency's legitimacy in the eyes of tourists. As for the tours offered by the company, Wilhelm assured Maestri that company officers "registered . . . only accredited French Quarter guides."[58]

Sentiments such as those voiced by Wilhelm reflected the maturation of the tourism industry under Maestri's leadership. In the summer of 1938, New Orleans businessmen debated municipal regulation of the city's tourism industry. George Toye, owner of the Yellow Cab Company, pressed for an ordinance that licensed tour guides. He expressed concern regarding the dangers of "misinformation . . . given out by irresponsible guides." Fellow businessmen looked to Montreal, where "competent professors of the Tourism School" affiliated with the University of Montreal trained tour group leaders. The school forced potential guides to take oral and written exams, after which graduates received a diploma, a requirement in the Canadian city. New Orleans businessmen largely agreed on implementing a similar arrangement. Tourism promoters believed that having guides tell conflicting tales about the city unraveled the mythology on which the touristic city rested. The Association of Commerce threw its support behind a licensing program. As a prerequisite, some businessmen suggested guides attend an "evening school or clinic conducted perhaps under W.P.A. sponsorship with lectures given by persons versed in New Orleans history, business, culture and the like." The proposed classes would use "some sort of text book, giving authentic facts about the city." Licenses, in other words, were useless without a means of supervising and instructing guides. Members of the business community closely observed tour companies by checking the qualifications of guides as well as the information they disseminated.[59]

New Orleanians had crafted tourism into a vital component of city life. Schools and textbooks for tour leaders regulated the tourism industry. Sites such as the French Quarter were identified and protected. Various projects improved the cityscape. Key events, like the Spring Fiesta and Sugar Bowl, permanently settled into the calendar of Americans nationwide. Equally important, tourism-related taxes and licenses buoyed city finances. With a tourism infrastructure in place by the start of the Second World War, New Orleans businessmen and politicians committed themselves to making New Orleans a major, year-round travel destination.

Playing the Part of Santa Claus

Within two years of taking office, Maestri's endeavors to resurrect the New Orleans economy gained national praise, reversing years of negative publicity stemming from the political war between Huey Long and the Old Regulars. Kathryn Cravens of the Columbia Broadcasting System informed American radio listeners in 1936 that New Orleanians, "tired of the detrimental headlines," looked forward to a city administration promising peace and progress. In 1938, the *Chicago Daily News* summarized the good fortune enjoyed by the city after Maestri grasped the reins of power: "Less than two years ago the city of New Orleans was in bankruptcy in the federal courts, its credit exhausted, its streets and public buildings going to ruin and political forces at odds." "Today," continued the article, "New Orleans's credit is restored, all of its bank loans repaid, its liabilities reduced 21 per cent and, better still, its operations placed on a cash basis for the first time in history. Its streets and public buildings are being improved on a 'pay-as-you-go' basis, no borrowings having been resorted to in more than a year, and bills are being discounted and expenses have been cut." Maestri's accomplishments certainly deserved national attention. His success had come rapidly and despite a 1937 national recession. Americans showed great interest in the New Orleans success story.[60]

Maestri's campaign to improve the tourism industry rested on a firm foundation of community support. New Orleanians thanked him for his financial reforms as well as for his citywide improvement program. Just one week after Maestri took office, a radio news broadcast on WDSU informed New Orleans and the coastal communities surrounding the city that the mayor was "playing the part of Santa Claus" by restoring city finances with a low-interest state loan. These arrangements allowed the city to pay its outstanding bills and to give its employees their paychecks. Other locals simply appreciated the end of the conflict between Longites and Old Regulars. Civic activist Judith Douglas, speaking for local "women representing various social agencies," thanked the new mayor for bringing "political peace" to New Orleans. Maestri was so successful at reversing the city's fortunes that some New Orleanians feared the consequences. One concerned citizen wrote to the mayor, "If the Chamber of Commerce and state officials keep on broadcasting about LA. prosperity, wont be long before floods of people with out any Financial responsibility will be flocking to Louisiana." Such a risk was the price of financial stability during an economically volatile time. Many New Orleanians and Louisianans in general likely thought the risk a pleasant worry after years of municipal budget cuts and political strife. In the fall of 1936, just a few months after Maestri took office, state residents amended the state constitution to skip the 1938 New Orleans mayoral elections, thereby giving Maestri a six-year term to carry out his already successful policies.[61]

Most New Orleanians embraced Maestri and his devotion to tourism. The mayor's enthusiasm inspired residents to assist boosters. An increasingly packed calendar of events along with the establishment of year-round attractions reshaped life in the Crescent City. Tourism no longer meant a seasonal influx centered on Mardi Gras. Furthermore, the intensifying dependence of municipal finances on tourist-oriented taxes and licenses led city administrators to keep a keen eye on the desires of out-of-towners. Maestri may have been a Santa Claus in the late 1930s, but his labors, along with those of his predecessor, revealed how an urban community in a severely depressed economy could cultivate fresh sources of revenue through tourism. New Orleans civic leaders had no trouble remembering the lesson.

CHAPTER 3

A NEW BABYLON

Vice and Gender in New Orleans

In 1925, after months of living in New Orleans, a young William Faulkner put to ink his initial impression of the port city. The sketch likened the city to a "courtesan, not old and yet no longer young, who shuns the sunlight that the illusion of her former glory be preserved." She surrounded herself with dull mirrors and worn furniture, a decor that conveyed an "atmosphere of a bygone and more gracious age." Her deteriorating residence reflected the taming of the city's flamboyant nightlife, which had centered on elaborate Storyville brothels. The closure of the red-light district and the victory of Prohibitionists after the First World War forced commercial sex and alcohol into the shadows. The astute Mississippian noted that the aging woman now received "few in number" despite her captivating allure. Her fortunes, like her youth, had slipped away. Drunken revelries and colorful madams faded into legend. Many travelers who had patronized the city's carnal attractions no longer came. To Faulkner, only one title seemed appropriate for his sketch: "The Tourist."[1]

As Faulkner suggested, the pleasures of New Orleans had been a profitable attraction. Brothels and bars unleashed men from the subdued behavior practiced at home, where wives and children lived. Reform-minded local politicians had sought to regulate carnal pleasures by establishing the nation's largest red-light district, Storyville, but the graft and profits resulting from the concentration of brothels, bars, and music halls reinforced the popular image of New Orleans as a harbor for wanton immorality. This image ignored the many ways Storyville meshed with the interests of businessmen in the age before mass tourism. Male-oriented attractions formed the backbone of local nightlife, drawing male visitors and, more importantly, providing a place to entertain business clients—at the time, predominantly men. After a hard day's work, Storyville provided a place to relax, a place that fit neatly with the business community's desire to spatially segregate work from leisure as well as foster a work-intensive city by controlling vice.

The closure of Storyville and the suppression of the city's male-centered attractions paved the way for the creation of a tourism industry structured for the enjoyment of both genders. Nightlife and gender conventions, both closely linked, would change significantly as women pressed for an expanded role in society during the first two decades of the twentieth century, from the right to vote to participation in organizations committed to the moral cleansing of American life. According to historian Alison Isenberg, women "established the field of *municipal housekeeping*—a domain in which they attacked and struggled to reform the shabby conditions of America's business streets." The "feminizing adornment agenda" introduced garbage receptacles and ornamental streetlights to the urban scene. Overhanging wires were buried. Trash-filled lots and gutters were cleaned. Streets were paved. But women did not stop at physical enhancements of the cityscape. Shutting taps and closing brothels helped erase the stigma placed on women who left the domestic sphere to work in public spaces long considered the cultural domain of women of questionable, even purchasable, virtue. By 1920, the actions of these crusaders had suffocated New Orleans's largely male-oriented nightlife. As a result, women during the interwar years felt increasingly comfortable venturing into the tamed streets.[2]

New Orleans politicians and businessmen responded by making the best of the situation. They secreted away a remnant of the city's formerly flamboyant nightlife, allowing men continued access to the pleasures they craved while making city streets more hospitable to the growing numbers of women entering public spaces. Over time, the repression of drinking and prostitution permitted carnal behavior, previously strictly associated with male entertainment, to lose its gendered identification. Urban reforms thus prepared the way for businessmen and elected officials to craft a tourism industry as well as an urban space suited to both sexes.

New Orleans Nights

In 1922, Pastor L. T. Hastings of the Coliseum Place Baptist Church joined fellow religious leaders and concerned parents in praising Mayor Andrew McShane after he steadfastly refused to permit a 3 July parade considered too offensive for public streets. Hastings informed McShane that his decision heartened "the confidence of all decent, self-respecting citizens of New Orleans in your purpose and efforts to make our city a suitable place for rearing boys and girls to become citizens with high ideals." In a letter simply signed "A Grandmother from Algiers," an elderly matron also thanked McShane for safeguarding morality: "If there was more like you," she wrote, "we old timers would not fear for our grandchildren and have to blush for our self." In a city known for ribald Mardi Gras celebrations, the ruckus might have seemed odd. But this was no ordinary procession preparing to roll down city avenues. The affair involved "so-called 'Bathing Beauties,' " women clad in skin-revealing and, for many locals, scandalous swimsuits. Showing skin without the pretense of masking was a far cry from what many New Orleanians deemed acceptable. New Orleanians could tolerate Carnival excesses during the extraordinary few days given over to bacchanalia. Liberating the body of clothing for an Independence Day celebration was another matter. Staid locals agreed with McShane when he declared, "I draw the line at bathing suits."[3]

The controversy over bathing beauties revealed the impact of changing gender conventions and moral reform on the urban space. "Sex appeal," to use the term coined during the period, was a powerful force in marketing goods and services. Yet the display of flesh along Canal Street, the downtown shopping district popular with middle- and upper-class white women, created an outcry. An older generation, including the grandmother from Algiers, the religious community, and social reformers took offense at the exploitation of the female body as an advertising gimmick meant to attract shoppers. In a city that had banned the sale of sex only a few years earlier, the public display of female bodies shocked many locals. The questionable exhibit of women in bathing suits clashed with reformers' efforts to make streets more hospitable for a genteel, respectable womanhood. Like the earlier traders in commercial sex and alcohol, the bathing beauties encountered an inhospitable cityscape. The now restrictive urban environment forced men to ferret out the carnal entertainment found with ease in previous years.

In the years preceding McShane's 1920 mayoral victory, the city and nation were so caught in the fervor of winning the First World War that long-prominent entertainment venues were forced to close. New Orleanians, accustomed to a city with close to five thousand bars, reluctantly accepted prohibition of alcohol as a war measure. Concerns over the conservation of foodstuffs such as grain and corn, along with the need to maximize the efficient use of labor for the war effort, justified restrictions on intoxicating beverages. Hard liquors and wines were viewed as luxuries, and the association of beer with Germans discredited the brew. Many Americans, galvanized by news from the battle lines, considered a consumer of alcohol unpatriotic and a sober public efficient. Likewise, many citizens believed that prostitution, in New Orleans concentrated in Storyville, hindered wartime mobilization efforts. The U.S. military, eager to calm family fears and secure the ranks from an outbreak of venereal disease, ordered cities to close all red-light districts within a five-mile radius of navy and army installations or risk losing those economic prizes. Reformers believed that alcohol and prostitution sapped American energy and corrupted the men in arms. Even as the opposing nations negotiated peace terms in the Hall of Mirrors at Versailles, Americans persisted in their efforts to maximize productivity, considering what was good for wartime just as good for peacetime.[4]

Nevertheless, Martin Behrman, New Orleans's mayor since 1904, cited the negative impact on tourism to justify his opposition to the reform efforts energized by wartime euphoria. Behrman sneered, "You can make prostitution illegal in Louisiana, but you can't make it unpopular." Brothels and bars, according to the mayor, merely provided the services men sought from a city. In Behrman's opinion, moral crusaders, especially vocal rural residents of northern Louisiana who supported Prohibition, were hypocrites: "There are thousands of voters who are devoted to prohibition at home so long as they may take a train to Alexandria, Eunice or New Orleans and go wet for a few hours." Maintaining New Orleans as a wide-open city not only brought profits from servicemen but also ensured a steady flow of visitors eager to indulge themselves.[5]

In the decade prior to 1920, the status of New Orleans as a pleasurable resort for men had ironically benefited from the success of reformers in the rural hinterlands. Long before the state legislature sanctioned the Eighteenth Amendment on 8 August 1918, much of the state had already removed alcohol from shelves. Under a local-option law passed in 1902, most rural parishes went dry—thirty Louisiana parishes totaling 81.8 percent of the state's territory and 52.9 percent of its population had banned alcohol. As a result, urban areas in wet parishes enjoyed an economic boon by providing escape from these restrictions. Because many saloons also harbored prostitutes, thereby satisfying some men's sexual hunger as well as their thirst, the success of Prohibitionists in rural areas as well as the availability of legal prostitution enhanced New Orleans's allure. Behrman, the boss of the Old Regulars, applied his sharp sense of humor to explain both the success of the Prohibition movement and the persistent presence of alcohol in the urban environment during the 1920s. Dry advocates were "strictly local option" supporters: "Their option is (or was) to be dry at home and wet when off on a visit."[6]

Behrman firmly believed in keeping New Orleans a permissive oasis. A controversy with Commissioner of Public Safety Harold Newman exposed Behrman's agenda. In June 1917, Newman made headlines by resigning, marking the culmination of five years of friction between the reform-minded Newman and the Old Regulars. The political machine hoped the pretense of reform would protect the status quo, and

Newman had been an unwitting part of a ploy to quiet protest against the Old Regulars. With pressure mounting in the years before the First World War, Behrman orchestrated a brilliant countermove. In 1912, he and the machine pushed through the state legislature a city charter creating a commission council. Newman joined a carefully selected slate—a front—put forward by the machine in hopes of maintaining control of municipal politics while appearing to give voice to urban reformers. Over the ensuing years, however, Newman and the Old Regulars frequently clashed. The question of enforcing the law against the sale of alcohol on Sundays proved the final straw. With Behrman incapacitated as a result of illness, Newman instructed the police chief to use plainclothes officers to identify violators. After recovering, Behrman overturned the order. Although detectives regularly patrolled out of uniform, Behrman disapproved of allowing ordinary officers to do so. When the mayor announced that he believed that no police force should " 'spy' on business people" and that the practice of allowing such officers to "snoop about town" was contrary to the concept of "good public police," Newman expressed outrage. The mayor's pretense of safeguarding business interests thinly veiled his deep concern with maintaining the city's male-oriented attractions. Saloons supplied valuable financial support to his political machine. Closing businesses on Sunday cut into profits, and restrictions on alcohol threatened social life within the city. Elite businessmen, who frequented private clubs and closed deals over glasses of alcohol, quietly supported Behrman's actions.[7]

Behrman's commitment to protect dispensers of alcohol was eclipsed only by his support of Storyville as an attraction for men eager to satisfy their sexual appetites. Throughout the 1910s, the mayor and his allies fought rearguard actions against restrictions on the red-light district. Seeking to head off reformers, Philip Werlein, president of the Association of Commerce, joined protests against Storyville but considered calls for closing the district too extreme. He instead tendered a proposal on the eve of the First World War to place screens around the neighborhood, particularly near the recently constructed Terminal Station for railroad passengers. The compromise failed after serious debate, partly because of Behrman's opposition. Nevertheless, the measure set a precedent: civic leaders were willing to disguise the district in response to public outcries but drew the line at completely eliminating the questionable activities allowed in the highly profitable neighborhood. A few years later, Behrman and his associates tempered the excessive displays in which prostitutes exposed themselves to potential customers passing in the streets, displays that also served as a magnet for public protest. Police cracked down on such behavior by enforcing an ordinance that required brothel owners to place opaque glass in their front doors and blinds on their windows. City Hall balked at more serious restrictions, however, even those demanded by the formidable U.S. military. Federal officials struggled to stop soldiers from patronizing prostitutes, and New Orleans's sex trade persisted despite the stationing of military guards to prevent enlisted men from entering Storyville. To circumvent the order, soldiers donned civilian clothes, passing themselves off as locals or tourists. The fruitless efforts of the military led Behrman to quote Rudyard Kipling: " 'Single men in barracks don't grow into plaster saints.' No kind of men do that." All cities with military personnel suffered the "same trouble," declared the New Orleans mayor. Behrman, who ardently defended Storyville against its detractors, observed that "no regulation or law . . . cannot be 'beat' by a few if hundreds try to get around it." Federal officials agreed but thought stricter measures might help the cause of chastity. A hesitant New Orleans leadership finally submitted to federal pressure, passing an ordinance closing Storyville at midnight on 12 November 1917.[8]

Reformers in New Orleans were a diverse group, with the exception that many were women. Activism among women in New Orleans, as historian Pamela Tyler has shown, emerged most prominently from graduates of Sophie Newcomb College, a women's college affiliated with Tulane University that maintained a separate faculty and campus. Most of the school's instructors were female, thereby providing intellectual role models to students at a time when society offered few opportunities for women outside the home. Tyler argues that the Newcomb experience "acted as a powerful acid to dissolve [graduates'] traditional women's reluctance to become involved in civic affairs, and particularly in the 'male' world of politics." Other women not affiliated with Newcomb College also left a legacy of reform that grew during the Progressive Era. Sophie Bell Wright, who pressed for government legislation to improve welfare until her death in 1912, made a strong impression on activists in New Orleans. Like many women at the time, she worked through the Women's Christian Temperance Union, the United Daughters of the Confederacy, the State Congress of Mothers, and the Prison Reform Association. Wright was not afraid to act independently as well. She operated a night school for working boys that won widespread praise from New Orleanians. Eleanor McMain, who died in 1934, served as director of Kingsley House, a New Orleans settlement house, and elite women such as Elizabeth Werlein regularly participated in its programs for the poor. Kate and Jean Gordon worked through the Era Club to address the key issue facing women at the time, obtaining the right to vote. Some supporters saw the franchise as a symbol of gender equality, while for others it provided a means to pressure politicians to pass reform legislation. The Gordon sisters advocated child labor laws, legislation protecting women workers, better tuberculosis treatment centers, and the creation of a juvenile court system. Through the Women's League for Sewerage and Drainage, of which Kate Gordon served as president, the Gordons facilitated the implementation of a better water system in New Orleans to prevent street flooding and outbreaks of yellow fever. All of these issues pushed women into politics.[9]

Despite the success of New Orleans politicians and some businessmen in prolonging the open existence of male-oriented attractions, each attempt to circumvent reformers' efforts further motivated the forces urging change. In the aftermath of Newman's resignation, the *Item* cried, "Booze and Bossism blunder along in a ghastly marriage, each infecting the other with its worst evils." Sensible police enforcement of the laws demanded "gum shoes and disguises," not legions of officers who hunted down "speakeasies" by marching down dark alleyways with "torches, flags and brass bands." In a 1917 letter, Jean Gordon expressed disgust with the Old Regulars and revealed the intersection of wartime fervor with reformist zeal: "Talk of going to fight Prussianism!! Better start at the City Hall!" This potent combination led to McShane's hard-fought 1920 victory. Even in triumph, however, reformers found little comfort. Concerned citizens recognized that the moral cleanup of New Orleans nightlife demanded close supervision. Colonel Allison Owen, president of the New Orleans Social Hygiene Society, joined prominent women such as Ida Weiss Friend and Jean Gordon, the press, and other interested organizations in forming a coalition to ensure that McShane fulfilled at least some of his campaign promises, especially in regard to the suppression of vice. Such persistence seemed wise given that the Old Regulars retained partial control of the city government and claimed loyalists in such powerful departments as the police force. A "little light" might indeed have begun to "fall into the dark places," as Permelia Shields of the Bureau of Protective Social Measures rejoiced, but the shadows still provided sufficient cover for politicians and businessmen to hide remnants of the sex and alcohol trade.[10]

Leaders of the New Orleans Association of Commerce, in which Behrman exercised considerable authority, expressed dismay at the reformers' efforts and the subsequent decline of practices long part of the city's national appeal. Businessmen fretted over an uncertain future. Association President Arthur Parker voiced serious concern in a 1921 message to his fellow businessmen: "Prohibition laws, while not resulting in the Sahara predicted by their advocates, have adversely affected some of New Orleans's attractions and even the famous eating places, which long have been a charm to the visitor, now close early in the evening." Moral reform hurt business. Famed for their culinary skills, New Orleanians proved especially reluctant to discard wine, a beverage that not only accompanied traditional meals but also held a prominent place in local recipes. The passage of blue laws rankled most members of the New Orleans business elite not just by closing popular attractions but also by making the city inhospitable to the male camaraderie businessmen sought when entertaining clients. "Sunday closing laws," announced Parker, "annoy not only our own people but our visitors as well, and our Latin-American and European friends who come among us neither understand nor appreciate the spirit of a community which denies them the right to purchase a cigar on Sunday." The closure of stores and carnal attractions made coming to the Crescent City less exciting. Boosters watched anxiously as New Orleans was forced to behave more like a backwoods hamlet than a national metropolis capable of enticing investors, tourists, and shoppers with a stunning array of entertainments. Parker crystallized the fears of the business community: "New Orleans, it seems to me, cannot hope to prosper under the strict conditions that obtain in some interior towns." A city such as New Orleans contained a population consisting of "many kinds of people from many lands, and of many minds." Plurality required a liberal attitude. Parker warned, "An unnecessary condition that jars a large percentage of our population does not make for tranquility." The concerns of businessmen stemmed not from a desire to make New Orleans a leisure center but from an interest in optimizing business opportunities. Even businessmen opposed to brothels and seedy bars hesitated to support the absolute measures of reformers who banned all alcohol and infringed on an urban atmosphere that fostered business both in the streets traversed by out-of-town shoppers and in conferences between men who wanted to discuss deals over brandy and cigars.[11]

Despite the delaying tactics of the Old Regulars and members of the Association of Commerce, Prohibition immediately affected city revelry. New Year's Day celebrations, popular with winter tourists and a draw for those within a day's traveling distance, were noticeably quieter during the Prohibition years. A *Times-Picayune* reporter commented in 1920, "The first day of the new year was observed, rather than celebrated by New Orleans, with hushful Sabbatical ceremony." Most locals awoke without hangovers. Reported injuries declined. New Orleanians were solemn in their dry city. "People appeared like actors in a play who were not quite sure of their part, and it must be confessed that New Orleans is the veriest amateur in sedate behavior on New Year's day." Not everyone accepted sobriety. In a few instances "through the Lenten 'atmosphere' came like a hurtling shell the advent of a[n] occasional individual with the ancient hang-over." Some women in evening gowns were seen breakfasting downtown after a night of alcoholic revelry. Clubs operating just outside the city limits still satisfied local thirsts, providing a refuge for those determined to party. For the most part, however, life in New Orleans remained subdued. Many police patrol wagons stayed parked. Churches greeted larger-than-usual crowds. "Precedents were broken and traditions utterly smashed," concluded the reporter. New Orleans had passed into a more temperate era.[12]

Long-popular landmarks disappeared from the cityscape. The Tango Belt, a seedy entertainment district bordering Canal Street and stretching between Royal and Rampart Streets, withered under the new restrictions on vice. So quiet had the belt become that the *Times-Picayune* ran a sarcastic 1920 lost-and-found ad for the area known as the "twin sister" to Storyville. Formerly packed with cabarets, the Tango Belt "followed the route traveled by John Barleycorn, and all that is left of it is a row of unkempt houses, a nauseous appearance of ramshackle insanitation." Other famed bars and stores vanished. Owners of such popular restaurants as the Moulin Rouge and Quartier Club attempted to ignore the Prohibition law, only to face fines and jail sentences. Federal agents padlocked the premises of violators. As a result, the character of entire neighborhoods changed. The closing of Solari's in the French Quarter in 1926 led the *Times-Picayune* to announce "Old Royal Street Is Being Rebuilt by Prohibition." The same held true for many other New Orleans thoroughfares.[13]

Social commentators such as W. J. Cash noted that prostitutes after the First World War increasingly conducted business from hotels, which he labeled "public stews." The suppression of red-light districts and streetwalking gave hotel personnel a "virtual monopoly of the trade of pander and pimp." In early 1919, Captain Harold Wilson, a member of the War Department Commission on Training Camp Activities, compiled a report on the persistent problem of soldiers visiting prostitutes. The confidential study of vice conditions in New Orleans intended for War Department officials contained a notorious "List of 42" hotels and cafes where commercial sex flourished. Although meant only for the eyes of federal administrators, a copy fell into the hands of the *Times-Picayune*, which printed excerpts of the document in July 1919. The publication of the exposé shocked readers. Of all the city's hotels, Wilson cleared only the prestigious St. Charles Hotel. At other establishments, "clerks, bell hops, house detectives, porters, maids and bar-tenders" secretly tolerated or even "aided and abetted" the sex trade.[14]

Facing public scrutiny, enraged hotel owners responded by condemn-ing Wilson's "grave" accusations that "all hotels in New Orleans were houses of assignation." Members of the New Orleans Hotelmen's Asso-ciation pressured the Association of Commerce to rebuke Wilson with the goal of having him "withdraw," "substantiate," or "apologize" for the unfavorable publicity. Although the leaders of the Association of Commerce distanced themselves from several telegrams sent by hotel operators to Louisiana's U.S. senators requesting that the War Depart-ment remove Wilson, the association worked behind the scenes to un-dermine him. In reaction to the outcry, the secretary of war expressed regret over the report's publication and offered to transfer Wilson. The risk of a public backlash made transferring Wilson untenable, however, and federal officials instead quietly reprimanded him. The operators of the Hotel Grunewald also attempted to intimidate the *Times-Picayune* staff by filing a baseless two hundred thousand dollar libel suit. Overall, the incident publicly embarrassed hotel operators, who sought to hide the sex trade within their establishments. Their reaction to the Wilson report stemmed less from shock that prostitution existed in their midst than from anger at the exposure of their involvement in protecting com-mercial sex. The vehement stance taken by the hotel operators and al-lied businessmen served as a clear warning to anyone else investigating prostitution in New Orleans.[15]

Nevertheless, the electorate wanted to enforce prohibitions against alcohol and commercial sex, as evidenced by McShane's election. Boot-leggers and sex merchants thus were forced to adopt less conspicuous marketing methods, and prostitution subsequently became much more clandestine. In 1920, two investigators for the U.S. Interdepartmental Social Hygiene Board reported that prostitutes rarely appeared in highly visible areas and described conditions on "streets, boats, movies, the-atres and cafes . . . as 'good.'" Streetwalking, though much subdued, existed primarily between 7 p.m. and 1 a.m. Many downtown prosti-tutes stepped out of hidden brothels only in the afternoon to "sun them-selves" and refrained from soliciting. Very few were approachable. One prostitute explained the importance of maintaining a low profile: "The police men are good fellows but can't help themselves. If they see anything they must make an arrest." Although discretion did not always keep prostitutes unmolested by law enforcement, the same prostitute clarified that officers "make no efforts to see anything, and they give warnings." To ensure smooth operation, women in the sex trade befriended and bribed police to ignore activities. One of the investigators recounted that one policeman "disappeared around the corner and out of the way" when he saw men hesitate to enter a brothel within eyeshot of the officer. Other brothel operators claimed powerful political allies.[16]

During the interwar years, the veil of race hid public solicitation of sex. White reformers were primarily concerned with preserving the virtue of white womanhood and generally ignored black involvement in the sex trade. Vice on the dark side of the color line was culturally invisible in a predominantly white society that stereotyped blacks as promiscuous. Blatant sexual behavior by blacks reinforced faith in white supremacy. Furthermore, white women, the backbone of reform movements, generally denied the sexual interaction between white men and black women. The Social Hygiene Board study identified 123 white and 283 black prostitutes and found that black participants in the sex trade operated free of harassment, whereas police adopted a firmer stance against white prostitutes, whom officers perceived as "fallen" women. As the *Item* reported, "Most of the law's activities are directed to the whites, and the blacks are allowed to run rampant up and down the street soliciting." As a result of the racially unequal enforcement of antiprostitution laws, the Social Hygiene Board found conditions among blacks "worse than ever before in the history of New Orleans." Storyville continued to operate on the "sly," with blacks dominating the old district. City officials fully realized that black women, long a part of New Orleans's sex trade, helped fill the void created by the intensifying suppression of white prostitution. By permitting black women to fill the vacuum caused by the moral crusade against white prostitutes, purveyors of the sex trade applied the camouflage of race to hide prostitution in full view.[17]

Persons tied to the tourism industry, such as cab drivers, safeguarded the less visible prostitution trade involving white women. Investigators for the Social Hygiene Board concluded, "Taxicab conditions are bad. I spoke to not less than forty taxi drivers and they were all wise and stated that they could put me next to anything and that they were all real young girls and pretty as can be." Drivers crowed that the women were "just as safe as they could be" from police harassment. Unlike streetwalkers, the women who solicited customers through cabbies were most plentiful in the afternoons, after downtown offices closed and college classes ended. Taxi drivers served as middlemen, marketing women engaged in the sex trade in the same way they marketed speakeasies. As such, these individuals provided a service both to men eager for sex and to prostitutes, who used the cab drivers to reduce the risk of arrest or harassment. Women did not need literally to flash their bodies publicly to attract customers. Investigators noted the secrecy shrouding the cab driver–prostitute relationship: "These drivers are a wise and tough bunch of men and make their living in this fashion. They will not give out any information, but all are willing to drive you to the houses." City officials soon recognized the new role of cab drivers in the post-Storyville sex trade. In 1921, the Commission Council passed a municipal ordinance prohibiting the use of taxis for solicitation, but the measure barely hindered the evolving sex trade. According to a guide writer from the early 1940s, cab drivers remained "gold mines of information," telling customers about nightclubs and places to meet "pretty girls." [18]

Despite the reduction in the public nature of the sex trade, hotels, New Orleans's most tourist-dependent business sector, continued to play a major role in prostitution. Given the increased secrecy surrounding the sex trade and the ability of hotel personnel to check customers, unearthing information about hotel prostitution proved daunting to reformers, especially after the Wilson fiasco. The 1920 Social Hygiene Board report found only fifteen prostitutes in hotels. Large hotels received a "clean bill of health," while the overall hotel situation was branded "fair." Only one establishment appeared to be a full-fledged brothel. It seems quite unlikely, however, that the report reflected genuine changes within the hotels instead of a more clandestine sex trade. By 1927, the line between hotel and brothel had blurred to such a degree that the *New Orleans Times-Picayune* called for a state law, modeled after legislation developed by outraged reputable hotel owners in California, that defined a hotel as an establishment possessing a minimum of fifty rooms, a dining area, and a ground-floor lobby. For the newspaper, establishing a definition was "important as all know who, misled by the name 'hotel,' have found themselves in rooming places quite different from what had been expected." The "other type of hostelry" would just have "to think up some other name for their establishments." But even larger hotels harbored prostitutes. Like taxi drivers, bellhops and elevator operators recruited customers and carried lists of available women located either on the premises or near enough to arrive quickly after a telephone call. Hotel personnel guaranteed quality to customers and protected prostitutes from undercover agents or potentially violent patrons. Not surprisingly, some prostitutes preferred the safety of hotels to the brothels, which were more vulnerable to police raids.[19]

Brothel operators took their own measures to safeguard the uninterrupted flow of male clients. Places devoted to sexual commerce fronted as rooming houses, and madams facilitated the ruse by calling themselves "landladies." The coded language extended to potential customers, particularly out-of-towners, who were known as "vidalias." Gaining access to brothels was a complex procedure for customers unknown to sex merchants. In a series on gambling, illegal alcohol, and prostitution that ran under the title "New Orleans Nights," the *Times-Picayune* in the early 1920s sent a young undercover reporter, Lyle Saxon, to examine conditions in the city. Armed with a reference from a cab driver named Julian, Saxon posed as a customer seeking sex. He knocked on the door of a Bienville Street rooming house located just off Bourbon Street. An electric buzzer struck from inside unlocked the door, allowing him to enter a dim hallway, where a voice asked what he wanted. The reporter responded, "Julian sent me." A housekeeper relayed the message upstairs, where another voice exclaimed, "Tell him that I've got enough whiskey here!" After Saxon clarified that he sought sex, the second woman invited him upstairs, where he met the "pretty, well rounded, and apparently young" madam. The woman asked if he wanted a cigarette and spoke of sex only after the reporter showed a card he had received from the taxi driver. No prostitutes were on the premises. Instead, customers chose sex partners from a list not unlike that carried by hotel bellboys and elevator operators. The madam then telephoned the selected prostitute, charging four dollars as room rent. To Saxon, the madam recommended a "nice kid who goes to a business college" and was only available "right after school." She charged a minimum of ten dollars. In regard to the police, the madam promised, "You won't be disturbed; I've got police protection." As in this instance, brothel owners regularly employed maids to answer the door to screen customers and delay the police during their occasional raids. Prostitutes entertained their patrons in the upper stories of the building. High prices restricted commercial sex to well-to-do clients, persons less likely to raise the ire of public officials or neighbors.[20]

When men pursued sexual entertainment, they frequently patronized the most public branch of New Orleans's reorganized sex industry—dance halls. Although far from the spectacles common in Storyville, dance halls encouraged ribald interaction between the sexes. Operators often opened their establishments near hotels, particularly places popular with conventioneers or men on business trips. In 1925, guests at the upscale Roosevelt Hotel complained about the noise coming from Tortorich's Dance Hall across the street, where the managers kept the windows open to cool the hall as well as lure passersby. The mayor subsequently asked the head of the police to order the windows closed so that the late-night doings would no longer keep hotel guests awake. Another complaint from the same year revealed what occurred inside such businesses. A New Orleanian objected to the lurid activities found in the Arcadia Dance Hall on St. Charles Avenue, a well-traveled thoroughfare popular with locals as well as tourists. The concerned citizen raged, "The things they are pulling off at this particular time had they been in vogue in the years gone by when our restricted district was in full blast the inmate of that district would have blushed with shame and would not have stood for the things that are being pulled off at this Dance Hall nightly almost opposite one of our most prominent hotels." The establishment employed thirty-six scantily clad women who did not have sex with patrons but instead had been instructed to "shake in order to make tickets." No money directly changed hands between the male customer and female entertainer. Patrons purchased tickets from the manager and then exchanged them for dances with the various women working for the house. The women then redeemed the tickets for payment. The system, common in all dance halls, prevented intrusions from freelance prostitutes. Ribald behavior reigned inside. At the Arcadia, the "girls . . . almost stand in one spot and go every movement of sexual intercourse and it is a common by-word . . . that if you want to get (DRY F.) go to the Arcadia and you can get it for a dime." All of this activity occurred under the watchful eye of a pair of police officers. Even the detailing of one of the city's first female officers, a hiring practice begun in the 1920s to regulate places such as dance halls, failed to interfere with the close contact between dancer and patron. Nevertheless, arrests for lewd dancing were not unusual at the Arcadia and at similar establishments throughout the city. Police may have ignored the occasional excessive display, but officers at least prevented the constant practice of explicit behavior. The mere presence of policemen and policewomen forced managers, dancers, and patrons to exercise caution. More importantly, the New Orleans Federation of Clubs, a civic association of prominent local women, kept an eye on the activities of dance halls and the hiring of female officers.[21]

Illegal alcohol lubricated the commercial sex trade. In 1926, one citizen complained to Mayor Arthur O'Keefe about conditions at 1110 South Franklin Street, where "Rosa Smith is making whiskey giving hands telling fortune and running furnish rooms selling beer every thing bad women meeting men at night from all around the neighborhood." Apparently the degree of vice did not disturb the complainant as much as the profits reaped by Smith. Signing the letter "a neighbor," the writer concluded by saying that Smith was "often brash about how much money she makes dead easy." On another occasion, patrolmen raided the 1517 South Rampart Street rooming house operated by Luciele Garner, a twenty-five-year-old white woman, after several neighbors complained about "drinking parties and vile language" heard "at all hours of the night." Particularly grating were the customers, who frequently knocked on the doors of neighboring houses by mistake and requested rooms. New Orleans police officers rarely raided a house known for prostitution without uncovering a stash of alcohol. Arresting the prostitutes rooming at 709 Burgundy Street, for example, the officers discovered an icebox packed with forty-two bottles of homemade beer.[22]

Like prostitutes, bar operators camouflaged their activities. Taverns commonly fronted as soft drink stands, which often operated near popular nightspots and served as the city's most prolific dispensers of alcohol. Father O'Slattery of St. Francis De Salle Church joined with the Mount Olive Baptist Church and Borean Presbyterian Church to protest the 1926 opening of a cabaret located directly across a back alley from a "soft drink establishment." Although the type of available refreshments went unstated, the complainants well understood the potential for liquor running between the two businesses. Worse, the presence of alcohol threatened to make the contact between dance partners strutting to the latest jazz hits all the more sexual. A Catholic priest might forgive a bar disguised as a soft drink stand, but the potential for lewd behavior within the cabaret proved too sinful a possibility. Despite occasional crackdowns on alcohol sales, soft drink stands maintained a foothold in the New Orleans bootleg trade. Owners developed clever ways of hiding alcohol on their premises: because police required a search warrant to frisk individual patrons, employees disguised as customers served as "walking bars," carrying flasks of alcohol in their pockets and dispensing drinks as requested.[23]

Though alcohol remained available, the purchase of liquor involved an intricate process not unlike that used to safeguard prostitution. Peter "Pappy" Gracianette, a French Quarter bartender, recalled the procedure by which patrons bought alcohol. Only known customers obtained alcohol with ease, and Gracianette used finger signals rather than words to let the liquor runners know what a purchaser wanted: "I would hold up either one, two, three, or four fingers, according to the grade of liquor wanted and the waiter would see that and go next door where he had the whiskey hidden." As with many rooming houses, where prostitutes did not stay on the premises but came when telephoned, speakeasy managers kept their supplies of alcohol offsite. Runners brought one-ounce bottles back from the secret stash, and Gracianette then mixed the drinks. Local politicians leaving City Hall could readily, though secretly, down bootleg booze. At 3 p.m., Gracianette regularly closed his lunchroom so that he could accommodate thirsty public servants. [24]

After reclaiming the mayor's chair from McShane in 1924, Behrman showed barely any concern with enforcing the Volstead Act. A policy of salutary neglect pervaded City Hall. Shortly before the election, City Attorney Ivy Kittrege informed the Commission Council that the city government, due to a legal loophole, lacked the authority to revoke a municipal license issued to a soft drink business even though the license holder used the permit "as a cloak or screen to conduct the illegitimate business of selling liquor." With the Old Regulars back in office, the municipal government showed little interest in closing the loophole. Doing so would have halted the flow of dollars into the pockets of corrupt public officials. Moreover, strict enforcement of Prohibition lost popular support over the course of the 1920s, as was evidenced by the victories of Old Regular candidates at the ballot box. One concerned resident rebuked Behrman in 1925 for his administration's failure to enforce laws against alcohol, charging, "Can you or any of the rest say that they are following their oath when you allow saloons to run unmolested in your city. It is well known that offenders of the 18th Ammendment are protected by the city administration and in fact encouraged and furthered by many city employes." Despite bouts of public outrage at the blatant disregard for the law, Behrman and subsequent civic leaders, along with the majority of the electorate, remained steadfast in their commitment to keep New Orleans wet. [25]

Violation of the law raised few eyebrows in City Hall or in the conference rooms of the Association of Commerce. Conventions and local organizations even put into print their desire to have alcohol present at their meetings. The Southern Amateur Athletic Union, for example, sent an invitation to Mayor Arthur O'Keefe, a member of the Old Regulars who succeeded Behrman in 1926, that not only listed the menu for the group's annual meeting but emphasized in large, underlined capital letters that the affair was "B.Y.O.L."—Bring Your Own Liquor. Politicians and businessmen saw little problem in ignoring what they considered a foolish law against alcohol.[26]

In a classic 1936 study of Behrman and the Old Regulars, George Reynolds portrayed the political debate over moral reform as an urban-rural struggle: "This tolerant City with its cosmopolitan moral standards presents an atmosphere that might better be termed unmoral than immoral. It has had to oppose the forces in the state that would impose rural, political, or moral standards unsuited to its peculiar tastes and habits." Prostitution and alcohol, vices long popular in the port, played major day-to-day roles in the city during the Prohibition years. In an urban center increasingly interested in tourism, complete repression of those vices was unpopular. Many New Orleanians paid lip service to the law while quietly protecting the highly profitable practices attacked by reformers.[27]

A New Business Need

When New Orleanians in the early 1920s opened their daily editions of the *Item*, they found not just a chronicle of such newsworthy events as the persistence of urban vices or the continued presence of political corruption but also a war of words over the proper role of women in American society. In a popular column, "Is Marriage a Success?" locals voiced their opinions about the nature of heterosexual relationships and the behavior deemed proper for each sex. Letters flooded the newspaper's editorial office. One female New Orleanian clearly identified the central tension in changing cultural concepts of womanhood after the First World War when she argued that the "modern up-to-date young woman" lacked the knowledge to cook, sew, keep house, or "do anything practical that would fit them for their place in the world as a woman, wife and mother." She believed that a growing number of women lived "for show only" and simply wanted "pleasure, gayety, . . . automobiles, furs, paint and fashion." These women ventured outside the household, where they not only pursued jobs but spent the money they earned so that they enjoyed their time off from labor. Their choices irked more traditional-minded Americans like the one who wrote to the *Item*.[28]

As women during the interwar years expanded the boundaries defining gender, New Orleans and other cities responded to this new market of female consumers. The establishment of an underground commercial sex and alcohol trade capable of satisfying the desires of male tourists constituted but a part of a much more important development born of successful moral crusades. Women claimed greater freedom to roam streets tamed of formerly male-dominated attractions. The stigma of being labeled a public woman faded as prostitutes hid in hotels and so-called rooming houses. Alcohol also lost its association with rowdy male behavior as speakeasies came to represent an edgy sophistication open to both genders, giving birth to the flapper stereotype made synonymous with the popular phrases *Jazz Age* and *Roaring Twenties*. Historian Lewis Erenberg has noted how the "Eighteenth Amendment led to increased emphasis on drinking and sexual styles as private rights that were not the business of the state or the society." Enjoying alcohol became an act of civil disobedience. Civic leaders slowly discovered that young women were joining men in seeking what had been male-oriented activities. By the time Prohibition was repealed, both men and women entered bars and even sex shows with little trepidation and much curiosity. However, politicians and businessmen carefully regulated the return of bars and nightclubs to allay public concerns. By the 1940s, New Orleans politicians and businessmen had forged their metropolis into a tourist resort that accommodated the change in gender conventions.[29]

The First World War accelerated women's push for equality. Women filled jobs vacated as men enlisted. Efficiency campaigns called on women to can goods or plant gardens. Volunteer work associated with the war, such as campaigns to sell Liberty Bonds, regularly fell to women. Lillian Burk, who spoke to her 1919 graduating class at Esplanade High School, emphasized that her female peers looked to the "future of women in business" rather than merely seeking husbands. The war itself destabilized notions of marriage for many Americans. With doughboys away in far-off trenches, the period of separation often weakened ties between husbands and wives. Some women, free from the presence of their husbands, gained a greater sense of independence. With the end of the conflict, women continued to work their way into the job market. Exposure to European cultural standards expanded many soldiers' worldviews by introducing them to more liberal sexual attitudes, especially among the French. The developing ideal of companionate marriage allowed wives greater expression of their sexuality as well as a more equal voice in their relationships.[30]

A double standard nevertheless persisted in popular attitudes toward proper male and female behavior. According to contemporary cultural mores, men, free to roam in public, experimented with vices such as prostitution and alcohol. Women, bound to their private households, were expected to remain chaste. Writing to the *Item*, a New Orleans man named Bobbins exemplified the hypocritical stance taken toward gender roles: "The man who has sown a few wild oats is far more experience[d] and better able to make a better husband than the poor mollycoddle who knows nothing of life." Sex, booze, and other vices ensured virile masculinity. Women, however, should remain virginal. Since ideal wives did not work outside of their homes, they had no need to become streetwise like their husbands. Bobbins boldly concluded, "There has always been a separate code of morals for men. It has existed since the beginning of time, exists today and always will exist." Frank M'Ger, another New Orleanian, also defended the difference between the sexes. In reference to smoking, a practice increasingly popular with both sexes during the 1920s, he combined arguments about women's natural weakness of body with statements about the strength of their virtue: "Man's constitution is built more strongly than a woman's and naturally can stand or resist the nicotine which the tobacco contains more effectively than a woman, who belongs to the weaker sex." Moreover, female smokers "set a bad example" for children. Most importantly, women were "entrusted [with] all the goodness of humanity," and cigarette smoking betrayed that "sacred trust." Smoking, like drinking alcohol or indulging sexual desires, endangered gender roles by equalizing women with men.[31]

The crusade against commercial sex and alcohol, in New Orleans as in other cities, stemmed in large measure from a continued public concern with protecting the few but increasing number of women who ventured into the workforce. With young, unmarried women drawn outside the patriarchal home by opportunities to gain wages and by the freedom afforded by the city, many Americans feared what might happen not only to their daughters but to the nation's future. Brothel owners and barkeeps came to be seen as body snatchers who seduced unsuspecting maidens into lives of debauchery. A large segment of the American population read with alarm the lurid, exaggerated accounts of white slavery carried by the national press. Near paranoia gripped reformers. Crusaders pressed their efforts to eliminate the modern slave markets—saloons, dance halls, and other establishments connected to the male-oriented commercial sex trade where many of America's white daughters allegedly lived in bondage to vice lords. The heightened military presence resulting from the Great War galvanized the reform movement against vice as fathers and mothers wanted to safeguard both their daughters (from the young men in uniform) and their sons (who were being sent to military bases near cities, which were notorious for carnal debauchery). The physical threat that venereal disease posed to young soldiers and their sexual partners further stirred anxiety about prostitution.[32]

Moral reformers' rhetoric rationalized the effort to protect the apparent virtue of womanhood. Alcohol and the sex trade went hand in hand with the consumerism fostered by businessmen. Ferdinand Iglehart, a lecturer in sociology at Syracuse University, voiced the concerns of reformers in a 1919 book, *King Alcohol Dethroned*. Alcohol flowed in America, according to Iglehart, because the "human heart" harbored "two thirsts, one for drink, one for gold." Liquor devastated lives by destroying the mind and body: wrote Iglehart with the fervor common among moral reformers, "Alcohol not only deteriorates the brain cells, befuddles the intellect and furnishes the tottering drunkard and wretch with the delirium tremens, but it becomes the devil incarnate in its assassination of the intellect, making the victim unwittingly a mental suicide, and society, by its license, his torturer and mental murderer." Reflecting the intellectual currents of the time, his analysis blended religious overtones with psychological evidence. For reformers, alcohol caused not only physical deterioration but social chaos as well. The effects of alcohol appeared "in the giggle and gabble of the girl in the street car, who, usually reserved, inflamed with wine makes a fool of herself, in the man who, not usually bold, without voice or invitation, befuddled with rum, insists on singing a solo in a crowded railway car . . . in the poor fellow who walks out of the corner groggery and incoherently undertakes to enter conversation with every stranger he meets to tell him how much he loves him." These kinds of public confrontations with drunkards fueled reformers' concerns. Furthermore, Iglehart referred to fellow experts who agreed that the fight against alcohol proceeded "thanks to women," who defended civic virtue by seeking a less offensive urban society devoid of rowdy behavior.[33]

The need for secrecy during Prohibition calmed city streets and produced the unanticipated effect of inviting women to enjoy public spaces. Traversing city streets no longer filled tourists and residents with angst. J. Torrey Drennan of New Brighton, New York, visited New Orleans for New Year's Eve in 1925 and found the city amazingly dry. Drennan mused, "I never saw so large a crowd, on a holiday night, where there was so little drunkenness. It was almost nil." The miraculous sobriety in which New Orleans celebrated holidays was matched by an altered cityscape. T. W. Evans, a resident of nearby Gulfport, Mississippi, expressed amazement at the change in New Orleans and the surrounding area. Whereas before Prohibition, "barrooms were at every corner and crossroad," a drinker found very few such sites in the 1920s—at least not in open view. Women, who had previously entered the vice-filled Louisiana metropolis with trepidation, no longer voiced concern. Explained New Orleanian Rosella Bayhl, "In former times, it was almost impossible for a woman to be on the streets at night, and in still older times, 8 o'clock was a dangerous hour, for drunken men abounded." The crusade against alcohol and prostitution at last quieted the urban space, opening it to Americans, especially women, who had previously feared venturing there.[34]

So quiet had the streets become that New Orleans politicians and businessmen soon discovered that visitors and locals hunting for excitement found their thrills as spectators in municipal courtrooms. In 1928, city officials heard a report from Commissioner of Public Safety P. B. Habans regarding the large audiences drawn to the night court. In a city where nightlife was subdued, the most titillating entertainment was found in court cases, which gave full view to the otherwise secretive trade in sex and alcohol. Habans emphasized that the court had "long since been a source of attraction to the pleasure loving public who on frequent occasions witness the Court more as sources of amusement than as places of serious administration of public business." Prostitutes, joined by booze dealers and drunkards, paraded before judges. Respectable men and women watched and listened intently to the parade of carnality on their excursions into New Orleans's seedy underworld.[35]

While moral crusaders against alcohol and prostitution calmed the urban environment, the extensive improvement projects begun by city leaders around the turn of the century and continued through the 1920s physically cleaned New Orleans streets. For women who genuinely believed themselves to be the weaker sex, urban improvements alleviated worries about filth and disease. Health concerns brought sewerage systems and garbage incinerators that treated and safely disposed waste. Waterworks eliminated disease-breeding cisterns. Ordinances against spitting in public spaces were strictly enforced. New Orleans politicians, like municipal leaders elsewhere, paved roads, laid sidewalks, and installed electric streetlights. The improvement projects included the removal of the tar-soaked wooden blocks used to improve traffic flow on some streets, which oozed sticky tar during the hot summers. Paving also lessened the number of dirt roads regularly sprayed with oil by city workers in an effort to curb dust. By constructing a car-friendly cityscape, local leaders encouraged automobile use, thereby sharply reducing the previously overpowering stench of horse manure and urine. A travel brochure from 1921 told how city leaders understood that "you didn't want a visitor to have to hold his mental and physical nose when he saw the open gutters which were all the sewers the Vieux Carre possessed." Streets subject to flooding "every time

Jupiter Pluvius tipped over the watering can" only worsened the outsiders' impressions. Evidence from other cities suggests that politicians persisted in their alliance with vice lords in part because the revenue gained through occasional fines for alcohol and prostitution violations helped fund the massive projects designed to better the physical appearance of the urban space.[36]

A gadfly to New Orleans boosters, author Sherwood Anderson lamented the erosion of masculinity within American cities brought by Progressive Era urban improvement campaigns and moral crusades. Anderson believed that the nineteenth-century urban environment had allowed masculinity to flourish. A sense of struggle had permeated public spaces populated by bearded and "rough-handed" men who slogged through muddy streets. Some urban spaces had even possessed "too much maleness." By the early 1920s, however, "speed, hurried workmanship, cheap automobiles for cheap men, cheap chairs in cheap houses, city apartments with shining bathroom floors, the Ford, the Twentieth Century Limited, the World War, jazz, movies" sapped men's virility, leaving a sterile, homogeneous consumer culture.[37]

A growing number of women took advantage of the freedoms afforded to them by the morally and physically cleansed urban space to adopt practices long associated with so-called "public" women, thereby making possible a tourism industry aimed at both sexes. Women's actions increasingly blurred traditional gender conventions. Boyish-looking flat chests and bobbed hair became fashionable. The use of cosmetics and provocative clothing gained acceptance. Experimentation with sex, tobacco, alcohol, gambling, and other "evils" chipped away at the cultural pedestal on which womanhood had long rested. One New Orleans "business woman" who claimed ten years in the workforce refuted attacks on working women as brewers of marital infidelities and social disruption, arguing that working women merely served as scapegoats for conservative, nagging wives who failed to keep their spouses' attention by adopting modern fashions and cosmetics. Puffing on cigarettes likewise signified an assertive femininity. Suffragist Kate Gordon cringed when she witnessed the more radical Elizebeth Werlein not only light a cigarette but blow the smoke out her nose.

Even a churchgoing mother of ten recognized that women possessed the "same right to liquors, gambling and living an unchaste life as men." Because definitions of acceptable behavior had changed, "some fashionable women admire men who use rouge and powder and probably some men admire the women who smoke with them. As for copying the tobacco habit from men, women copy and recopy, produce and reproduce in this age until it's hard to distinguish the sex." Female presence in the public sphere slowly came to appear normative rather than scandalous.[38]

The stylish popularity of speakeasies in the 1920s eased the stigma that places serving alcohol were purely male refuges where women of purchasable virtue gathered. Prohibition encouraged rebellion. To growing numbers of Americans, the Eighteenth Amendment reflected backward, conservative, rural America, while drinking symbolized the cosmopolitan. Urban residents resented government agencies' and moral reformers' interference in an individual's private choice to consume alcohol or mingle with the opposite sex. Historian Catherine Murdock has noted that the "elimination of alcohol's associations with brewers, saloon keepers, and abusive male drinking patterns allowed Americans of both sexes to consider the substance alcohol without its most negative trappings." Under these circumstances, alcohol became a "symbol of . . . individuality and liberation." Movies glamorized cabarets, while radio and records gave mass audiences to bands that frequented clubs where illegal booze flowed. A night on the town or even better a vacation to a large city became laden with political meaning about personal freedom.[39]

One of the clearest links between the attack on urban immorality, the liberalization of cultural attitudes toward women, and the emergence of a less male-oriented tourism industry was the practice of dating. Dating, a term appropriated from the jargon of prostitutes, emerged as a respectable practice among the middle class in the mid-1910s, just as the assault on commercial sex and alcohol neared a climax. Historian Beth Bailey has shown that early dating practices mimicked the exchanges between prostitutes and their customers. A man spent money to take a woman on the town. The more money he spent, the more his date felt pressured to provide sexual favors in return. Dating made sex more available, especially as the automobile decentralized the walking city and provided Americans with greater privacy. On these unchaperoned outings, women increasingly wore finery and cosmetics, practices previously associated with women in the commercial sex trade. As more women experimented with their sexuality, they undermined the conviction that commercial sex supplied men with physical release while preserving womanly virtue from the taint of sexual desire. Herbert Asbury, who wrote during the 1930s about the decline of Storyville, commented that prostitution had waned throughout the United States because women were more willing to express themselves sexually, leading to a "radical change in . . . pre-marital relations." To support his argument, Asbury quoted a prominent New Orleans madam, Countess Willie V. Piazza, on why she closed her brothel: "The country club girls are ruining my business!" [40]

In New Orleans, even the most guarded and tradition-bound bastions of high society—Mardi Gras krewes—accommodated the more publicly assertive women of the interwar years. Membership in krewes had originally been open only to men. Although the first female krewe, Les Mysterieuses, formed in 1900 and hosted balls for several years, the idea of woman-dominated organizations did not become common until after the First World War. A group of adventurous young female socialites formed an exclusive Mardi Gras organization, the Krewe of Iris, in 1922. The female members not only exercised authority within their newly established krewe but, as the press reported, reversed tradition by "calling out" male dance partners and selecting their male royalty. Even renowned all-male krewes such as Rex faced insurgent wives and daughters. In a 1924 message to New Orleanians, the krewe's "Royal Scribe" announced, "It seems that the ladies of His Majesty's household have all become infected with modern, occidental ideas." Although Rex maintained a male-only membership dominated by the city's business elite, wives and daughters pressured the leaders to accept bobbed hair and fashionable dress at the organization's festivities and demanded a more active voice within the krewe. "I fear that there is some notion in their pretty heads that they ought to have a prominent place in the Carnival festivities," observed Rex's spokesman. Rex's leaders tried to make light of the reforms advocated by their mothers, sisters, and daughters but could not ignore the demands for change. By 1936, social commentator Margaret Dixon published a *Times-Picayune* article under the title "Women's Role in Carnival: The Era When New Orleans Women's Major Part Was to Look Beautiful Is Definitely Past." Women's growing participation in Carnival culminated in 1941 with the Krewe of Venus, the first all-female organization to parade through the streets.[41]

Although some New Orleanians attempted to dismiss women's demands for more say in society, most local businessmen supported the increased presence of women outside their homes. Resort owners on the Mississippi Gulf Coast, for example, worked closely with New Orleans businessmen to encourage women to be outgoing. Advertisements for beachfront communities commonly pictured female figures. The Biloxi Chamber of Commerce sponsored an annual swimsuit contest, with the organizers using letterhead that presented a female waterskier clad in what was a revealing swimsuit for the time. Such images on letterheads and brochures, however, symbolized youthful fitness, not a streetwise seductress. Gone were the images common prior to the First World War, in which bare-breasted women and suggestive corsets bursting with flowers figured prominently. Ad designers at New Orleans area resorts deemphasized the sexual allure of women, presenting the female body as innocently flat chested, young, energetic, and athletic. Women were no longer depicted as shadowy seducers or hopeful matrons but as active participants in society. Their sexuality implicitly rested in their outgoing, friendly nature and their ability to join men in activities previously considered unladylike. Advertisers emphasized the same image in campaigns for products ranging from electric appliances to automobiles to tourist destinations. These marketing tactics neutralized the concerns of more conservative Americans who expressed unease with the liberalization of female sexuality.[42]

A few businesses, however, only reluctantly accepted the presence of women in formerly male spaces. Barbershops, for example, long catered solely to a male clientele. With the popularity of bobbed hair, which required frequent trimming, a growing number of businesswomen, venturesome socialites, and female visitors demanded the services of New Orleans haircutters. The Association of Commerce, responding to letters of complaint, joined the attack on hesitant barbers, with Walter Parker arguing that "business women have no more spare time than business men have." But Louis Edwards, president of the Master Barber's Association, defended regulations for women in barbershops: "I believe that throwing open the barber shops without any restrictions to women would ruin them. Why, the men customers—those who are really in a hurry I mean—would desert them!" Edwards personally "put a tax" on haircuts for women as a means of discouraging them from entering his shop. Nevertheless, he admitted that conditions for women were "unfair" and that men received "superior" service at half the cost charged female patrons, and he was willing to make concessions in the face of changing times. As long as women agreed not to expect "particular courtesies or exceptions," Edwards would accommodate female clients: "If women want equal rights, they must bear equal inconveniences." An investigator for the Association of Commerce and another for the *Times-Picayune* discovered a general acceptance of women at haircutting establishments despite the reluctance of Edwards and a few other owners. Describing the situation, the reporter declared, "Looks as if the city has a new, and very real, business need!"[43]

The issue of constructing public restrooms brought the shift to a more gender-equal urban space to the foreground. In 1931, businessmen argued that New Orleans desperately needed restrooms in the "center of the community" given the large numbers of people "who centralize there to see the sights or to spend their money." Existing businesses provided few toilet facilities. A study of the situation found that locals and tourists who ventured through the streets "and without whom the purveyor of service, or merchandise, or entertainment, or what not, could not operate, have been given little or no consideration in this respect." In the "pre-Volstead days, the saloon very well supplied the need as far as males were concerned," although "the woman visitor into town has never been very much considered and practically the only resource for them is provided by the department stores and that but for eight or nine hours in the day only." By the early 1930s, when women regularly entered public spaces from the sidewalks outside Canal Street stores to the alleyways of the French Quarter and from places of employment to places of recreation, the absence of public facilities became a major problem, particularly for female locals and tourists who participated in the burgeoning nightlife. The committee of businessmen who studied the bathroom situation recommended the construction of three "public comfort stations . . . to serve the white people of New Orleans." Members identified Canal Street, Jackson Square, and the Dryades Market as spots most in need of restrooms. More and more women—many of them from out of town—frequented the shopping centers of Canal and Dryades Streets along with the popular Jackson Square.[44]

With the repeal of the Eighteenth Amendment in 1933, New Orleans emerged from Prohibition a much quieter city. Over the preceding thirteen years, the city had lost its seedier dives and prostitute havens. Although some returned with repeal, Americans in general and New Orleanians in particular had changed their habits in regard to drink and sex, and the male-oriented city had become a thing of the past. Citing police reports, a January 1934 editorial in the *Times-Picayune* stated that "the most pessimistic have had to admit that predictions of an orgy of intoxication after the return of licensed liquor have not been borne out." The newspaper declared ridiculous the gloomy predictions of Leon Sloan, leader of the Anti-Saloon League, and concluded, "Carnival is coming soon, and if conditions are what Mr. Sloan reports, an unusually large number of right-minded tourists probably will come down to investigate. Especially since he says that all 13 of the girls he saw at one bar were beautiful." Alcohol's threat to the moral state of American society, especially its women, no longer preoccupied the citizenry.[45]

Repeal did not bring back the halcyon days of carnality associated with Storyville but nevertheless gave New Orleans tourism a boost by permitting men and women to drink and socialize without fear of the law. Most Americans by the 1930s no longer thought of alcohol as a great evil and of women in bars as prostitutes. An advertisement for a newly opened bar, Marble Hall, depicted an upscale couple being served a bottle of alcohol. A promotional piece for Bourbon Street's Vanity Club showed a well-dressed man and woman watching a burlesque dancer and sipping cocktails. Proprietors of the Cadillac Nite Club and Bar a few blocks away on Common Street illustrated an ad with a couple toasting each other. The *Roosevelt Review*, a monthly publication issued to guests of the upscale Roosevelt Hotel, celebrated the mingling of men and women in a sexually charged atmosphere. In the hotel's Hawaiian Blue Room, guests danced to the rowdy sounds of prominent white musicians. The Abe Lyman Orchestra, visiting in 1938, was celebrated for its "musical pyrotechnics" and for one performer in particular, a three-hundred-pound trumpeter named Red Pepper who " 'gets off' during the dance sets, and sets the dancers crazy." Musicians and singers were freely described as "hot." A set of three pairs of dancers known as the Six Jitter-bugs added "spice" to the nightly "extravaganza." The language not only hinted at sex but also blatantly flaunted the interaction of men and women in a ballroom awash in alcohol.[46]

Women also entered areas of New Orleans nightlife much more risqué than sexually charged ballrooms. The Powder Puff, the city's first club featuring female impersonators, opened in the French Quarter during the mid-1930s. Although forced to close for ordinance violations, the owners quickly reopened as the Wonder Club on Lake Pontchartrain. The cabaret flourished until 1947, when Club My-O-My, a staple of New Orleans tourism through the 1970s, appeared. Sex merchants adapted to the demand for entertainment as well. French Quarter madam Norma Wallace remembered how conventioneers' wives began coming to the strip shows and displays of simulated sex acts at her Dauphine Street brothel during the 1930s. Although women rarely attended without their husbands or boyfriends, Wallace recalled nights when couples outnumbered the single men in her establishment. Adult entertainment venues began factoring women into their profit-seeking ventures.[47]

Some female tourists certainly hesitated to enter an urban space where good times again rolled. In 1938, visitor Catherine Vidokovich wrote to Mayor Robert Maestri that New Orleans possessed a "magnetic force," especially in regard to the architecture and history of the French Quarter. She had enjoyed her visit but voiced regret that her tour group was "unable to go through [several buildings] because they were occuppied [sic] (as taverns). It would have been a place of interest (since it did have history in it) to be able to see these." Vidokovich, a teacher, probably shunned saloons to avoid the possibility of being confused with a less morally upright woman. Evidence suggests that a sizable portion of Americans, especially women, shared her concerns. A national survey conducted by *Fortune* in January 1938 showed that 29.3 percent of women but only 15.1 percent of men favored complete Prohibition. In contrast, 41.9 percent of men and 28.4 percent of women favored no restrictions other than liquor licenses. Other respondents expressed a desire to limit alcohol to sales by the bottle, to state stores, or to light wines and beers. Trepidation about the sale of alcohol clearly remained a force, especially among American women.[48]

To minimize public outrage about alcohol and the sexually permissive atmosphere of bars, New Orleans leaders carefully controlled the urban nightlife tourists of both genders enjoyed in the years after repeal. The city government, along with local businessmen, worked to create a more sedate urban space. A city increasingly devoted to its tourism industry desired to attract as many guests as possible. Unregulated debauchery produced negative press and limited tourism to a small number of adventurous souls. Mayor T. Semmes Walmsley thus pleaded with council members to regulate nightlife even before repeal went into effect. In November 1933, he asked New Orleanians to "remember the evils that brought about prohibition." Public officials worked to ensure that past "abuses, leading as they did to that obnoxious and hypocrisy-breeding amendment, even though well intentioned by some people, may be avoided in the future." Politicians kept a much closer eye on barroom activities than had been the case in the pre-Volstead years. Male indulgence, the keystone of New Orleans nightlife before 1920, was abandoned in favor of a carefully regulated tourism industry meant to attract a broad range of visitors of both genders and with a wider variety of interests. The money spent by women such as Vidokovich could not be ignored.[49]

City leaders carefully guarded the city's popular image. On learning that a 1934 film starring Mae West would bear the name *Belle of New Orleans*, officials protested loudly. That title had been selected after an earlier name, *St. Louis Woman*, had provoked opposition from Missourians. Film executives again buckled under the pressure, eventually releasing the movie as *Belle of the Nineties*. New Orleanians proudly boasted that West's suggestive antics in what they considered her "worst picture" had failed to soil the city's reputation despite the fact that West modeled her character on Lulu White, a notorious Storyville madam. Civic leaders wanted the memories of Storyville to fade into a romanticized haze. West's vivid portrayal of aggressive womanhood raised too many eyebrows and her possible association with New Orleans threatened to vulgarize the peaceful though enticing image of the city's nightlife that local leaders had so carefully cultivated. A very sexualized female character set in New Orleans who spouted, "It's better to be looked over than overlooked" suggested a return to a time when streets were filled with purchasable women who competed for attention and customers. Although the movie addressed fictional events in the past, memories of the era when respectable women only hesitantly entered public spaces were too recent to permit those days to be recalled without protest. Nightlife grew more spirited with the return of legal alcohol, but municipal officials and urban businessmen worked hard to supervise drinking, sex, and the city's reputation.[50]

Civic leaders and tourism boosters showed no desire to eliminate completely the city's ribald reputation, however, balancing the wild with the mild. They used descriptions of the city's lurid past and Latin heritage to mask appearances of prostitutes and drunks, packaging such persons as fading remnants of New Orleans's culture. Tour guide writers reassured visitors that whatever carnal celebrations might be uncovered in the post-Volstead era did not compare with the much more notorious past. In the 1936 *Guide to New Orleans and Environs*, Laville Bremer treated tourists to a voyeuristic journey through the city. At the Old Absinthe House, Bremer urged tourists to explore the ruins of

Prohibition: "Ask to see the devices used in prohibition days for giving the alarm if a police raid was being made; see the secret door that opened at the pressure of a match-end in another room, so that patrons might escape upstairs, or out of doors; formerly there was a trap into which the liquor disappeared—concealed by a picture on a wall." Lyle Saxon, who published several books about Louisiana and directed the Louisiana branch of the Federal Writers Project while working closely with local businessmen and politicians, likewise packaged commercial sex and alcohol as part of the city's exoticism. In one instance, he went so far as to romanticize the existence of prostitution in 1930s New Orleans, identifying the sex trade as a shadowy relic of the once extravagant Storyville. Any commercial sex still remaining emerged in local guidebooks as a precious, dying remnant of a more glorious age. The difference separating the writings of Bremer and Saxon from the performance of Mae West was the medium. Black-and-white pages allowed readers to apply their imagination. Celluloid brought the past to life in a blatant display of questionable morality.[51]

In his *The Bachelor in New Orleans*, published in 1942, Robert Kinney offered a comprehensive guide to New Orleans nightlife that reflected the changed cultural views of proper male and female behavior. His richly colored, no-holds-barred booklet supplied insights for both men and women. Kinney defined the bachelor as "any man or woman who gets off a train or bus or plane or out of a car or wheel-chair alone and unguarded, minus wife, husband, mother-in-law or detective to watch him or her while here." Bachelors were "out for one hell of a good time." A few establishments, such as the Sazerac Bar, still accepted only male patrons, a reflection of past attitudes linking female patrons with prostitution; however, the vast majority of nightclubs provided a "happy place for Bachelors, men and women, of spirit and bravado." Women who patronized Pat O'Brien's Bar, for example, joined men in celebrating at a place where the center of entertainment was a "very remarkable girl-team at the piano." Not even prostitutes came under attack. Kinney warned male bachelors, "Speak kindly to prostitutes, should you encounter them, unless they paw you. They work hard, poor creatures, and probably approve just as little of their trade as do you. After all, why shouldn't they: they know more about it." Kinney considered women vital and equal players in New Orleans's nightlife.[52]

Our Enthusiastic Way of Living

Repeal of Prohibition brought loud rejoicing from most New Orleanians, a population weary from the collapse of the stock market and years of economic depression. In particular, Association of Commerce members sang out in thanksgiving. The organization's *News Bulletin* announced, "With Volstead's shrouds at last removed, we of New Orleans have gotten rid of something we never did understand." New Orleanians "love life and we show it in our enthusiastic way of living." Winking at the years during which local politicians and businessmen had subverted the liquor law and antiprostitution legislation, the editorial stated, "We are patriotic, but not hypocritical." Support for Prohibition in the city had never been great, claimed civic leaders. However, circumventing the law did not mean that New Orleanians were any less American. The business community likened the repeal of Prohibition to the abolition of slavery. Happy days had finally returned. New Orleans came to "life again," and many Americans joined in its "new emancipation." The *News Bulletin* reflected that for "14 long and weary years in our restaurants and in our homes we have tried to eat our special Creole dishes without wine . . . but all along, we've felt that something was wrong when Rex was called upon to toast his queen in mineral water." New Orleanians gleefully prepared for a restoration of past customs.[53]

The years of sobriety greatly altered the urban space and the way the sexes interacted in the streets. Repeal brought emancipation not just for drinkers of alcohol but also women, whom cultural convention had long denied the ability to indulge in ribald nightlife without loss of reputation. A few bars restored tradition, but overall, the new urban scene differed vastly from the one that had existed since the market revolution and appearance of Victorian mores in the early nineteenth century. A tourism industry thus emerged in which both sexes freely traversed city streets.

The city that had attracted William Faulkner in the early 1920s drew another Mississippi writer more than a decade later. Tennessee Williams stepped off a bus at Lee Circle in December 1938 and rented an apartment in the French Quarter, staying for two months. Recalling his days at 722 Toulouse Street, Williams near the end of his life wrote an autobiographical play, *Vieux Carré*. His landlady, committed to fading standards of propriety, attempts to reform the neighborhood, even pouring boiling water through the floorboards of her residence to douse what she believes is an orgy in the downstairs apartment. Williams's landlady cannot fathom the cultural redefinition of decency. At one point, she spouts against the moral depravity—real and imagined—surrounding her: "I tell you—the Vieux Carré is the new Babylon destroyed by evil in Scriptures!" New Orleans remained a carnal playground, seemingly permissive of all sorts of ribaldry. The city's position as a major port had long made it a Babylon to the morally upright, but by the time Williams arrived, the city had become more open to both sexes than ever before in its two-hundred-year history. Progressive reforms and changes in gender roles had altered the conditions that made New Orleans a sin city. New Orleans remained a Babylon, but the way Americans of both sexes experienced the urban space was certainly new.[54]

The French Quarter, seen here in the 1920s at Jackson Square, was a working-class neighborhood home to various ethnicities and light industries. Note the smokestack and smoke rising above the buildings as well as the absence of pedestrians. By the 1940s the St. Louis Cathedral came to symbolize New Orleans. (New Orleans Public Library)

On 17 August 1936 Robert Maestri, center, became New Orleans's mayor, ending years of bitter political battles between the city's Old Regular machine and the supporters of Huey Long. During his administration Maestri worked tirelessly to enhance the city's appeal to tourists. (New Orleans Public Library)

Boosters democratized Mardi Gras festivities by emphasizing masking and neighborhood celebrations. Here, locals decorated their private float. Women worried less about their reputations and safety after reformers tamed the influence of prostitutes and alcohol on the festivities, as is demonstrated by the presence of equal numbers of men and women on the float. (New Orleans Public Library)

Advertisers turned the mammy into a symbol of quality goods created for white buyers. The image appealed to buyers' nostalgia for the past and to concern for maintaining white supremacy. In this photograph from 1921, the Elks of New Orleans don blackface to sell pralines for their annual fundraiser. (New Orleans Public Library)

Martin Behrman, seated on the far left, dominated New Orleans politics during the early twentieth century. Despite Prohibition and the closure of Storyville, the city's red-light district, Behrman worked to keep New Orleans a carnal oasis stocked with booze and prostitutes. He was also instrumental in developing the convention trade. (New Orleans Public Library)

As growing numbers of tourists searched for exotic locales, New Orleans boosters increasingly blended nostalgia for the past with the traditional message of progress in industry and commerce, a development reflected by this advertisement published in newspapers across the United States during the late 1920s. (New Orleans Public Library)

Motor vehicles supplied a convenient means of transporting groups of visitors to a wide range of sites spread across New Orleans. The Crescent Sight Seeing Company was one of several tour companies that responded to the growing demand for professional guides capable of providing accurate information about the city. (Loyola University)

 map OF THE ORIGINAL CITY OF NEW ORLEANS

ABOVE PLAN SHOWS NEW ORLEANS
AS IT WAS IN 1778 WITH FORTIFICATIONS AND PRESENT
LOCATION OF HOLMES

This map, from a 1930s guide published by D. H. Holmes department store, reveals the extent to which businesses capitalized on the French Quarter. The guide emphasizes Holmes's modernity by noting the store's presence outside the original city borders even while equating the store with the neighborhood's historic landmarks. (Loyola University)

Canal Street, seen here in a circa-1930 photograph looking toward the river, served as the city's main shopping district. The rise in automobile ownership led to crowded streets and heightened concerns over preservation. The building on the left under the U.S. flag is the Southern Railway Terminal. (New Orleans Negatives Exposures Prints, 17620029dp, Louisiana and Lower Mississippi Valley Collection, LSU Libraries, Louisiana State University)

Ohio native Alberta Kinsey popularized the painting of French Quarter scenes in an impressionistic style that disguised squalor. Here Kinsey stands in front of some of her paintings. (The Louisiana Collection, State Library of Louisiana, Baton Rouge, Louisiana)

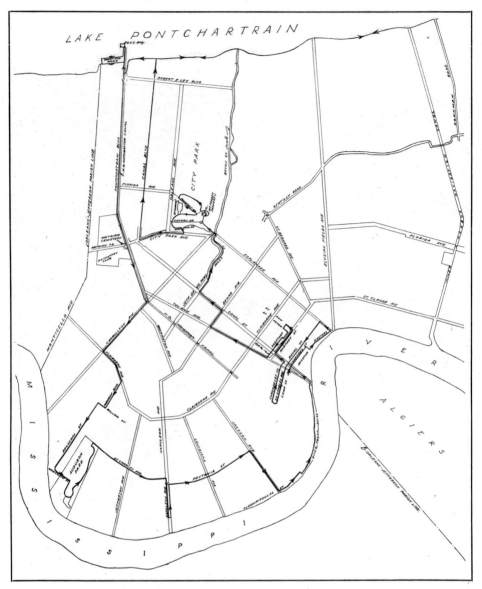

The Visitors Route represented Robert Maestri's efforts to convert New Orleans into a tourist city. The fifty-plus mile route, shown by the arrows in the map, begins in the French Quarter. Motorists then drive through the central business district before heading to City Park and Lake Pontchartrain. Motorists return by passing Metairie Cemetery, Audubon Park, the uptown mansions, and finally, the docks and warehouses of the riverfront.

CHAPTER 4

FRENCH TOWN

The Reconstruction of the Vieux Carré

As the nation demobilized after the Great War, New Orleanians in the newly founded Vieux Carré Society prepared their campaign to preserve the city's oldest neighborhood. Success hinged on the society's efforts to convince the Commission Council, the city's governing body, to pass an ordinance establishing safeguards for the historic district. The idea outraged a large number of businessmen such as William Schultz who in the early 1920s failed to see the profitability of a tourism-oriented city. He considered any plan for preservation "inconceivable." Infringement of property rights seemed outrageous. Property had long possessed near-sacred status in the United States. Even demands for renovation remained out of the question because the buildings, in Schultz's words, were "badly, unscientifically planned, and closely hemmed in on either side by adjacent buildings, which excludes light, and air in that good old mediaeval European fashion." Schultz continued, "There is no doubt that tourists and local art enthusiasts have indulged in a great deal of sentiment over the artistic and antiquarian aspects of the French Quarter. But art and sanitation do not always go hand in hand. If the tourists were to put in a few months living in this locality they would soon change their views." Pointing out that "only a very small part" of the structures in the French Quarter were more than fifty years old, Schultz argued for an end to any more foolish talk about government-enforced preservation. "In its present condition the Vieux Carre renders valueless a big slice of our commercial section. . . . It is quite certain that a general demolition of the tumbledown shacks in the Vieux Carre will be necessary for the expansion of the city within the next decade," concluded Schultz. Preservation, in other words, conflicted with businessmen's efforts to develop industry and commerce. Plans to renovate the French Quarter seemed to retard growth rather than permit the advance of modern enterprise. Pleasing tourists and artists was a silly reason for preservation.[1]

Schultz and others failed to consider the impact of activist women on the cityscape and on the tourism industry. Whereas businessmen largely conceded the district to extinction and deemed preservation both hopeless and unwise in an evolving metropolis, elite women exercised their voting rights and redirected energy from other reform campaigns to save the oldest part of New Orleans. They saw preservation rather than the wrecking ball as the answer to neighborhood ills. Their actions served as a catalyst that changed civic leaders' laissez-faire attitude toward the French Quarter. Prominent preservationist Elizebeth Werlein recalled that local businessmen initially dismissed her work, frequently patting "me on the back, [telling] me I was a nice girl, who didn't know that 'progress' meant destruction of old buildings." Preservation was largely deemed women's work—not to be taken too seriously. As lawyer James Wilkinson commented to Mayor Robert Maestri in 1937, "I have found that when it came to reunions and perpetuating the memories of the historic dead women are always prominent." Despite the difficulties, the development of the French Quarter into a year-round tourist attraction depended on the devotion of prominent local women who flocked to the neighborhood during the interwar years and labored tirelessly to carry out their agenda as well as gain public support. Only slowly, as political and economic leaders recognized tourism as a worthwhile endeavor and after preservation-minded women established an enclave of restored buildings that became popular with tourists, did the French Quarter receive official protection. However, the measures implemented failed to provide for the full restoration or strict regulation of the neighborhood. Businessmen remained hesitant to trample property rights or to lock themselves out of a developing tourist hub by restricting access to the area.[2]

Women in the preservation movement left an indelible mark on the French Quarter, influencing both how the district was eventually marketed and why the neighborhood appealed to tourists. Women concentrated their preservation efforts on Royal Street and the streets around Jackson Square. Over the course of the 1920s, these areas evolved to reflect the domestic traits long associated with womanhood but did so in a historic setting that cast a nostalgic glow on fading social mores. The attractions in these areas thus catered to women grounded in female-oriented domesticity without denying the achievements and rights won by women at the start of the interwar years. Bourbon Street in turn developed into an adult entertainment center, appealing to more carnal tastes. Free of the vice common on other French Quarter streets, Bourbon Street offered an ideal location where businessmen could open nightclubs and burlesques, tapping into the risqué presence of nearby brothels and sex shows while remaining largely untainted by illegal activities. Running immediately parallel to Royal Street, the neon glitz of Bourbon Street provided an outlet for adventurous men and women eager to explore a changing social world in which the genders mingled in a sexually charged atmosphere outside the domestic sphere. By the late 1930s, the French Quarter emerged as a fixture of the city's year-round tourism industry.

The Ideal Spirit of the Vieux Carré

Writing to a local newspaper in early 1922, a self-described "Admirer of New Orleans" commented on the need to salvage the historic French Quarter. The language used recalled Lyle Saxon's famed eulogy to the French Opera House written shortly after the structure burned to the ground in December 1919, an event so significant that he declared that the "heart of the old French Quarter has stopped beating." On that "fatal night," explained the "Admirer," the centerpiece of the quarter had fallen. All was not gloom, however. "The women of New Orleans have very recently started a movement to bring before her people the great need of the French Opera House and when these women come to you and ask for help remember that they are helping you—they are building a monument to be known the world over, a monument to tradition." At issue was the preservation of New Orleans's heritage. The French Opera House, though never rebuilt, symbolized the romantic way of life local activists associated with the neighborhood. Rescuing the district from destruction became a mission to salvage the Crescent City's historic past. The "Admirer" warned, "Remove the 'Vieux Quartier,' and all the traditions that have made New Orleans famous are gone and you behold a modern city with smoke and dust and skyscrapers, but after all only a city modelled after New York, Chicago and innumerable other cities." To the activists, the fight to restore respectability to the French Quarter represented a fight to maintain New Orleans's distinctiveness.[3]

For preservationists, especially the white women who rallied to the cause, salvaging historic buildings gave vent to reformist zeal. Just as reformers had acted to save American civilization by eliminating alcohol and the vices bred wherever bartenders sold drinks, they now asserted themselves in an effort to protect cultural landmarks. Elizebeth Werlein, the figure who would come to dominate the preservationist cause, aimed to rescue the city's historic French Quarter, which symbolized the civilization brought to New Orleans by its white founders. According to preservationists, this noble site floundered in the filth of poverty, the decadence of black and immigrant lifestyles, and the neglect of white businessmen and politicians who saw profits in modernization. Werlein founded the Quartier Club, located in the Pontalba Apartments on Jackson Square, and participated in performances at the nearby Le Petit Theatre du Vieux Carré. Le Petit Theatre, which opened in November 1919, was born from the efforts of Louise Nixon, a woman known fondly as Mother Nixon who served as president of the organization until her death at age ninety in 1947. The Arts and Crafts Club, another of several groups emerging in the decade after the First World War with the aim of restoring the French Quarter as a cultural center, likewise benefited from the strong support of women. Mrs. P. J. Ford served as the club's first president in 1921, and three-quarters of its members were female. The organization aimed to develop an artist colony educated in modern techniques in a variety of media. Sarah Henderson, who served in various offices within the club, including president, was the organization's chief financial backer until her death, regularly guaranteeing money for exhibits and underwriting the group's school and rent costs. As Werlein's daughter, Betty Werlein Carter, recalled, such groups were among several meant "to demonstrate that respectable women could safely go into the French Quarter." According to Carter, the social clubs also sought "to focus interest of women uptown on the charm" of the historic neighborhood.[4]

The disappearance of major landmarks and other buildings evidenced the neglect affecting the French Quarter. Construction of a white marble courthouse had wiped away an entire rundown block of the neighborhood just after the turn of the century. Across the street from the courthouse stood the historic St. Louis Hotel. Formerly an elegant establishment that hosted wealthy planters, slave auctions, and even the Louisiana legislature for a brief stint during Reconstruction, the St. Louis Hotel suffered serious damage in 1915, when a hurricane caused the domed roof to collapse, leaving the structure beyond repair. It too was razed. Even the St. Louis Cathedral seemed on the verge of collapse until local banker and tobacco magnate William Irby donated funds for a complete restoration of the historic church in 1916. Most significant was the loss of the French Opera House three years later. The expansion of area businesses led to numerous other demolitions. Although most structures lacked the history or significance of the St. Louis Hotel or French Opera House, the persistent removal of less noted buildings threatened the identity of the Vieux Carré. "Modern needs are pushing the Quarter farther and farther from" the Canal Street shopping district, commented a guidebook issued by the *Times-Picayune* in 1924. Many New Orleanians saw the district as teetering on oblivion.[5]

Life in the French Quarter furthered preservationists' and locals' opinion that the neighborhood was in decline. As a result of low property values, poor blacks and immigrants—as well as prostitutes and speakeasies—moved into the district. Exaggerating the ethnic homogeneity of the Vieux Carré, Sherwood Anderson described the neighborhood in the early 1920s as becoming "more and more Italian." Fellow author Oliver LaFarge more accurately captured the residents' diversity: "The population included Negroes, Creoles, and Cajuns, an occasional Malay drifted in from the Barataria marshes, Italians, Greeks, Jews of both French and North European origin, and a great many Latin-Americans." "There were sailors of all kinds," continued LaFarge, "antique dealers, second-hand dealers, speakeasies galore, simple workmen, a fair variety of criminals, both white and coloured nuns, the survivors of a few aristocratic Creole families clinging to their ancestral homes, merchants of all sorts, and whole blocks of prostitutes." The quarter's motley population stigmatized the neighborhood in the eyes of white New Orleanians, who believed in their own racial and cultural supremacy. Furthermore, poverty plagued those living in the district. Illegal activities, hard labor, and the sale of goods from the neighborhood's no-longer-prestigious homes defined life in the district. Along the riverfront, streets were "littered with trash and dirt—old shoes, broken barrels, rotting fruit." The thoroughfares reeked from "decaying garbage." Other areas of the French Quarter were only slightly cleaner. Residents frequently kept chickens, goats, and even calves. Many purchased live animals at the French Market, returned home, and slaughtered them on the patios common throughout the neighborhood. Well into the 1920s, numerous buildings lacked plumbing. "Except for part of Royal Street and a section around the Cathedral which had been brushed up and enjoyed the tourist trade," LaFarge concluded, "this was the real thing in slums."[6]

The same low rents and cheap meals that attracted poor immigrants to the French Quarter also brought a colony of prostitutes, adventurous writers, and bootleggers. Police turned a blind eye to their activities, allowing a permissive atmosphere to pervade the district. Like fellow artistic types William Faulkner and Anderson, LaFarge leased an apartment in the French Quarter, where he and his friends gathered to "laugh and sing without causing parents to protest or scandalizing the neighbors." Illegal alcohol enlivened such parties. A thriving commercial sex trade encouraged ribald behavior. The closure of Storyville forced prostitutes to migrate the few blocks toward the riverfront docks and the cheap housing found in the French Quarter. Most prostitutes operated from brothels and soft drink stands in an area marked off by Rampart, Bienville, Dauphine, and St. Peter Streets. The 700 block of Conti and 800 block of Orleans also harbored the sex trade. Robert Tallant, an author and New Orleans resident, compared the French Quarter to "the worst districts of Marseilles, of Honolulu, of Singapore." In Faulkner's 1927 novel, *Mosquitos*, a French Quarter street became a gauntlet where men were "accosted" by whispers of "come in boys lots of girls cool you off come in boys." The voices came "from every doorway, hands unchaste and importunate and rife in the tense wild darkness." As with alcohol merchants, however, sex workers exercised restraint. Prostitutes refrained from streetwalking, except for occasional forays along the riverfront. Although aggressive when soliciting men from doorways and windows, prostitutes were wary of offending any elite women who might be within earshot. The few who took to the streets exercised caution to avoid attracting too much attention. Maria Smith, for example, used her automobile to solicit customers. Often enjoying police protection, prostitution thrived in the French Quarter blocks with the least traffic.[7]

The Vieux Carré of the 1920s was largely abandoned at nightfall. J. L. Jenkins, reporting for the *Chicago Daily News* in 1925, described a district forgotten by visitors eager for nightlife. "A few wistful spirits may be encountered about the doors of the old absinthe house, which has now fallen to the dispensing of orangeade, red pop, and like drinks, and an occasional taxicab may be met cruising over old pavements that can only handle two cars abreast," wrote Jenkins. Aside from patrons of restaurants, particularly Antoine's and La Louisiane, and hotels "on the fringe of the district," few people traversed the streets. The French Quarter after sunset was "a mysterious and somewhat sinister district . . . freed from its persistent swarms of visitors." Jenkins urged out-of-towners seeking entertainment to journey through the "rest of New Orleans," which escaped the "curfew habit of its world famous parent-town."[8]

People venturing into the neighborhood after dark most likely sought mischief rather than entertainment. In 1926, Robert Glenk of the Louisiana State Museum asked the city government for aid in preventing widespread vandalism. "We are utterly unable to cope with the destructive element of the population around J[ackson]. Square to prevent the breaking up of the railings and benches and destruction & theft of the plants & flowers," explained Glenk. The famed statue of Andrew Jackson astride his horse was a particular target. As late as the 1930s, vandals stole the sword hanging at Jackson's side, forcing Glenk to house the piece in the museum after police recovered the sword. The vandalism recalled an incident some years earlier when police halted hoodlums who were attempting to remove Jackson's head with a sledgehammer. In 1934, another group of boys successfully decapitated the statue, leaving the scratched head lying in the dirt near the base of the monument. The *Times-Picayune* called for increased police protection of the popular tourist spot. In an editorial, the city's leading newspaper commented, "In numerous other instances Jackson Square has been a shining mark for ruffians with destructive mania." The haunting image of a headless rider silhouetted against St. Louis Cathedral damaged the peaceful aura of the French Quarter promoted by preservationists. Furthermore, the *Times-Picayune* reminded readers that vandalism, if unabated, threatened lives as well as property. Evidence of the danger already existed. According to the newspaper, the "real high spot" of "outrageousness" at Jackson Square had occurred in the late 1910s, "when, in the shades of the night, a crew of marauders loaded an ancient cannon under the shadow of the museum and sent a solid shot that with a roar straddled the Mississippi, struck a dwelling house in Algiers, passed two feet above a sleeping lady, dropped to the floor and rolled down the steps." Hooliganism had strong traditions in the city's long-neglected Vieux Carré.[9]

The women and small number of men who gathered to preserve the neighborhood saw the French Quarter as the quaint home of a formerly prosperous, refined white people, the Creoles. The activists depicted the quarter as a graceful, romantic neighborhood filled with elegance and history rather than trash, poverty, crime, and ethnic groups of questionable character. From preservationists' point of view, the decay of the structures within the district came to symbolize the ruins of a gracious

French culture, a society to which prominent New Orleanians sought to tie themselves via genealogy or the preservation movement. Elizebeth Werlein's *The Wrought Iron Railings of Le Vieux Carre New Orleans* and Helen Pitkin Schertz's *A Walk through French Town in Old New Orleans*, both published in the decade after the First World War, revealed the way two major players in the preservationist movement envisioned the district. Werlein, a native of Michigan and widow of a prominent New Orleans music store proprietor, declared that a journey into the neighborhood was a pilgrimage into "sacred confines." The French Quarter stood as a holy relic offering communion with one's ancestors in time if not blood. "The link that binds the past and the present, the romance and the reality into the charm of fascinating old New Orleans," wrote Werlein, "is irrevocably enshrined in the memory of all passers through its Vieux Carre." Schertz, who organized the annual Spring Fiesta in the French Quarter during the 1930s, shared Werlein's sentiments. Rather than a threatening, vice-filled neighborhood, Schertz envisioned "homes snuggled together with an instinct for safety." [10]

With such strong claims about the French Quarter, the dingy, crass, and immoral aspects of the district were either ignored or interpreted in such a way as to avoid tarnishing the favorable image cultivated by preservationists. A 1928 booklet, *Vieux Carré Guide: Souvenir of Old New Orleans with Its Latin Quarter of French and Spanish Old-World Romance*, written by G. William Nott with an introduction by noted local author Grace King, revealed how preservationists focused on the neighborhood's quaint aspects. The guide not only reiterated the romantic charms frequently referred to in the works of Werlein, Schertz, and others but also outlined the geographic boundaries initially defended by preservationists. King gave the guide a ringing endorsement. She beckoned readers, "Book in hand, now, we wander through old streets, and pause before the age-stricken houses; and, strange to say, the magic past lights them up; and dull must he be of mind who does not yield to that subtle illumination!" The booklet discouraged tourists from entering the back areas of the quarter except for Rampart Street, a major, well-traversed thoroughfare that figured prominently in the guide precisely because of its "quaint" buildings and "picturesque characters." The choice of words reflected both Nott's and King's paternalistic attitudes toward the area's largely black population. A description of the built-over Congo Square, where antebellum "negroes decked in their most gorgeous colors were wont to dance" and where "Voudous" had practiced their incantations, furthered the depiction of happy, harmless darkies. Given whites' paternalism, the tour of the blocks along Rampart Street appropriately ended at the cloister of the Discalced Carmelites, where "the good sisters pray for the sinners of the world without." Other streets, especially those areas well stocked with vice, received much less consideration. Burgundy Street offered "little of interest to the visitor, having early fallen upon evil days, and only by making forays into the intersecting streets will the explorer of the Vieux Carré find his trouble rewarded." Although Nott selected a few buildings for praise, he also discouraged tourists from strolling Dauphine Street by explaining that the thoroughfare "has not figured so prominently as some of its sister streets." Only when the author turned to Bourbon Street did the descriptions become more glowing. Not yet a nightspot lined by music clubs and burlesque shows, Bourbon Street was a place to enjoy without fear of being morally offended. Nott rejoiced, "Named after the French royal family, what memories does this ancient street recall! Mardi Gras, the French Opera House, mirth and revelry, music and drama, all are associated with this delightful street! For is not Bourbon Street one of the elect of the Vieux Carré?" Of Royal Street the guide exclaimed, "What delightful memories cling to it, and what a host of picturesque characters, real and imaginary, are associated with the name!" Nott emphasized to tourists the superiority of Royal to all other French Quarter thoroughfares. The street boasted "some of the finest examples of early Spanish and French architecture" as well as numerous "surprises and contrasts." No ethnic groups marred the gracious Creole neighborhood described by Nott and King. Moreover, the presence of prostitution and poverty was erased from accounts told by those looking to restore the French Quarter's sullied reputation.[11]

Local women supplemented their written descriptions of the French

Quarter with colorful impressionistic art. Beginning in the 1920s, members of the Arts and Crafts Club, Art League, and various other groups sketched and painted neighborhood scenes. At the center of the art colony supported by local elite women stood Alberta Kinsey, "one of the pioneer painters to popularize the old courtyards as a theme for pictures." A native of Ohio, Kinsey taught a plethora of artists the techniques needed to capture the romantic aura of faded stucco, tropical plants, and iron lace balconies. Irene Cooper, an admirer of the movement, recognized that romantic imagery permeated artistic standards in New Orleans, writing, "Sooner or later almost every artist who wields a brush in the Crescent City tries his or her hand on the French quarter scenes, striving to catch the quiet, quaint air and the atmosphere which sets New Orleans apart from every other city." By painting hazy buildings and blurry figures, artists disguised the neighborhood's poverty and filth while preserving on canvas structures that seemed doomed to destruction. Nostalgia hinged on the perception that the buildings were in such poor condition and in such conflict with modern demands that the French Quarter seemed destined for oblivion. As a result, artists as well as tourists took the opportunity to seize the day in a neighborhood where the days were apparently numbered.[12]

French Quarter preservation—and tourism, for that matter—depended on the careful crafting of the neighborhood's malleable image. For visitors to New Orleans during the early 1920s, the French Quarter stood as a popular but not overly impressive attraction. One observer commented that tourists who gathered in front of a four-story Royal Street building saw not the oldest "skyscraper" in the country popularized by guides but "simply a tenement with a grocery store on the ground floor." Without the romantic writings and sentimental stories of tour guides or the proliferation of admiring artwork, the quarter remained a place of "glamour and squalor" with visions of poverty intruding on tourists' interpretation of the neighborhood. Podine Schoenberger witnessed the extent to which tourists' perception of the area reflected the way the French Quarter was packaged rather than what they actually observed: "Almost any day you can see them, following soldierlike in the wake of guides, listening wide-eyed to stories of the haunted house, the quadroon ballroom, the exploits of Jean and Pierre Lafitte. At first they are struck only by the dinginess of the buildings and the lack of modern architecture. But as they walk along, inspecting ancient patios and listening to stories of the Old City, they become imbued with the spirit of adventure and, like explorers of old, decide to leave no stone unturned." Prominent figures such as tour guide Flo Field and author-preservationist Lyle Saxon encouraged the romantic depictions, friendly style, and masking of reality that fostered interest in the neighborhood as well as the services and works of guides who revealed the "authentic" French Quarter. [13]

While artists and authors cast the neighborhood in a favorable light, civic activists worked to rescue the French Quarter from the wrecking ball. The agenda put forward by the Vieux Carré Society in February 1920 linked domesticity and preservation. Society members aimed to restore the French Quarter as a respectable place to live as well as to preserve area buildings. The organization brought together "property owners, dwellers of the Vieux Carre, and Orleanians interested in restoring the Quarter to its original state." Rather than simply safeguard a historic treasure, the society's seven-point program attempted to eliminate a slum. Members called for paved streets, better schools, the development of apartment buildings as well as "family hotels," and the "right kind of living conditions . . . so more families may be encouraged to live there." The society urged reconstruction of the French Opera House and the "marking" and "permanent preservation" of historic buildings. The members wanted primarily to draw middle- to upper-class whites to the French Quarter, thereby displacing blacks and ethnics, raising property values, and reducing the presence of vice. These preservationist goals were limited to the protection of a few select buildings, not a wholesale program meant to control renovations or demolitions within the entire neighborhood. Although the society found a sympathetic ear in tourism-conscious Mayor Martin Behrman, he was defeated in the 1920 election. [14]

A small group of New Orleans men and, more importantly, a larger number of women took matters into their own hands. Community organizations, led by the Arts and Crafts Club, motivated private individuals and area businesses to restore French Quarter structures by encouraging the purchase of buildings as they appeared on the real estate market. As early as August 1917, the leaders of the Association of Commerce, hesitant to support municipal regulation of the neighborhood, endorsed private efforts "as patriotic and public spirited and worthy of emulation." Observing the trend "just beginning" in 1922, Lyle Saxon joyously proclaimed the breathing of "new life" into the old neighborhood. He identified a "dozen or more" houses bought for restoration purposes. Saxon urged New Orleanians to join him in purchasing French Quarter property. "There are hundreds of splendid houses in the Vieux Carre," Saxon warned, "and the only way to save them is to buy them, to restore them as best you can—to change them in no important detail of construction—and, finally, to live in them." The private-purchase movement reached its apex in 1927, when a group of prominent locals organized the Vieux Carré Community Million Club. With the goal of gaining a one dollar contribution from one million locals and tourists, club leaders hoped to establish a fund for buying, restoring, and maintaining French Quarter structures. Organizers hosted members-only functions with descendants of old-line New Orleans families donning costumes similar to the clothes worn by their ancestors. The increasing popularity of French Quarter real estate brought a sudden rise in property values. By the late 1920s, the purchase of homes in the district by such distinguished socialites as Elizebeth Werlein began to reverse the opinions of many New Orleanians who had believed that the neighborhood was a slum beyond hope of renovation.[15]

Women had staked a clear claim to the neighborhood, sanitizing the area and suppressing the attractions associated with male entertainment before the First World War. Walter Loubat of the Vieux Carré Association, one of the numerous organizations founded to improve the French Quarter, wrote to the mayor in 1926 requesting the greater presence of municipal cleaning crews. Besides the "great many of the business people" who complained about street conditions, Loubat emphasized the loud protests of resident women and woman-run social clubs headquartered in the neighborhood: "The ladies who operate the

Patio Royal, and La Boutique du Patio Royal say that the block that they are in, which is the four-hundred block [of Royal Street,] has not had a good sweeping in many many weeks." Further away from the enclave of preservationists and tourist shops along Royal Street and around Jackson Square, however, streets received much less attention. A woman who had made extensive renovations to her residence at 711 Bourbon Street told Loubat that she had "never seen a street sweeper in her block." Activists also resisted the intrusion of certain businesses. In 1926, the Vieux Carré Association presented the receptive municipal government with a petition signed by property holders who "vigorously disapprove of pool rooms on the ground floor of Royal Street." Five years later, owners of properties near the St. Louis Cathedral advocated a municipal ordinance banning any "cabarets, night clubs, or dance halls" from the vicinity. Given the cathedral's location on Royal Street, the development of the thoroughfare and Jackson Square as a nightspot decreased as preservationists continued to purchase property. The bastion of New Orleans high culture was well defended.[16]

Mounting pressure from preservationists forced the municipal government to provide official protection for the French Quarter. Le Petit Salon du Vieux Carré, an organization of female socialites founded in 1924 and led by Grace King, joined with the American Institute of Architects to campaign for the protection of the French Quarter. The "circle of distinguished ladies, animated with the desire to maintain the social prestige of the old Creole quarters and preserve its social traditions," as King described the salon members, quickly threw its support behind Behrman in the upcoming mayoral election. With a victorious and grateful Behrman back in office, the municipal government soon passed an ordinance creating the Vieux Carré Commission. The measure officially recognized the deterioration of the buildings and the need to preserve some of the most historic structures. Members of the Commission Council feared that encroaching businesses and parking lots threatened to erase the "historic and ideal spirit of the Vieux Carré." But the ordinance granted the Vieux Carré Commission only the "authority to make a study" of the French Quarter and to offer "recommendations" to the Commission Council. Although the Vieux Carré

Commission provided a mechanism to supervise construction and renovation projects in the French Quarter, the failure to grant the agency legal authority prevented direct intervention with such work even when the character of the district was threatened. Moreover, the commission had authorization to study only the area from Esplanade Avenue to St. Louis Street and Royal Street to Dauphine Street. These blocks marked the geographic core preservationists had carved out and promoted as an exceptional part of the neighborhood, but more than half the district remained beyond the commission's reach. The riverfront area and its warehouses, sections near Canal Street department stores, and several blocks near business-lined North Rampart Street remained open to development. Because tourism was only beginning to capture area businessmen's attention, the idea of forging the district into a perpetual attraction had yet to take hold. That the ordinance restricted the territory supervised by the commission revealed New Orleanians' continued conception of the French Quarter as a marginal area containing a few scattered historic homes. Economic growth, for many New Orleanians, still meant the expansion of local manufacturing and downtown retail stores, not the maintenance of a tourist attraction. Effective preservation of the neighborhood would have to wait.[17]

The limited protection of the French Quarter was also manifested in the parking plan installed by the municipal government in late 1928. The plan treated much of the French Quarter as part of the retail business district anchored by Canal Street. The blocks surrounding the preservationist enclave remained linked to commerce, the longtime heart of the New Orleans economy. Almost a decade would pass before civic leaders reconceptualized those blocks as a buffer protecting the core attraction in the Crescent City's developing tourism industry.[18]

The niche carved onto the cityscape by the preservationist movement slowly increased local consciousness concerning the value of the French Quarter to the New Orleans economy and to the city's culture. By the early 1930s, the need for parking lots to meet the sharp rise in automobile traffic intensified concern with salvaging the French Quarter. Recognizing the importance of Jackson Square as a tourist site, Mayor T. Semmes Walmsley in 1930 fulfilled an agreement made by his predecessor, Arthur O'Keefe, for the city to take possession of the Pontalba Apartments bordering the famous park. According to the *Times-Picayune*, the takeover added "very greatly to the attraction of our original civic center, for our city's visitors, as well as, of course, for our many citizens who are interested, as well they should be, in the historic past of our community and its famous dead." Such efforts reflected the increased civic anxiety that the French Quarter remained too vulnerable to modernization. The Association of Commerce went on record in 1931 decrying the fact that the Vieux Carré Commission had "no set method of preserving . . . points of interest, which are a distinct asset to the City of New Orleans, both commercially and aesthetically." For businessmen, the tourist value of the French Quarter had grown too important to ignore. The presentation of the neighborhood demanded an agency "clothed in authority." The association argued that removal of "unsightly objects" and regulations designed to enforce "uniformity without standardization" served as the best means to "insure the continuation of the old city's romantic aspects." Furthermore, the increasing popularity of the Vieux Carré among tourists justified the protection of the district as a means of bolstering New Orleans's economy during the Great Depression. Controlling the intrusion of such modern devices as combustion engines and neon lights was a necessity if the popular image of the French Quarter as a relic of a simpler yet exotic time was to be sustained. In 1936, the Association of Commerce sharply criticized the "forces tearing away the charm and the beauty" of the Vieux Carré. Trampling on property rights seemed less and less outrageous. The city's leading business organization proclaimed, "The French Quarter no longer belongs even to those who own and occupy the property down there. It is the priceless possession of all the people of New Orleans, of all Louisianians, of all the people of the United States who appreciate its capacity to remind us of the colorful days of our history and the greatness of our community's tradition."[19]

Political tensions between New Orleans leaders and the Huey Long–dominated state legislature prevented efforts to strengthen the Vieux Carré Commission until after Long's assassination in 1935 despite anxious preservationists' relentless pressure for a more effective commis-

sion. In 1936, the legislature crafted an amendment to the state constitution that authorized the city to expand the powers of the Vieux Carré
Commission. Louisiana voters ratified the measure, granting popular
support for preservation through stricter regulation of private property.
Empowered by the mandate, the New Orleans Commission Council re-
vamped the Vieux Carré Commission in 1937. Despite the reform, the
agency clung to its passive ways, in part because of confusion over the
range of buildings covered by the new municipal ordinance. The ambi-
guity stirred Frank Waddill, with the support of another preservationist
group, La Renaissance du Vieux Carré, to issue Waddill's Vieux Carré
Creed in August 1937. Preservationists pled with "authorities of the
city of New Orleans, not to interpret the meaning of the law as applying
only to half dozen or so buildings surrounding the Jackson Square, as
alone historical and worthy of preservation, but to consider, and so de-
termine, that THE BROAD INTENT OF THE LAW is to preserve THE
WHOLE OF THE VIEUX CARRE, as a perpetual historical monument
to the builders of this great city and state." Preservationists' heightened
expectations increased their displeasure with the commission. Members of the agency showed persistent negligence in policing changes to
French Quarter buildings. According to the revised law, candidates for
the commission were to be nominated by the Louisiana Historical Society, Louisiana State Museum, the American Institute of Architects, and
the New Orleans Association of Commerce. The mayor then selected
six members from among those nominated and appointed an additional
three at-large members. The law promised to breathe life into the Vieux
Carré Commission by requiring quarterly meetings at City Hall. Legal
questions about the extent of the agency's power, however, hindered
an organization that failed to reach a quorum of five members even
once during 1938. Other serious shortcomings plagued the regulatory
agency. Under the act, the commission organized the Law and Finance
Committee to plan an annual budget, the History Committee to review
applications from property owners who requested special privileges,
and the Architectural Committee to screen applications for all alterations or construction projects within the French Quarter. Nevertheless, many shops and residents skirted the bureaucratic requirements.

"You know how building operations are all over the country. . . . They take building inspectors around the corner to a barroom and buy them a drink. That goes on in all cities. Later they may get a permit," explained commission member Walter Keenan to a reporter. As structures continued to fall at the hands of wrecking crews, preservationists' frustration with the commission mounted.[20]

Anger over the impotence of the Vieux Carré Commission finally erupted into public protest guided by Elizebeth Werlein, who was serving as the first president of the Vieux Carré Property Owners Association. The watchdog group, formed in June 1938, attempted to fill the regulatory void left by the ineffective commission. When the Nut Club, one of the numerous nightclubs squeezing onto Bourbon Street, proposed replacing a nearby structure with a parking lot in January 1939, the plan sparked loud protests. The vice president of the property owners' organization, Alberta Kinsey, dug in her heels: "If [the Vieux Carré Commission lets] this building go, we might as well give up all of our efforts to save this most historic part of our city. If this movement succeeds, then we'll have another and then another fine old structure wiped out for parking lots." She supported her domino theory by pointing to the growing number of "night clubs" in the neighborhood, each one wanting its own parking facility. Werlein enlisted the support of the New Orleans Association of Commerce, the Hotelmen's Association, and the Young Men's Business Club. At a meeting of the Vieux Carré Commission in late January 1939, Werlein directly confronted the commission members with her charges of negligence. As officials evaded Werlein's questions, her frustration grew. When Chairman Louis LeSage explained that Keenan was responsible for inspecting activities in the French Quarter, Werlein thundered, "He doesn't have the time; none of you have; you have your own businesses. You need people whose job it is to make those inspections. . . . You haven't listed the buildings that should be saved. . . . You haven't asked for a budget? You haven't arranged to give advice to people who are not sure about how they should proceed in changing a building." Rather than directly address Werlein, the commission quickly adjourned its meeting with a resolution requesting that the Vieux Carré Property Owners Association submit its complaints in writing.[21]

Werlein and the property owners not only rallied public support but also offered a list of specific recommendations that would energize the commission. "Mrs. Elizabeth [sic] Werlein has performed a courageous and distinguished civic service in spotlighting the inefficiency—and apparently the indifference—of the Vieux Carre Commission," commented the *Item*. The proposal urged the commission to hire one or more inspectors to patrol the French Quarter and supervise the removal of ironwork, doors, balconies, gates, or windows. Inspectors were also to report on paint pigments, store signs, and the styling of cement or stucco used in renovations. Most importantly, the association considered all buildings in the district architecturally and historically valuable. Addressing the neighborhood as an aesthetic whole eliminated any questions about the value of any single structure. The demands included a ban on parking lots as well as a thorough Works Progress Administration survey detailing the architecture and history of French Quarter buildings for future reference. In addition to stricter zoning to exclude "certain objectionable industries now permitted," the property owners argued that the "immediate importance in this respect is that the New Orleans Public Service Inc. be persuaded to remove all streetcars from the streets of the Vieux Carre and that arrangements be made . . . so that all heavy trucking shall be detoured," since the vibrations from these vehicles weakened fragile walls and disrupted the "quaint" atmosphere.[22]

Maestri responded positively to Werlein's requests. The mayor detailed an inspector to patrol the French Quarter twice a week to keep the Vieux Carré Commission informed of any alterations to neighborhood structures. For renovation or construction projects to receive official sanction, the commission, under pressure from the mayor, now required the submission of precise sketches showing the proposed alterations to building fronts. The commission would need to approve the changes before the municipal government would issue a permit for the work. Court cases over the next few years confirmed the legality of the commission's expanded powers. Maestri further appeased preservationists by intensifying police enforcement of municipal litter ordinances. Officers cited French Quarter residents for "the unsightly placing on the sidewalks of garbage and trash in boxes, dilapidated containers and paper bundles" or for merely sweeping trash into "little piles which a passing foot or gust of wind scatters all over the street." The mayor even cracked down on prostitution in the neighborhood. Preservation of the Vieux Carré as a romantic oasis became the order of the day.[23]

The French Quarter revival encouraged locals and even tourists to see sections of the district, especially Royal Street, as a feminine space. New Orleans differed little from the Charleston described by historian Stephanie Yuhl, where women involved in the preservationist movement "bestowed a decidedly female cast to the public image they constructed . . . they infused their restored buildings and paintings with objects and images out of their own feminine understanding of history." The Vieux Carré was not a captivating place for male tourists to visit, especially during the Prohibition years. Carl Meyer, who headed a delegation of St. Louis businessmen and their wives on a trip to New Orleans in 1925, asked Mayor Behrman about possible entertainment opportunities, writing that his wife would "probably entertain the ladies at the Patio Royale [in the French Quarter], but what will I do with the men? Do you suppose we could get hold of a boat, show them the harbor and feed them on oysters, or something unusual like that?" Men found few attractions in the neighborhood. Billy Henerty, a long-time resident of Royal Street, confided to Saxon in 1926 that the street had become a "prosaic business street: a respectable business street, all shops and hotels and souvenir shops and restaurants. The old roistering days are gone." Whereas Royal Street once reflected the needs of French Quarter residents, especially its men, the thoroughfare now increasingly catered to the burgeoning tourist trade and preservation-minded elite women. Restoration efforts had removed the gambling dens and wild saloons, places Henerty fondly remembered. Businessmen thought much the same. Although the Association of Commerce curtailed its complimentary program between the First and Second World Wars the organization continued to supply informal tour guides to conventions less for the benefit of attending businessmen than for their wives. Area business leaders welcomed the tours because they "afforded the ladies a chance to see New Orleans in a very delightful way, and at the same time become acquainted with local ladies who were thoroughly familiar with the city and able to help them in enjoying their stay." Despite increasing opposition by professional tour companies, the persistent use of local women to guide and entertain out-of-towners revealed New Orleans businessmen's lingering perception that the French Quarter and its history were in the hands of women.[24]

Royal Street thus came to embody the characteristics fostered by preservation-minded New Orleans women. A 1928 guide, *The Charms of New Orleans*, described Royal as "one of the most interesting streets of America." On its thirteen blocks "full of historic associations," tourists encountered "the lighter and gayer side of life of New Orleans." Such descriptions became a mainstay of the tourist trade. Preservationists had successfully marked the thoroughfare as vital to local culture. Here tourists encountered supposedly exceptional places worthy of their time and money. Restored residences joined shops filled with antiques, candy, and other fare popular with tourists. "Rue Royal, main artery of the New Orleans Vieux Carre, is by far the most interesting street of 'America's most interesting city,'" boasted a 1938 tourist magazine issued by the Louisiana Department of Commerce and Industry. On "pleasant" Royal Street, tourists discovered "perfumeries, book stores, cabinet makers, doll hospitals, gift shops, and praline kitchens" along with "Persian rug marts, saloons, grocery stores, tea rooms, fortune tellers, ivory colors, linen and lace makers, oyster bars, and a hundred other quaint and colorful stores." The article emphasized an emporium where women could indulge interests culturally identified as female—cooking, dolls, perfumery, and housewares. The presence of a few saloons and fortune-tellers only spiced up the shopping experience.[25]

Women manifested their vision of the French Quarter most clearly in the annual Spring Fiesta. Helen Schertz's nephew remembered how his aunt and Caroline Jones regularly drove to Natchez to visit their friend, Katherine Grafton Miller. Miller, called by one historian the "exalted empress" of the annual Natchez Pilgrimage inaugurated in 1932, inspired Schertz and Jones to develop a similar festival in their beloved French Quarter. Plans became reality in 1937, when the first Spring Fiesta took place a few weeks after Mardi Gras. As in Natchez, private homes were opened to visitors, but this constituted but a small part of what organizers envisioned as a major weeklong (and by the 1940s monthlong) celebration. The event eventually came to include a night parade through the French Quarter and candlelight tours of the celebrated patios, thereby casting a romantic glow on the neighborhood. A preliminary announcement for the festival called attention to the balls, blooming flowers, music, Major League Baseball spring training games, horse racing, river rides, golfing, "etc., etc., etc." available in New Orleans during the springtime, when "snow may be elsewhere." Organizers arranged a fencing tournament, a puppet show, an art exhibition, various concerts, and numerous other activities. An editorial in the *Times-Picayune* labeled the packed event schedule "concentrated entertainment." The Spring Fiesta showcased the city's wide variety of attractions while further establishing the French Quarter as the centerpiece of New Orleans tourism.[26]

The women instrumental in creating the Spring Fiesta carefully linked their romantic display of the French Quarter to businessmen's interest in profits. Organizers balanced preservation with exploitation to ensure widespread support from business leaders and politicians. "We brought over one thousand people to New Orleans," boasted one organizer, "and while this is not as large a number as we had hoped for, it is not bad for the beginning of a brand new, unusual proposition, particularly since our budget was less than $6000.00." The quality of participants offset any disappointment about the small size of the crowds. The Spring Fiesta targeted a tourist audience packing fat wallets and eager to bring home expensive mementos of their visit to the Crescent City. Antique dealers praised the event, noting that the "type of people who bought were of the substantial class, and [merchants] made more than usual." A public exposition by French Quarter artists also raked in impressive profits. In 1939, more than three thousand tourists arrived for the Spring Fiesta, and the festival continued to grow, becoming New Orleans's second-biggest celebration (trailing only Mardi Gras) until the advent of Jazzfest in the 1970s.[27]

Preservationists packaged Royal Street, Jackson Square, and an expanding area within the Vieux Carré as an exceptional space liberated from modernity. In a perceptive editorial from the 1920s, the *Times-Picayune* clearly related the district's function within the emerging tourism industry. The "wiser tourists" who "jam the narrow streets of the Vieux Carré, their Northern haste lost in the dreamy bypaths of romance," discovered a "real New Orleans" with an "utterly uncommercial spirit in the air." In the "old town," tourists learned that to "eat, to drink and to be merry is the native creed . . . for the sombre brooding undertone of the city tells them that tomorrow they die and imparts interest even to that fact by offering its 'quaint' cemeteries in proof." New Orleanians, in other words, taught tourists that life was to be enjoyed and that carnal indulgence was mere participation in local culture. The French Quarter presented a sharp contrast from the business-oriented skyscrapers located just a couple of blocks away on the other side of Canal Street. The quarter's architecture presented a more relaxed way of life, one passed off to tourists as French, as contrary to the standards of hard work central to American commerce. "The heart of the city's soul beats a muffled cadence," explained the *Times-Picayune*, "too soft and sweet for common ears. To hear it it is almost necessary to walk, alone and between midnight and dawn, in the gray and ghostly Vieux Carre." The French Quarter offered a realm outside modern time and space. Entering the neighborhood was like stepping away from the hassles of everyday life into a more relaxed, romantic past. In addition, the district united the seemingly contradictory American perceptions of the French as both civilized and deviant. Truly knowledgeable tourists, after all, knew that in the Vieux Carré, "Carnival isn't just in February, . . . it's always."[28]

Restored homes offered temporal portals into the past. The renovation of one French Quarter residence led a local commentator to praise the owners because when entering the structure, "the visitor [leaves] the twentieth century waiting without, and gazes upon a scene that might have greeted a caller in the year 1800." Flo Field, a local writer, preservationist, and tour guide, explained that to walk down Royal was to step back in time: "It is a few moments before the Present dies away on a balcony, an iron grill, the delicate modeling of an upper façade. Something comes over you—the spirit of an older world." Tourists agreed. Kathryn Randolph from Toledo, Ohio, praised the contrast between the business district and the French Quarter: "In one part of town everything is new and comfortable and shiny; cross a street and you are in a different world, old and quaint." Many tourists concurred with Randolph's exclamation: "What more could one want?"[29]

Ironically, the presentation of the French Quarter as a near-holy relic supplied tourists with not only an exotic site but also a space that excused behavior otherwise deemed unacceptable by Americans. The district seemed to rest outside the normal passage of time. Here, modern standards of behavior could be ignored as an homage to the old seaport and its former inhabitants. Reporting on his visit to New Orleans in 1938, J. B. Priestley complained of boosters' celebration of past iniquities. "New Orleans, we are told over and over again, is beyond any other American city the city of Romance. But what is Romance? If it is simply a combination of the odd, picturesque, and raffish, then the supremacy of the old New Orleans cannot be challenged." He noted that over time, New Orleanians had reformed the city's most decadent ways: the worst debauchery was "in the past." Speaking from the perspective of tourists temporally separated from the indulgent lifestyle of wealthy antebellum New Orleanians, Priestley explained, "We are not reformers faced with a stinking city to clean up. We can afford to be tolerant." Tolerance allowed tourists to admire—even mimic—the figures honored in guidebooks. Carnal indulgence became a means of reviving history. But Priestley criticized the ploy, targeting in particular the writings of Saxon, who described Creoles and planters as part of a culture fixated on sensual pleasures and often invited readers to seek out remnants of this decadent past. According to Priestley, "It is possible to play the fool—to drink and gamble and fornicate away all one's resources and health and manhood—with a certain amount of style; but I do not catch a glimpse of style here. On examination, the wild wicked legend of the gay city of the South begins to shrivel to a mumbled tale of waterfront harpies and sots." For Priestley and a few other visitors, New Orleans's reputation wore thin. The increase in the number of tourists during the late 1930s and early 1940s, however, suggests that Americans generally embraced rather than scorned the ribald New Orleans described in guidebooks.[30]

Cloaking the French Quarter as a harbor for French mores also aided in transforming the city into a carnal fantasyland. Exploiting popular preconceptions to excuse risqué behavior was a practice common among emerging tourist centers. In his study of Las Vegas, Hal Rothman shows that the image of the Wild West as lawless allowed boosters during the interwar years to transform the desert town into a cultural oasis where the "ribald could be packaged as individual freedom." New Orleanians played a different cultural hand to win a share of the tourist pot. One contemporary observer noted that American popular opinion held that the French were preoccupied with the enjoyment of food, alcohol, and sex. The repeal of Prohibition facilitated the French connection by bringing a wave of cabarets to the district. To enhance the association with France, Louisiana Governor Richard Leche in the late 1930s urged city leaders to place bilingual street signs throughout the French Quarter. The Louisiana State Museum supported the effort, stating that the policy returned "to the Vieux Carré in the words of the Governor 'its historic atmosphere.'" Francophilia was furthered by private enterprise. In 1944, Paul Schrecker published his impressions of New Orleans in *Harper's Magazine*: "Strolling through the Vieux Carré with its sad relics of French glory, its innumerable 'French antiquity shops' filled with horrors that a concierge in the outskirts of Paris would not hesitate to throw into the garbage, its strange tendency to emphasize its French character by making alcoholism easy and night clubs the most frequent institutions, you can perceive remnants of genuine French civilization only by moments and, as it were, through a thick fog." Nearly everything in the district seemed "got up for naïve tourists by some travel agency or chamber of commerce." In the Crescent City, tourists did not do as New Orleanians did but as the French supposedly did. Tourists indulged themselves. Tourists consumed.[31]

Bourbon Street, running parallel to Royal Street, emerged as Royal's alter ego, giving vent to the less dignified pursuits and merchandise desired by tourists. Businessmen wanted to establish a foothold near if not on the highly popular tourist draws of Royal Street and Jackson Square. With preservationists vigorously defending Royal, however, prospective operators of nightclubs and tawdry entertainment venues found Bourbon much more accessible. Here the gaudy commercialization often associated with tourism—from neon signs to trinket-filled souvenir shops—forged a glitzy strip through the center of the Vieux Carré. Largely free of prostitution, Bourbon Street bore none of the stigma burdening other French Quarter streets located further away from the river. Nor did the thoroughfare suffer from the heavy traffic carried by streets closer to the Mississippi. The development of cabarets and nightclubs, many with burlesque revues, capitalized on the close proximity of the thriving commercial sex trade but lacked the shock of actual encounters with prostitution. Bourbon Street businesses thus remained accessible to respectable men and adventurous women without offending their sensibilities.

Despite the empowerment of the Vieux Carré Commission, preservationists conceded most of Bourbon Street to profiteers. By the early 1940s, guide writers proclaimed Bourbon the center of New Orleans nightlife: "Here are honky-tonks and gilt-and-silver supper clubs; here are clubs with 'B-girls' by the score and clubs with strip-tease entertainers; here are floorshows with dozens of lovely dollies and floorshows with a few boney old hags grinning through their routines in horrible travesty; here is the gamut of nightlife." The influx of soldiers during the Second World War accelerated the trend. A 1948 guide reported that tourists found hawkers announcing "girlie shows" and "hot spots" vastly different from the "more select Royal Street vicinity patios." In a guidebook from the early 1950s, Ernest Vetter recognized that "sound-minded businessmen" had moved to exploit the burgeoning tourist trade in the French Quarter. Whereas Royal possessed "beautiful architecture, old residences, and romantic spots," Bourbon became "perhaps the rowdiest, loudest, heaviest-drinking, least inhibited, half-dozen blocks in the world today." The glitz amazed Vetter, who declared that Bourbon appeared more like "an oldtime movie set rather than an actual street."[32]

The French Quarter thus emerged as a fantasyland of adult desires. Tourists within the district seemingly encountered an old world of Creole culture born of Spanish and French ancestors in which mores, especially in regard to sex and alcohol, seemed vastly different from American ways. Local establishments emphasized the exoticism of the Vieux Carré. La Lune at 800 Bourbon Street even offered a Mexican decor, a Mexican band, and Mexican drinks—the house specialty was the Tequila Sunrise. Also on Bourbon Street, the proprietors of Café Lafitte operated a restaurant and bar in a building once used by pirate Jean Lafitte as a blacksmith shop. For adventurous tourists, the bar specialized in Obituary Cocktails. Tourists in the French Quarter encountered both a supposedly foreign space, as suggested to the patrons of La Lune, and a place where behavior usually considered taboo could be enjoyed, as at Café Lafitte. In the French Quarter, New Orleanians developed a tourist attraction capable of sustaining year-round interest.[33]

But This Is the French Quarter

Nationally acclaimed author and French Quarter resident Roark Bradford wrote a play that perceptively examined the neighborhood's role as a tourist attraction. For Bradford, women left an indelible mark on the preservationist cause. "Club women are push-overs, when they get a chance to do their civic duty in a romantic setting," declares one character early in the script, which was never published. Preservation trumped concerns over other urban ills. "Just say, 'Vieux Carre' to a bunch of club women, they'd damned quick forget about slot machines" and other vices, continues Bradford's insightful character. "And their husbands, too," quips another. Although local elite women nurtured the French Quarter art community, resident artists resented the stifling standards of socialites concerned mainly with capturing the neighborhood's romantic essence. "That fat bunch of dowagers," barks a frustrated young artist named Betty. The most venomous criticisms targeted Le Petit Salon du Vieux Carré. Bradford saw the salon, located in a building on Jackson Square, as representing elite women's artistic tyranny over life in the district. One of Bradford's characters fondly recalls the artist who sat in his attic window across from the salon and shot "those old dames" with his BB gun as they stepped from their cars for their Thursday meetings. The character was modeled on the antics of William Faulkner and his friend William Spratling, who later in life gained fame as a silversmith in Mexico. Although the policing of the neighborhood by elite women curtailed artistic ingenuity, the impressionistic style they promoted and financially supported ensured that the French Quarter captivated many curious tourists.[34]

Bradford also understood that tourists embraced the French Quarter as a liberating oasis from everyday life. Hester, a tour guide in Bradford's play, urges visitors to enjoy alcohol, justifying drinking absinthe—a "French drink in the French Quarter"—as a way to explore New Orleans's supposedly foreign lifestyle. Because Americans associated sexual and alcoholic indulgence with the French, such claims easily convinced tourists to loosen their moral moorings despite preservationists' attempts to downplay the neighborhood's seedier side. Responding to Hester's offer of an absinthe frappe, a female tourist hesitates, "I wonder if I dare? It sounds so wicked!" Hester's friend responds, "But this is the French Quarter!" The otherworldly atmosphere pervading the neighborhood unleashed hedonism among tourists. Visitors even deemed illegal activities an integral part of the New Orleans experience. In Bradford's play, a pair of tourists search for marijuana, explaining, "We come two thousand miles, just to see New Orleans, and we don' want to miss a thing." Many tourists in the Crescent City could easily have uttered such words.[35]

Neighborhood residents in turn learned to exploit visitors' expectations. Bradford's script presents shopkeepers, artists, and vendors fixated on the profits to be gained from tourists. The play begins with Sinclair, an art instructor, teaching a class to paint an iron-laced balcony. When Hester and her tour group approach, Sinclair and his students quickly dishevel their clothes "to affect an arty carelessness." When the tourists arrive, Sinclair discreetly pulls Hester aside to ask if there is any "chance of them buying anything." The artists understand the firm connection between meeting tourists' expectations and making sales. Like the impressionistic paintings they create to hide reality, the enterprising artists disguise themselves to appeal to visitors. But the subterfuge also hides a system of kickbacks. Local desires to exploit out-of-towners, as Bradford suggests, influence the stories told about the French Quarter and the places tourists are instructed to visit. Hester, for example, receives payments from French Quarter businesses for leading tourists to particular bars and souvenir shops. Everything in the French Quarter—from the buildings to the people—could be packaged as either "interesting" or "charming," no matter how mundane.[36]

CHAPTER 5

A CITY THAT CARE FORGOT

The Reinvention of New Orleans Mardi Gras

Tourists and locals packed city streets in expectation of the first Mardi
Gras parade of the 1947 season. The Krewe of Cynthius slowly rolled
down the traditional New Orleans parade route of St. Charles Avenue
to Canal Street, where it would then turn onto Bourbon Street and then
onto Orleans Street on its way to the debarkation site at the Municipal Auditorium. Patrons of French Quarter bars eagerly waited. Many
repeatedly darted out into the street to check if the first float was yet
in view. Even the buildings heralded the arrival of Mardi Gras royalty. Robert Tallant, a local writer and authority on the New Orleans
holiday, remembered, "The old houses in the French Quarter of New
Orleans were all dressed up in the carnival colors of purple, green and
gold." As the flickering orange glow from Cynthius's flambeau carriers came into view, "customers and entertainers rushed from the night
clubs." The horse-drawn floats lit by torch-bearing attendants cast a
spell over the crowd, sending them back to a romantic past free of
mechanized vehicles, electric lights, and the tensions of modern life. The
narrow street and unique architecture accentuated the magical transformation, converting otherwise upstanding Americans into drunken, ex-
uberant revelers eager to embrace their carnality. Maskers on the floats
heightened the frenzy by tossing trinkets. Those lining the narrow street
and cramming the balconies yelled and waved and leaped in an effort to

catch a share of Carnival treasure. Marching bands "blazed with jazz music," while band majors and majorettes "strutting and dancing and hurling batons" captivated the crowd. When the parade finally ended, recalled Tallant, the "honky-tonks of Bourbon Street began to fill again with customers, and more kept coming, for after a parade a drink is generally sought." The passage of more parades over the next week guaranteed that the partying had just begun.[1]

The arrival of Mardi Gras in the French Quarter marked the annual high tide of New Orleans tourism, with thousands flocking to the festivities from throughout the United States as well as from foreign countries. As popular as Mardi Gras was, however, the holiday served only as a momentary attraction. The abandon enjoyed by tourists walking New Orleans streets on the handful of days leading up to Fat Tuesday depended on the definition of Mardi Gras as an exceptional time. Inverting the standards of social behavior offered brief release from the behavioral norms expected during the other fifty-one weeks of the year. The French Quarter, however, supplied a year-round getaway. Here, in a neighborhood possessing a French and Spanish heritage, visitors could indulge themselves and justify doing so as part of their adventure into a foreign space. The passage of Mardi Gras parades through the French Quarter appropriately served as the climax of the Carnival processions. As Tallant showed, the movement of the parade drew celebrants into the city's entertainment district, where the partying could freely continue after the parade ended. Mardi Gras did much the same for New Orleans as a whole.

During the interwar years, New Orleans participated in a national trend in which Americans preserved traces of the past, invented (or reinvented) traditions, and sought encounters with those cultural remnants. Historian Roderick Nash has suggested that, during the 1920s, a "sense of change had penetrated to the roots of popular thought." Faced with rapid economic expansion, urban growth, and the rise of new technologies such as the automobile and radio, many Americans expressed a desire for certainty that translated into a widespread interest in salvaging traces of the past. Preserved houses or resuscitated folk celebrations carried into the present influential links to previous generations, thereby providing guidance—if not certainty—in disorienting times. The women in Charleston, South Carolina, set a precedent for preserving distinguished homes and fostering a romantic memory of the southern past. Their actions restored to life celebrated men and women to serve as role models for the living. J. D. Rockefeller rebuilt Colonial Williamsburg as a reminder of the nation's august beginnings. Similar restoration efforts blossomed throughout the United States. Folk festivals proliferated as well. Interest in the primitive led to the emergence of art colonies such as that in Taos, New Mexico, where Native American designs captivated painters and writers. As Americans entered an increasingly urbanized, mechanized, consumer-oriented world, they fondly remembered the age of handmade goods, uncommercialized music, and a supposedly simpler way of rural life but did so without rejecting the conveniences of modernity. Ironically, the same attempts to rescue old ways and relics produced a flood of fresh tourist attractions that dragged those practices and sites into the growing consumer market. New Orleanians, like people throughout the country, turned their attention to their architectural and cultural treasures, eventually exploiting both for profit.[2]

Mardi Gras underwent a revolutionary change in the years after the First World War. Businessmen's evolved understanding of tourism, the moral crusades of Progressivism, changes in attitudes toward women, and the economic and political turmoil of the Huey Long years dramatically altered the way civic leaders perceived and promoted the longtime mainstay of New Orleans tourism. Although they occasionally frowned on subsuming the city's reputation for business to images of Carnival revelry, businessmen considered Mardi Gras vital to the city's economic health. The celebration was a necessity for suffering hotels and restaurants. Furthermore, the holiday supplied a means of condensing festivities within the heterogeneous, heavily immigrant population and thereby maintaining an orderly urban environment the rest of the business calendar. As Tallant observed, "Mardi Gras is very old, but it is also very young. It belongs to the past, yet also to the present and to the future." Though the holiday claimed a lengthy history, the traditions the festival came to symbolize during the 1920s and 1930s were reinvented by a New Orleans society eager to capitalize on a growing tourist trade. New Orleanians donned the green mask of commercialization while costuming Mardi Gras in the garb of romantic authenticity.[3]

The Very Word "King" Has a Stigma Placed upon It

When Rex returned to the streets in 1920, the king of Carnival confronted a social climate much changed from the last time he appeared in 1917. The wartime suspension of Mardi Gras broke decades of tradition. Worse, the meaning of royalty, real and make-believe, had undergone a dramatic transformation. The *Times-Picayune* pointed out that of the nineteen kings and emperors who had ruled Europe prior to the First World War, one was "dead, with his entire progeny, and nine others are in exile." As for the remainder, "in several instances their crowns rest uncomfortably upon brows that seem scarcely to possess the proper contour to fit the diadem." The social hierarchy suggested by Mardi Gras krewes, with their dukes, kings, and queens, faced a cultural landscape where such titles bore ridicule and political impotence. The *Times-Picayune* solemnly concluded, "Today, because of the world transformation brought about by Armageddon, the very word king has a stigma placed upon it and misrule has been such a vivid and terrible reality that we cannot look upon even mock monarchs with the same mental freedom we once did." The social moorings presented by Mardi Gras's regal hierarchy no longer went unquestioned.[4]

The legacy of the First World War and the onset of Prohibition altered the purpose of Carnival krewes. Since the end of the Civil War, the Rex, Comus, Momus, and Proteus parades had displayed white elites' status within the city. Regal titles reaffirmed the paraders' economic and social prestige, and although such honors were fanciful parts of a brief celebration, the possession of a title carried definite currency among the upper classes. Even into the 1930s, many New Orleanians sneered that "Carnival is for society and the rich." But businessmen's increasing acceptance of tourism during the interwar years spurred the re-creation of Mardi Gras. Over the 1920s and 1930s, Mardi Gras slowly became a holiday fashioned less for homage to the city's elite than for the maximization of public pleasure and interest—and, of course, profit.[5]

The lack of public interest in the 1920 Mardi Gras shocked New Orleans businessmen, especially hotel and restaurant operators. Although, as one concerned citizen complained, "a lot of business men" during the 1920s thought Mardi Gras sent an antibusiness image to the nation and should therefore be deemphasized if not abandoned, a significant number had no desire to see the festivities fade. The city enjoyed a larger-than-usual winter tourist crowd in 1920, partly the result of continued upheaval in Europe, but the arrival of Carnival revelers was noticeably reduced. Only one parade, Rex, returned to the streets. Rain kept maskers indoors. To make matters worse, even those already visiting the city were ignorant of the holiday. A dismayed Alfred Amer, manager of the prestigious St. Charles Hotel, observed, "But many of the guests did not know that a Carnival was on. There is not the great rush from the surrounding districts this year." Mardi Gras flopped.[6]

Hit by postwar inflation and crippling strikes, railroads, which usually arranged discount fares and special trains to transport extra revelers, failed to adequately promote Carnival during the early 1920s. The Illinois Central announced that its travel load lingered "considerably below" the six thousand persons usually carried to New Orleans for Mardi Gras. New Orleans Association of Commerce officials thought that the 1920 crowd measured just half of prewar levels. The *Times-Picayune* mourned, "There was little animation in the crowds—there was practically no 'Mardi Gras spirit.'" The next year brought limited relief. Arthur Van Pelt, a prominent member of the Association of Commerce, estimated that crowds were "practically" as large as before the First World War, putting a typical, positive spin on another lackluster Carnival. A guidebook issued by the local chapter of the Hotel Greeters of Louisiana more accurately declared that "New Orleans' great Carnival was revived in all its former glory in 1922," completely ignoring the previous two disappointing celebrations.[7]

The most serious threat to Carnival came from Prohibition. Businessmen looked with deep concern at the Volstead Act. They had good reason. As a Mississippi newspaper reported in 1921, few locals were heading to the downtown railroad depot to catch New Orleans–bound trains. "The Sazerac cocktail, the Ramos gin fizz and those delightful concoctions in Ye Old Absinthe House," explained the *Jackson News*, "are mere memories, and the bars over which they were passed are now desecrated with vapid tasteless soft drinks." Areas known for their alcohol-induced revelry, such as the famed Tango Belt, faded from the urban landscape. To make matters worse, federal officials increased investigations into bootlegging activities in the weeks leading up to Mardi Gras. Such crackdowns often coincided with increased Coast Guard patrols against smugglers. Efforts at moral reform, from Prohibition to blue laws, stirred one New Orleanian to sneer that legislators sought "to bring to pass the words of the man of the sight-seeing auto as it passes St. Louis Cemetery: 'The people of New Orleans are all buried above ground.' " [8]

The resurrection of Carnival, though partly reflective of Americans' return to normalcy, stemmed in large measure from the concerted efforts of New Orleans businessmen. In 1920, Association of Commerce President Arthur Parker directed the Convention and Tourism (C & T) Bureau to "give careful thought to the problem that has arisen and to the local factors that are standing in the way of a larger influx of desirable visitors each season, and suggest a plan for the creation of attractions that may take the place of the attractions we have lost." Soon thereafter, another association member announced that "in view of prohibition and other restricted measures something should be done to add to the attractiveness of the City as a tourist resort." Resuscitating and improving Carnival soon emerged as the solution. Until the First World War, the tourist trade drawn by Mardi Gras was taken for granted. Yet as some economic leaders quickly realized, the holiday was too important to allow it to fade. Mardi Gras enhanced the city's popularity with out-of-towners. In particular, the festival allowed local businessmen to develop important contacts as well as to showcase the city's economic potential. Businessmen at times explicitly made this point, as in 1917, when the Association of Commerce proposed an "Industrial Parade" of floats honoring area industries and resources. The event would substitute for the regular Carnival processions since the

Mardi Gras organizations had decided not to parade during wartime. New Orleans businessmen usually let Carnival send an implicit message to potential investors about the supposedly contented, happy nature of the workforce. City leaders also believed that the vibrant street celebrations refreshed citizens for another year of hard labor. A November 1920 meeting of representatives of tourist-related businesses affirmed attempts to improve Mardi Gras, announcing the steadfast "opinion that efforts should be concentrated upon the restoration of the French Opera House and the many features of the Carnival season so that New Orleans might not lose its identity as one of the most attractive tourist cities in America." Mardi Gras served as the linchpin of the tourism trade as well as of promotional campaigns meant to attract industrial and commercial investors from across the nation and overseas.[9]

Intent on informing the world that "New Orleans is going to have a big Mardi Gras in 1922," the C & T Bureau launched a publicity drive, sending articles describing the "revival" of festivities to nearly 150 newspapers and magazines across the nation. The fruits of the campaign appeared quickly in the flood of mail from prospective tourists eager to learn everything from hotel rates to the number of parades. In 1923, the bureau hired the Harcol Film Company to capture moving images of the festivities. The films, shown in theaters and schools "in the north," proved "so popular that demands for bookings could not be met." Each passing year, New Orleans businessmen reported an increased number of requests for pictures, stories, and general information about travel to the city. By 1930, Mardi Gras made national news. The presence, according to the association, of "practically all of the important screen news weeklies . . . here to 'shoot' Mardi Gras" carried the sights and sounds of Carnival nationwide. A national hook-up broadcast the celebration via radio, enabling Americans to sit at home and listen to the screaming crowds and frivolity of New Orleans streets. In 1931, the Columbia Broadcasting System carried a one-hour program on Mardi Gras over its sixty-eight stations, while shortwave radio stations sent the signal abroad to stations in London, Paris, Berlin, Rio de Janeiro, Buenos Aires, Mexico City, Lima, Havana, Montreal, and Toronto. "With Mardi Gras in print, on the screen and on the air," businessmen looked to a promising future for Carnival despite the Great Depression.[10]

To protect Mardi Gras's popularity, the C & T Bureau policed price gouging among New Orleans businesses. Beginning in the mid-1920s, the bureau opened two information booths on Canal Street, the city's central thoroughfare and shopping district, two weeks prior to Mardi Gras. The booths supplied information about area attractions and provided lists of places with "approved" lodging whose proprietors had agreed not to raise prices above certain levels. As the 1927 Mardi Gras approached, businessmen learned from visitors that "some towns north of us were giving such information as ferry charges around New Orleans being extremely high and the roads bad, with the idea of securing some of the tourists for a day or two." To prevent the spread of such "mis-information" and thereby protect the city's financial interests, the association mailed rate schedules for area toll roads to tourist agencies and automobile clubs nationwide. E. P. Lowe, a local doctor, stressed the necessity of strict regulation. "If we would encourage tourists," Lowe explained in words that could have come out of the mouth of any New Orleans businessman, "we must meet them in a cordial, welcoming and liberal spirit." He emphasized, "We must not show any inclination to extortion. When such a spirit tends to arise we must promptly repress it." Forcing establishments to publish their prices in a single, approved booklet supervised and distributed via the association curtailed price gouging and reassured tourists that they were not being exploited.[11]

Although advertising campaigns and price regulations received attention, the reconstruction of Mardi Gras preoccupied local leaders. In June 1921, the Association of Commerce commended efforts aimed at the "revival of Carnival by the carnival organizations as it existed before the war" and advocated a conference between the C & T Bureau and Retail Merchants Bureau to expedite the return of former parades. Stretching the calendar of events lengthened tourists' stay and satisfied out-of-towners' expectations. Even with the return of Momus, Proteus, and Comus by 1924, large portions of the parading season remained void of entertainment. The failure to restore the Monday celebration involving the arrival of Rex's yacht at the riverfront left local leaders uneasy. "Without the king's coming there was a let-down of Carnivalism from Thursday night to Monday evening, and many visitors delayed their visit and missed the Momus parade because to see it added several days to their expenses without the assurance of entertainment over the week-end," commented the *Times-Picayune*. Only the masking and "impromptu street parades" of marching clubs on Mardi Gras itself supplied daylong festivities. City leaders continuously struggled to fill the "too wide . . . gap in our suite of entertainment." Nevertheless, by the mid-1920s, businessmen could breathe a sigh of relief. As the press reported, Mardi Gras had indeed regained most of its "old feeling." More importantly, tourists increasingly flowed into New Orleans. Few businessmen, however, expressed content with the simple restoration of Carnival.[12]

Attempts to revitalize Mardi Gras during the mid-1920s focused on having local businesses display Carnival colors. The Krewe of Rex had officially adopted purple, green, and gold in 1872, but acceptance outside the organization came slowly. For decades, residents and businesses blended American flags into their decorations, making Mardi Gras seem more a patriotic celebration than a holiday unique to New Orleans. Although postwar patriotism fueled interest in the proper use of the Stars and Stripes as well as the national colors, civic leaders recognized the added importance of marking Carnival as a special time. Years of murmurs finally led to action in 1925. General Allison Owen, who chaired the Association of Commerce committee responsible for spearheading the movement to institutionalize the color scheme, advocated "the exclusive use of the Mardi Gras colors and regalia for the occasion," asserting that "the effect will be much more striking if this is done." Mardi Gras would thus be marked as a festival outside of national time and American culture. Although the use of the Stars and Stripes was not prohibited, the strict application of the flag code, which required respectful display of the banner, sharply curtailed the presence of American flags along New Orleans streets during Carnival. Association member E. Davis McCutchon ordered, "Every merchant who expects to decorate his place of business should make sure right now that there will be nothing in his scheme of decoration which is in violation of the flag code." Businessmen, joined by patriotic organizations such as the American Legion, vigorously policed displays and turned in violators, causing the number of violations to drop from sixty-five in 1926 to thirty in 1927 and to just fifteen in 1928. This decline stemmed as much from the decision to avoid potential controversy as from the educational impact of the enforcement effort. Negative publicity about disgracing the Stars and Stripes carried significant weight in the patriotic postwar United States. Guidebook writer Stephen Curtis West commented in 1929, "The downtown streets and buildings are beautifully decorated with flying banners of . . . the Carnival colors. Gleaming, irridescent [sic] strings of colored electric lights loop across the main streets, a fitting stage for the Carnival Pageant." [13]

To complement a city cloaked in celebratory garb, civic leaders committed themselves to increasing the amount of masking among Carnival revelers. Parades might come and go with the political and economic winds, but masking made Mardi Gras more resilient. Costume contests, dancing contests, and the closure of city streets ensured both masking among revelers and tourists' concentration near downtown retail stores. As the 1923 Carnival approached, the Association of Commerce urged city officials to restrict traffic on Canal Street for a "few hours on Mardi Gras day." The arrangement provided maskers a place to be seen, thereby encouraging locals and tourists to masquerade. Furthermore, by giving maskers a place to congregate, officials converted Canal Street into a magnet for those eager to see the outrageous outfits donned by celebrants. As one businessman who studied the issue declared, the closure of Canal Street for more than just the passage of parades "would be much more attractive to the tourists and would bring Mardi Gras back to where it was years ago." The Lions Club hosted a Charleston contest on Canal Street in the mid-1920s. In 1927, merchants sponsored a Black Bottom dancing competition. A more overt effort to encourage masking appeared as well. In the early 1930s, the 500 Block Canal Street Boosters, an organization of merchants, organized a costume contest as a device to draw Mardi Gras revelers to their storefronts. By offering prizes and enlisting the aid of capable promoters such as Lyle Saxon, the businessmen increased the number of maskers. Such endeavors threw a lifeline to an activity feared to be fading in the depression years. "Any group or individual effort that brings out more maskers, more private floats and more novelties is a genuine service to all of us," explained the *Times-Picayune* in 1934 as financial hardships forced some krewes to hibernate in their dens and caused large numbers of New Orleanians to curb their private celebrations.[14]

Masking charged the festivities with a latent sexuality as disguised men and women mingled in the streets. At a time when gender conventions were rapidly changing, disguises facilitated the inclusion of women across class lines in street festivities. The *Times-Picayune* stated in 1930, "One of the most interesting and enjoyable features of our Carnival is the promiscuous masking on Mardi Gras. Not only do the maskers themselves delight in their fantastic disguises and the home-folk never weary of the colorful and constantly changing march and merry-making of the maskers, but our visitors find its charm unique and unforgettable." For the city's leading newspaper, the presence of a costumed crowd—a "kaleidoscopic tribe"—gave the celebration an erotic allure. The *Times-Picayune* in 1934 recounted an incident on Canal Street in which a policeman encountered a "bewildered" but "gaily bedecked" couple clinging to each other as if they were about to faint. When asked whether he could be of assistance, the woman assured him that she was "having a s-s-swell time." The officer then asked if her husband needed help. She quickly replied, "He's not my husband. I don't know who he is!" The humor of the tale lay in the implicit sexual contact between strangers in the streets, an activity that readers themselves likely had experienced at some moment during a Mardi Gras celebration.[15]

Maskers literally threw off their clothes, the fashions of modern civilization, to enjoy a primal fantasy. Costumed as lawless pirates, grass-skirted islanders, gangsters, or other figures from the social margins, tourists and locals visually displayed Mardi Gras's status as a holiday outside American cultural norms. The celebration inspired college student Hodding Carter to write the poem "Mardi Gras" in January 1925:

Reeling red devils, laughing and leering
Dance with fair dames of the Court of Make-Believe;
Scarcely clothed Circes, trembling, mock fearing
Sway neath the pressure of Bedouin sleeve.
Pierre La Fitte, Columbine, Pierrot, and Geni
Trifle with treacherous flame, sensuous and free,
Lethe draughts seeking in satyr-like frenzy
For the Despot of Pleasure has read his decree.
Bodies close pressed to a rhythm erotic,
Dark eyes beseeching an unspoken plea.
Hot blood run riot in revel exotic
For the Monarch of Madness has made his decree.

Carter clearly linked the masquerade with the unleashing of sexual urges. More importantly, the outfits donned by revelers recalled bandits, nomads, bewitching mythological figures, and saucy comedic characters. Carnival heralded the outrageous. Even the pretense of a costume could be discarded. In 1930, tourist Herbert Bell from Detroit staged "an all-night parade clad only in his underwear," discarding his shoes, necktie, and almost everything else in a vacant lot. Encountering policemen when he returned for his clothes, Bell explained that he had downed a couple of drinks and become envious of the costumes he saw, so he decided to "adopt a little novel exhibition." Bell's wanderings failed to raise any alarm among neighborhood residents, who probably considered such conduct part of the festivities. Everyone during Mardi Gras was, in some sense, an outlaw stretching social boundaries.[16]

Mardi Gras's success hinged on presenting the festival as a step back in time. When the *Times-Picayune* commented on the centennial of New Orleans Mardi Gras in 1927, masking defined the holiday as an ancient festival: "It is indeed this indiscriminate masking that ties our city not with similar festivities in Philadelphia, St. Louis and a few other American cities, but that links our gaieties into company with those of Italy and old Spain, of France and yet other lands that have received the Carnival spirit in direct unbroken inheritance not only from its earliest Christian manifestations but even from far beyond, from the pagan mysteries that sink deeper and deeper into the past until they unconsciously blend into the frolics of demideities and even of the whole deities of Olympus." The "spontaneous" appearance of costumes on city streets symbolized both a turning back of the clock and an authenticity lacking in the celebrations of other American urban centers. Businessmen and the press rarely missed an opportunity to point out to tourists a unique word in the local lexicon. New Orleanians used the term *mawdygraw* to describe a masker. For city leaders eager to prove to outsiders the indigenous quality of Carnival, no better evidence of popular support for the traditional holiday could be found than the slippage of *mawdygraw* from local tongues.[17]

The continued use of draft animals and torches further contrasted Mardi Gras from mechanized, electrified modernity. Local resident John Mendes saw the parades as "the one place where the spirit of modern times has not placed its mark." Mendes continued, "They have been given for about seventy years and the motive power has remained the same. Our Carnival parades have been a success and we have found an indispensable factor—mules and horses." The appearance of animal-drawn floats was all the more impressive given the prominence of skyscrapers, "costly" theaters, "modern" docks, and "hundreds of automobiles." In a city where horses and mules "rarely" appeared in the streets—except, of course, in front of carriages operated by tour guides—locals and tourists romanticized the slow tread of hoof-beats on paved streets. Night parades went a step further. The krewes used flambeau carriers, black men who carried torches, to illuminate the floats. The flames cast an orange glow along the length of the procession that recalled a time when gas street lamps and candles served as the primary means of lighting. In 1929, the *Times-Picayune* hammered home the point that despite the "ultra-modern developments" taking place in the city, "the spirit of the age-old Carnival survives as strong and vigorous as in the old days when aircraft and skyscrapers were not, and the electricity that lights our nightly paths and drives our mills and factories still went unharnessed." Carnival turned back the clock, allowing tourists and residents to imagine themselves in some premodern era in which revelry could reign.[18]

The desire to present Mardi Gras as a relic of the past was matched by the desire to democratize the traditional, highly exclusive balls hosted by the city's krewes. Tourists, attracted by the mystery of Mardi Gras krewes, with their regal titles and exclusive balls, flooded the mayor's office and the Association of Commerce with requests to see the private dances held after parades completed their routes. Like horse-drawn processions lit by torchbearers, the romantic realm of Carnival balls recalled an elegant, almost fantastic, past of waltzes and royal courts. In 1930, members of the Association of Commerce debated staging a "costume affair" for tourists to remedy the problem of "hotels and others who were considerably embarrassed by requests from Mardi Gras visitors for invitations to the various Carnival balls." The "reaction was unfavorably against New Orleans when these people returned home disappointed at their inability to take part in the festivities." Creating a ball for the enjoyment of tourists did not go without criticism, however. Another businessman protested "what he termed the 'commercializing' of a New Orleans Carnival and the placing of a dollar sign on this historic celebration." Particularly grating to some members of the association was the suggestion of selling tickets to the affair, thereby funding the event but also raising a profit. The sensibilities of businessmen concerned with hiding the commercial side of Mardi Gras were ruffled for another reason as well. One of the financial backers demanded that the "ball should be of a risque nature," or else the affair would not be worth the monetary risk. A committee studying the feasibility of the ball favored quick implementation, seeing the masquerade as a "means for a Carnival-minded and fun-bent host of people who are guests of New Orleans at Mardi Gras time to fully enter into the spirit of the occasion and feel that they have really taken part in this internationally famed event." Other businessmen, however, supported deferring action on this matter during the nadir of the depression.[19]

The idea of a tourist-oriented ball gestated until 1934, when the event was finally implemented. The Municipal Auditorium hosted a midnight "subscription affair" open to visitors who paid $5.50 a head to attend. By holding the event in the early morning hours of Mardi Gras, businessmen assured tourists a full day of festivities. The follow-up Mardi Gras Masquerade Ball in 1935, again intended "primarily for the entertainment of visitors," offered "a floor show given by nationally known theatrical talent, a spectacular tableaux and one of America's best known 'name' bands." The setting was disguised to convince vacationers that they were witnessing authentic New Orleans culture.[20]

To increase the number of parades and bolster the entertainment offered to tourists, New Orleans businessmen united to form two new krewes, the Krewe of Mid-City in 1934 and the Krewe of Hermes in 1937, carefully choosing the names to reflect specific goals. Mid-City's organizers deliberately avoided a classical name and the traditional parade route of St. Charles Avenue, instead taking Canal Street into downtown to draw attention to their area of New Orleans as well as to reinforce the perception that organized Carnival permeated the city. Hermes, the God of Commerce and Travel, supplied tourists the glitz some expected from Carnival by introducing neon lights into float designs. Despite the use of modern illumination, Hermes members sought to reinforce rather than overthrow tradition, a major selling point to tourists. For example, the Hermes ball replaced the subscription affair, thereby linking the dance with a parade and removing any sense that the ball was a mere sham staged for tourists. In terms of marketing, the members of Hermes were pioneers. The krewe in 1939 launched the first traveling Carnival exhibition, which visited Chicago, Minneapolis, Detroit, Kansas City, Memphis, and several other urban centers. According to the *New Orleans States*, the exhibition featured the krewe's costumes and jewels "to exploit the Mardi Gras season."[21]

The 1934 creation of the Krewe of Nor, a children's parade, marked businessmen's most significant contribution to Carnival and its popular image. The end of Prohibition meant the return not only of alcohol but also of public lewdness. Although businessmen avoided explicitly connecting their desire for a children's parade with their desire to mitigate the ribaldry of an alcohol-enhanced Mardi Gras, the timing of Nor's emergence was no coincidence. The parade tempered the public image of Carnival as a time of alcoholic and sexual indulgence. Moreover, the floats sought to represent the city's history and economic strengths, thus cloaking boosterism in the guise of school-level education. To downplay the ribaldry of Mardi Gras, local leaders chose the name of the children's parade very carefully. By selecting *Nor*, an acronym for "New Orleans Romance," businessmen and politicians deviated from the custom of using the names of mythic gods. The Greek and Roman deities who graced krewes with their names represented behavior most Americans in the 1930s considered outrageous if not blatantly immoral. Nor thus distanced Carnival from its bawdy heritage. To make the separation clearer, the children paraded under a different red, white, and green Mardi Gras flag. The Association of Commerce boasted that the annual parade would become an "outstanding feature" of Carnival. Timing the procession for the Saturday prior to Fat Tuesday also aided efforts to extend Carnival, encouraging tourists to extend their stay in New Orleans. The end result was a Mardi Gras capable of catering to a wide range of celebrants, from indulgent revelers to family vacationers.[22]

The introduction of schoolchildren into Mardi Gras parades did not go without some protest. The first Nor procession interspersed floats with eighteen school bands, and each public school in the city was responsible for constructing a float. Furthermore, schoolboys rather than the usual horses or mules pulled the floats, placing the children at street level. Although participation was optional, parents felt pressured to allow their children to work on what the *Times-Picayune* called a "pet school project." Outspoken parents and educators at Robert Usher Elementary and Audubon Elementary urged Nicholas Bauer, superintendent of the public schools, to discontinue the Nor parade. Some parents expressed outrage at the idea of exposing children to cold rains and the hazards of the streets, while others objected to fielding the costly parade at a time when the school system faced monetary shortfalls. Ignoring the outcry and acting quickly, before opponents could organize effectively, Bauer pushed through the school board a commitment to parade again in 1935. Whether Bauer caved to Association of Commerce pressure or truly believed that Nor's benefits outweighed its costs was unclear. Yet concerned New Orleanians such as Paul Jones saw the association as the obvious puppet master. He angrily asked, "Is the New Orleans Association of Commerce going to . . . pay for the parade it wants?" Already knowing that the answer was no, Jones condemned the association: "For shame, men! Don't hide behind children!" Despite lingering resentment, Nor became an annual supplement to the ever growing, ever more profitable Mardi Gras celebration. Although Nor ceased to parade after the United States entered the Second World War, schoolchildren's participation in Mardi Gras expanded after the conflict, with krewes integrating school bands and cheerleaders into their processions.[23]

At the same time businessmen worked to invigorate tourists' Mardi Gras experience, leading New Orleanians prepared for the gathering of Mardi Gras memorabilia in an attempt to make Carnival a year-round attraction. Businessmen in 1929 rallied support for a perpetual display memorializing past Carnivals. For the *Times-Picayune*, the "preservation and display of the jewels and rich costumes worn for a day or a night by Rex, his royal brethren, and the lords and ladies of the Carnival courts" promised to augment tourists' fascination with the festival. The proposed Carnival museum would open to permanent public view the otherwise exclusive items of elite krewes. If the invitation, dresses, and other regalia were donated or loaned to a museum, the New Orleans press, along with a large number of social and business leaders, including Association of Commerce President Alfred Danziger, expressed "no doubt" that the collection "would prove an added attraction to New Orleans visitors in and out of the Carnival season." Henry Dart, president of the Louisiana State Museum, quickly responded by preparing space in the French Quarter's Cabildo for the elegant presentation of Mardi Gras treasures to tourist crowds. The newspapers urged residents to comb through their heirlooms for exhibit items. By creating "so uniquely interesting" a collection, business leaders hoped to entice even more tourists to the city. Costumes, scepters, badges, ball invitations, and sketches of float designs from past Carnivals poured into the museum. To accommodate the artifacts, the museum opened a new exhibition hall in late 1931.[24]

Carnival boosters sustained the popular impression of Mardi Gras as a traditional relic from the past by stressing the role of profits in shaping festivals in other cities. A 1929 editorial in the *Times-Picayune* explained, "City after city has attempted to outdo New Orleans, imagining that money can purchase the true essence of Mardi Gras, the inner spirit of Carnival enjoyment. Uniformly such undertakings have been solemn affairs, mere stage setting without the histrion[ic]s to perform the extravaganza as it should be played." Businessmen and politicians rarely missed the opportunity to urge tourists to venture into less visited neighborhoods to see that the festivities were not contrived. Another piece from the *Times-Picayune* published in the early 1930s encouraged visitors to "escape from the big centers of festivity . . . and journey everywhere, anywhere throughout our city and see . . . that this famed New Orleans Mardi Gras is not a mere artifice, resorted to, as is the Tournament of Roses in California, Philadelphia's fanciful parades, St. Louis' Veiled Prophets, or Tampa's piratical review." According to the newspaper, competing holidays in competing cities stood as "stage shows" that paled in comparison to the revelry found in New Orleans. The editorial ignored the fact that many other such events, especially those in Philadelphia and St. Louis, possessed long histories. That businessmen consciously stimulated masking and neighborhood parades to improve tourists' experiences only showed how the ruse of authenticity succeeded. "There ever exists the unexpected just around the corner, the something new and surprising in its inventiveness," boasted the *Times-Picayune*, subsequently echoing the refrain sung by businessmen throughout the city: "It is, indeed, the general good nature prevailing here that largely differentiates our annual gay season from all attempts at imitation that thus far have failed so signally." In New Orleans, the fabricated remained well concealed.[25]

The introduction of throws at parades disguised the commercialism of Mardi Gras. As longtime resident Louise Glynn remembered, prior to the 1920s, float riders merely threw kisses to the bystanders. This changed as businessmen explored ways to enliven the festivities. Krewe members, beginning with Rex's introduction of beads in 1921, increasingly tossed items to the crowds. In a 1924 article for a tourist magazine, prominent socialite Elizabeth Werlein described how krewes offered spectators "colored bead necklaces, boxes of candy, or small amusing gimcracks." The throws turned once passive observers into active participants, and jostling for beads added to the sexually charged atmosphere. In streets packed with New Orleanians and out-of-towners, physical contact was inevitable. In his 1929 guide to New Orleans, Stephen Curtis West reassured tourists about the safety of the crowded streets: "Hoosiers from Indianapolis bump into dignified professors from Boston, apologize profusely, and then break out into hilarious laughter." Moreover, "couples meet up in the street," explained West, "and dance to the impromptu music of wandering minstrels." West emphasized that women standing along the parade route "smile and titter, for it is Carnival, whose imperial command is: Be sure and have a good time. A GOOD TIME!" Concerns with propriety—especially among middle- and upper-class women disturbed by the close contact with men—merely dampened the festivities and detracted from the enjoyment of Carnival. Mardi Gras throws both encouraged and excused such contact. Beads served as trophies, allowing couples to bestow gifts on each other and permitting singles a means of introduction to members of the opposite sex. Exchanging trinkets tossed from floats substituted for the practice of treating and gift giving common when couples dated. More importantly, the items tossed from floats supplied souvenirs of tourists' experience in New Orleans. West concluded his snippet on Carnival by encouraging tourists to grab a throw. He wrote, "You've caught one? A string of bright-colored beads? Ah, but you're lucky to get it, because good luck goes with it. Did you see all the hands flying for the token? Ah, yes, they know the rich value of a MARDI GRAS SOUVENIR!" Krewe members understood that the locals and tourists crowded along the parade route could not resist the challenge and opportunities offered by the capture of a throw. A strand of beads served the multiple purposes of souvenir, trophy, and calling card.[26]

Civic leaders did not keep tourists ignorant of the expense of Mardi Gras. Nothing signified the elegance and high quality of Carnival better than the amount of money spent on parades, throws, and balls. In a 1928 *Times-Picayune* article, "Before You See the Parade," writer K. T. Knoblock emphasized that Rex alone spent between forty and forty-five thousand dollars annually on its floats, costumes, and expenses associated with parading. Yet Knoblock posed the question of why elite New Orleanians who enjoyed a life of leisure put forth such "hard work, strenuous work." The answer varied. Some, according to Knoblock, stressed the "educational" value of the floats; others claimed that the event was "traditional" and therefore had to be continued. Still more "hard-headed businessmen" pointed to the "fifty thousand visitors" and the "commercial benefits to the city through the advertising that is Mardi Gras." In Knoblock's eyes, however, even blatant talk of commercialization served as a ruse, providing justification for men to spend money on what everyone supposedly knew to be a wasteful celebration "without the hope of return" on money invested. According to Knoblock, "Even hotel men don't make enough out of the crowds to compensate them for the black eyes they get when they have to turn late reservations away." Packed hotels and crammed restaurants, in other words, represented only greater expenses, not greater profits. Knoblock stretched his argument thinner: "It is obvious to the first-grader in arithmetic that there can't possibly be a financial return to those who spend the $200,000 or so that goes into the Carnival parades. It is just, to the prosaic, so much money wasted, so much effort spent that could as easily be put into getting more factories." At a time when factories remained symbols of progress and prosperity, the idea that tourism was a major industry could still be hidden. The "real thing behind Carnival," according to boosters such as Knoblock, was not a "mere advertising instinct" but a commitment to an expensive tradition in which everyone forgot "his business, his dignity, even his identity." Mardi Gras served as a convenient excuse to abandon the American business ethic of hard work.[27]

The depression forced New Orleanians to reassess their commitment to Carnival excess. A holiday described as a traditional money pit during the fat times of the 1920s seemed sheer folly in the lean years of the 1930s. "There have come to us of late the echoes of scattered protests against the Carnival merry-making in a time of depression," remarked the *Times-Picayune* in 1931. To curb criticism, the newspapers and the business community sought to enlighten locals as well as the nation regarding the economic benefits brought by organized merrymaking. As Perry Young from the Krewe of Comus declared, "Those who criticize the holding of Carnival parades do so because they have taken a wrong slant of the matter." "There are black boys who carry lights, grooms for the horses, musicians, electricians. For the ball there must be florists, caterers, decorators," Young continued. Explaining that Comus operated solely for the "entertainment of the public," Young stressed that Carnival tourists spent a "six or seven-figure total." Young, like Knoblock, clearly split hairs by discussing the beneficial impact of Mardi Gras on the city economy while emphasizing how krewes, many with members from the business community, failed to gain a return on their expenses. According to the Comus spokesman, the krewes financially benefited everyone but themselves. Furthermore, the city government and businesses (especially hotels, restaurants, and nightclubs) hired additional personnel. Carnival meant not only a weekend of festivities but short-term and long-term employment. Young concluded with a vision that was utopian, at least from the perspective of a well-off member of the social blue bloods: "Even the panhandlers on the street will benefit, because when a storekeeper makes a nice profit he can afford to drop a quarter in the beggar's cup."[28]

Despite such blatant discussions of profiteering, the defenders of Carnival proclaimed the celebration less an economic salve for local woes than an affordable safety valve for anxious Americans. Argued the *Times-Picayune*, the "genial spirit, enjoyment and good feeling generated by this brief play-time of ours have themselves a psychological value as solvent of the depressed and fearful state of mind which rewards the nation's recovery." The newspaper and New Orleans's other dailies repeatedly lampooned the "local cynics" who persisted in throwing "up their hands in holy horror" while crying that "Carnival should be banned." If businessmen failed to reason their Mardi Gras opponents into submission, convincing New Orleanians that such protesters were comical figures served well enough.[29]

Overt advertising or profiteering remained taboo because both endangered the image of Mardi Gras as a festival where concern over ordinary cares or money were discarded. Advertising trucks tagging along at the end of parades in the late 1930s, for example, outraged a significant portion of the business community. Although the Association of Commerce did everything in its power to increase profits from Mardi

Gras vacationers, members of the organization persisted in the belief that the holiday "differs from events in other cities in that it is distinctly a celebration and not a promotion." New Orleans Carnival possessed "no inherent commercial features," and the understanding that "everything is free or by invitation is well known nationally." By disguising the event's economic significance, New Orleanians portrayed the festivities as a purely cultural event. Blatant advertising threatened to expose the sham. "This lack of commercialism," continued the association's board of directors, "gives it individuality and helps to maintain and increase its popularity." The association called for a city ordinance to prohibit infringement on parades' noncommercial aura so that tourists could visually consume the procession without blatant reminders of their role as free-spending consumers.[30]

Despite local businessmen's best efforts, the artificiality of New Orleans Carnival occasionally showed through the carefully constructed facade. During the 1930s, the formerly rowdy festival lacked the edge previously associated with its street festivities. Organized dance and costume contests, a supervised color scheme, parades harking back to premodern times, sophisticated promotional techniques, and shrewd arguments about Mardi Gras economics came to dominate the way Carnival was celebrated. In addition, the tourist trade galvanized interest in reinventing the New Orleans festivities to disguise the profit motive. In 1937, editors for *Life* magazine called national attention to the changes Carnival had undergone in the preceding two decades, running a spread on Mardi Gras in Mobile, Alabama, rather than New Orleans. Photographers from the magazine explained their decision by pointing out that New Orleans was "tamer than usual." The orchestrated celebrations lacked spark and made Mardi Gras, despite local leaders' best efforts, appear contrived. *Life* editors concluded that in Mobile, the holiday was simply more social and "less commercial" and therefore held greater interest for the magazine's readers.[31]

Although the reworking of Mardi Gras to accommodate the tourist trade could backfire as in the somewhat negative publicity in *Life*, tourists continued to flock to the New Orleans Mardi Gras and businessmen continued to exploit the holiday. As a result, the profits kept flowing into private pocketbooks as well as municipal coffers. Carnival became big business—as big and important as river traffic and factories. No color gleamed brighter during Mardi Gras than that of gold.

From the River's Mouth to All of America

Few people understood local businessmen's hold on Mardi Gras better than author William Faulkner. In his 1935 novel *Pylon*, Faulkner cut to the heart of Carnival by thinly fictionalizing New Orleans as "New Valois." The name given to the city suggested much about Faulkner's vision of the festival. Following the Capetian dynasty, the Valois family rose to power in France in the fourteenth century. To reinforce their authority and cast an aura of magnificence around themselves, the rulers developed elaborate processions and rituals with strict color codes, music, and organized groups of children. The parallel with New Orleans businessmen was too much for Faulkner to ignore.[32]

Faulkner's businessmen dictated city affairs from Grandlieu Street, the novel's version of Canal Street. No matter where people traveled, they could feel the "glare and pulse of Grandlieu Street miles away." In city leaders' pursuit of money, Faulkner saw New Valois (and New Orleans) as no different than any other American city. The urban space described in *Pylon* was inescapable, "symbolic and encompassing, it outlay all gasolinespanned distances and all clock or sunstipulated destinations." Green, a symbol of money, appears everywhere within the city. Newspapermen, for example, work beneath "greenshaded light" and publish their articles on "pale green paper"; streets are lighted with "bloodless grapes of lampglobes" and "pariahgreen globes." From "paid monkeymen" janitors to the "rented cunts" of prostitutes, money dictates every aspect of urban life.[33]

Faulkner's New Valoisian Mardi Gras seems free from commercialization. Despite the prevalence of green throughout the city, Mardi Gras is celebrated with only purple and gold. No pamphlets or banners praise a sponsor or express gratitude to any businessman. In contrast, the opening of New Valois's first airport is commemorated with stunt pilots, programs, and the expected booster hoopla. In an allusion to the opening of New Orleans's Shushan Airport in the early 1930s, the airport's terminal and runways bear the initials of the facility's namesake, who is also the city's leading economic decision maker. Purple and gold appear throughout the ceremonies held to inaugurate the new means of tourist travel, thus cloaking the celebration of local economic and political power in the noncommercial mirage of Carnival and making the airport an extension of the holiday but not part of the core festivities downtown. Carefully masking otherwise blatant commercial interests benefited both fictional New Valoisians and real New Orleanians. Yet as Faulkner shows, traditional interests in industry and commerce were changing. The future of urban development rested not along the riverfront, with its ties to industry and commerce, but at the lakefront airport on the opposite side of the city. Tourist travel and leisure promised the greatest economic benefits, a point New Orleanians increasingly recognized.[34]

By the late 1930s, then, New Orleans businessmen had expanded Mardi Gras into a powerful tourist magnet complete with numerous parades, a masked ball, and costume contests. More importantly, the public image of Carnival as a time for the city's elite to display their wealth and social standing became secondary to the public's general enjoyment and participation in all aspects of the festival. Mardi Gras emerged as a national holiday celebrated in the unique setting of New Orleans. A reporter in Faulkner's novel, standing at the train station after Mardi Gras, observed the mass exodus of tourists: " 'Because they can go home now'; thinking of all the names of places which railroads go to, fanning out from the River's mouth to all of America; of the cold February names: Minnesota and Dakota and Michigan, the high iceclad riverreaches and the long dependable snow; 'yair, home now, knowing that they have got almost a year before they will have to get drunk and celebrate the fact that they will have more than eleven months before they will have to wear masks and get drunk and blow horns again.' " New Valoisians, like New Orleanians, converted their long-standing trade relationship with cities in the Mississippi River Valley from one of goods to one of people. In Carnival, tourists found reason to cast aside their everyday mores for a brief period of indulgence. And, more importantly, they planned to return in a yearly pilgrimage. "Every train, bus, airplane and passenger ship brought fresh loads of Carnival visitors, many from the frozen North, and every highway was a parade of automobiles whose license plates showed that practically every state in the nation will be represented in what authorities have predicted will be the greatest Mardi Gras throng on record," boasted the *Times-Picayune* in 1936, echoing Faulkner's observation. The emergence of the automobile and bus, along with the airplane, was part of the reason for the expansion of Mardi Gras crowds, but the Carnival crafted by New Orleans businessmen during the interwar years assured that travelers journeyed to the city again and again.[35]

CHAPTER 6

OLD NEW ORLEANS

Race and Tourism

As Fat Tuesday dawned in 1930, a rowdy bunch of Tulane University athletes crowded into a rented truck to sing, drink, and make merry havoc in the New Orleans streets. Groups of revelers commonly meandered in wagons or trucks or on foot to celebrate Mardi Gras. They started innocently, but after sipping some bootleg alcohol, the college boys quickly took to another tradition of Jim Crow New Orleans, the harassment of blacks. The white Tulane students threw eggs at black bystanders. Several black pedestrians retaliated by cursing at the students as they drove down St. Philip Street in the French Quarter. Eager to teach their victims a lesson in respecting white privilege, the athletes got out of their vehicle but faced more resistance than expected. A loud pop sounded above the melee. Joseph Lawrence, a white medical student, lay bleeding to death on the street, shot by black French Quarter resident Son Robertson.[1]

The incident revealed the racial tension underlying tourism and tourist sites, which, in the years after the First World War, were constructed by and for whites. New Orleans tourism reflected whites' acceptance of white supremacy. Blacks were expected to give whites leeway and to swallow their pride even in the face of insults. A black man who transgressed the white world of touristic New Orleans—whether on Canal Street, in the French Quarter, or along a parade route—risked his life if he did not show deference. White authority was not limited to policemen or prominent citizens but also included unruly adolescents and drunken college students. Although violence against blacks was common in Jim Crow New Orleans as well as across the country, whites expected blacks quietly to accept the assaults. Just a few days prior to the violent confrontation in the French Quarter, an incident occurred that revealed the complicity of even white officials in such racist actions. Ten white boys had accosted a black bystander while he awaited the arrival of the Momus parade. An eyewitness recalled them making the "usual request, 'move on nigger,'" only to turn to "combative force" when the man refused to comply. A disinterested white policeman feebly asked the youths "to leave the 'nigger' alone," but the boys paid no heed and chased their victim several blocks before they beat him unconscious with a "blunt instrument." Although racial violence was commonplace, forceful retaliation against white supremacy, such as the shooting of Lawrence, was rare. Whites usually denied that offenses to the black community had taken place. One of the college students, Edward Hebert, claimed that his friends had just picked up five sailors and were "going on happily enough" when a "crowd of negroes began following the truck and pulling at us, shouting insults to such an extent that eventually we clambered off and began fighting them." To Hebert, tossing eggs at black revelers—a practice that whites enjoyed—seemed a natural part of Mardi Gras revelry. The local press quickly exonerated Lawrence and his cohorts of any wrongdoing. According to white popular opinion, unruly blacks had attacked without provocation, taking the life of a promising young white man.[2]

In Jim Crow New Orleans, tourism sites and guides were developed to either erase traces of black culture or present blacks as subservient to whites. Blacks, with only a small middle class located primarily in large urban centers, lacked economic power during the interwar years. In New Orleans, they also lacked numbers, forming less than a third of the city's population.[3] Segregation laws and racial customs restricted black travel to and within New Orleans. The relationship of black culture, particularly jazz and Creole history, to the urban image forged by politicians, businessmen, and social activists reveals the extent to which leading white New Orleanians structured tourism in accordance with their belief in white supremacy. Jazz, a musical style created by black musicians, was suppressed in the 1920s. The wild wailing, the improvisational style, and the musicians' ties to vice encouraged what many whites, especially those of the upper classes, deemed lewd, sexually suggestive behavior. Jazz remained popular with the youth of both races despite the criticisms, and the fresh sound slowly entered mainstream American culture. In time, New Orleans tourism boosters seized on the city's role in birthing the musical form. The jazz embraced by civic leaders, however, was a whitened version that reinforced the racial hierarchy.

Concerns regarding miscegenation led tourism promoters to propagate the belief that white New Orleanians, especially the elite, had been racially pure throughout the city's history. The bugbear of race mixing not only threatened the lineage of white families but also tarnished the reputation of Creoles, the descendents of the city's French and Spanish settlers who figured prominently in the developing tourism industry as a romantic, exotic, noble, and above all white people. The light-skinned blacks who claimed Creole identity evidenced an urban history contrary to the mirage of racial purity constructed by whites. Given the international fame gained by such Creole jazzmen as Jelly Roll Morton and Sidney Bechet, white New Orleanians urgently needed to assert their claims of racial purity. Tourism provided boosters an opportunity to buttress the racial image of the city and its inhabitants, allowing Jim Crow a free hand in the marketing of area attractions.

Blacks were a curiosity for tourists to ogle. The rhetoric of boosters stripped blacks of agency. Those living on the dark side of the color line were described as contented servants eager to please white New Orleanians and tourists alike. Tourism businesses that employed blacks often dressed them in costumes, reinforcing their servile status as well as crafting an urban space that retained traditions that reached back into slave times. Marginalized blacks were thus essential to the urban myths cultivated by boosters.

Invented by Demons

In the winter of 1932, future blues legends David "Honeyboy" Edwards and Big Joe Williams left the juke joints and barrelhouses of the Mississippi Delta for the bars and dives of New Orleans. "In New Orleans, that was good hustling there," recalled Edwards. The men made a living on the streets, moving from time to time along a circuitous route that stretched east to Alabama and west to Texas, north to Chicago and south to the Crescent City. For a young guitarist such as Edwards, his first sojourn in a "big city" such as New Orleans with its "bright lights" left an indelible impression. The volume of activity captivated the troubadour: "There was streetcars and the Canal Ferry was running then, men loading banana boats on the river, people everywhere on wagons and in old cars and on horses. It was beautiful." Edwards and Williams stayed in the French Quarter with one of Williams's girlfriends. To earn money, the two men "would play around Rampart Street at the little joints, go in the bars, get chairs, and set down and play." The duo drifted through black neighborhoods and into areas traversed by white downtown shoppers and tourists. "We'd play in them bars, serenade in the streets, play for the whores, play at the train station, different places all over New Orleans," remembered Edwards. The musicians prospered in a city where it seemed they were the "only ones" strumming the rhythms of the Delta blues. New Orleans, after all, had "always been a jazz town."[4]

Making jazz an acceptable part of the New Orleans tourism industry took time. Although Edwards used the term to describe a musical style, *jazz* was laden with cultural meaning during the interwar years. Until the early 1930s, most white Americans, along with middle- and upper-class blacks, looked with disdain on the prevalence of jazz among culturally rebellious teenagers and young adults of both races. Political, business, and social leaders largely shared the view that the urban space should function as a machine, with each part—each citizen—contributing to the efficient production of prosperity. The arts supported by elites reflected the same structured harmony. Symphonies performed what businessmen and socialites saw as "real" music by bringing a disparate range of instruments into concord; conversely, the jarring turmoil of improvisational jazz shattered any attempt at order and bordered on chaos. As a result, jazz emerged not simply as a musical style but as a word synonymous with danger and disarray. Jazz also reflected white supremacist characterizations of blacks, who were thought to lack self-control. For New Orleans whites, Edwards might not have been playing jazz, but he was certainly jazzing—roaming from place to place with little purpose other than self-gratification. White civic leaders there, as elsewhere in the United States, diligently worked to mute the popular new musical form.

When New Orleanians glanced at the front page of the *Times-Picayune* on 28 February 1921, the largely white audience read an article that summarized popular opinion about the new musical style. Princeton University professor Henry Van Dyke sharply attacked jazz as a public menace. He decried the wild sounds and dancing, especially as a segment of American youths embraced the new rhythms. "Jazz music was invented by demons for the torture of imbeciles," declared Van Dyke. Furthermore, jazz was a "deadly art" threatening society's moral fabric. Those who heard Van Dyke expound on the dangers of jazz were no archconservatives or religious fanatics pushed to the margins of mainstream American society: they were teachers. Van Dyke had spoken at the National Education Association convention in Atlantic City.[5]

Whether to lampoon or celebrate, whites linked jazz to blackness. White revelers during Mardi Gras, for example, frequently donned blackface and stepped to jazz-related dances in the streets. They carried with them instruments or simply pretended to play instruments, like the six "black-faced" celebrants in 1923 who "warbled" while one man cut loose on a paper flute. Even many of the names given to the faddish dances of the 1920s recognized the role of African American culture in giving birth to what many whites deemed immodest moves. White women and men happily performed the Black Bottom in the streets during Mardi Gras or in halls throughout New Orleans during the rest of the year.[6]

Jazz's assertiveness clashed with the white vision of submissive blacks.

Tales about the past regularly harped on black musicians who catered to a white audience by playing reels and waltzes. Longtime New Orleans resident George Kernion fondly recalled the days of his youth in the late 1800s, when the white elite held private social gatherings at which " 'Snow Ball' shone in all his glory." Kernion continued, "Snow Ball was a negro, black as an ace of spades and a natural-born musician. He led an orchestra composed of violins, drum, cello, cornet and piano and was much in demand by all good dancers and among the best people of the Vieux Carre." Kernion's memories denied Snow Ball his real name, recognizing only his nickname, an ironic reference to the extreme blackness of his skin. The nickname also reflected black subservience to white authority and to white definitions of music. Kernion flatly stated, "He played real music and not that kind of abomination known today as Rag Time, which so many claim to be tuneful and agreable [sic] to the ear." The grandeur of the past depended on the maintenance of racial barriers and black submission to white authority.[7]

Whites labored to perpetuate so-called real music. In 1921, for example, New Orleans businessmen expressed concern about the plight of local musicians. Working through the Association of Commerce, a group of businessmen urged the creation of a municipal band, explaining that "it is practically impossible for musicians in New Orleans to make a living unless they are employed in one of the theatres, and not only is the demand outside of theatres small, but it is decreasing with the popular demand for music other than classical." The word *musicians* strictly applied to performers of classical styles. To play other forms of music threatened to demean the performer.[8]

Commentators connected bad music with bad behavior. Numerous black jazz innovators, including Louis Armstrong and Jelly Roll Morton, learned their art in Storyville before signing record deals during the interwar years. The scarlet dens of New Orleans blended sex, music, and race into a potent elixir young Americans found difficult to resist. However, older Americans considered the musical form troublesome. Jazz rhythms spurred wild, suggestive dance steps that led to close interaction between the sexes, leading many observers to associate the music with sex and rebellious youth. A series of articles in the *Times-Picayune* during the late 1920s and early 1930s asked readers and numerous prominent personalities a question: "What Is Sex Appeal?" One respondent noted that concern with the subject simply reflected the times: "The public picked it up because it fit into the jazz era of frank discussion. Youths discussed it without even a blush. It gave them an excuse to talk about things their grandmothers had never breathed." Jazz music represented a breakdown of taboos.[9]

White critics argued that the physical and social refinement attributed to a person with an appreciation for symphonic music easily crumbled from the vibrations of a wailing jazz band. Although people might not appreciate high art, constant attention to it supposedly led to uplift. The Association of Commerce explained to its members that attempts at self-improvement forced many individuals "to enjoy BACH, when we really would much rather hear tuneful melodies." Admirers of classical music entered a "better environment with the result that before long we become a part of that sphere—we begin to understand—and thus on through a constant progression." The more attention people gave to high art, the more quickly they improved themselves. This reasoning easily operated in the reverse as well. Jazz degraded its listeners: "If we appreciate and receive only the lowest forms of music, those that are simplest in construction and therefore easiest to understand— i.e. JAZZ—we must admit that in at least a musical respect, we are uncultured." Despite the effort to withhold an indictment of jazz admirers as degenerates, the implication was clear. Jazz contrasted with classical music in style and effect. Blaring horns and wailing woodwinds retarded character.[10]

Prominent local blacks such as the supporters of the city's black-operated *Louisiana Weekly* shared white concerns about jazz and the damage the music inflicted on efforts at racial uplift. The publishers expressed their disgust in a parable: "When the animals held a convention once upon a time the story says that all went well until a jackass brayed. Then everything left the hall in disgust except the snakes, alley-bats, cats, dogs[,] donkeys and monkeys." Part of the success of the new musical form—and part of the reason middle- and upper-class blacks dreaded jazz—stemmed from whites' perception of black performers as primitive. For middle-class blacks, many of whom adopted white cultural standards as a sign of racial progress, jazz reinforced white biases. Rather than reveal artistry, jazz supposedly showcased the lack of sophistication within the black race. The *Louisiana Weekly* advocated extreme measures to control the musical contagion: "The jazz and the public dance has its grasp upon the public so strong that it's a question of time when this menace will have to be checked by law." [11]

That any whites embraced, even celebrated, a black musical form caused great consternation among elite white New Orleanians. "One of the strangest of human inconsistencies is that while Americans actually love the tuneful, soulful and stately old songs more than these maniacal travesties on the beautiful, the big commercial demand is for jazz," remarked the *Times-Picayune* in 1923. The newspaper's musings came in response to a survey that found that most white Americans cherished old-time tunes such as "Old Folks at Home," "Dixie," "Home, Sweet Home," and "My Old Kentucky Home"—songs clearly grounded in a white viewpoint. The focus was on a wholesome home life defined by white cultural standards. "Dixie," the battle hymn of the Confederacy, and "My Old Kentucky Home," a tribute to a society in which blacks showed complete contentment, glossed over black grievances. The racial hierarchy stood firm. Although the persistent admiration of old-time tunes reassured white defenders of taste, the same survey revealed that the respondents purchased stacks of jazz records. The newspaper carefully explained the paradox in veiled racial terms. In a constant pursuit of "something 'new and different,'" white Americans certainly enjoyed jazz. But the *Times-Picayune* denied the "decadence on the part of public taste." White supremacy demanded racial unity. Americans, after all, remained devoted to the "grand old songs." Instead, the New Orleans press blamed the composers for peddling "decadence" and "rubbish." [12]

The concerns about jazz stemmed as much from the feared loss of aesthetic music as from the actual transformation of the listener. Charles Deutschman, national president of the Association of Piano Tuners, informed a 1927 gathering at a prominent Canal Street store of the physical harm inflicted by jazz. "The constant clubbing of jazz masters rings on natural musical ears until they become perverted and cannot appreciate the wrist and finger piano music of artists," exclaimed Deutschman. Jazz did not merely change musical taste but actually damaged listeners' ears to such an extent that their hearing was "forever ruined." The loss of musical taste made one no better than those who enjoyed jazz—that is, members of the black community that nurtured the musical form. For white commentators, it was as if jazz resulted in the devolution of white listeners. The jazz debate echoes the findings of historian Joel Williamson in his study of race in the early decades of the twentieth century. Blackness and whiteness were malleable concepts. Consequently, as Williamson has written, "It was possible in the South for one who was biologically pure white to become black by behavior." Jazz therefore threatened to lead to both cultural and racial deterioration by making whites the equivalents of blacks.[13]

To sandbag civilization against the rising tide of black music, white New Orleanians expanded school music programs with the idea that fostering appreciation of classical music at an early age would immunize children against infectious jazz rhythms. A policy established in the mid-1910s brought phonographs to every white school in the city, enabling educators to use recordings to acquaint children with symphonic composers. According to a 1921 *Times-Picayune* report, the school system tied music to a litany of topics. School standards dictated "the correlation of selections with pictures, story telling, history, English, geography, drawing, and nature study." Furthermore, students increasingly learned to play instruments. Student orchestras "sprung up like mushrooms dotting the expanse of the school system." The *Times-Picayune* declared that "children are being taught to appreciate good music and to reject the bad." New Orleanians had high praise for the expanding program. "The cultural standards of thousands of future United States citizens are being raised every year by the appreciation of music as taught in the public schools of New Orleans," the paper concluded. To ensure students' cultural development, the Orleans Parish School Board in 1922 explicitly prohibited jazz music or dances related to jazz within its jurisdiction. Some New Orleanians even sought to safeguard the lessons taught within the schools by hiring former students to perform music for the rest of the community. As late as 1935, local businessmen advocated the formation of a symphony orchestra, with "the nucleus therefor to be drawn from graduates of our public schools."[14]

While schools strove to bolster youngsters' affection for classical performances, civic leaders in 1923 joined fellow Americans in inaugurating the first national Music Week aimed at the general population. The city adopted the measure, according to M. A. Caruso, chair of the local Music Committee, "for the purpose of developing in New Orleans an appreciation of good music with a view to recovering for our city some of its lost musical prestige." The annual celebration was designed to foster grassroots-level appreciation for quality music. Organizers of Music Week wanted to stop the encroachment of jazz into American culture, a culture defined by whites. The program included "the playing of special music in the churches of the city on the first day (Sunday) of the period; a band concert in the business district at noon Monday; and the rendering of special programs by theatres and musical schools throughout the week," thereby tying respectable music to religion, business, and education. Jazz was banned from entertainment venues. "Theatres will be asked to play a special selection as part of the evening's program and, in the case of photoplay houses, to abstain from the use of jazz music," reported the Association of Commerce, which fully supported Music Week. Area universities played chime music, and local churches hosted organ recitals. Establishments with dance floors were asked to play waltzes. In addition, area blacks were urged to participate in "a 'Jubilee Sing.'" Spirituals and slave songs packaged black music in a form acceptable to white ears. Music, according to organizers of the annual festivities, affirmed the social order.[15]

White supremacy underlay the Music Week movement. In 1927, New Orleans organizers proclaimed, "Music Week is set aside each year with the object of helping to maintain human interest in good music, one of the fundamental arts of the race." Though speaking in terms of the human "race," the focus of Music Week revealed a bias toward white achievements. Classical music tied American whites to Europe—in particular, to the Germanic composers who, some contemporary racial theorists held, had descended from allegedly pure white Nordic stock. Waltzes, church hymns, and the work of composers such as Bach linked whites to European traditions. As the objectives outlined in 1932 demonstrated, Music Week sought to "advance the art of music" among institutions of "accepted standardization" as well as civic projects of a "legitimate kind." The litmus test for music as well as other forms of artistry rested in the ability of art to promote "worthy citizenship." Whites, of course, defined such qualifiers as "accepted," "legitimate," and "worthy." [16]

In the 1930s, however, the purpose of Music Week began to shift from combating jazz to easing anxieties caused by a languid economy. Edification became a secondary concern. At the start of the decade, public schools during Music Week gave performances exhibiting the "evolution of the brass band." How much, if any, jazz slipped into the program is unknown. However, New Orleanians, aware of the prominence of brass instruments in jazz, were very likely reminded of the controversial art form, especially given the role of traditional march music and jazz in Mardi Gras. Later music programs made the link with leisure more explicit. Music Week coordinators announced in 1934 that the "primary purpose of the week is to develop a more fruitful use of leisure through music." Though still significant in fortifying civic virtue, music now served more as a means of uplifting human spirits. As New Orleans planners explained, the program was "especially important . . . since music offers a salutary form of recreation and serves to strengthen the general community morale." By the late 1930s, the Music Week program aimed to "direct the attention of each community upon its own constructive musical forces, and to stimulate and encourage them." Promoting local unity mitigated the alienating effect of unemployment and poverty. In addition, celebrating indigenous musical creativity proved locals' ability to adapt to change, an important lesson given the times. Charles Behre, a prominent member of the Association of Commerce and chairman of the committee responsible for arranging the 1938 Music Week program, argued that the national movement gave "praise to the local musical and other cultural forces whose influence promotes the best interests of the community." [17]

The range of musical styles accepted as worthy of white ears broadened. By the mid-1930s, Music Week became as much a folk festival as a celebration of classical music and church hymns. The inclusion of folk songs left intact a racial barrier between blacks and whites. Contemporary scholars argued that folk songs, especially those recorded in the isolated hollows of the Ozarks or Appalachians, exhibited the vitality of white America. Mountaineers were believed to be Anglo-Saxons untainted by the influx of immigrant Italians, Jews, Slavs, and other ethnic groups as well as the large U.S. black population. In New Orleans, however, the songs of the Creoles, a people defended by local writers as racially pure whites, substituted for the music of the old English folk. The 1936 Music Week included "traditional songs and dances of the white people of New Orleans in the period prior to 1860." The growing acceptance of indigenous forms of music opened the door to styles previously shunned. But the door cracked only wide enough to allow black groups variety in voicing their subservience to whites. Plantation songs and dances joined river songs and "local street cries, Indian songs or cries of French Market sellers of herbs" as part of the Music Week celebration. The rhymes of black street vendors as well as the songs of Italian and other ethnic groups received attention. Although storytelling and handicrafts also became part of the festivities, the emphasis remained on music. Folk songs, as defined at the time, lacked a tone of social criticism. Indeed, work chants and cries celebrated service to white consumers while maintaining racial and ethnic stereotypes. Such folk tunes, according to the New Orleans press, sprang from the "heart of the people" and reflected the "wholesome happiness" of Americans. At a time of paralyzing economic crisis, folk songs and practices represented the vitality of the nation but did so without jeopardizing white supremacy.[18]

Even jazz slowly emerged from the cultural dungeons. Disdain for jazz waned in New Orleans public schools. Throughout the interwar years, blatantly underfunded black schools existed in neighborhoods where brothels and bars cradled jazz. The close proximity of jazz bands fostered students' appreciation of the sounds drifting from area establishments. Teachers began instructing students on the alluring musical style. White schools also failed to resist the intoxicating, fresh rhythms. Students at Samuel J. Peters Boys' High School formed a popular jazz band in the late 1920s, and legendary performer Pete Fountain remembered his participation in a group organized at Warren Easton Boys' High School in the mid-1930s. Though the school system continued to ban jazz, the music gained a foothold in the classroom. The prohibition of jazz became a dead letter.[19]

White anxiety about jazz further dissipated as black musicians became culturally isolated from the musical form they had created. The trend reflected not only New Orleanians' reluctance to credit blacks but also white Americans' continued discomfort with jazz as played by blacks. From the earliest performances of jazz bands, segregation played a role in the way listeners enjoyed the music. Louis Armstrong recalled the cardinal rule of bands that played aboard steamboats in the years just after the First World War: "We were colored, and we knew what that meant. We were not allowed to mingle with the white guests under any circumstances. We were there to play good music for them, and that was all." Some whites nevertheless befriended the musicians, even inviting the performers home. Yet such experiences constituted exceptions to an otherwise rigid racial system common in the halls frequented by white aficionados of jazz. Bassist George Murphy "Pops" Foster, a New Orleanian who plied the Mississippi River with Armstrong, recalled an incident from 1926 in which a jazz band violated racial protocols in Miami, Florida. While playing a gig, several band members stepped from the stage with the intention of teaching "some white girls to dance." A group of outraged white men who witnessed the interracial contact subsequently ambushed and tarred and feathered the musicians. One musician died from the assault. Foster's band, which was scheduled to travel to Miami shortly after the murder, asked the local police chief if he could provide protection given the racially charged atmosphere. As Foster remembered, "He said he couldn't because down there they didn't want colored playing for whites and we didn't go." Fear of future incidents of racial interaction had led to the removal of black performers from bandstands.[20]

During the 1930s, many black jazz artists suffered despite the growing popular interest in indigenous art and cultural forms. Jelly Roll Morton had fashioned a lucrative career as a recording artist in the 1920s; by the late 1930s, however, he found the doors of the music industry harder to pry open. Although American tastes had changed somewhat, Morton recognized that his declining fortunes had much to do with the recording industry's attitude toward black performers, and the frustrated New Orleans pianist soon took an anti-Semitic view of the various New York record labels and radio programs that ignored him, writing to a friend that "the Jews are in the dominating position at this time, they are in control of the Union, Radio Stations publishers, booking agents & etc. . . . [T]hey have put most everyone out of business but the jews or communist." Morton, a proud Creole, hesitated to see his blackness as a factor barring his continued success, focusing on Jews to disguise his anger at the success of white jazzmen over their black counterparts. Similarly, Morton's fellow New Orleans musician, Bunk Johnson, who had taken to the rice and sugarcane fields around New Iberia, Louisiana, returned to his trumpet at the start of the Second World War, hoping to find work in bustling San Francisco, where wartime mobilization brought a flood of military personnel and war industry workers. Johnson's dreams soon burst on the harsh reality of race relations in America. In a 1944 letter to close friend and jazz historian William Russell, Johnson decried the "dam big City." "I'm not doing a dam thing here in San Francisco and they aint nothing to be done here at all in the line of Music for a Colored Musician as I told you before in my letters that it is only the White Musicians that is making the big money here." Even Johnson's attempt to be the front man for a white band failed to open opportunities: as he wrote in another letter, "I thought by having a white band that I would of been playing Every night making real good money here in San Francisco but I was all out the way about it but now I know for shore so the white band donot mean a Dam thing a colored musician donot have a chance out here Calif." The mainstream popularity of jazz offered most of Louisiana's black musicians only empty promises of financial success.[21]

New Orleans venues likewise promoted white rather than black jazz musicians. Captain Verne Streckfus headed a family that had plied the

Mississippi and Ohio Rivers with excursion steamboats since 1903. The vessels had carried some of the earliest jazz bands, but Streckfus noted that his family always emphasized "pretty" music. Dancers heard fox-trots, waltzes, and one-steps. For a time, the Streckfus family hired the director of music for New Orleans's Saenger Theater to instruct bands on the graceful performance of traditional dance steps. Moreover, according to Streckfus, each summer, when steamboats docked at towns and cities to offer entertainment to local citizens, the deluxe vessels carried white bands, while black bands entertained on the less lavish craft, and the admission price was cheaper.[22]

Land-based venues shared much the same concerns. White musicians commonly performed at the more prestigious clubs, thereby contributing to the redefinition of jazz as a white rather than black musical form. Writing about dance bands for *Harper's Magazine* in 1941, Irving Kolodin noted the discrimination against black musicians in the nation's hotel ballrooms. Even the most prestigious New York establishments hesitated to break the color line: "There is a widespread legend that the transient trade of the large 'commercial' hotels in New York includes many persons from the South, and that they would be offended to find themselves in a dining room where the musicians were colored." Hotels erred on the side of caution. New Orleans certainly fit the pattern. During the late 1930s, the Roosevelt Hotel's famed Hawaiian Blue Room featured a white band headed by Abe Lyman. "The Lyman dance music is superior to any ever heard in New Orleans," boasted the hotel's publication, the *Roosevelt Review*. Beneath the typical hyperbole of such advertisements lay disregard for black music in the city. The first issue of *Louisiana Tourist*, a monthly magazine inaugurated by the state tourist bureau in 1938, carried a small photo of a white clarinet player with the caption, "Jazz music originated in Louisiana." The meaning was clear: white men played jazz.[23]

Promotional literature about New Orleans reshaped perceptions of jazz into a form more acceptable to whites. In 1948, the New Orleans Hostess Service issued a booklet that proudly boasted of the city's role as the birthplace of jazz: "This new, pulsing rhythm spread like fire across the nation. Feet began to tap and New Orleans had given a folk music to the world which gained immortality." Although the Hostess Service pointed to jazz's origins in "the folk songs, the waterfront ballads, the music which the Negroes and West Indians played so energetically at their shakedowns," the publication downplayed black contributions when it declared the city the "birthplace of jazz, or swing music." Swing, with its big bands capable of performing hit tunes with little variation, tamed the dangers of improvisation. By adopting the word *orchestra*, many bandleaders linked themselves to a classical tradition. Although a few big bands were integrated and some all-black swing orchestras gained success, the emergence of swing began an era in which black musicians found employment increasingly difficult. To emphasize the difference between wild, black jazz and the milder, whitened swing, the Hostess Service included two articles on facing pages. On the left, readers were informed about "Nightlife." The accompanying illustrations showed a photograph of Canal Street at night and a sketch of a dance hall filled with white couples with a white female singer sitting on a piano played by a white male. On the right, new residents learned about "Folklore." Although the article focused on voodoo, the illustration for this piece showed two bare-chested black men beating on drums deep in a swamp. Near a campfire, a topless black woman danced. The contrast between the two illustrations was sharp. Whites supposedly possessed a refined culture, even if New Orleans's attractions included "girlie shows" on Bourbon Street. Blacks, conversely, were presented as crude, superstitious, and sexually aggressive. The curious, according to the Hostess Service, could still find believers in voodoo, though the practice was "confined solely to the sale of harmless powders in Negro drug stores and to the occasional harmless charms which are found about." [24]

Even when they received credit in white publications or at tourist-oriented events, black jazz performers were forced to bow to white supremacy. In 1949, for example, the New Orleans Jazz Club publicized an inaugural season of concerts. The *Old French Quarter News*, a weekly neighborhood newspaper for Vieux Carré residents and businesses, reported the popularity of the events with locals and tourists. Black musician Papa Celestin and his band, the Tuxedoes, concluded the series, drawing a record crowd as more than one thousand tourists and locals crammed "all available tables and chairs and standing room in the rear of the enclosure." Although the concert series celebrated black jazzmen, the musicians performed in Beauregard Square. The park, built in honor of local Confederate General P. G. T. Beauregard, had erased from city maps the black meeting ground known as Congo Square. A space famed for black music and dance was converted into a site that reassured whites, locals and tourists alike, of their superiority.[25]

A celebration of a black jazz pioneer such as Celestin could easily turn into a celebration of Jim Crow society. In 1953, Celestin visited the White House, where he shook hands with President Dwight Eisenhower. In a radio interview with Louisiana Congressman F. Edward Hébert, who had introduced Celestin to the White House in a "wonderful speech," the jazzman recalled how the president received him as a soldier, treating him with respect—as an equal. Hébert praised Celestin and his art in the radio program carried on WNOE, a New Orleans station. By visiting the president, Celestin and his Dixieland jazz band honored the state and the region. The Louisiana politician, however, manipulated the meeting into a message supportive of the racial status quo. Hébert concluded the interview by condemning the actions of desegregationists who sought to interfere with race relations below the Mason-Dixon Line. Hébert thereby defused a White House event suggestive of racial equality, reinterpreting the encounter to preserve Celestin's role as a black minstrel subject to white rule.[26]

By the 1940s, white popular opinion in New Orleans had come to embrace jazz as an integral part of the tourist image presented in guidebooks and promotional literature. The soulful musicians blowing into clarinets and trumpets at local nightspots popular with whites looked much different from the performers who originated the sound that brought fame to the Crescent City. Civic leaders honored the city's importance as the birthplace of jazz but did so by denying blacks the fruits of the style they had invented. To suit the tastes of white, middle-class tourists as well as well-to-do locals, jazz was whitened. Although dancing to jazz might cause a person to act out primal impulses, the presence of white performers ensured that white listeners did not degrade themselves to the point of behaving like blacks. Camaraderie between musicians and dancers, both male and female, was much more palatable when the two were of the same race. Any racial transgression was not merely figurative in New Orleans, where light-skinned blacks boasted a proud independence and frequently passed as white, even marrying into white families. In such a city, the enjoyment of jazz called into question racial lineage as well as taste. But turning jazz into a white musical form offered only a partial solution to the problem of tying the city's musical heritage to its burgeoning tourism industry. Boosters still needed to interweave the color line through the urban history recounted to tourists.

Class and Caste

When Frances Oliver, the sister of legendary jazz pianist Jelly Roll Morton, sat down for an interview in 1969, she remembered a family uneasy about the young musician's choice of careers. A black pianist in the years before the First World War found little work outside the brothels of Storyville. Morton's grandmother regularly scolded him for "staying out all night," and Morton attempted to hide his pursuit of a musical career by claiming to work the night shift at a local cooperage. The family tension Oliver remembered had as much to do with questions of race and status as with Morton working in a brothel. "At one time some of the Creole people in downtown New Orleans believed in *class* and *caste*, but my brother wasn't prejudiced against dark people," recalled Oliver. Nevertheless, the light-skinned Morton emphasized his European lineage rather than his African blood. He learned as a youth that music was a serious matter, a lesson emphasized by the Morton family's patronage of the French Opera House. A brothel-based piano man, in contrast, served baser tastes both in style and showmanship. He was seen as degrading himself, becoming not a refined performer—no matter what his talents—but simply a black man putting into action his primitive impulses. By embracing and developing jazz, Morton transgressed a racial boundary vital to some members of his family who still prided themselves on being light-skinned, cultured Creoles, not merely descendents of Africans. He had little choice, however. Jim Crow laws had collapsed the city's multiracial heritage into two tiers, white and colored.[27]

Elite New Orleans whites went to great lengths not only to deny the identity of black Creoles such as Morton but also to downplay black contributions to the city. The rush of white youths to hear jazz bands put parents on edge for fear that the music might lead to disorder and immorality, traits whites linked with blacks in the same way Morton's grandmother looked down on those with darker skin. Among whites, however, the efforts of families such as the Mortons were in vain. City leaders did not stop at segregation but also whitewashed the past by actively erasing traces of black history from New Orleans culture. Only picturesque blacks—clearly caricatures—remained. In a city that increasingly marketed itself to white American tourists, the reduction of blacks to stereotypes eliminated the threat of black agency, with its potential to disrupt the carefully constructed image of New Orleans as an exotic, romantic leisure site defined by white American middle-class standards.

White civic leaders structured the cityscape to reflect their vision of the past and to reinforce their values in the present, thus giving New Orleans a white supremacist tint. Black residents long recognized the dangers of traversing Canal Street, a thoroughfare popular among female shoppers and out-of-towners, "most of them white," according to New Orleans writer Robert Tallant. Random acts of racial violence regularly occurred on Canal Street. The message of white supremacy had been physically manifested on the street since 1891. Only a year after the state legislature segregated railroads in a law subsequently made famous by *Plessy v. Ferguson*, prominent citizens erected a large obelisk on the Canal Street median near the Mississippi River. The monument paid homage to the Crescent City White League, an organization that attempted to liberate Louisiana from the supposed tyranny of Radical Republicanism during the September 1874 Battle of Liberty Place. According to a guidebook published in the 1910s, some locals fondly recalled the pitched battle as the "Bunker Hill of New Orleans." The monument's prominence in guidebooks reinforced the message that the downtown retail center belonged to the city's hegemonic white population.[28]

Numerous sites culturally important to black New Orleanians vanished in the early twentieth century. In addition to the replacement of Congo Square by Beauregard Square and the Municipal Auditorium, the St. Louis Hotel, a center for slave auctions during the antebellum period, deteriorated until a 1915 hurricane inflicted irreparable damage. More significantly, a 1919 fire destroyed the French Opera House, which had long stood as a prominent symbol not only of the city's artistic sophistication but also of its racially mixed population. Creoles with black ancestry proudly subscribed to the performances, a tradition cherished by anyone of French descent. Jelly Roll Morton recalled, "We always had musicians in the family, but they played for their own pleasure and would not accept it seriously, and always considered a musician (with the exception of those who would appear at the French Opera House, which was always supported with their patronage) a scalawag, lazy, and trying to duck work." The elegant hall served as a marker of refinement within the Creole community of black ancestry. When white civic leaders decided not to rebuild the facility, blacks of French heritage permanently lost part of their urban legacy.[29]

Elite white families closely guarded their bloodlines and carefully crafted the city's image to reinforce the illusion of white racial purity. The suggestion that "black blood" contaminated prominent white families scandalized socialites, businessmen, and politicians. In nationally popular novels written in the late nineteenth century, George Washington Cable, who was white, suggested that some blacks were more honorable and successful than their white relatives. Public outrage forced Cable to abandon his residence in New Orleans, and several New Orleanians took up their pens to refute his accusations. Charles Gayarré, a white Creole and a historian, took it upon himself to respond in print and in lecture halls to Cable's allegedly libelous works, forging an image of Creoles as a white people of the highest character. When Gayarré died in 1895, his close friend, Grace King, seized the banner of Creole racial purity and held it high until her death in the 1930s. In her autobiography, King decried Cable's "preference for colored people over white" and the assumed "superiority—according to his theories—of the quadroons over the Creoles." "He was a native of New Orleans," explained King, "and had been well treated by its people, and yet he stabbed the city in the back, as we felt, in a dastardly way to please the Northern press." Whereas Gayarré remained a local figure, King sought to introduce his noble, romantic Creole population to a national audience, using her popularity as a writer to counteract the negative impressions spread by Cable. King soon gave birth to a racial history of New Orleans that became the dominant version accepted by local whites and marketed to tourists well into the twentieth century.[30]

In *New Orleans: The Place and the People*, published in 1907, King outlined the city's once unique three-tiered racial system: "During the *ancien régime* in Louisiana, the pure-blooded African was never called coloured, but always negro. The *gens de couleur*, coloured people, were a class apart, separated from and superior to the negroes, ennobled, were it by only one drop of white blood in their veins." Though King defended Creoles' racial integrity, she did not deny the existence of light-skinned blacks within New Orleans. She took great care, however, to exonerate local whites of charges of miscegenation, arguing that the various groups of light-skinned blacks had been brought to Louisiana rather than made there: "The caste seems to have existed from the first introduction of slaves."[31]

To further ease white anxiety over miscegenation, King contrasted the laxity of racial standards in France with the rigorous separation of races enforced by the United States to explain why many light-skinned blacks fled to Europe. No figure was more dangerous than that of the quadroon woman. According to King, the desire of quadroons to "rise from a lower level to social equality with a superior race" led light-skinned black women to a "relaxation and deviation from, if not their complete denial of, the code of morality accepted by white women." Whites responded to the threat with legislation. The children of black mothers were classified as black no matter the race of the father. Stern laws separated the races, making New Orleans less hospitable to quadroons who attempted with "great ambition" to pass themselves and their children as white. King sharply criticized qua-droons: "Unscrupulous and pitiless, by nature or circumstance, as one chooses to view it, and secretly still claiming the racial license of Africa, they were, in regard to family purity, domestic peace, and household dignity, the most insidious and the deadliest foes a community ever possessed." Their "unwholesome notoriety" proved too alluring to white men, whom King saw as victims of quadroon advances. King even allowed that bribery "could be" used to circumvent race laws. Quadroons' intense desire to enter refined society led to many an "honourable marriage," although King remained silent on whether such unions joined light-skinned partners or interracial couples. Despite her vagueness on this point, King made certain to argue that the quest for social legitimacy by the quadroon wife resulted in the couple "removing" themselves to France, where they "obtained full social recognition for themselves and their children." France served as a melting pot that kept white New Orleans families racially pure.[32]

By the 1920s, King had carved a mold of white Creole society that cast an attractive image of New Orleans. Her influential 1921 book, the aptly titled *Creole Families of New Orleans*, chronicled the histories of several prominent white French families with lineages dating to the colonial era. The choice of the word *Creole* for her study, which focused only on whites, revealed the extent to which King ignored black New Orleanians' rich cultural heritage. According to King, the "genealogical records bear witness to [whites'] good blood; their 'maintenances de noblesse' are still in existence, brought with them from France, in simple accord with what they considered a family necessity, as much so as a house and furniture." King's landmark work argued that the French colonial settlers defended their racial purity just as vigorously as later Anglo-American residents. The slaves of white Creoles were "the best of servants, purchased with a careful eye from a market stocked with samples of the best tribes of Africa, and bought without regard to price." White Creoles had considered light-skinned slaves better than their darker counterparts and had consequently preferred to import paler bondsmen and -women. Although King remained consistent in her claims that New Orleans's light-skinned slaves had been imported rather than born in the city, she now denied that any blacks could penetrate white ranks. White Creoles lived in a "society that, although gay, was kept within the bounds of the proper and the discreet by the rigid maintenance of the etiquette of society in Paris, and the strict enforcement of French laws for preserving the purity of blood and family prestige." No bribery, as suggested in her previous books, could circumscribe the racial integrity laws. Officials stringently guarded civil and church records. Moreover, families carefully arranged marriages using "private ways" to ensure the legitimacy of the engaged couple. "The scrutiny was keen and inexorable," King assured her readers.[33]

Maintaining the racial purity of white Creoles meant that only two colors—black and white—mattered to the creators of New Orleans's touristic image, who completely denied the claims of light-skinned black Creoles with ties to old-line white families. Although the presence of variant skin colors within the black community was obvious, the white New Orleans elite jokingly discounted any evidence that light-skinned blacks might pass themselves off as whites. One civic activist and friend of King frequently recounted a tale about a black domestic servant who testified in a libel case involving accusations of miscegenation. According to the story, the woman told the court, "You see, Judge, it's like this; when you pour black coffee into your breakfast cup, and then pour in milk, the coffee gets whiter and whiter; but you know that the black coffee is there, no matter how white it looks!" Keeping alive the servant's words comforted whites by suggesting that blacks understood the futility of crossing the color line. In white popular opinion, the stain of black blood indelibly marked those of mixed lineage.[34]

Freed from the taint of miscegenation, Creoles became a valuable means of packaging New Orleans culture. Their traditions helped make New Orleans unique. Local writers, themselves interested in selling products or services to tourists, reinforced arguments about Creole racial integrity. Tourism boosters such as Lyle Saxon and Harnett Kane, both of whom followed in King's footsteps, emphasized that remnants of Creole culture survived into the present, hinting to tourists that actual encounters with an honorable, exotic people remained possible. Saxon penned numerous newspaper articles and books describing the grandeur of Creole life. In a piece frequently republished verbatim in guidebooks throughout the interwar years, Saxon lectured, "What does 'Creole' mean? No, of course not. I don't know why tourists always say that. The Creole is not of colored blood. The word means French and Spanish." Saxon's Creoles descended directly from white Europeans. None of their bloodlines reached to the slave quarters. His piece admonished tourists for thinking that Creoles were of black ancestry, and he could not contain his praise of the city's white ancestors: "The New Orleans Creole is our finest product. The women are lovely. The men are brave. They have charming manners. They are exclusive. They are clannish." Saxon certified the racial purity of the Creoles by emphasizing their strong attachment to their culture and lineage. Creoles' supposedly reclusive qualities not only supplied tour guides and writers with a means of justifying their services to tourists, who might not otherwise gain access to the secretive world of the Creoles, but also sheltered the Vieux Carré's legendary French inhabitants from accusations of miscegenation. As for the confusion regarding racial identities, Saxon explained that "the reason the word 'Creole' has been so often misunderstood is because their slaves spoke Creole dialect, bearing about the same relation to pure French as our Southern negro talk does to English purely spoken." Saxon's close friend, Flo Field, also stressed the purity of Creole blood and culture. A tour guide and playwright, she told visitors about the elegance found in the homes of former white French residents of the Vieux Carré. In a 1929 guide to New Orleans, an associate of Field praised her "rendition of Creole and 'Cadgin' stories," which were deemed "inimitable, full of a superb and rich charm." In one of the earliest examples of the blurring of Creole and Cajun culture, Field implicitly linked the French residents of New Orleans to the Acadian refugees living in southern Louisiana. Like the secluded Appalachian mountain folk, the isolated Cajuns were viewed as free from the taint of black blood. By intermingling stories from both cultures, Field cleverly tied tourists' perception of the racially pure Cajuns to the Creoles in New Orleans.[35]

Businesses possessed a vested interest in clarifying the meaning of *Creole*. Marketing campaigns aimed at tourists benefited from allusions to the exotic, and New Orleans's French heritage served as a prime means of advertising goods and food. Gluck's Restaurant, for example, issued a small souvenir booklet for tourists that presented the history of the city. The definition of *Creole* played a prominent role: "Everything that is 'good' in New Orleans is 'Creole.' The highest praise that can be bestowed upon any article for sale along the streets and in the country is to declare that it is 'Creole.'" Yet the booklet made a point of clarifying the racial meaning of the word: "One hears, too, the term 'Creole Negroes,' but it must be remembered always that this is a fine distinction, meaning blacks and colored people that are Louisiana-bred and born and French-speaking as distinguished from the Negroes of other States." Racial mixing was beyond the pale: "Creole means 'white,' though . . . it has been given many shades of signification—shades which have been taken up by ignorant scribblers and gradually accepted by many Northerners as meaning Louisianians of mixed blood." The Gluck guide informed readers that nothing was more "erroneous" than the conception of Creoles tainted by miscegenation, for "never was a nobler or more pure-blooded race than the Creoles of Louisiana." A comparison to the colonial Dutch settlers of the Hudson Valley provided an analogy northern tourists could readily comprehend: "In Louisiana 'Creole' has much the same meaning that 'Knickerbocker' has in New York."[36]

So important was the question of Creole whiteness to tourism and the image of New Orleans that even city officials joined efforts to safeguard the bloodlines of the celebrated French and Spanish. When tourist Harry Bowman asked City Hall for information about Creoles in 1926, he promptly received a letter from Mayor Arthur O'Keefe's secretary explaining that *Creole* applied only to "white descendents of French or Spanish settlers in Louisiana, or their colonies, who preserve the speech and culture of those countries." The municipal government's official stance pointedly excluded local ethnic groups as well as blacks: "It does not apply to negroes, or descendents of negroes, nor does it apply to persons of nationalities or their descendents, born either in Louisiana, or French or Spanish Colonies." Creoles stood as pillars of white civilization worthy of tourists' admiration.[37]

With Creole culture a major selling point to visitors curious about the Crescent City's exotic food, history, and architecture, maintaining the fabled racial purity of the city's French families took on added importance. To heap praise on a supposedly noble, fiercely independent people who might carry black blood contradicted the racial hierarchy. The agenda of tourism boosters, social activists, and city administrators reinforced the political and social barriers of Jim Crow while preserving their own bloodlines against suggestions of miscegenation. Rewriting history provided a lengthy tradition of racial separation in an urban center that had formerly possessed an attitude of French liberality on such matters. The whitening of Creoles brought New Orleans and its past into the mainstream of American thought on race.

Typical New Orleans Characters

The 1935 film *The Green Pastures* begins with the sounds of a black choir singing "City Called Heaven." Filmmakers adapted the movie from a popular play based on Roark Bradford's novel, *Ol' Man Adam an' His Chillun.* A New Orleans resident, Bradford depicted blacks as prone to sex, gambling, and alcohol but also as a deeply religious people. His book, a literary example of white paternalism, retold biblical stories from a black perspective, using heavy dialect and comical racial stereotypes. In writing the screenplay, Bradford maintained his condescending view of black life. As the introductory film credits flash, the camera focuses on church bells and then, through a mist, on the picnic grounds where a congregation of blacks enjoys a fish fry. Beyond the picnickers appears "a rise in the ground, topped by 'the golden gates,' shining in the sun." These are no ordinary doors to heaven. The script emphasizes that the "gates resemble in pattern the beautiful wrought iron gates one can still see in the old houses of the French Quarter of New Orleans." For Bradford, the Crescent City harbored a pious black population, though one still prone to mischief. More importantly, New Orleans—the city called heaven—seemed to possess a social order blessed by a higher authority. The film represents a southern paternalist's racial fantasies recorded on celluloid, offering a message entirely in compliance with the stereotypes fostered by New Orleans tourism boosters.[38]

In their attempts to craft a tourist-friendly city, white New Orleanians did not stop at denying the artistic genius of black jazz performers or the Creole heritage of the city's mixed-race population. Although boosters whitened the city's culture, New Orleans still retained a sizable black population whose physical presence could not be erased. Denied their history and their musical achievements, blacks appeared largely as caricatures within the tourism industry.[39]

Black New Orleanians discovered few opportunities within the tourism industry. An African American newspaper, the *Louisiana Weekly*, recognized that black New Orleanians languished in low-paying jobs as "a working class of people. . . . [W]e cook [whites'] food, wash their clothes and nurse their children—This is done well, so well that we are persistently seen in places with the little white children, when we would be thrown out if we attempted to go thither on our manhood." The local situation varied little from that of other popular travel destinations, including Atlantic City, New Jersey, where blacks pushed rolling chairs containing white vacationers down the Boardwalk. In *An American Dilemma*, Gunnar Myrdal identified "traditional 'Negro jobs,' those of waiter, bell-boy, porter, jobs where the over-all hours are long and where the men must be on call at all times."[40]

Attitudes toward attracting black travelers, in contrast, varied during the interwar years. The issue initially split the white power structure. Despite their unwavering support for segregation, New Orleans mayors regularly urged black organizations to meet in the city during the 1920s. The Association of Commerce, dominated by leaders in industrial and commercial enterprises, likewise favored the attraction of black organizations. For many elite white New Orleanians, the arrival of black conventions not only raised profits but also suggested satisfaction with the racial status quo. Hotel owners, restaurant operators, and other tourism-centered businesses, however, frowned on the idea of black tourists wandering the city. The tourism industry had been constructed for whites' enjoyment, and catering to black vacationers and professionals threatened to undermine the illusion of black servility.

Furthermore, the presence of black conventioneers raised the specter of racial equality since they often sought access to the same services and facilities as whites. The Woodmen of Union sparked a sharp controversy in late 1927 when representatives scouted New Orleans as the site for their next gathering and a group of white hotel operators rebuffed the black delegation. Stunned at the action, representatives of the Association of Commerce and the Whitney Bank invited the Woodmen to visit New Orleans in August 1928. As the tourism industry based on white travelers grew in importance to the New Orleans economy over the 1930s, attitudes toward attracting black conventions became more uniform. The development of an infrastructure to accommodate white out-of-towners made area businessmen increasingly nervous about hosting black conventions since such events emerged as lightning rods for civil rights advocacy. Charles Favrot of the Association of Commerce summarized the organization's stance in late 1935, explaining that the association had "not extended invitations to Colored Associations to come to New Orleans, because [the group is] not in a position to offer them any facilities when they come, and it may be the cause of some unpleasantness, for which they would in no way be responsible."[41]

The Municipal Auditorium stood as a symbol of racism within the New Orleans tourism industry. Shortly after the hall opened in 1930, blacks began to request usage of the facility. When a convention of undertakers sought access, the Association of Commerce responded that the Commission Council should not grant such permits since "the possibilities are that will preclude the use of the Auditorium for social purposes on the part of the white people." Any black presence threatened to taint the structure. Administrators expressed particular concern because a "good portion of the [building's] revenue will come from social functions of the white citizens of New Orleans." In a compromise meant to thwart black protests, whites granted use of an annex to the building but then hedged even on this concession. In 1936, the National Baptist Sunday School Convention pressed feverishly for access to the facility, but white officials blocked all such efforts. The *Louisiana Weekly* reported, "Like the song, the committee [representing the Baptists] 'went round and round,' contacting first one official and then another, always to be told that the person with authority to grant them the privilege of paying for the use of the auditorium was some one else and the grand old game of 'passing the buck,' was played to the fullest extent." Money paid to the "white press for publicity" failed to produce editorials critical of the city's actions. "The hundreds of dollars were simply accepted in, perhaps, the light of a gift," grumbled the newspaper. The refusal insulted a large segment of the black community. For black New Orleanians, the National Baptist Sunday School Convention combined two major cultural forces, education and religion, and the conventioneers personified respectability and intelligence. The *Weekly* concluded its biting commentary, "It is humiliating for those ambitious and optimistic men and women who worked so diligently to bring the great Baptist group here to have such a decided rebuff come from the majority and ruling group, nor is it one easily forgotten."[42]

Race influenced the preservationist agenda as well. In 1944, for example, white citizens railed against the War Shipping Administration's proposal to convert the whites-only Senator Hotel into a housing facility for mariners of both races. Although located near the docks in an area some commentators described as "in part a Negro center," preservationists saw the admission of blacks to the Senator as a severe threat to the nearby French Quarter. Preservationists, including Elizabeth Werlein, argued that a Senator Hotel that accommodated members of both races would interfere with "restoring the Vieux Carre section." The Vieux Carré Commission, a government agency created during the interwar years to safeguard the neighborhood, joined the Vieux Carré Property Owners Association in expressing serious concerns about the historic district's future racial integrity. John Fletcher told a group of seventy individuals called the New Orleans Citizens' Committee on Race Relations that the Vieux Carré Commission "believes that by converting the Senator Hotel to the use of Negro merchant seamen it will encourage other Negro enterprises in the neighborhood and danger of trouble between the races will be increased by bringing additional Negroes into a neighborhood which has already undesirable elements." U.S. Representative Hébert was no less troubled by the War Shipping Administration's "diabolical scheme." He voiced the popular opinion that allowing blacks into the Senator Hotel meant the "further desecration of the historical Vieux Carre of New Orleans." The intrusion of blacks threatened to undo the image of the neighborhood, a place praised as both a refined enclave of white Creole culture and a carnal fantasyland. Given the concern with miscegenation that underlay Jim Crow restrictions, the mere presence of any but servile blacks in the French Quarter endangered the romantic allure fostered by tourism boosters and preservationists.[43]

New Orleans civic leaders made certain that white tourists rarely met blacks as equals downtown, on Bourbon Street, or anywhere else popular with out-of-towners. Even as prominent a black figure as Haile Selassie, the leader of Ethiopia, suffered the indignities of segregation when he visited the city in 1954. State Department requests that the dignitary and his entourage receive treatment appropriate for a head of state meant little to civic officials more concerned with maintaining racial protocol. Mayor DeLesseps Morrison and his advisers and area businessmen made only slight concessions. Haile Selassie received a room in the prestigious whites-only Roosevelt Hotel, but hotel managers demanded that none of his party enter the hotel bar, restaurant, or famed Blue Room. Enjoying the local nightlife remained out of the question. Glen Douthit, Morrison's public relations director, spied on the Ethiopian delegation late into the night to ensure that none of them ventured onto Bourbon Street. Although blacks were not barred from walking the popular strip lined with burlesque clubs and jazz dens, the establishments served only white customers. A party of blacks claiming equal status with white tourists carried the potential for a violent clash. Luckily for city officials, Haile Selassie did not test the tourism industry's tolerance.[44]

Mardi Gras exemplified how tourism buttressed white supremacy by depicting the city's blacks as joyfully acquiescing to the racial status quo. White crowds often looked forward to the appearance of celebratory blacks. Whereas the highbrow parades conducted by elite white krewes occasionally disappointed the largely white bystanders, blacks dependably provided entertainment with their dancing, singing, and dress. In 1925, Lyle Saxon recorded in his diary that the Momus parade was "exceedingly banal except for the prancing niggers." Many whites looked on blacks as jesters, comic figures in service to their superiors. With tourism a developing part of the urban economy, civic leaders slowly focused more attention on blacks. "No one enters into the spirit of Carnival more whole-heartedly than the New Orleans negro," remarked the *Times-Picayune* in 1936. The same article explained how nothing displayed the fun-loving character of blacks better than the Zulu parade, which consisted of "floats depicting African scenes and personages." In grass skirts and blackface, the all-black Krewe of Zulu supplied nonthreatening caricatures that reinforced white stereotypes. White opinion considered the Zulu parade, blacks' most public means of critiquing New Orleans's white order, to be nothing more than a natural outgrowth of the childlike foolery expected from blacks. Joyful black float riders suggested to white tourists and locals a contentment with the social order. Furthermore, the *Times-Picayune* explained that the chicanery associated with blacks was essential to the success of Mardi Gras: "There is something individualistic about the negroes' street-masking that stands out in the fun they create—the music and color and grotesque antics of the fun-makers in their equally grotesque costumes, which all together play a distinctive role in making Carnival the happy event it is." The emphasis on the grotesque warned white visitors and locals not to join black revelers in their extreme behavior.[45]

Accounts of slavery constituted another prominent aspect of New Orleans's tourism industry. In a region that often downplayed the institution's brutality, Crescent City tourism boosters regularly recalled Madam Lalaurie, an antebellum slave owner living in the French Quarter who starved and tortured slaves to death in her attic. When the public eventually learned of her sadism, angry mobs expelled Lalaurie from the city. According to a typical description printed in a guidebook from the 1920s, the ghosts of her slaves still haunted the French Quarter, especially "on dark and stormy nights." Lalaurie's abuse of slaves was seen as an aberration from the paternalism that usually prevented such cruelty. Moreover, the paranormal manifestations entertained visitors. Tales about Lalaurie thereby reinforced the servile role of blacks within the tourism industry even while excusing slavery as a generally benevolent institution.[46]

White commentators emphasized the practice of voodoo as a sign of blacks' propensity toward questionable—if not immoral—behavior. Tales of voodoo rituals in New Orleans flowered as tourism took root. Far from the serious accounts of religious practices captured by Zora Neale Hurston in her 1935 book, *Mules and Men*, the narratives crafted by tourism boosters depicted half-naked celebrants engaged in sinister nighttime rituals. In his 1928 volume, *Fabulous New Orleans*, Saxon explicitly linked voodoo to racial stereotypes, writing, "To understand properly the workings of this black magic, one must understand something of the negro's characteristics." Saxon explained that a black person "is intensely emotional, that he possesses a childlike credulity, that his imagination is easily inflamed, and that the powers of darkness are potent powers." Even visitors to the city adopted the views of white locals. In his 1938 travel account, *A Southerner Discovers the South*, Jonathan Daniels used voodoo to describe, from a clearly white point of view, both the primitive nature and the base lifestyle of black New Orleanians. "I noticed that the Negress servant of my friends had her nails lacquered red as any heiress,' " wrote Daniels. "In a town in which voodoo is harder and harder to find they might have been recently withdrawn from bloody entrails of beasts of augury." Voodoo offered an interpretive lens through which whites observed black culture, in the process reinforcing their sense of racial superiority. Tallant introduced his 1946 *Voodoo in New Orleans* by taking readers from the "white world" of Canal Street to the "much darker" world of South Rampart Street, where the odor of "stale beer and whiskey, oyster barrels too long in the hot sun, [and] a musky mingling of perspiration and cheap perfume" made an impression that the "white man will never forget." A white who could withstand the stench and curious looks from black pedestrians soon met a more powerful barrier. Tallant explained, "It is almost as if some metaphysical force had driven him out of a place in which he did not belong." Even with voodoo fading from the urban landscape, the religious practice provided whites with a powerful means for castigating blacks and excusing segregation.[47]

Jim Crow customs required blacks to dress as well as to act as subordinates to white authority when they ventured into otherwise white areas of the city. Entering a neighborhood normally off limits without a reason could lead to a life-threatening turn of events. Jazzman Punch Miller recalled a time early in the twentieth century when he entered the Irish Channel to sign his annual contract to play for a neighborhood Carnival organization. A gang of whites quickly stopped Miller, demanding to know his reasons for trespassing. Only the intercession of Miller's benefactor prevented what likely would have been a sound beating. Black domestic workers donned uniforms, thereby permitting them access to white residential neighborhoods and whites-only parks. From hotel bellhops to restaurant waiters, black laborers who regularly interacted with whites were required to wear outfits—costumes—marking them as servants. For blacks not employed by white households or businesses, a shoddy appearance and the avoidance of eye contact offered a degree of safety when transgressing white districts.[48]

The black street musician epitomized blacks' dependence on white benefactors, much like the dark-skinned waiters, bellhops, and other workers in the service-oriented tourism industry who received tips for their congenial compliance. A 1941 issue of the *Roosevelt Review* paid particular attention to the "dozens" of one-man bands who wandered city streets with guitar, drum, harmonica, and several horns, looking for handouts from passing tourists. Each musician collected donations in a "tin cup, securely attached to his drum." "Coins dropping into this receptacle provide music more dear to the maestro's heart than any his diverse props can produce," commented the *Roosevelt Review*, thereby denying the meaning of the songs performed. The same article revealed that street musicians most commonly played "St. Louis Blues," "Basin Street Blues," "Way Down Yonder in New Orleans," and, most significantly, "Every Man a King," Huey Long's anthem. Blues songs suggested the hardship of black life in a white-dominated society. Conversely, by playing "Every Man a King," black musicians declared their appreciation for the politician who, according to the *Louisiana Weekly*, fought "for the common man." Blacks gained from Long's construction, medical, and educational programs, although not as much as whites. Many blacks even believed that Long had planned to remove voting restrictions in an effort to widen his electoral base before running for president. Black street musicians likely chose the song as more than just an ode to Long, however: its populist message of social uplift also resonated with blacks. Long's anthem stretched beyond a single man's political agenda to encompass the hopes of African Americans, who sought an egalitarian society pulled free from the mire of economic and racial inequality. The *Roosevelt Review* downplayed any sense of such assertiveness, depicting black street musicians as performing only to collect tips rather than to voice opinions about societal conditions. Tourists were assured that audience superseded any intended message. According to the *Review*, "Every Man a King" was simply a popular tune. The call for equality dissipated with the rattling of a cup filled by white handouts. The image of racial harmony as well as the racial hierarchy remained unshaken.[49]

Arnold Genthe's 1926 *Impressions of Old New Orleans*, for which Grace King wrote a foreword, described black residents of the city as part of the scenery rather than the citizenry. In Genthe's words, "The negro population however has retained a good deal of its southern picturesqueness, in spite of the tendency to dress in an up-to-date American fashion." Black New Orleanians, at least according to Genthe, remained encased in the region's racial social structure. The local black population was a colorful remnant of the romanticized past. Blacks were also servile, at least from the white viewpoint. In 1937, for example, the Garden Study Club held a French Quarter flower show that "reached a climax . . . when the excited ladies appeared at half past eight, each with a colored man to assist her, and vases, flowers, fancy tables, draperies, and all manner of confusion were spread all over the shop in no time. The ladies were very pleasant, but singularly helpless, possibly due to the state of their nerves." Given southern sexual and racial conventions, the black men entered the white-oriented playground of the French Quarter as little more than emasculated figures paid to serve their benefactors.[50]

A select few black occupations received particular attention from the tourism industry. Although largely absent from local guidebooks, black men and women received credit as excellent cooks. Relegated to the kitchen, blacks catered to whites much as slaves did in the antebellum years. According to King, formerly enslaved servants safeguarded the recipes loved by the Creoles who once owned them, loyally "follow[ing] their old families faithfully into lowering degrees of ill fortune, producing their masterpieces of cooking with a proud self-consciousness of what they had been worth in slavery." Such depictions packaged black waiters and cooks as loyal servants who gleefully perpetuated white Creole culinary traditions by preserving old recipes and serving other whites. In New Orleans, as elsewhere in the region and nation, the services provided by black cooks and waiters reinforced black social and economic subservience to white patrons.[51]

Moreover, tourism boosters' claims about black devotion to traditional ways offered visitors the opportunity to role-play, substituting themselves for antebellum masters. A trip to the dining table was a journey through time. The popular *Gourmet's Guide to New Orleans*, first published in 1933, described the delicacies of the city as if the clock had stopped in the 1850s. In her foreword, social commentator Dorothy Dix traced the history of New Orleans foodways: "Founded originally on the French cuisine, it was pepped up, so to speak, by the Spanish, given body and strength by the New England influence, a bit of warmth by the hot breads of Virginia, and finally glorified by the touch of the old negro mammies who boasted that they had only to pass their hands over a pot to give it a flavor that would make your mouth water." The book's cover reflected the message found inside. A black man in chef's garb appeared with a platter of steaming food. Daniels also observed the role of race in the city's restaurants, finding the signposts of Jim Crow so important to the tourism industry that even the Roosevelt Hotel, where "not a single Negro servant is visible," made a point to serve a "Mammy Dinner," implying that blacks were busy in the kitchen. Such a dish offered a nostalgic (and mythical) return to antebellum life, when blacks were joyful, proud servants.[52]

The mammy was the most common image of black subservience. According to the post–Civil War nostalgic myths created about the plantation South, the mammy was a slave devoted to her owner's family who remained fiercely loyal even after emancipation. In the postwar South, hiring a black domestic servant to care for children and assist around the household became a symbol of a white family's middle-class status. Furthermore, as historian Grace Hale has argued, "Mammies rooted the new southern world within the paternalistic race relations of the antebellum South." The mammy, an ideal servant, recalled slave times, and in New Orleans and other cities across the South, she became a central figure within businesses that catered to tourists.[53]

With their heads wrapped in elaborate headdresses and wearing clothes reminiscent of antebellum mammies, costumed locals appeared on New Orleans streets to pander to the needs of tourists. The mammy image was frequently used to market pralines, a candy consisting of brown sugar and pecans. The matriarchal guardian of white families merged with the image of formerly enslaved house servants who preserved Creole recipes. Combining the two stereotypes placed a New Orleans twist on a southern fiction. A woman dressed as a mammy brought the myth of contented blacks to life, reinforcing tourism boosters' efforts to present the Crescent City as a portal to a simpler past while affirming contemporary racial mores. In addition, the use of mammies to market pralines excused the presence of black women in white tourist-oriented spaces. In a city that had featured prominent black madams in Storyville, costuming black women remained particularly important. The depiction of mammies as robust, motherly figures tempered any sexual allure. Even white women and men disguised their sexuality by donning outfits associated with mammy figures. In 1923, members of the Business and Professional Women's Club raised money selling pralines during Mardi Gras while dressed as "white-skinned 'mammies.'" White women who tested still-strong gender taboos by accepting employment outside the home served themselves well by masquerading in a traditional garb that recalled submissive loyalty to the patriarchal family. Men also had reasons for dressing up. In the early 1920s, the Elks of New Orleans wore blackface and mammy outfits during their annual fund-raiser, a praline sale. The costumes protected the masculinity and pride of participants who felt embarrassment about soliciting buyers in the streets.[54]

New Orleans businesses capitalized on the mammy image. The Green Orchid, a prominent French Quarter store, offered tourists a booklet that explained how the "outstanding candy of the old Negro mammies, has become synonymous with New Orleans." Delicious pralines, loyal mammies, and the Crescent City were tightly bound together. Léda Plauché, who operated the Green Orchid, named the confections "Ma-Lou Pralines," an abbreviation for "my old Negro mammy, Marie-Louise." The shortened version, done for "commercial purposes," not only stripped the black figure of a name suggestive of her Creole roots— and possibly mixed bloodline—but also presented her as motherly. Playing on tourists' curiosity, Plauché had cooks don costumes and opened the kitchen to the public, providing "the only place in New Orleans where you may see mammy making pralines." The Green Orchid was not alone in manipulating the mammy image for financial gain. One local shop used the name Aunt Sally's and packed pralines in "souvenir cotton bales" with a picture of a big-eyed, smiling mammy printed on the side. In addition to pralines, the store offered "leisurely" and "old-fashioned" carriage rides through the French Quarter conducted by a "reliable old-time driver." The description was accompanied by an illustration that showed a black driver steering a carriage occupied by a white gentleman in a top hat and two white ladies in hoopskirts. A small pamphlet distributed by Aunt Sally's in the late 1940s instructed tourists to search "for Mammy with Blinking Eyes," a reference to the signs marking the chain's four stores. Other businesses also capitalized on the mammy image. In the early 1940s, Bacino's Bar and Cocktail Lounge on Bourbon Street beckoned tourists to "hear Genevieve Hub, negro mammy Blues Singer and pianist, par excellence." The ad depicted Hub in mammy garb, banging on a piano.[55]

Souvenir stores reinforced the message that blacks happily served white interests. Gift shops sold mammy dolls and comical figures of blacks. Crumb Gifts, a store appropriately located on Lee Circle in the shadow of the city's towering monument to the Confederate general, headlined ads with "Souvenirs of the South." The shop offered silks, shawls, and items for children, but the main line of goods recalled the antebellum southern social order. "Mammy Dolls a Specialty," boasted the proprietors. Crumb Gifts faced ample competition. Doll maker Flo Salter subtly advertised her "Typical New Orleans Characters," including mammies, pickaninnies, and black street criers. In the early 1940s, Stanley Arthur, an author and the executive director of the Louisiana State Museum, organized an exhibit of "appropriately garbed character dolls illustrating old-time folk of Old New Orleans." Arthur expressed particular interest in the city's street-wandering chimney sweeps, whom he called "the nigger[s] in the chimney flue." The purchase and display of adult black figures—a Jim Crow–era phenomenon that permitted whites to acquire or ogle stereotyped blacks—proliferated in a city notorious for having harbored the largest slave market in the antebellum South.[56]

Believe It or Not

When James LaFourche, a black man, examined New Orleans race relations from the vantage point of 1938, he surprisingly found a city much improved over the previous three decades. "Believe it or not, I know the time when Colored people, viewing a Carnival parade on Canal Street or any other downtown thoroughfare, were usually recipients of a good fist beating administered by scores of white ruffians, mostly in their teens," remarked LaFourche in the *Louisiana Weekly*. He remembered being charged by "little white hoodlums, and some larger ones too" when he braved Canal Street during one Carnival. LaFourche claimed that such incidents were no longer common. The roots of this change were easily found—the expansion of the tourism industry. As white New Orleanians created a more tourism-based economy, blacks discovered employment opportunities that demanded their increased presence in previously white-dominated urban spaces. To the question of why local blacks witnessed a sudden reduction in harassment and beatings during Mardi Gras, LaFourche responded, "My answer is the white Carnival clubs, white street maskers and white merry-maskers who crowd trucks, all employed Colored musicians and Colored men in various other capacities in their Carnival set-up." Whites needed blacks to efficiently run Carnival. The change LaFourche described had been rapid. "In the course of a few years the demand for Colored musicians, truck drivers and Negroes in other capacities increased and with the increase of this kind of labor, prejudice was driven from the streets." Although LaFourche overstated his argument when he declared that white New Orleanians no longer acted with prejudice, he nevertheless called attention to tourism's importance in opening the urban space to blacks, even if they were permitted only to assist or entertain whites.[57]

Like LaFourche, civic leaders recognized the importance of maintaining at least the semblance of racial harmony in streets filled with tourists. New Orleanian Arthur Schott voiced a sentiment that grew among whites over the course of the 1930s when he criticized the "assaults on negroes in the crowd along Canal street by young white men for no apparent reason except that they are black." Tourism boosters and citizens such as Schott worried about the "bad impression" such incidents gave visitors. The permissive attitude toward racial violence made matters worse. According to Schott, tourists who "witnessed the unmerciful beating and kicking of negroes by the police when making arrests" saw evidence of racial tension and a tyrannical municipal government. For tourism to flourish, New Orleans needed to maintain peaceful streets that did not undermine civic leaders' carefully constructed illusion of harmony. The greatest symbolic act of white acceptance of blacks within the tourism industry occurred in 1939, when Mayor Robert Maestri became the city's first head to toast the king of Zulu, a gesture that granted official sanction to blacks' right to enjoy public streets.[58]

LaFourche's optimistic appraisal of New Orleans race relations was tempered by his realization that blacks occupied stereotypical positions within attractions such as Mardi Gras. "With fear banished, the Colored people ventured more into the streets, and to the extent that the comical and most picturesque maskers were to be found among them," boasted LaFourche. His glee at the decrease in violence belied persisting white attitudes that made blacks laughable figures. LaFourche noted as much when he looked at costume contests conducted by white businesses. "Hardly a reviewing stand in the city giving prizes frowned upon the colored maskers who came seeking awards for their original designs," reported LaFourche. Black buffoonery fit into a tourism industry structured to make blacks appear harmless and servile. Furthermore, white visitors were led to believe that grass-skirted participants in the Zulu parade and colorful Mardi Gras Indians were primitive. Although the black community used Zulu to ridicule the pageantry of the white parades and adopted Indian garb to honor those who resisted white authority, whites interpreted the same festivities as evidence of a childlike black race still in need of paternal care. Blacks may have been safer walking downtown streets, but the cost of that freedom—their continued degradation—was high.[59]

LaFourche and other black New Orleanians witnessed the creation of a white-dominated tourism industry during the interwar years. White civic leaders erased black history and contributions to the city, shaping the touristic image of New Orleans in the likeness of whites. Jazz, the wild musical style created by blacks, slowly evolved into a white art performed at upscale clubs. Fears about the popular perception of Creoles as a people with black ancestry led to the affirmation of the two-tiered race system of Jim Crow America. Whites moved quickly to purify Creole bloodlines and ennoble the early inhabitants of the city's primary tourist attraction, the French Quarter. Although the glorification of the Creoles as pure-blooded whites had begun in the late nineteenth century, the growth of tourism renewed concerns about the city's image and heritage. By the end of the interwar years, white New Orleanians had constructed a tourism industry that accommodated blacks only as colorful characters decorating the landscape. Blacks were packaged to fit white expectations, either as servants in restaurants and other establishments or in symbolic form as purchasable figurines. Such was the foundation of southern hospitality on which local whites constructed New Orleans tourism.

EPILOGUE

Boomtown

> For New Orleans did look lovely. But I thought I had seen its loveliness
> somewhere before, and I couldn't remember where. . . . I felt I was
> being teased by the view through the shutters: it was equally full of
> come-hither looks and keep out notices. It was also trying for its effects
> a shade too hard, as if it were using me as a mirror in which to inspect
> its own fresh paint and powder and ingenious twiddles of mascara. I
> was supposed to say, Yes, you do look beautiful; no, that's just exactly
> right. I wanted instead to say what truthful mirrors do: Watch it, or I'll
> crack, you vain old bitch. —Jonathan Raban, *Old Glory*

For a brief period during the Second World War, the *New Orleans
Item* entertained readers with a running dialogue about the virtues and
sins of tourism. The language used in letters to the editor by several
of the more than one hundred thousand out-of-towners who flooded
into nearby military bases or area industries often wounded local pride.
"New Orleans never was more than a dingy river town with mouldy
ruins, into which French frugality placed bars and cafés, to charge ex-
horbitant prices. Its culture and color has been manufactured in miserly
style and promoted with cheap imitation of the most repulsive California C[hamber]. of C[ommerce]. tactics," barked Richard Dyer, an
officer in the U.S. Marines. "Profiteers, prostitutes, pimps, bookies,

hopheads, and hotel owners vie in the merry-go-round to rob the serviceman," he continued. Having previously been stationed at several posts around the country, Dyer felt confident in his claim that the Crescent City was "a madhouse of avariciousness and war greed without equal in the United States." Wartime price controls, described by Dyer as "a joke," failed to hinder profit-minded New Orleanians. The marine was not alone in his sharp remarks about the local desire to fleece out-of-towners. One temporary resident of New Orleans, a self-proclaimed " 'Happy' Visitor," recognized locals' success in promoting their city and commended them for their "ability to perpetuate the greatest swindle in history—the French Quarter."[1]

Despite much publicly aired dissatisfaction, New Orleanians fully realized the profitability of tourism during the Second World War. Resident Bill Broussard observed how wartime mobilization brought "people from every city and town in the country," creating a popular image of New Orleans as a boomtown. For a city that already had its eyes on tourism, the influx of military personnel and wartime laborers powerfully boosted the economy. The municipal government prospered as a result of expanded tax revenue. Restaurants, nightclubs, hotels, and other entertainment venues flourished as soldiers and sailors, flush with sizable government paychecks, indulged themselves before boarding ships headed for the front. Workers likewise spent their earnings on the exciting attractions of urban life. The boon was magnified by the long economic drought caused by the Great Depression. War industries and military service provided regular pay and evaporated the pool of unemployed Americans who had languished for much of the 1930s. As Broussard noted, many of those who flooded New Orleans streets came from small towns or farms. New Orleans offered not only steady jobs but also encounters with big-city glitz and excitement. Furthermore, U.S. involvement in the Second World War dragged on for four years, bringing far more Americans into contact with the port than had been the case during the First World War, which gave the city barely a year of activity. The military personnel and workers who moved to the Crescent City were supplemented by an untold number of Americans who passed through the port, spending only a handful of days there on their way to other locations. As men flocked into the military, women filled openings in war-related industries. The city became a romantic rendezvous where young, single women, seeking employment and freedom from small-town eyes, met uniformed men preparing for the fight in Europe or the Pacific.[2]

With thousands passing through, New Orleanians took comfort in having a tourism industry that, despite high wartime prices, could capture Americans' imaginations and glow bright in postwar memories. Resident Cedric McNeil fumed over the criticisms of the city but recognized that New Orleans would linger in popular memory: "To the dissatisfied visitors of the city, we and the world need you here *now* but after the war, GO HOME, but I am sure, that you will tell your friends some good about us, we can't be all bad." Other New Orleanians simply dismissed complaints with a confidence befitting many area businessmen. As Felix Aitkens bluntly declared, "About the service people seeing New Orleans and not recommending it later. Well old timer for every one who doesn't like it there are ten who do like it."[3]

With a tourism infrastructure firmly in place, New Orleans became increasingly accessible in the postwar years as the national economy underwent a major expansion. Government restrictions on metals, rubber, gasoline, and other supplies reserved for the war machine had sharply curtailed the production of consumer goods as well as opportunities for shopping or travel in the early 1940s. When the federal government lifted the restrictions, Americans again hit the stores and highways. The nest eggs saved by military personnel and war industry workers hatched into a burst of spending. Government programs furthered the expansion of the economy. Returning soldiers benefiting from the G.I. Bill worked their way through a growing network of public colleges and into the ranks of the well-paid business professionals, while women, though encouraged to surrender the jobs they filled during the war, maintained a hold on a wider variety of occupations than before the conflict and thereby gained greater independence. Even those women who retreated from the workplace to adopt traditional roles at home found increased resources and opportunities as a result of the prosperity provided by their salaried husbands. The Cold War expansion of the military-industrial complex provided more employment and job security. Americans worked shorter hours, received higher salaries, and gained more vacation time. In turn, weekend getaways and weeklong trips became increasingly affordable. As historian Lizabeth Cohen has put it, the nation evolved into a "consumers' republic."[4]

The unprecedented expansion of suburbia also benefited New Orleans tourism. Government housing loans spurred nationwide construction in the years immediately after the Second World War. Suburbs sprouted around major cities in what urban scholar Kenneth Jackson has called a "crabgrass frontier" of identical houses surrounded by manicured lawns. As a result, automobiles became a necessity. Car sales, stagnant since the onset of the depression, blossomed. Improvements in automobiles' style, speed, and comfort stoked the American love affair with their vehicles and with travel. Shiny new cars resting in suburban driveways also conveyed social and economic status. Americans' desire for status symbols was far from limited to what they drove or where they lived, however. In the proverbial race to keep up with the neighborhood Joneses, vacations joined houses, automobiles, appliances, and other consumer products as part of the social status arsenal. Photo albums, home movies, and souvenirs served not only as personal mementos but also as signs of a family's financial success. A tin of New Orleans pralines, a bundle of Mardi Gras throws, a sketch of Jackson Square, a shot glass commemorating a jaunt down Bourbon Street, or an antique purchased on Royal Street displayed the economic ability to pursue leisure.[5]

Nothing aided the New Orleans tourism industry as much as the construction of the interstate highway system. Engineers in Louisiana had paved a way through the swamps surrounding the city and had bridged the Mississippi River during the interwar years, but New Orleans still suffered at the hands of less spirited road construction and maintenance efforts in Mississippi, through which northern and eastern motorists had to pass. Access to New Orleans improved as the federal interstate highway project firmly tied the Isle de Orleans, as the French pioneers had named the land on which they founded the Crescent City, to the rest of the country. Originally intended to quicken the military's response to potential threats, the gridlike ribbons of concrete permitted Americans to travel at higher speeds over longer distances. By the 1970s, the roads not only permitted speedy travel but also eased northerners' anxiety about venturing into the Deep South, particularly the rural expanses of Mississippi and Alabama. Even southerners had entered Mississippi with trepidation. Nashville's Richard Schweid recalled that during the 1960s, "Any time I drove to New Orleans from Tennessee, for instance, I would schedule the Mississippi stretch of the drive for the daylight hours. Don't let the sun set on you in Mississippi if you're in a car with out-of-state plates, is what I used to think." At a time when Americans recalled images of segregationists using intimidation and lethal violence against outsiders—even those not involved in the civil rights struggle—the interstates offered a comforting familiarity. Out-of-state drivers whizzed past name-brand gas stations, hotels, and fast-food outlets strategically stationed near interstate exits while bypassing the sundry towns scarred by battles for racial equality. The simultaneous expansion of the airline industry, another beneficiary of government largesse, made New Orleans even more accessible to vacationers. From high above, air travelers faced none of the concerns of motorists such as Schweid.[6]

Pop culture reflected Americans' obsession with the metropolis near the mouth of the Mississippi River. New Orleans was hip during the Cold War. Trumpeter Louis Armstrong's nostalgic 1946 hit, "Do You Know What It Means to Miss New Orleans?" resonated with listeners, many of whom had worked in or passed through the city during the Second World War. Ignoring the jazz musician's biting criticism of Jim Crow in his hometown, white New Orleanians understood the power of Armstrong's music as a promotional tool. When the all-black Zulu Social Aid and Pleasure Club invited Armstrong to serve as king of the organization's 1949 parade, publicity-minded Mayor DeLesseps Morrison used the opportunity to host a public ceremony in which he handed the legendary jazzman the key to New Orleans, the same city that forced Armstrong to bed in a "colored" hotel during his stay. Other jazz performers, particularly whites such as Louis Prima, Al Hirt, and Pete Fountain, fostered interest in the city as they gained international audiences. Hirt and Fountain even opened clubs on Bourbon Street to satisfy tourists eager to hear the music associated with New Orleans. Movies now gave the public classic images of the Crescent City: the chiseled Marlon Brando and elegant Vivian Leigh in *A Streetcar Named Desire*; the soulful, rebellious Elvis Presley in *King Creole*; and the bohemian acid-droppers Dennis Hopper and Peter Fonda in *Easy Rider*. All of these popular films presented the city as sexually charged, mysterious, and enticingly decadent. Television executives, developing programs to air on the sets that revolutionized home entertainment in the late 1950s, also tapped the allure of New Orleans with such shows as the hourlong primetime crime drama *Bourbon Street Beat*, which began airing on the American Broadcasting Company network in 1959.[7]

In a society fixated on racial barriers, however, the New Orleans tourism industry and the city's image remained white oriented through the early 1970s. Pop-cultural images such as those found in film commonly restricted the presence of blacks to cameo roles. Advertisers, art, and pulp fiction focused on white experiences, particularly those of the middle class. White residents accounted for the majority of New Orleans's population until the 1970s, when they fled a desegregated New Orleans by traveling newly constructed Interstate 10 to neighboring parishes, leaving the urban population predominantly black. Arthur Vernon's privately published guide from the early 1970s, *New Orleans Nonsense*, reflected these changes in an essay that declared, "I am sick of riots, marches, protests, demonstrations, confrontations, and the other mob temper tantrums of people intellectually incapable of working within the system." The verbal assault on the civil rights movement continued: "I am sick of those who say I owe them this or that because of the sins of my forefathers—when I have looked down both ends of a gun barrel to defend their rights, their liberties and their families." Factual tidbits informed readers that blacks were responsible for more than 80 percent of New Orleans crimes. Although Jim Crow restrictions on lodging, transportation, and other services vital to a thriving tourist trade disappeared from law books during the 1960s, attitudes such as those printed in Vernon's guidebook persisted; nevertheless, blacks exercised their newly won rights. When an interviewer asked one young black woman how the civil rights movement affected her life, she looked to her mother, who had grown up when segregation and the racial hierarchy stood firm: "Now she travels. She does things that before she thought only white people did."[8]

Although by the end of the twentieth century tourism boosters had adapted to the changes in racial attitudes, the legacy of Jim Crow continued to linger in the city. Arrivals at Louis Armstrong International Airport could shop at Lulu White's Lingerie Store, named for a seductive, light-skinned madam who operated in Storyville. French Quarter tourists could still buy pralines from Aunt Sally's, a name that reminded visitors of the old-time mammies. Sambo and mammy imagery abounded in souvenir shops. Significantly, the biased guidebooks produced during the interwar years, including those written by Lyle Saxon, remained in print, and even updated guides usually paid homage to the works of the 1920s and 1930s in their bibliographies. Events promoted for black travelers were relegated to dates whites had long shunned: the Essence Music Festival in the heat of July and the Bayou Classic football game held on the weekend after Thanksgiving. Some French Quarter businesses closed during these events.

A foundation had clearly been laid during the interwar years that secured the development of tourism in New Orleans. To tap the expanding vacation market energized by the mass production of automobiles, urban boosters in New Orleans turned from homogenizing symbols of modernity such as skyscrapers to an elaboration of the city's unique heritage. Mardi Gras and the French Quarter exemplified the French past—or at least such was the tale constructed in the advertising campaigns designed by the New Orleans Association of Commerce and City Hall. Boosters painted a trip to the Crescent City as a journey to an exotic, foreign place. Preservation efforts and festivals merged with elaborate publicity campaigns to draw crowds downtown. Images of modernity were subsumed by romantic descriptions of the quaint, centuries-old community rich in history and memories. After the Great Depression hobbled industry and commerce, tourism rose as a vital pillar supporting the economy and the municipal government.

The shift in American culture regarding gender conventions played an equally significant part in jump-starting the mass tourism industry. Progressive Era reforms prepared the urban environment for vacationers by modernizing the cityscape. Outbreaks of disease, a major problem in swampy southern Louisiana, dramatically decreased. Paved roads, closed gutters, water systems, and sundry other improvements facilitated the conceptual change that allowed Americans to envision cities not as harsh environments but as pleasant places worth visiting. The temporary disappearance of saloons and other so-called dens of iniquity reassured women of the safety of urban spaces. At the same time, a younger generation of women who joined the workforce embraced the alleged vices of cosmetics, alcohol, and even sex. By the time Prohibition ended, both conservative and adventurous women entered the streets with little if any trepidation. Civic leaders ensured such ease of movement by carefully regulating the reappearance of barrooms while continuing to secret away the commercial sex trade.

Few people confronted the permissiveness of New Orleans, its tourism industry, and the unleashed desires of American vacationers like Joel Harrington, nicknamed the Chaplain of Bourbon Street. Like many other Americans, Harrington had been introduced to the city during the Second World War—the Alabama native was formally discharged from the navy in New Orleans. After living in the rural South and spending a dull period at a military base in Illinois, Harrington found the Crescent City's allure too much to ignore, and he quickly took to the streets with an old girlfriend. "I spent practically all my mustering-out pay visiting the dives and strip joints of the Quarter," recalled Harrington with some embarrassment. He returned to New Orleans in 1961 as a born-again evangelist and headed to Bourbon Street wearing a bright red tie, red socks, and red-covered Bible to save the souls of tourists and locals. Harrington opened a small Salvation Shop across from the Sho-Bar, one of the street's better-known burlesque clubs, and even arranged to preach from the Sho-Bar's stage each Sunday afternoon. The preacher, often ogled by tourists but accepted as another French Quarter character by locals, dreamed of opening similar missions in Greenwich Village, Las Vegas, and the Sunset Strip, other places catering to the leisurely decadence associated with tourists. Despite his intentions, the dynamic Harrington remained well ensconced in the New Orleans nightlife: "Wherever I am in the world, all roads, finally, lead back to Bourbon Street." The Crescent City, according to the unorthodox evangelist, was the "devil's Disneyland," a tourist mecca that seemingly gave vent to every desire. In New Orleans, vacationers discovered, as Harrington did, "a world of total unreality" where visitors forgot their everyday lives and the social conventions that usually restricted their behavior. Although he criticized Bourbon Street's strip clubs and bars, Harrington argued that the city merely reflected Americans' taste for self-indulgence. He did not realize that Bourbon Street constituted only a segment of a complex tourism infrastructure built to appeal to a wide variety of expectations. After all, New Orleans also catered to vacationing families and other more sedate visitors. Music clubs, antique stores, steamboat cruises, street festivals, and an ever-growing range of attractions widened the city's tourist market and solidified the city's place in the pantheon of American vacation destinations.[9]

So successful had the tourism industry become that Americans began calling New Orleans the Big Easy. The epithet, drawn from the jargon of black jazzmen, referred to an obscure jazz hall popular in the early twentieth century. As the city embraced its first black mayor and white flight left the city with a majority black population during the 1970s, many local whites began to use the term to refer to New Orleans. The term appeared in the title of a crime novel by James Conaway and in a *Times-Picayune* column by Betty Guillaud. Echoing the cultural politics of the interwar years, white opinion now used the phrase to cast New Orleans as black. Demographic maps of the metropolitan area presented the city as a black hole in the center of a white suburban ring. The nickname, a play on many whites' long-held racial attitude toward blacks, branded the city as lazy and sexually promiscuous. Furthermore, the term drew attention not only to the variety of leisurely attractions but also to the permissive attitude of local officials. *The Big Easy*, a 1987 hit movie starring Dennis Quaid that popularized the phrase across the country, reassured the nation that the largely white police force was too busy collecting payoffs, enjoying free meals at restaurants, and even trafficking in confiscated heroin to impinge on the vices available to travelers. When not violating the law, the police (Quaid's character, a detective, is a Cajunized New Orleanian) seemed to work hardest at keeping the black population under thumb. It seemed that little had changed since the interwar years.[10]

White boosters after the First World War cultivated the popular image of New Orleans as uncalculating, leisurely, and morally lax. But despite tour guides' claims, New Orleans's cultural penchant for indulgence was no gift from the past. Mass tourism developed from the hard work of shrewd New Orleanians as they adapted to rapidly changing conditions within American culture. In short, the Big Easy was made.

NOTES

Abbreviations

AJSPC   Anthony J. Stanonis Pamphlet Collection, Loyola University
New Orleans, J. Edgar and Louise S. Monroe Library, Special
Collections and Archives

LSM   Louisiana State Museum

NOACM   New Orleans Association of Commerce Minutes, University of
New Orleans, Earl K. Long Library, Louisiana Collection and
Special Collections

NOACNB   *New Orleans Association of Commerce News Bulletin*

OPCC   Official Proceedings of the Commission Council of the City of
New Orleans, New Orleans Public Library, City Archives and
Special Collections

RAJM   Records of Mayor Andrew J. McShane, New Orleans Public
Library, City Archives and Special Collections

RAJO   Records of Mayor Arthur J. O'Keefe, New Orleans Public
Library, City Archives and Special Collections

RMB   Records of Mayor Martin Behrman, New Orleans Public
Library, City Archives and Special Collections, New Orleans
Public Library, City Archives and Special Collections

RRSM   Records of Mayor Robert S. Maestri, New Orleans Public
Library, City Archives and Special Collections

TU   Tulane University, Howard-Tilton Memorial Library, Special
            Collections Division
UNO   University of New Orleans, Earl K. Long Library, Louisiana
            Collection and Special Collections
WRPC   William Russell Pamphlet Collection, Historic New Orleans
            Collection, Williams Research Center

Introduction: The City of Myths

1. Yuhl, *Golden Haze of Memory*, 119–26, 168–69; Chiang, "Novel Tourism," 312–13, 317–28.

2. Kammen, *Mystic Chords of Memory*, 299–300.

3. Onuf, *Jefferson's Empire*, 53–58; Roger Kennedy, *Mr. Jefferson's Lost Cause*, 53–55; Filler, *Appointment at Armageddon*, 71–79, 140–79; Tichi, *Exposés and Excess*, 76–87.

4. Pitot, *Observations*, 1, 31.

5. Schultz, *Travels*, 27; Latrobe, *Impressions*, 142; Duffy, *Parson Clapp*, 49, 107; McMurry, *John Bell Hood*, 202–3.

6. Frink, "Spectacles of the Street," 37–41; Timothy Reilly, "Heterodox New Orleans," 533–45; Fredrika Bremer, *Homes of the New World*, 239; "New-Orleans as a City," *New York Times*, 29 December 1884.

7. Early, *New Orleans Holiday*, 142; "Philadelphia," *New York Daily Times*, 11 October 1852; Halttunen, *Confidence Men and Painted Women*, 34–55; Ryan, *Cradle of the Middle Class*, 65–104, 155–79; Mason, *Making of Victorian Sexuality*, 109–73.

8. Flint, *Recollections*, 223–24.

9. Olmsted, *Cotton Kingdom*, 228–29; Walter Johnson, *Soul by Soul*, 1–2, 6–8; Jerah Johnson, "Colonial New Orleans," 46–57; Tregle, "Creoles and Americans," 149–50; Gossett, *Uncle Tom's Cabin*, 164–238.

10. Buel, *Mysteries and Miseries*, 498, 590, 592; Alecia Long, *Great Southern Babylon*, 10–13, 203–14.

11. Brady, *George Washington's Beautiful Nelly*, 223, 214–15.

12. "The Coup d'Etat in New-Orleans," *New York Times*, 7 June 1858. For information on antebellum New Orleans and immigration, see Frink, "Spectacles of the Street," 38, 48–52, 58, 65–93; Tansey, "Prostitution and Politics," 450–51, 470–79; Lachance, "Foreign French"; Timothy Reilly, "Heterodox

New Orleans," 533–51; Tregle, "Early New Orleans Society," 20–36; Tregle, "Creoles and Americans," 131–85; Pagliarini, "Pure American Woman."

13. "The Dangerous Classes at the South," *Harper's Weekly*, 9 January 1875, 37–38; "The Papal Democracy and Civil War," *Harper's Weekly*, 27 January 1877, 70.

14. Joy Jackson, *New Orleans in the Gilded Age*, 17–19, 244–53; Summers, *Rum, Romanism, and Rebellion*, 78–83; Botein, "Hennessy Case"; Kenneth Jackson, *Ku Klux Klan in the City*, 241–49; MacLean, *Behind the Mask of Chivalry*, 91–97, 127–48; Blee, *Women of the Klan*, 76–93; Finan, *Alfred E. Smith*, 157–285.

15. Leathem, "Carnival," 183–91; Gilfoyle, *City of Eros*, 176, 213–14, 233–37, 264.

16. Tager, *Boston Riots*, 88–101; Fry, "Quebec's Relations."

17. Campbell, *Romantic Ethic*, 179–201; Sheriff, *Artificial River*, 27–62; Sears, *Sacred Places*, 49–71.

18. Löfgren, *On Holiday*, 19–40, 43–55, 58–68, 172–73, 216–20; Peiss, *Cheap Amusements*, 115–38; Lencek and Bosker, *Beach*, 127–31, 139–40, 153–71, 197–217; Simon, *Boardwalk of Dreams*, 21–24; Shaffer, "Seeing the Nature of America," 155–77; Shaffer, *See America First*, 11–39, 172–202; Withey, *Grand Tours and Cook's Tours*, 7, 33–35, 40–45, 105–32, 202, 299–336; Rothman, *Devil's Bargains*, 30–49.

19. "Sights in New-Orleans," *New York Times*, 9 March 1884; Walkowitz, *City of Dreadful Delight*, 81–134, 191–228; Srebnick, *Mysterious Death of Mary Rogers*, 61–83.

20. Olmsted, *Cotton Kingdom*, 239; Warner, "New Orleans," 186, 189–190.

21. Rydell, Findling, and Pelle, *Fair America*, 18–71; Rydell, *All the World's a Fair*, 3–8, 17–37, 73–104; Gilbert, *Perfect Cities*, 78–130.

22. "The 'Mistick Krewe,'" *Harper's Weekly*, 29 March 1873; Twain, *Life on the Mississippi*, 466–67; Cocks, "Chamber of Commerce's Carnival."

23. Hesse-Wartegg, *Travels*, 169–72.

24. Nye, *Electrifying America*, 287–335.

25. Twain, *Life on the Mississippi*, 424, 442–44; Starr, *Inventing New Orleans*, xii–xxvi.

26. Rebecca Harding Davis, "Here and There," 601; Phelps, "New Orleans and Reconstruction," 129.

27. Cocks, *Doing the Town*, 117; Harris, "Urban Tourism."

28. Alecia Long, *Great Southern Babylon*, 169–71.

29. Diary, 19–27 February 1903, Telling-Grandon Collection, UNO.

30. Ibid.

31. Belasco, *Americans on the Road*, 7–173; Berkowitz, " 'New Deal' for Leisure," 185–207; Jakle, *Tourist*, 84–198, 245–300; Weiss, "Tourism in America," 291, 295–96, 301, 309–18.

32. Embury, "Old New Orleans," 85.

33. Urry, *Consuming Places*, 147, 151; MacCannell, *Tourist*, x, 3; Hardy, *Mardi Gras Guide*, 34.

34. Colleen Long, "Iconic Locations in New Orleans Damaged by Katrina," Associated Press, 3 September 2005.

Chapter 1. A City of Destiny: New Orleans Businessmen and Modern Tourism

1. "Adopt New Slogan," *NOACNB*, 25 July 1922.

2. Harvey, *Urbanization of Capital*, 189. For a discussion of time and space within cities, see Harvey, *Consciousness and the Urban Experience*, 2–35; Benson, *Counter Cultures*, 12–116.

3. Fogelson, *Downtown*, 188.

4. Booster rhetoric offers a view into the concerns and beliefs of urban businessmen. The *New Orleans Association of Commerce News Bulletin*, though only slightly informative about tensions within the organization, provides excellent insight into businessmen's general concerns. Often opinionated and hopeful regarding progress, the editors of the *News Bulletin* strictly emphasized accuracy of information and realistic urban improvements. For a discussion of booster rhetoric, see Abbott, *Boosters and Businessmen*, 109–22; Gaston, *New South Creed*, 47, 63–79; Doyle, *New Men*, 136–88; Rothman, "Selling the Meaning of Place." Abbott shows that booster rhetoric reflected businessmen's need for "realistic and often precise knowledge about the economic bases" of their cities (*Boosters and Businessmen*, 109). Modern tourism, as Rothman suggests, differs little from previous economic enterprises. Business leaders need accurate information "to anticipate and cultivate trends in American society" ("Selling the Meaning of Place," 525) and require realistic calculations about transportation and capital to make successful investments.

5. Rae, *City*, 185–90.

6. "Larger Tourist Crop Object of Month's Personal Contact Trip," *NOACNB*, 9 August 1932; "Tourist Crop Best, Says Publisher," *New Orleans Item*, 9 February 1939. For information on the southern economy during the early twentieth century, see Arneson, *Waterfront Workers of New Orleans*, 244–52; Kirby, *Rural Worlds Lost*, 49–79, 115–54; Tindall, *Emergence of the New South*, 318–472; Wright, *Old South, New South*, 156–238.

7. "George Creel First Speaker for Council," *NOACNB*, 15 September 1919; David Kennedy, *Over Here*, 60–63, 90–91.

8. "The New Ideal," *NOACNB*, 22 December 1919. For information on business leaders' involvement in the First World War, see David Kennedy, *Over Here*, 45–92.

9. "The New Ideal," *NOACNB*, 22 December 1919.

10. "Annual Report—Membership Department," 1920–30, NOACM. For insight into New Orleans's pre-1918 business community, see Alecia Long, *Great Southern Babylon*, 64–82, 98–101; Tansey, "Prostitution and Politics," 449–64; Joy Jackson, *New Orleans in the Gilded Age*, 63–65, 215–23, 234–35.

11. "Things Other Than Trade," *NOACNB*, 12 August 1924; "Annual Report of President B. C. Casanas to the Members of the New Orleans Association of Commerce," 31 December 1919, NOACM; Brownell, *Urban Ethos in the South*, 125–55.

12. "Asleep," *NOACNB*, 18 August 1919.

13. "As Collier's Sees It," *NOACNB*, 20 June 1922.

14. "Boosting Becomes Disease with Californian, Says Native Son," *NOACNB*, 17 May 1921. In the 1920s, California used its scenery and climate to fuel land speculation similar to the land craze in Florida. Flood-control projects provided temporary jobs during the depression, opening more land to settlement and speculation (Mike Davis, *Ecology of Fear*, 61–72; Susan Davis, "Landscapes of Imagination," 173–77; Zimmerman, "Paradise Promoted"). Zimmerman reveals the importance of railroads to the development of southern California. In competition with San Francisco, Los Angeles formed powerful advertising campaigns. The Chamber of Commerce led the way. According to Zimmerman, the 1920s was the "golden age of Southern California boosterism" when advertising became "more visual in its appeal, and hedonism became acceptable as a motif" ("Paradise Promoted," 26). Developing year-round tourism gained particular attention. Since one of the main transcontinental railroad routes to the region ran through New Orleans, the city's residents were well aware of booster activities along the Pacific coast. Yet despite being

residents in a city with a long history, people in New Orleans were handicapped when competing against a region of relatively recent development.

15. "Summer Wonderland," 615; Portes and Stepick, *City on the Edge*, 74.

16. Convention and Tourism Bureau, 1919, NOACM. For Florida towns such as Tarpon Springs, middle-class tourists in automobiles in the 1920s replaced the upper-class tourists who had previously defined tourism. Since these early tourists often carried their own supplies, the development of the local culture became essential to getting tourists to spend money on food and souvenirs. Tarpon Springs boosters promoted the local Greek community involved in the sponge industry. Curio shops and Greek restaurants tapped tourist dollars. Boosters of Sarasota, conversely, pressed to develop the city as a deepwater port and metropolitan resort. They also recognized New Orleans as a prime competitor. Sarasotans even developed a local festival that they compared to the New Orleans Mardi Gras (Simpson-Walker, "Tarpon Springs"; Bauer, "Sarasota," 135–38).

17. *Biloxi News* clipping, 24 March 1933, NOACM; "'Outlook for Big Season Is Good,' Says C.-T. Bureau," *NOACNB*, 19 October 1920.

18. "5-Mile Chain of Islands to Protect, Develop, Beautify Lake Is Suggested," *NOACNB*, 26 August 1924; "Canals No Bar to Developing of Lake Front," *New Orleans Times-Picayune*, 26 February 1922; "New Seawall Will Wipe Out Historic Lakeside Resort," *New Orleans Times-Picayune*, 31 December 1922; "On Lake Pontchartrain," *New Orleans Times-Picayune*, 3 February 1923.

19. Brownell, *Urban Ethos in the South*, 61–97; Gaines M. Foster, *Ghosts of the Confederacy*, 80–91; Gaston, *New South Creed*, 86–116, 158–60, 167–77.

20. "Let 'Em Holler," *NOACNB*, 31 May 1921.

21. "Philadelphia's Loss," *NOACNB*, 16 August 1921.

22. "Sympathize with Galveston," *NOACNB*, 9 September 1924; "Galveston Has No Claim to Rank of Second Port," *NOACNB*, 5 January 1926.

23. "Flood Lies Written by Chicago Daily News Reporter about the South Brings Storm of Protest," *NOACNB*, 30 August 1927. For information about the 1927 flood and its impact, see Barry, *Rising Tide*, 399–411; Daniel, *Deep'n as It Come*; Saxon, *Father Mississippi*.

24. "National Ads Impressive Say Men Who Know," *NOACNB*, 12 April 1927; "Advertising De Luxe," *NOACNB*, 3 July 1928. For a typical mass publicity campaign before 1927, see "C. and T. Starts Campaign to Tell World about 1922 Mardi Gras," *NOACNB*, 23 August 1921. The Association of

Commerce undertook a campaign to raise one hundred thousand dollars for a sustained, three-year ad campaign to begin in the late 1920s. However, the 1927 flood altered the priorities of the marketing strategy (Fort Pipes to Martin Behrman, 4 August 1925, RMB).

25. "Municipal Flags," 244; Andre LaFarge, "The Story of Three Flags," 1922, RAJM.

26. "Minutes of Regular Weekly Meeting of the Executive Committee," 19 June 1929, NOACM; "Minutes of Regular Weekly Meeting of the Executive Committee," 5 August 1931, NOACM.

27. Anderson, "New Orleans."

28. "Anderson's Sneer," NOACNB, 3 August 1926.

29. "Reorganized C. & T. Bureau Hot on Trail of Many Conventions for 1924," NOACNB, 2 October 1923. For an in-depth examination of the close relationship between the New Orleans political machine and the business community, see Reynolds, Machine Politics in New Orleans, 104–5, 138–41.

30. For information on the concerns and conditions influencing the emergence of associations and chambers of commerce, see "Members Should Read This History of the Organization," NOACNB, 23 May 1922; Grantham, Southern Progressivism, 276–83; Painter, Standing at Armageddon, 173–79; Wiebe, Businessmen and Reform, 16–41; Wiebe, Search for Order, 123–32, 164–95.

31. "Seeing Is Believing," NOACNB, 22 March 1920.

32. "Annual Report of the New Orleans Association of Commerce Presented by Ernest Lee Jahnke," 7 January 1918, "Annual Report of President B. C. Casanas," 13 January 1919, both in NOACM.

33. "Report of the Budget Committee," 1919, "Minutes of the Annual Meeting of the Convention and Tourist Bureau," 15 December 1921, both in NOACM.

34. Aron, Working at Play, 9; Maunder, James Greeley McGowin, 40.

35. "Reports to Board of Directors for Month of September 1916," NOACM.

36. "Minutes of the Meeting of the Entertainment Committee of the Wholesale Merchants Bureau for the 1920 New Orleans Fall Buyers Convention," 1920, NOACM.

37. Entertainment program, National Association of Commercial Organization Secretaries' Convention, 23 October 1938, NOACM.

38. "Annual Report of President Arthur Parker," 10 January 1921, "Report

of the Finance Committee to the Board," 14 May 1915, "Director, T & C Bureau, to Board of Directors," 10 November 1920, "Minutes of Meeting of the Committee of Management of the Convention and Tourist Bureau," 17 April 1923, "Meeting of the Executive Committee of the Board of Directors," all in NOACM.

39. "Martin Behrman Is Re-Elected Head of the Convention Bureau," *NOACNB*, 2 January 1923; "Perkins and Paglin Re-Elected by C & T Bureau," *NOACNB*, 10 December 1929; "Conventions to Be Held in New Orleans, Issued by the Convention and Tourist Bureau of the New Orleans Association of Commerce," 1 February 1925, RAJM.

40. Harold Furlong to Andrew McShane, 23 October 1922, T. S. Walmsley to Andrew McShane, 4 October 1922, Ringling Brothers and Barnum and Bailey to Andrew McShane, 4 October 1922, all in RAJM; "Minutes of Meeting of the Local Hotel Men with Chairman Walmsley and Members of the American Legion Hotels and Housing Committee," 1922, "Minutes of Meeting of the Hotel Men," 6 December 1922, both in NOACM.

41. "Facts for Strangers," *NOACNB*, 16 June 1919.

42. "The Direct Way," *NOACNB*, 28 July 1919.

43. "Know Your City," *NOACNB*, 4 August 1919.

44. Parham Werlein to Andrew McShane, 26 February 1921, RAJM; "Committee Presents Plans for Great Civic Auditorium," *NOACNB*, 16 May 1922; "Site of French Opera," *New Orleans Times-Picayune*, 22 January 1921.

45. "Minutes, Meeting, Memorial Committee with Representatives of Various Civic Organizations," 10 June 1919, "Committee on Restoration of French Opera," 6 January 1921, "Minutes of Meeting of the Campaign Committee of the Civic Council," 24 October 1922, "Minutes of Meeting of the Coordination Committee of the Civic Council," 27 October 1922, "Annual Report of President Harold W. Newman," 8 January 1923, all in NOACM.

46. "Eight Years' of Effort Preceded Construction of Orleans Auditorium," *New Orleans Times-Picayune*, 30 May 1930.

47. "Rex, Porteus [*sic*] and Comus Make N.O. an All-Soul City, Says Schermerhorn," *NOACNB*, 20 February 1923.

48. "N.O. One of 5 Distinctive Cities in U.S., Says University Chief," *NOACNB*, 27 November 1923.

49. "As You Like It," *NOACNB*, 14 July 1919; Lyle Saxon diary, 9 February, 2 March 1925, Melrose Collection, Northwestern State University of Louisiana, Watson Memorial Library, Cammie G. Henry Research Center.

50. Flink, *Automobile Age*, 169–71; Huey Long, *Every Man a King*, 236–41; "Governor Long's Plan for Louisiana's Good Roads Improvement Program," 1929, NOACM; Leuchtenburg, *Franklin D. Roosevelt*, 118–42.

51. "The Association of Commerce Details—Good Roads Bureau," *NOACNB*, 10 July 1923; "Motorcade to Ponchatoula for Road Dedication April 27 Being Organized," *NOACNB*, 5 July 1927; "Motor Trips Planned to Give Orleanians Better Knowledge of Points of Interest Around City," *NOACNB*, 25 June 1929; "N.O. Terminus of More Highways Than Any Other City," *NOACNB*, 23 July 1935. For an excellent study of road construction and its meaning in a rural community, see Keith, *Country People*, 103–17. In Keith's study, roads were the basis of an efficient society: "Good roads would facilitate access to markets, churches, and schools; schools would teach good citizenship, proper consumer attitudes, and market-oriented farming; better-educated citizens would support law and order" (104). For a broader account, see Grantham, *Southern Progressivism*, 307–10.

52. "'Detour' No More," *NOACNB*, 13 April 1926; Lynd and Lynd, *Middletown*, 251–63; Lynd and Lynd, *Middletown in Transition*, 265–69; Allen, *Only Yesterday*, 227–28; Belasco, *Americans on the Road*, 7–39.

53. According to a 1927 survey by the General Federation of Women's Clubs, 60.5 percent of American families in towns with fewer than one thousand inhabitants owned automobiles. Only 54 percent of their counterparts in cities with more than one hundred thousand inhabitants owned automobiles. A total of 2.7 million of the nation's 27.5 million families owned two or more cars (Flink, *Automobile Age*, 129–35; Flink, *Car Culture*, 167; Belasco, *Americans on the Road*, 142–55).

54. "10,000 Tourists," *NOACNB*, 1 March 1927; "Tabulation Shows a Growth of Alien Auto Visits Last Summer," *NOACNB*, 18 September 1928; "New Orleans Again South's Leader in Conventions," *NOACNB*, 28 July 1931.

55. "Annual Report, Membership Department," 31 December 1929, "Annual Report, Membership Department," 1 January 1934, both in NOACM; "144 Conventions Bring $651,805 in New Money to N.O.," *NOACNB*, 11 December 1934; Flink, *Automobile Age*, 129–35; Flink, *Car Culture*, 167; Belasco, *Americans on the Road*, 142–55.

56. "Fortune Quarterly Survey: V," 158, 161.

57. "Universal," *NOACNB*, 27 February 1934; "Mardi Gras Visitors Set Records at Association Information Desk," *NOACNB*, 8 March 1938.

58. "Sightseeing Tours to Be Tested for N.O. Sales Value," *NOACNB*, 5 July 1927; "How N.O. Can Better Profit from Bus Tours Is Topic," *NOACNB*, 19 July 1927.

59. "Practices Obsolete," *NOACNB*, 27 November 1928.

60. Ibid.

61. *Original Cookes Tour of the City*, circa 1910s, AJSPC; *Seeing New Orleans*, circa 1940s, AJSPC.

62. "Will Write Out 'Louisiana,'" *NOACNB*, 9 October 1928; "Help Advertise N.O.," *NOACNB*, 26 August 1930; "N.O. Bumper Signs on Outgoing Cars," *NOACNB*, 2 December 1930.

63. "A. of C. Sends Out 12,000 Tourist Bids," *NOACNB*, 7 May 1929.

64. "100,000 Tourist Bids," *NOACNB*, 14 May 1929.

65. "Board Changes Name of C. & T. Bureau to C. & V. Bureau," *NOACNB*, 14 October 1930; "Selling Technique of C & V Bureau Outlined," *NOACNB*, 4 February 1936.

66. Arthur O'Keefe statement, 27 November 1929, RAJO; "Annual Message of President A. M. Lockett," 11 January 1937, NOACM; "Five-Phase Program Outlined by Lockett," *NOACNB*, 3 November 1931; "Five-Plan Referendum," *NOACNB*, 10 November 1931.

67. Brownell, *Urban Ethos in the South*, 193.

68. "Your City Is Growing," *NOACNB*, 5 August 1930. Terry Cooney points out that during the depression, the present, "filled with frustration and confusion," was often "set against visions of a more cohesive, more romantic, or more purposeful past" (*Balancing Acts*, 24–25).

69. "Without New Orleans, All Western America Is Valueless," *NOACNB*, 28 April 1931.

70. "Pictures of Prominent Visitors with Typical N.O. Settings Planned," *NOACNB*, 21 October 1930; "Annual Address of the President of the New Orleans Association of Commerce," 9 January 1933, NOACM.

71. "Everybody Agrees on N.O.," *NOACNB*, 4 October 1932.

72. "Minutes of the Regular Monthly Meeting of the Board of Directors," 10 August 1932, NOACM; "Plans Laid for Intense Tourist Campaign," *NOACNB*, 20 September 1932; "New WSMB Series Inaugurated by Commissioner Pratt with Talk on 'The Visitor,'" *NOACNB*, 15 November 1932.

73. "Annual Report, Convention and Tourist Bureau," 6 November 1932, NOACM; "First of Series of Newspaper Ads," *NOACNB*, 8 November 1932, 8; "Vieux Carre," *NOACNB*, 22 November 1932; "Vieux Carre," *NOACNB*,

29 November 1932; "Golf Courses," *NOACNB*, 15 November 1932; "Mardi Gras," *NOACNB*, 6 December 1932; "The 'Old World' City So Close to You," *NOACNB*, 6 November 1934; "Cuts to Advertise New Orleans Available to Members," *NOACNB*, 29 August 1939; "Visit Quaint New Orleans," *NOACNB*, 7 November 1939.

74. "Biennial Report of the Board of Curators for 1920–21," 53, "Biennial Report of the Board of Curators for 1928–29," 50, "Biennial Report of the Board of Curators for 1930–31," 55, "Biennial Report of the Board of Curators for 1944–45," 9, all in LSM. Although the figures failed to separate locals from out-of-towners, the museum staff, local press, and Association of Commerce recognized the Cabildo numbers as the most accurate means of gauging the size of the tourist crop. The *Times-Picayune* reported in 1939 that "the Structure is a No. 1 stop for a certain portion of all visitors from afar and its guest books may safely be said to reflect a steadily increasing flow of pilgrims to the city." Museum officials agreed. The institution's 1942 biennial report declared the attendance figures "an unfailing barometer of the number who flock to the Old Square annually" ("Biennial Report of the Board of Curators for 1938–39," 13, "Biennial Report of the Board of Curators for 1941–42," 14, both in LSM).

75. "Offering over $100 for $1," *NOACNB*, 2 October 1934; "Biennial Report of the Board of Curators for 1941–42," 15, LSM.

76. "More Rooms for Visitors Needed," *NOACNB*, 9 May 1939.

77. "New Orleans' Largest Industry Has No Smoke Stack," pamphlet produced by the Convention and Visitors' Bureau, no date, RRSM; "144 Conventions Bring $651,805 in New Money to N.O.," *NOACNB*, 11 December 1934; "Annual Report, C & V Bureau," 30 November 1937, NOACM; "The Tourist: A Business Builder," *NOACNB*, 20 June 1939.

78. "President Hoover Says 'A City of Destiny,'" *NOACNB*, 28 January 1930.

79. "Playing the Game," *NOACNB*, 19 February 1924.

Chapter 2. New Era New Orleans: The Great Depression, Taxation, and Robert Maestri

1. "Presentation to Mayor Walmsley by Employees of the New Orleans Welfare Committee," 6 December 1932, OPCC.

2. Cobb, *Selling of the South*, 5, 21–35, 157, 228; T. Harry Williams, *Huey*

Long, 155–80, 693. Other cash-strapped governments nationwide tried a variety of innovative ways to raise money. In 1931, sparsely populated Nevada legalized gambling. In 1936, Mississippi developed the Balance Agriculture with Industry Program, supplying subsidies to attract factories. Several states quickly followed Mississippi's lead. For a discussion of the economic depression in agriculture, a major contributor to New Orleans's commercial trade, see Garraty, *Great Depression*, 52–61; Kirby, *Rural Worlds Lost*, 27–49; Tindall, *Emergence of the New South*, 111–14, 122, 354–57.

3. "Special Report of Commissioner of Public Finances," 6 December 1932, "Special Message of the Mayor," 6 December 1932, both in OPCC. Cities and local governments throughout the United States depended on property taxes, which amounted to more than 80 percent of local taxes in the late 1920s and more than 90 percent in the early 1930s. With the depression, median tax delinquency for cities with populations greater than fifty thousand rose to 10.5 percent in 1930 and peaked at 26.35 percent in 1933. Shreveport, Louisiana, endured a rate of 68.6 percent. The highest delinquency rate in the country, an incredible 96 percent, plagued Lake County, Indiana (Beito, "National Pay-Your-Taxes Campaign," 388–89; Ortquist, "Tax Crisis," 97–98).

4. "Canal Street Beautified," *New Orleans Times-Picayune*, 23 February 1930; "New Orleans," *New Orleans Times-Picayune*, 24 February 1930; Heleniak, "Local Reaction," 293–94. The fate experienced by New Orleans and the actions taken in the early 1930s closely paralleled other American cities, such as Baltimore, which also faced debts from improvements undertaken in the 1920s, and Newark, which confronted high property tax delinquency rates. For comparison to other cities, see Fogelson, *Downtown*, 218–21; Kimberly, "Depression in Maryland," 191–94, 197–201; Beito, "National Pay-Your-Taxes Campaign," 388–89, 392–93, 395; Ortquist, "Tax Crisis," 96–119.

5. Hoover, *Memoirs of Herbert Hoover*, 16, 39; Galbraith, *Great Crash*, 168–86; David Kennedy, *Freedom from Fear*, 58–60, 65–66, 69. Galbraith argues that no evidence shows that Americans' "desire for automobiles, clothing, travel, recreation, or even food was sated. On the contrary, all subsequent evidence showed (given the income to spend) a capacity for a large further increase in consumption. A depression was not needed so that people's wants could catch up with their capacity to produce" (*Great Crash*, 173). An estimated 13 million people were unemployed in 1933.

6. "Relief of Unemployment," *New Orleans Times-Picayune*, 14 March 1930.

7. Runyan, "Economic Trends in New Orleans," 8, 21–22, 36, 45. Based on total population New Orleans suffered from an unemployment rate of 4.3 percent in 1930, 9.7 percent in 1937, and 8.4 percent in 1940.

8. "Prayer," 5 May 1930, OPCC; Runyan, "Economic Trends in New Orleans," 57.

9. "Annual Report of the Commissioner of the Department of Public Finance for the Year Ended December 31, 1924," 26, "Annual Report of the Commissioner of the Department of Public Finance for the Year Ended December 31, 1925," 30, "Annual Report of the Commissioner of the Department of Public Finance for the Year Ended December 31, 1926," 14, "Annual Report of the Commissioner of the Department of Public Finance for the Year Ended December 31, 1929," 26–27, 53, "Annual Report of the Commissioner of the Department of Public Finance for the Year Ended December 31, 1945," 35–55, all at UNO; "Walmsley Objects as Banks Call City Loans of $653,000," *New Orleans Times-Picayune*, 31 May 1930. During the 1920s, the city treasury typically received $25,000 to $55,000 annually in interest from overdue taxes. In 1930, the city owed American Bank and Trust Company ($8,400), Canal Bank and Trust Company ($323,700), Hibernia Bank and Trust Company ($110,200), Interstate Trust and Banking Company ($19,600), New Orleans Bank and Trust Company ($11,200), and Whitney National Bank ($162,400).

10. "Special Message of the Mayor," 5 May 1931, "New Business," 22 August 1934, "From the Mayor, Special Message," 22 March 1932, all in OPCC; "Mayor Recounts History of City's Welfare Effort," *New Orleans Times-Picayune*, 5 January 1933; Heleniak, "Local Reaction," 298–300. The city had previously allowed residents to defer personal tax payments for up to three years before sending property to auction. Deferments added interest and legal fees to the original tax debt. In a stable or growing economy, such a procedure tantalized city financial officers. That many politicians possessed ties to the legal profession only sweetened the deal. Yet economic decline quickly shocked City Hall out of its complacency. Even the money raised by the bond issue and close supervision of funds could do little in the face of rising unemployment. By the end of 1932, the city found itself harboring seven thousand families desperate for relief. The money available to the Welfare Committee only permitted the expenditure of $60,000 per month from local sources met with an additional $90,000 from the state. With the going rate of $2.50 for a day's worth of labor, the Welfare Committee faced a severe financial crunch. Families usually represented several able-bodied men, plus a wife, daughters,

and young sons. To make matter worse, each day more needy citizens appeared outside New Orleans's relief offices.

11. "From the Mayor," 25 October 1932, "Report of Commissioner of Public Finance," 9 March 1932, "From the Mayor, Special Message," 22 March 1932, all in OPCC; Heleniak, "Local Reaction," 303; "Financial Condition of City of New Orleans as Result of Freezing of Funds in Banks—Taxpayers Delay in Paying Taxes," 11 October 1933, NOACM; "Suggests Change in Taxation Plan," *New Orleans Times-Picayune*, 31 December 1933. The budgetary plans prepared in March assumed the worst. The Commission Council, anticipating a $17 million drop in property values rather than the $35 million proposed by the Louisiana Taxing Commission, carefully trimmed the city budget. Salaries dropped by 15 percent while other expenditures were slashed from an already lean municipal government. The average 10 percent salary cuts were expected to save $24,000 per month. By June, however, property assessment revenue declined by more than $421,000, much more than the measures taken by Walmsley and Pratt could absorb. Although expediting tax collection and streamlining expenditures gained priority, the Walmsley administration understood the need for leniency as well. Many New Orleanians could not afford the burden of taxes in a depressed economy. Given the times, Walmsley announced his intention to "proceed with care and discrimination in order not to increase burdens already too heavy." Pratt worked with Walmsley to meet the expected $236,000 shortfall.

12. "Financial Condition of City of New Orleans as Result of Freezing of Funds in Banks—Taxpayers Delay in Paying Taxes," 11 October 1933, NOACM; "Statement by Mayor Walmsley," 22 May 1933, OPCC.

13. "Gasoline Taxation," *New Orleans Times-Picayune*, 9 December 1930; "Gasoline-Tax Diversion," *New Orleans Times-Picayune*, 16 April 1932. Louisiana levied a five-cent per gallon tax on gasoline, while New Orleans added another cent per gallon within its city limits. Those figures certainly placed the state in rare company, since only three states possessed a six-cent tax. Nationally, gas taxes for the first six months of 1930 sent $230 million into public treasuries, compared with $175 million for the same period in 1929. For the first half of 1930, $13 million went to projects other than road construction.

14. "Ordinances on Final Passage," 16 October 1934, OPCC; "Annual Report of the Commissioner of the Department of Public Finance for the Year Ended December 31, 1935," 74, "Annual Report of the Commissioner of the

Department of Public Finance for the Year Ended December 31, 1937," 46, both in UNO; Robert Maestri to John Mirt, 6 June 1938, RRSM.

15. "Anti-Gambling Committee Asks the Governor's Co-Operation toward Suppressing of Evil of Illegal Practice around N.O.," *NOACNB*, 3 July 1928; Annual Report of Members' Council for the Year 1920, 4 March 1920, "Minutes of the Meeting of the Anti-Gambling Committee," 25 June 1928, both in NOACM; Joy Jackson, *New Orleans in the Gilded Age*, 63–64, 268–69.

16. "Permission Given for Fair Grounds Races on Sunday," *New Orleans Times-Picayune*, 11 February 1933; Heleniak, "Local Reaction," 298; Frank Smidtt to Robert Maestri, 14 June 1937, RRSM; Haas, *DeLesseps S. Morrison*, 48, 172, 177–78.

17. "If Only We Could Use It!" *New Orleans Times-Picayune*, 26 March 1932.

18. "The Beer Tax," *New Orleans Times-Picayune*, 22 March 1933.

19. "Beer Ordinance for New Orleans Voted; Promptly Signed by Mayor," *New Orleans Times-Picayune*, 8 April 1933; "Ordinances on Final Passage," 4 December 1933, "Ordinances on Final Passage," 7 January 1934, both in OPCC; "Annual Report of the Commissioner of the Department of Public Finance for the Year Ended December 31, 1935," 74, "Annual Report of the Commissioner of the Department of Public Finance for the Year Ended December 31, 1937," 46, both in UNO. Prior to 1937, city officials charged a flat fee of $360 for a liquor license, arguing that differentiating between hard liquor and beer and wine would simply cause beer sellers to draw on their long experience in circumventing the law to bootleg whiskey. In that year, however, the Commission Council separated licenses for hard liquor from those for just beer and wine, charging $500 for a hard liquor permit and dropping the fee to $100 for beer and wine. The higher fees charged to bars more than offset the lower cost of wine and beer licenses, resulting in the dramatic jump in alcohol-related revenue ("A New Liquor Ordinance," *New Orleans Times-Picayune*, 19 December 1936).

20. "Walmsley Orders Closing of City's Speakeasies to Protect Beer Taxpayers," *New Orleans Times-Picayune*, 9 April 1933.

21. "From the Mayor, Special Message," 10 August 1934, OPCC.

22. Ibid.

23. "Ordinance on Final Passage," 22 August 1934, OPCC; "Amusement Tax Problems," no date, Robert Maestri to John Mirt, 6 June 1938, both in RRSM.

24. "Soaking the Poor Again" (flier), 29 October 1937, "Statement by Mayor," 24 January 1938, both in RRSM; "Annual Report of the Commissioner of the Department of Public Finance for the Year Ended December 31, 1937," 46, UNO; L. E. Himler to Jess Cave, 9 September 1937, 13 January 1938, 12 July 1938, RRSM. The luxury tax did not apply to supplies purchased by vessels traveling through New Orleans (John Conway to Robert Maestri, 22 May 1938, R. E. Tipton to Robert Maestri, 27 May 1938, E. H. Murphy to Robert Maestri, 18 May 1938, George Norton to Members of the Legislature of the State of Louisiana, 12 June 1937, H. Van R. Chase to Robert Maestri, 7 June 1938, all in RRSM).

25. "An Epistle to the Pharaohs," *Anti-Taxer* (circa 1935), RRSM; Runyan, "Economic Trends in New Orleans," 23–48.

26. "Important Facts About N.O. Hotels Revealed by Moore," *NOACNB*, 17 June 1930; "The Tourist: A Business Builder," *NOACNB*, 9 May 1939.

27. J. Walker Ross Jr. to Jesse Cave, 17 March 1937, RRSM.

28. "Financial Statistics of City Government of New Orleans for 1936," 3 January 1938, Department of Commerce, Bureau of the Census, RRSM; Walker, *Research Papers, Issues Forum*, 30–33, 139. A 1937 movement sought to include football games, philharmonic concerts, and little theaters under the 2 percent amusement tax because persons who attended these functions were deemed most able to afford the tax. A year earlier, the amusement tax had been revised to exempt movie theaters that charged less than fifteen cents for admission, taking $2,500 a month from city coffers (Richard Foster to Robert Maestri, 15 February 1937, "Amusement Tax Problems" [memo], no date, both in RRSM). Tourists spent $3.8 million in sales taxes according to the 1969 study.

29. "Statement by Mayor Walmsley," 22 May 1933, OPCC, "From the Mayor," 9 October 1934, both in OPCC; "Says Lack of Coordination Hurts Recovery," *Berkeley Gazette*, 20 March 1934, RRSM.

30. "Unfavorable Publicity for City as Result of Fight between Political Factions—Partial Martial Law, Etc.," 8 August 1934, NOACM; "Long Offers to Let Federal Land Bank Be Taken from City," *New Orleans Times-Picayune*, 26 June 1935. For insight into Long's tactics and public reaction, see Brinkley, *Voices of Protest*, 65–67; Cortner, *Kingfish and the Constitution*, 59–64.

31. "Mayor's Inaugural Address," 7 May 1934, OPCC.

32. "Special Message from the Mayor," 5 February 1935, OPCC. Accord-

ing to Walmsley, a large part of the $112 million in official property value reductions since 1930 had come at the hands of Long's henchmen.

33. "Radio Talk Station WWL," transcript, 15 October 1936, "Public Welfare Digest," Department of Public Welfare of the City of New Orleans, August 1936, "Census of Partial Employment, Unemployment, and Occupations," 25 April 1938, all in RRSM; Moore, "New Deal in Louisiana," 145–50. For an excellent comparative study of New Deal programs in southern cities, see Smith, *New Deal in the Urban South*. The city's Department of Public Welfare in 1936 served five thousand families at a cost of well over one hundred thousand dollars per month. Federal programs, which were trimming their rolls, aided twenty thousand additional families. A November 1937 survey of unemployment in New Orleans listed close to thirteen thousand persons as partially unemployed, meaning they possessed part-time work with earnings below what they needed for survival. The figure excluded persons lacking any employment or workers in federal relief programs such as the WPA. New Orleans administrators thus clearly required whatever funds they could collect to care for the city's still serious unemployment problem.

34. Miller, "Tourist Trap," 222–23; Moore, "New Deal in Louisiana," 145–50; Stanonis, "'Always in Costume and Mask,'" 35–52.

35. "Motion," 13 July 1935, OPCC.

36. "Report of Commissioner of Public Finance," 21 November 1935, "From the Mayor, Special Message," 3 December 1935, both in OPCC.

37. T. Semmes Walmsley to Commission Council, 9 March 1936, OPCC.

38. Haas, "New Orleans," 286–88, 295.

39. Jack Williams, "Huey's Scepter Still Rules in Another Hand," *Kansas City Journal Post*, 15 March 1938, Irv Kupcinet, "Shades of Huey Long! Mardi Gras Steals All," *Chicago Times*, 25 February 1938, both in RRSM.

40. Haas, "New Orleans," 289–95; "Annual Report of the Commissioner of the Department of Public Finance for the Year Ended December 31, 1945," 45, 59, UNO.

41. Haas, "New Orleans," 289–90; Moore, "New Deal in Louisiana," 151–52, 156–63; Runyan, "Economic Trends in New Orleans," 58.

42. Charles Thorn and Jonathan Taylor, "Our Dynamic Mayor," *NOACNB*, 2 March 1937.

43. Edward Rapier to Ben J. Williams, 29 September 1938, RRSM.

44. Deputy Commissioner (no name) to J. O. Fernandez, 4 June 1937,

Robert Maestri to M. E. Polson, 27 January 1939, Edward Rapier to Robert Maestri, 1 February 1939, Edwin Heaton to Robert Maestri, 21 June 1939, all in RRSM; "Report," 17 August 1938, 11–12, OPCC.

45. A. Miles Pratt to Robert Maestri, 5 January 1938, Joseph Skelly to Robert Maestri, no date, both in RRSM; James Lee Reilly, "Street-Cleaning Problems," 54–56; "Glean Bucketful of Gum a Night on Canal Street," *New Orleans Times-Picayune*, 29 January 1939.

46. Robert Maestri to Commission Council, no date, James Fortier to Robert Maestri, 30 September 1937, H. Van R. Chase to Robert Maestri, 1 October 1937, all in RRSM.

47. Helen Schertz to Robert Maestri, circa 1938, Warren Miller to Robert Maestri, 12 January 1938, both in RRSM.

48. "Minutes of the Regular Weekly Meeting of the Executive Committee," 4 November 1931, NOACM; Fred Corcoran to Robert Maestri, 22 February 1938, Fred Salmen to Robert Maestri, 21 February 1938, both in RRSM.

49. "Minutes of the Regular Weekly Meeting of the Executive Committee," 18 November 1931, NOACM; Warren Miller to E. M. Rea, 11 June 1935, Joseph Cousins to Robert Maestri, 16 December 1937, 15 January 1938, R. H. Fleming to Robert Maestri, 22, 29 December 1937, both in RRSM; "Sugar Bowl Crowd of 42,000 Sets New Orleans Attendance Record," *New Orleans Times-Picayune*, 2 January 1937; "Fans See Great Fullback Lead Aggies' Triumph," *New Orleans Times-Picayune*, 2 January 1940; "Boston College Takes Back Sugar Bowl Crown by 19–13 Defeat Handed to Tennessee," *New Orleans Times-Picayune*, 2 January 1941.

50. "Biennial Report of the Board of Curators for 1936–37," 67–69, LSM; A. Sidney Nunez to Robert Maestri, 8 July 1938, RRSM.

51. "Movie of the Week: *The Buccaneer*," *Life* 4 (10 January 1938): 54; radio conversation between Cecil B. DeMille and Lyle Saxon, 10 January 1938, Lyle Saxon Papers, Manuscripts Department, TU; "Biennial Report of the Board of Curators for 1936–37," 69–71, LSM; "City Commemorates 125th Anniversary of Battle of New Orleans; Units March," *New Orleans Times-Picayune*, 8 January 1940.

52. Franklin Roosevelt to John Overton, 17 July 1937, E. L. Hawes to Robert Maestri, 15 May 1937, J. D. Fernandez to Robert Maestri, 26 June 1937, all in RRSM.

53. Chris Valley to Robert Maestri, 9 December 1937, "Elks Outdoor Xmas

Lighting Contest to All Citizens of New Orleans," 30 November 1937, both in RRSM.

54. "Minutes of the Meeting of the Civic Affairs Committee," 18 November 1936, NOACM.

55. "Fireworks Victims," *New Orleans Times-Picayune*, 3 January 1935.

56. Edward Estalote to Robert Maestri, 2 January 1938, F. W. Thompson to Robert Maestri, 6 January 1938, W. E. Sherwood to Robert Maestri, 4 January 1938, J. W. Hanson to Robert Maestri, 4 January 1938, S. O. Brisburn to Robert Maestri, circa 1938, Francis Badeaux to Robert Maestri, 4 January 1938, all in RRSM.

57. "Outlaw Fireworks in New Orleans!" *New Orleans Item*, 2 January 1938; George Reyer to Robert Maestri, 4 January 1938, RRSM; "Arrest 9 for Firecrackers," *New Orleans Item*, 1 January 1939.

58. A. M. Billie Wilhelm to Robert Maestri, 19 December 1936, RRSM.

59. "Minutes of the Regular Semi-Monthly Meeting of the Board of Directors," 21 September 1938, "Minutes of the Meeting of the Executive Committee," 25 May 1938, both in NOACM.

60. "Pontiac Program over Columbia Broadcasting System through KMQX," 27 August 1936, John Mirt, "New Orleans Out of Red in 2-Year Economy Drive," *Chicago Daily News*, 1938, both in RRSM.

61. WDSU press sheet, 25 August 1936, Judith Douglas to Robert Maestri, 26 July 1938, J. C. Corbin to Robert Maestri, no date, all in RRSM; "What Every Citizen Should Know," 2 November 1936, Bureau of Governmental Research, RRSM.

Chapter 3. A New Babylon: Vice and Gender in New Orleans

1. Faulkner, *New Orleans Sketches*, 49–50.

2. Isenberg, *Downtown America*, 14–28, 39–40, 68–72; Hickey, *Hope and Danger*, 58–60, 77.

3. L. T. Hastings to Andrew McShane, 5 July 1922, "A Grandmother from Algiers" to Andrew McShane, 2 July 1922, both in RAJM; "Mayor Forbids Bathing Beauties to Stage Parade," *New Orleans Times-Picayune*, 2 July 1922.

4. Joy Jackson, "Prohibition in New Orleans," 262–65; Kerr, *Organized for Prohibition*, 199–210. Brewers attempted to distance themselves from distillers

of hard liquor to avoid possible restrictions on beer. The split eliminated any chance at a united front against Prohibitionists.

5. Behrman quoted in T. Harry Williams, *Huey Long*, 131; Behrman, *Martin Behrman*, 279–80.

6. Behrman, *Martin Behrman*, 279–80; Joy Jackson, "Prohibition in New Orleans," 261–63. For an insightful examination of Storyville as a tourist attraction in a region in which rural towns fell increasingly under laws restricting vice, see Alecia Long, *Great Southern Babylon*, 160–72; Alecia Long, "Notorious Attraction"; Ownby, *Subduing Satan*, 167–84, 203–11. For information on red-light districts, prostitution, and reform movements nationwide prior to 1918, see Hobson, *Uneasy Virtue*, 139–64; Rosen, *Lost Sisterhood*, 28–33, 70–111.

7. "Commissioner Resigns When Aid of Plain Clothes Men to Close Saloons Is Refused," *New Orleans Item*, 19 June 1917; Reynolds, *Machine Politics in New Orleans*, 61–62.

8. Behrman, *Martin Behrman*, 303–4, 307–8; "District House Owners Accused by Police," *New Orleans Item*, 30 May 1917; Asbury, *French Quarter*, 451–52; Reynolds, *Machine Politics in New Orleans*, 156–61; Hobson, *Uneasy Virtue*, 166–72.

9. Tyler, *Silk Stockings*, 14–27; Gordon, *Gender and Higher Education*, 177–88; Stanonis, "Woman of Boundless Energy," 8–13.

10. "A Decision That Flavors Liquor Lawlessness," *New Orleans Item*, 20 June 1917; Jean Gordon to Ida Weiss Friend, 17 December 1917, Permelia Shields to Ida Weiss Friend, 18 March 1921, Ida Weiss Friend Papers, Manuscripts Department, TU.

11. "Annual Report of President Arthur Parker," 10 January 1921, NOACM.

12. "Punctiliousness, Primness, and Prudery Prevail Here," *New Orleans Times-Picayune*, 2 January 1920.

13. "Tango Belt Joys Turned to Gloom," *New Orleans Times-Picayune*, 18 February 1920; "Quartier Club Café Is Raided by Dry Agents," *New Orleans Times-Picayune*, 9 February 1924; "Noted Cabarets Included in List by Judge Foster," *New Orleans Times-Picayune*, 1 March 1924; "Old Royal Street Is Being Rebuilt by Prohibition," *New Orleans Times-Picayune*, 28 March 1926.

14. "City Tight in Grip of Organized Vice, Says Capt. Wilson," *New Orleans Times-Picayune*, 13 July 1919; "163 'Houses' in Orleans Listed by U.S. Agents," *New Orleans Item*, 26 January 1921; Cash, *Mind of the South*, 320.

Cash emphasizes the role of blacks in the hotel industry and, with racist overtones, criticizes moral reforms that made white women dependent on black pimps.

15. "Minutes, Regular Meeting Board of Directors," 29 July 1919, NOACM; "Grand Jury Says Hotels Are Trying to Prohibit Vice," *New Orleans Times-Picayune*, 20 July 1919; "Hotel Sues Times-Picayune," *New Orleans Times-Picayune*, 20 July 1919; "Meeting of Special Committee of Members, Council on Investigation," 17 January 1921, NOACM.

16. "163 'Houses' in Orleans Listed by U.S. Agents," *New Orleans Item*, 26 January 1921.

17. Ibid. For insight into contemporary attitudes toward white and black sexuality, see Gilmore, *Gender and Jim Crow*, 70–75; Hale, *Making Whiteness*, 32.

18. "163 'Houses' in Orleans Listed by U.S. Agents," *New Orleans Item*, 26 January 1921; Ordinance #6359, 29 July 1921, City Council City Ordinances, City Archives and Special Collections, New Orleans Public Library; Robert Kinney, *The Bachelor in New Orleans* (1942), 57, AJSPC; Vyhnanek, *Unorganized Crime*, 134. So strong was the taxi company–prostitution link within New Orleans that reform mayoral candidate DeLesseps S. Morrison felt it necessary to cut a deal with cab drivers on the eve of Election Day 1946, guaranteeing that his administration would not interfere with the sex trade. Conditions became so bad, however, that a crackdown ensued in 1950 as public pressure mounted. For information on the taxicab-sex trade in the 1940s and early 1950s, see Haas, *DeLesseps S. Morrison*, 38–39, 48–50, 181–83.

19. David Jackson to Thomas Healy, 1 December 1925, RMB; "What Is a Hotel?" *New Orleans Times-Picayune*, 2 March 1927; Reichert and Frey, "Organization of Bell Desk Prostitution," 516–25; "163 'Houses' in Orleans Listed by U.S. Agents," *New Orleans Item*, 26 January 1921. Although they study Las Vegas in the late 1970s, Reichert and Frey provide insights into a system that has changed little since the appearance of telephones and automobiles. For information on hotel prostitution, see Duis, *Saloon*, 150–215; Gilfoyle, *City of Eros*, 243–48. In New York and Boston, attempts to restrict alcohol to hotels merely pressed saloon owners to install bedrooms. In cities unlike New Orleans or Chicago, which had vice districts, prostitution flourished in small hotel-saloons as early as the turn of the century.

20. "New Orleans Nights: Little Adventures in Devilment," *New Orleans Times-Picayune*, 14 January 1920; "Lyle Saxon," newspaper clipping, Arts and

Crafts Club Papers, Historic New Orleans Collection, Williams Research Center; David Jackson to Thomas Healy, 17 November 1925, RMB; Wiltz, *Last Madam*, 24–69.

21. Martin Behrman to Thomas Healy, 30 November 1925, "A Friend" to Martin Behrman, 9 October 1925, "Respectable Citizen" to Martin Behrman, 14 October 1925, James Dimitry to Thomas Healy, 21 October 1925, all in RMB; Grace Brandas to Arthur O'Keefe, 25 October 1926, RAJO; Vyhnanek, *Unorganized Crime*, 143–45.

22. "A Neighbor" to Arthur O'Keefe, 18 April 1926, "Second Precinct Station," 14 May 1926, "Third Precinct Station," 22 October 1926, all in RAJO.

23. William Azcona to Thomas Healy, 28 October 1926, RAJO; William Azcona to Theodore Ray, 26 November 1929, Records of Mayor T. Semmes Walmsley, City Archives and Special Collections, New Orleans Public Library; " 'Walking Bars' Latest Scheme of Bootleggers," *New Orleans Times-Picayune*, 14 February 1923.

24. Gracinette quoted in Joy Jackson, "Prohibition in New Orleans," 267.

25. Ivy Kitterege to Andrew McShane and the Commission Council, 12 February 1924, OPCC; "Citizen" to Martin Behrman, 16 July 1925, RMB.

26. "Southern Athletic Association Union Officials Club," no date, RAJO.

27. Reynolds, *Machine Politics in New Orleans*, 12.

28. "Is Marriage a Success?" *New Orleans Item*, 7 January 1921.

29. Erenberg, *Steppin' Out*, 236.

30. S. Lillian Burk, Graduation Speech at Esplanade High School, June 1919, Rene A. Steigler Papers, Williams Research Center, Historic New Orleans Collection; Cott, *Grounding of Modern Feminism*, 147–50; Cott, *Public Vows*, 157–74.

31. Bobbins to marriage editor, *New Orleans Item*, 25 January 1921; Frank Vernon M'Ger to editor, *New Orleans Times-Picayune*, 12 January 1920. For an example of how women engaged in activity previously considered taboo—in this case, cigarettes—see Tate, *Cigarette Wars*, 93–117.

32. Leathem, "Carnival," 225–26; Marone, *Hellfire Nation*, 258–73; Odem, *Delinquent Daughters*, 1–5, 129, 135–38; McDermott and Blackstone, "White Slavery Plays," 141–55; Lubove, "Progressives and the Prostitute"; Haag, " 'Commerce in Souls,' " 292–305; Hobson, *Uneasy Virtue*, 139–47, 150–54.

33. Iglehart, *King Alcohol Dethroned*, 1, 20–22.

34. "Prohibition," *New Orleans Times-Picayune*, 26 February 1926; "Less

Drunkenness," *New Orleans Times-Picayune*, 13 January 1925; "A Prohibition Anniversary," *New Orleans Times-Picayune*, 16 January 1925.

35. "Special Report of Commissioner of Public Safety," 3 July 1928, OPCC.

36. Mary Doiron, self-taped for her grandchildren, no date, Friends of the Cabildo Oral History Project, New Orleans Public Library, City Archives and Special Collections; "New Orleans: The City of Progress, Beauty, Charm, and Romance," Louisville and Nashville Railroad, 1921, 21–22, WRPC; Gillson, *Progressive Years*, 189–90, 204–6, 251–55, 260–70; Mohl, *New City*, 170–79; Bauman, "Disinfecting the Industrial City"; Rettmann, "Business, Government, and Prostitution." Rettmann reveals the profitability of municipally sanctioned prostitution. Fines charged monthly to prostitutes helped fill city coffers, suggesting the importance of commercial sex in funding urban budgets stretched by improvement projects and expanding population.

37. Anderson, *Story Teller's Story*, 80–81.

38. "Is Marriage a Success?" *New Orleans Item*, 1 January 1921; "Letters to the Editor," *New Orleans Times-Picayune*, 15 January 1920; Tyler, *Silk Stockings*, 24; Cott, *Grounding of Modern Feminism*, 42–45, 149; Kessler-Harris, *Out to Work*, 224–36; D'Emilio and Freedman, *Intimate Matters*, 229–49. Kate Gordon opposed a constitutional amendment to give women the right to vote, considering it a threat to racial harmony; Werlein, conversely, supported a suffrage amendment. See Tyler, *Silk Stockings*, 20–25.

39. Murdock, *Domesticating Drink*, 160–61; Erenberg, *Steppin' Out*, 234–52.

40. Bailey, *From Front Porch to Back Seat*, 16–28; Ullman, *Sex Seen*, 104–36; Asbury, *French Quarter*, 455.

41. "Women 'Call Out' at Krewe Dance," *New Orleans Times-Picayune*, 27 January 1923; "Disquieting News from Rex; Harem Ladies to Bob Hair," *New Orleans Times-Picayune*, 24 February 1924; Margaret Dixon, "Women's Role in Carnival," *New Orleans Times-Picayune*, 21 February 1936; Mitchell, *All on a Mardi Gras Day*, 170; Tallant, *Mardi Gras as It Was*, 43–45, 165.

42. Anthony Ragusin to Arthur O'Keefe, 18 June 1926, RAJO; Flink, *Car Culture*, 145, 158; Lears, *Fables of Abundance*, 148–53, 183–92; Brumberg, *Body Project*, 104–7; Cott, *Grounding of Modern Feminism*, 149–50; Tate, *Cigarette Wars*, 94–95; Lencek and Bosker, *Beach*, 200–217. Lears explains, "The voluptuous woman and the bearded man had been far more formidable figures than the perpetually boyish husband and his giggling girl-bride—two icons who came to dominate the fiction as well as the advertising pages of the

national magazines during the 1910s and 1920s" (*Fables of Abundance*, 184). According to Lencek and Bosker, swimsuits were also functional, reflecting contemporary concerns with efficiency.

43. "Demoralizing Feminine Invasion Ruinous to Shops, Barber Fears," *New Orleans Times-Picayune*, 13 January 1924.

44. "Report on Public Comfort Stations," 9 June 1931, NOACM.

45. "Drinking and Logic," *New Orleans Times-Picayune*, 11 January 1934.

46. "Famous New Orleans Drinking Places," *New Orleans Times-Picayune*, 8 February 1934; "Famous Drinks and Where to Get Them," *New Orleans Times-Picayune*, 21 February 1936; Washburn, "Hawaiian Blue Room," 36, 59.

47. Bartlett, "Vintage Drag," 44–49; Wiltz, *Last Madam*, 47.

48. Catherine Vidokovich to Robert Maestri, circa 1938, RRSM; "Fortune Quarterly Survey: XI," 88.

49. T. Semmes Walmsley to Commission Council, 8 November 1933, OPCC.

50. "Protest against Name 'Belle of New Orleans' Being Used in Connection with Mae West Picture Originally Titled 'It Ain't No Sin,' " 11 July 1934, "Annual Report of the Publicity Department," 20 November 1934, both in NOACM; Alecia Long, *Great Southern Babylon*, 208.

51. Laville Bremer, *Guide to New Orleans and Environs* (1942), AJSPC; Stanonis, " 'Always in Costume and Mask,' " 49–54. For comparison, see Rose, "Wettest in the West," 288.

52. Kinney, *Bachelor in New Orleans*, 10, 12, 14–15, 20, 26, 32–36.

53. "A 1934 Toast," NOACNB, 26 December 1933.

54. Tennessee Williams, *Vieux Carré*, 59.

Chapter 4. French Town: The Reconstruction of the Vieux Carré

1. "Vieux Carre," *New Orleans Times-Picayune*, 23 March 1920.

2. "2 New Moves to Preserve Vieux Carre Are Prepared," *New Orleans Item*, 1 February 1939; James Wilkinson to Robert Maestri, 25 February 1937, RRSM.

3. "Our French Opera House," *New Orleans Times-Picayune*, 7 March 1922; Lyle Saxon, "Fire Leaves Famous Home of Lyric Drama Heap of Ruins," *New Orleans Times-Picayune*, 5 December 1919.

4. Waldo Pitkin, interview by Adele Salzer, 10 August 1977, Friends of the

Cabildo Oral History Project; Gallup to Gideon Stanton, 12 May 1921, "Members," no date, Nellie Kelleher to Sarah Henderson, 15 April 1938, George Westfeldt to Sarah Henderson, 7 May 1938, Richard Koch to Sarah Henderson, 6 March 1941, all in Arts and Crafts Club Papers; Betty Carter, biographical sketch submitted to 1984 World's Fair, Betty Carter, "Notes for Notable American Women," 2 June 1966, both in Hodding and Betty Werlein Carter Papers, Mitchell Memorial Library, Special Collections, Manuscripts Division, Mississippi State University.

5. Embury, "Old New Orleans," 89–90; Curtis, "Creole Architecture," 433, 436, 442; Celestine Chambon, *The Saint Louis Cathedral and Its Neighbors* (1938), 32–34, WRPC; "What Visitors Can See in the Vieux Carre," *Tourists' Guide to New Orleans* (1924), 17, AJSPC. The article from the tourist guide frequently reappeared in the newspaper as authored by Lyle Saxon. See, for example, "What Visitors Can See in Famous Vieux Carre," *New Orleans Times-Picayune*, 15 February 1920; "French Quarter without a Guide," *New Orleans Times-Picayune*, 2 March 1924. Saxon later included a very similar piece in his *Fabulous New Orleans*.

6. Anderson, *Sherwood Anderson's Notebook*, 106; Oliver LaFarge, *Raw Material*, 117; "Gallatin Street," *New Orleans Times-Picayune*, 6 January 1924; Sinclair, *Port of New Orleans*, 316–17; Lewis, *New Orleans*, 53–54; Marc Antony, interview by Dorothy Schlesinger, 3 September 1977, Louise Glynn, interview by M. Colvin, 9 December 1978, Leon Zainey, interview by Dorothy Schlesinger, 19 November 1996, all in Friends of the Cabildo Oral History Project.

7. Anderson, *Sherwood Anderson's Notebook*, 59–60; Oliver LaFarge, *Raw Material*, 114; Faulkner, *Mosquitoes*, 335, 338; Tallant, *Romantic New Orleanians*, 309–10; New Orleans Police Department Arrest Records, Precinct 3, 1931–32, City Archives and Special Collections, New Orleans Public Library. Anderson even boasted of once picking "up a woman in the streets."

8. J. L. Jenkins, "New and Old Orleans Await Record Travel," no date, RMB.

9. John Tims to Martin Behrman, 1 December 1925, RMB; Robert Glenk to L. E. Schlessinger, 27 March 1926, RAJO; "Jackson Statue Vandalism Laid to Group of Boys," *New Orleans Times-Picayune*, 24 February 1934; " 'Old Hickory' Beheaded," *New Orleans Times-Picayune*, 24 February 1934.

10. Elizebeth Werlein, *The Wrought Iron Railings of Le Vieux Carre New Orleans* (originally published circa 1920s, 1986), AJSPC; Helen Schertz, *A*

Walk through French Town in Old New Orleans (circa 1920s), WRPC; Brown, "New Orleans Modernism."

11. G. William Nott, *Vieux Carré Guide: Souvenir of Old New Orleans with Its Latin Quarter of French and Spanish Old-World Romance* (1928), 3, 29–31, 35, 39, AJSPC.

12. "Vieux Carre Inspires Authors," *New Orleans Times-Picayune*, 23 February 1933; "Arts and Artists," *New Orleans Times-Picayune*, 21 February 1936; Yuhl, *Golden Haze of Memory*, 71–72.

13. "Old Quarter Draws Mardi Gras Visitors while Waiting for Rex," *New Orleans Times-Picayune*, 4 March 1924; "A Vieux Carre Stroll," *New Orleans Times-Picayune*, 21 February 1936.

14. "Vieux Carre Restoration Society Meets Thursday," *New Orleans Times-Picayune*, 1 February 1920; Raffray, "Origins," 284–85.

15. "Meeting of the Executive Committee of the Board of Directors," 28 August 1917, NOACM; "New Orleans' Vieux Carre Now Coming into Its Own," *New Orleans Times-Picayune*, 16 April 1922; "Vieux Carre Club Launches Million Members Drive," *New Orleans Times-Picayune*, 4 February 1927; "The Vieux Carre Held Heroes of Last Battle Here," *New Orleans Times-Picayune*, 18 March 1928.

16. Walter Loubat to Arthur O'Keefe, 12 February 1926, Vieux Carré Association to William Daly, 17 December 1926, both in RAJO; "Minutes of the Regular Weekly Meeting of the Executive Committee," 6 May 1931, NOACM.

17. King, *Memories*, 386; Rigney D'Aunoy to Martin Behrman, 15 October 1925, RMB; Ordinance #8735, 21 October 1925, City Council City Ordinances, City Archives and Special Collections, New Orleans Public Library; Raffray, "Origins," 288–90.

18. Raffray, "Origins," 285, 290; "Parking System Proposed by Experts," *New Orleans Times-Picayune*, 16 December 1928.

19. "Pontalba Building Site," *New Orleans Times-Picayune*, 7 May 1930; "Minutes of Regular Weekly Meeting of the Executive Committee," 1 July 1931, NOACM; Lydia Wickliffe to T. Semmes Walmsley, 20 January 1934, Records of Mayor T. Semmes Walmsley; " 'Save Vieux Carre or Be Sorry,' City Is Warned," NOACNB, 7 July 1931; "The Status of the Vieux Carre," NOACNB, 18 August 1936.

20. "Waddill's Vieux Carré Creed," 16 August 1937, RRSM; "By-Laws of the Vieux Carre Commission of the City of New Orleans," Vieux Carré Commission Minutes, 4 August 1937, City Archives and Special Collections, New

Orleans Public Library; Vieux Carré Commission Minutes, 8 April 1937–26 February 1940; "Views on French Quarter Slated by Mrs. Werlein," *New Orleans Times-Picayune*, 1 February 1939.

21. P. A. Gaudel to Robert Maestri, 12 July 1938, RRSM; "Map Fight for Quarter Building," *New Orleans Item*, 9 January 1939; "2 New Moves to Preserve Vieux Carre Are Prepared," *New Orleans Item*, 1 February 1939.

22. "Fizzle," *New Orleans Item*, 2 February 1939; "Plan to Preserve Vieux Carre Is Presented to Commission," *New Orleans States*, 9 February 1939.

23. "Following Through," *New Orleans Times-Picayune*, 18 February 1939; "Keep the French Quarter Clean," *NOACNB*, 15 August 1939; Betty Werlein Carter, notes to send to Elizabeth Kell, 2 June 1966, Carter Papers.

24. Yuhl, "Rich and Tender Remembering," 228; "Minutes of the Meeting of the Committee of Management of the Convention and Visitors Bureau," 12 November 1936, NOACM; " 'Billy' Henerty, 42 Years on Rue Royal, Watches Evolution of Noted Street," *New Orleans Times-Picayune*, 7 March 1926; Carl Meyer to Martin Behrman, 27 November 1925, RMB; Alecia Long, *Great Southern Babylon*, 82–88.

25. W. G. MacFarlane, *The Charms of New Orleans: The Vieux Carre, the Mardi Gras, the Color and Romance of French and Spanish Days* (1928), 39–41, WRPC; "The Fathers of Creole Furniture," *Louisiana Tourist* (1938), 16, AJSPC.

26. Pitkin interview; "Preliminary Announcement, New Orleans Spring Fiesta," circa 1937, RRSM; "Spring Fiesta," *New Orleans Times-Picayune*, 10 March 1937; Jack Davis, *Race against Time*, 53–67. For complete Spring Fiesta schedules, see *Annual New Orleans Spring Fiesta*, 1939, AJSPC; *New Orleans Souvenir Program Spring Fiesta*, 1942, AJSPC.

27. [Illegible] to Robert Maestri, 18 March 1937, RRSM; Helen Schertz to Lyle Saxon, 1 June 1938, Saxon Papers; "Spring Fiesta Plans Bigger 1939 Show," *New Orleans Item*, 15 January 1939.

28. "Tourists Gradually Grasp Spirit That Is New Orleans," *New Orleans Times-Picayune*, 21 February 1925.

29. *Sincerely Yours, New Orleans* (1948), 6, WRPC; "Modernized Mansions of Vieux Carre," *New Orleans Times-Picayune*, 2 January 1927; Flo Field, "Rue Royal," *The Orleanian*, 15 November 1930, 20, WRPC; "Carnival Visitors," *New Orleans Times-Picayune*, 4 March 1924.

30. Priestley, "New Orleans," 593–94.

31. Rothman, *Neon Metropolis*, 8; Borden, "Defense of French Morals,"

570–71; "Biennial Report of the Board of Curators for 1936–37," 85, LSM; Schrecker, "American Diary," 383.

32. Kinney, *Bachelor in New Orleans*, 98; *Sincerely Yours, New Orleans*, 48; Ernest Vetter, *Fabulous Frenchtown: The Story of the Famous French Quarter of New Orleans* (1955), 169–70, 184–86, WRPC.

33. Kinney, *Bachelor in New Orleans*, 27.

34. Roark Bradford, "Lousy with Charm: A Comedy" (1937), act 1, 9–10, Roark Bradford Papers, Manuscripts Department, TU.

35. Ibid., act 2, 16; act 3, 9–10.

36. Ibid., act 1, 7–9.

Chapter 5. A City That Care Forgot: The Reinvention of New Orleans Mardi Gras

1. Tallant, *Mardi Gras as It Was*, 3, 34.

2. Nash, *Nervous Generation*, 127. For information on the preservation and handicraft movement as well as the American interest in the past during the interwar years, see Becker, *Selling Tradition*; Dorman, *Revolt in the Provinces*; Cooney, *Balancing Acts*, 59–128; Brundage, "Reveil de la Louisiane"; Greenspan, "Shrine to the American Faith," 3–20; Löfgren, *On Holiday*, 41–154; Martin, "To Keep the Spirit," 249–60; Nash, *Nervous Generation*, 55–105, 126–63; Yuhl, "Rich and Tender Remembering," 227–48. Festivals chronicler Robert Meyer began his work with the words, "Ever since the 1930s, at least, it has been apparent that festivals should flourish in North America not only because there is so much to celebrate here, but also because of improved transportation, the shorter work week, longer vacations with pay, and labor saving devices on farms and in homes, offices, and factories" (*Festivals U.S.A. and Canada*, vii).

3. Tallant, *Mardi Gras as It Was*, xi.

4. "Kings of Misrule," *New Orleans Times-Picayune*, 17 February 1920.

5. "New Orleans and Mardi Gras," *New Orleans Times-Picayune*, 4 February 1934. For insight into the relationship between Mardi Gras and the white elite after the Civil War, see Gill, *Lords of Misrule*, 77–192; Mitchell, *All on a Mardi Gras Day*, 51–112.

6. "Carnival Visitors Not So Numerous as in Past Years," *New Orleans Times-Picayune*, 17 February 1920; "Brave Effort Unable to Revive Olden

Joys," *New Orleans Times-Picayune*, 18 February 1920; "Mardi Gras," *New Orleans Times-Picayune*, 27 February 1920.

7. "Carnival Visitors Not So Numerous as in Past Years," *New Orleans Times-Picayune*, 17 February 1920; "Tourist Travel Has Resumed Old Volume," *New Orleans Times-Picayune*, 9 February 1921; "The Charms of New Orleans," *Guide Book of New Orleans* (19 March 1923), AJSPC.

8. "Knocking 'Mardi Gras Festivities,'" *New Orleans Times-Picayune*, 19 February 1921; "Mardi Gras Revives Old Tango Section," *New Orleans Times-Picayune*, 14 February 1923; "Dry Agents Hunt Evidence Even while Rex Rules," *New Orleans Times-Picayune*, 1 March 1922; "Drys Hit Cabarets Double Blow as Contempt Charges Filed in Raiding Carnival," *New Orleans Times-Picayune*, 17 February 1926; "Dry Cordon Will Be Made Tighter before Carnival," *New Orleans Times-Picayune*, 21 February 1930; "Sunday 'Blue Laws,'" *New Orleans Times-Picayune*, 23 February 1920.

9. "Annual Report of President Arthur Parker," 10 January 1920, "Minutes of the Meeting of the Committee of Management of the Convention, Tourist, and Publicity Bureau," 8 October 1920, "Minutes of the Meeting of the Executive Committee, Board of Directors," 17 July 1917, "Minutes of the Annual Meeting of the Convention, Tourist, and Publicity Bureau," 29 November 1920, all in NOACM. Mardi Gras remained significant as a magnet for industrial and commercial development into the Cold War years. When Kaiser Aluminum rejected New Orleans as a site for a new plant in 1951, the city's mayor, DeLesseps Morrison, arranged a second appraisal of the city by company officials to coincide with Carnival. So impressed was the evaluation team that its members reversed their earlier decision and awarded New Orleans the plant project, valued at $145 million. For information on the Kaiser plant, see Haas, *DeLesseps S. Morrison*, 156–57.

10. "C. and T. Bureau Starts Campaign to Tell World about 1922 Mardi Gras," *NOACNB*, 23 August 1921; "Interest in Mardi Gras Increases Among Tourists," *NOACNB*, 7 February 1922; "Mardi Gras Movies," *NOACNB*, 27 March 1923; "Movie Tone Pictures of N.O. Made; A. of C. Co-Operation Given," *NOACNB*, 28 February 1928; "Bringing Them In," *NOACNB*, 31 July 1928; "A Comeback," *NOACNB*, 4 March 1930; "Plans Completed for Broadcast of Carnival," *NOACNB*, 17 February 1931.

11. "2 Information Booths for Carnival Visitors to Be Put on Canal St.," *NOACNB*, 26 January 1926; "Minutes of the Regular Monthly Meeting of

the Board of Directors," 20 January 1926, "Minutes of the Meeting of the Executive Committee," 26 January 1927, "February Report, Convention and Visitors Bureau," 1 March 1937, all in NOACM; "Cordiality to the Tourist," *New Orleans Times-Picayune*, 20 February 1931.

12. "Regular Monthly Meeting of the Board of Directors," 8 June 1921, NOACM; "Carnival Parade Suggestions," *New Orleans Times-Picayune*, 16 January 1923; "Carnival Events Crowding Calendar until Mardi Gras," *New Orleans Times-Picayune*, 4 February 1923; "Mardi Gras," *New Orleans Times-Picayune*, 4 March 1924; "New Carnival Club Needed," *New Orleans Times-Picayune*, 22 February 1928; "The Krewe of Chance," *New Orleans Times-Picayune*, 18 February 1928. In 1928, the Elks' short-lived Krewe of Chance took to the streets on Monday afternoon in an effort to enhance tourists' Carnival experience.

13. "Use Mardi Gras Colors," *NOACNB*, 20 January 1925; "Display Flag as Code Specifies, Is Appeal of Chairman McCutcheon," *NOACNB*, 5 January 1926; "Annual Report of the Flag Committee," 20 December 1928, NOACM; Stephen Curtis West, *French Quarter Guide* (1929), 37, WRPC. In 1928, the Association of Commerce registered a total of twenty-five flag violations, of which fifteen occurred during Carnival.

14. "Minutes of the Regular Monthly Meeting of the Committee of Management of the Convention and Tourist Bureau," 7 February 1923, NOACM; Mitchell, *All on a Mardi Gras Day*, 133–34; "Carnival Comment," *New Orleans Times-Picayune*, 22 February 1931; Morris Lakowsky to Lyle Saxon, 23 February 1938, Al Durning to Lyle Saxon, 3 March 1938, both in Federal Writers Project Collection, Northwestern State University of Louisiana, Watson Memorial Library, Cammie G. Henry Research Center; "Plea for More Maskers," *New Orleans Times-Picayune*, 6 February 1934.

15. "A Carnival Suggestion," *New Orleans Times-Picayune*, 22 February 1930; "Sidelights on the Merrymakers," *New Orleans Times-Picayune*, 14 February 1934; Leathem, "Carnival," 29–34, 51–63, 207–9, 219–23.

16. Hodding Carter, "Mardi Gras," in "Collected Poems: Bowdoin, 1923–27," Carter Papers; "Carnival Visitor Solves Mystery," *New Orleans Times-Picayune*, 6 March 1930; Mitchell, *All on a Mardi Gras Day*, 131–41.

17. "Carnival and Mardi Gras," *New Orleans Times-Picayune*, 27 February 1927.

18. "A Barely Noted 'Factor,'" *New Orleans Times-Picayune*, 18 Febru-

ary 1928; "Mardi Gras," *New Orleans Times-Picayune*, 12 February 1929; Mitchell, *All on a Mardi Gras Day*, 175.

19. "Minutes of the Meeting of the Committee of Management of the Convention and Visitors Bureau," 18 December 1930, "Minutes of the Annual Meeting of the Convention and Visitors Bureau," 13 December 1930, both in NOACM; "Plans Laid for Grid Epic, New Mardi Gras Ball," *NOACNB*, 20 January 1931.

20. "Minutes of the Annual Meeting of the Convention and Visitors' Bureau," 24 November 1933, "Minutes of the Regular Semi-Monthly Meeting of the Board of Directors," 28 February 1934, both in NOACM; "Masquerade Ball Added Attention for Mardi Gras Visitors," *NOACNB*, 29 January 1935. The 1934 Carnival ball began at midnight on 12 February and included a late supper and early morning breakfast ("Throng of Carnival Visitors Arrives by Train, Bus and Ship," *New Orleans Times-Picayune*, 21 February 1936).

21. "King Midcity I, Parading at Head of Gala Floats, Toasts Gracious Queen," *New Orleans Times-Picayune*, 12 February 1934; Tallant, *Mardi Gras as It Was*, 40–43; "Sponsor Traveling Mardi Gras Exhibit," *New Orleans States*, 2 January 1939.

22. "Chairman's Report, Convention and Tourist Bureau," 1933, NOACM; "Thousands Acclaim Children's First Carnival Pageant," *New Orleans Times-Picayune*, 11 February 1934.

23. "Report of Children's Carnival Pageant Committee," *NOACNB*, 20 March 1934; "School Carnival Parades," *New Orleans Times-Picayune*, 25 February 1934; "Children's Carnival Parade Will Be Repeated in 1935; School Heads Give Sanction," *New Orleans Times-Picayune*, 8 March 1934; "That School Parade," *New Orleans Times-Picayune*, 9 March 1934; "That Children's Carnival Again," *New Orleans Times-Picayune*, 1 April 1934.

24. "For a Carnival Museum," *New Orleans Times-Picayune*, 12 February 1929; "For the Carnival Museum," *New Orleans Times-Picayune*, 25 February 1929; "Biennial Report of the Board of Curators for 1928–29," 20–21, "Biennial Report of the Board of Curators for 1930–31," 32–33, both in LSM.

25. "Carnival at New Orleans," *New Orleans Times-Picayune*, 11 February 1929; "Mardi Gras in New Orleans," *New Orleans Times-Picayune*, 9 February 1932; "Carnival Days Are Here," *New Orleans Times-Picayune*, 27 February 1933. For information on historic festivals in other cities, see Meyer,

Festivals U.S.A. and Canada, 104–5; Spencer, *St. Louis Veiled Prophet Celebration*, 7–101; Welch, "Oh, Dem Golden Slippers."

26. Glynn interview; Elizebeth Werlein, "Way Down Yonder in New Orleans," *Lincoln*, February–March 1924, 9, Carter Papers; West, *French Quarter Guide*, 37, 39; Gill, *Lords of Misrule*, 177.

27. K. T. Knoblock, "Before You See the Parade," *New Orleans Times-Picayune*, 19 February 1928.

28. "Carnival and Its Benefits," *New Orleans Times-Picayune*, 11 February 1931; "Carnival's Glitter Brings Large Sums Which Benefit City," *New Orleans Times-Picayune*, 15 February 1931.

29. "Carnival's Glitter Brings Large Sums to Benefit Workers," *New Orleans Times-Picayune*, 8 February 1934.

30. "Minutes of the Regular Semi-Monthly Meeting of the Board of Directors," 6 April 1938, NOACM.

31. "Civic Fun in New Orleans and San Francisco," *Life*, 22 February 1937, 17; "Life Goes to a Party," *Life*, 1 March 1937, 64.

32. Knecht, *Valois*, 10–16; Seed, *Ceremonies*, 52–54.

33. Faulkner, *Pylon*, 10, 14, 57, 59, 73, 180, 186, 291.

34. Ibid., 35, 37. Abe Shushan, a supporter of Huey Long, was a leading advocate of state aid for a New Orleans airport. Fearing that a victory by anti-Long forces might result in a name change, Shushan arranged for his name to appear on the terminal's roof, floor, doorknobs, plumbing fixtures, and walls—both inside and outside. When asked about this, he declared, "We may lose out sometime, and they may change the name of Shushan Airport—but it'll cost 'em $60,000 at the least, and I doubt whether they could do it for $100,000." For information on Shushan Airport, see T. Harry Williams, *Huey Long*, 549–50.

35. Faulkner, *Pylon*, 288; "Throng of Carnival Visitors Arrives by Train, Bus, and Ship," *New Orleans Times-Picayune*, 21 February 1936.

Chapter 6. Old New Orleans: Race and Tourism

1. "Killings and Cuttings Are Sore Spots," *Louisiana Weekly*, 8 March 1930; "Negro Confesses Slaying Student in Carnival Riot," *New Orleans Times-Picayune*, 6 March 1930.

2. "Tulane Student Is Killed in Riot in Vieux Carre," *New Orleans Times-Picayune*, 5 March 1930. Although blacks certainly took to the roads and rails, as evidenced by the Great Migration begun just prior to the First World

War, the reasons for travel had less to do with leisure than the pursuit of improved living conditions. As Neil McMillan has shown in his insightful study of Mississippi under Jim Crow, blacks, whether walking down the street or driving the state's dusty byways, needed to show constant deference to whites or suffer potentially fatal consequences. Moreover, deferential practices varied from county to county, making travel particularly treacherous for blacks not familiar with local customs. For scholarship on race during the early twentieth century, see Fairclough, *Race and Democracy*, 5–35; Grantham, *Southern Progressivism*, 123–27; Grossman, *Land of Hope*, 13–19, 28–37, 99–119, 123–60, 168–79; Hanchett, *Sorting*, 116–44; Kusmer, *Ghetto Takes Shape*, 98–111, 136–39, 157–93; Litwack, *Trouble in Mind*, 8–47, 218–46, 284–312, 327–52; McMillan, *Dark Journey*, 3–32, 262–75.

3. *1950 New Orleans Population Handbook*, 21.

4. Edwards, *World Don't Owe Me Nothing*, 43–44.

5. "Professor Raps Jazz but Defends 'Nudity in Art,'" *New Orleans Times-Picayune*, 28 February 1921.

6. "Sidelights of Orleans' Day of Fun Illustrate Whimsical Rule of Rex," *New Orleans Times-Picayune*, 14 February 1923; Mitchell, *All on a Mardi Gras Day*, 51, 131–35. For a discussion of the origins of jazz, see Buerkle and Barker, *Bourbon Street Black*, 14–28, 41–48; Peretti, *Creation of Jazz*, 13–21, 24–37, 76–82.

7. George Kernion, "The Vieux Carre of Yester Year," no date, George Campbell Kernion Papers, Manuscripts Department, TU.

8. "Minutes of Meeting of Municipal Band Committee of the Civic Bureau with a Committee of Musicians and Interested Business Men to Discuss the Formation of a Municipal Band," 18 November 1921, NOACM.

9. "What Is Sex Appeal?" *New Orleans Times-Picayune*, 12 January 1930. For information about the origins of jazz, see Marquis, *In Search of Buddy Bolden*, 1–2.

10. "Business Jazz," NOACNB, 13 January 1931; Leonard, *Jazz and the White Americans*, 14–22, 30–41; Haas, *DeLesseps S. Morrison*, 253–54. Haas provides evidence that even during the late 1950s, New Orleans police possessed little tolerance for interracial jazz bands attempting to earn a living from the tourist trade.

11. "The Jazz and the Public Dance," *Louisiana Weekly*, 6 March 1926. For insight into the creation of a hierarchy of culture and the role of race, see Levine, *Highbrow/Lowbrow*, 176–77, 219–31; Erenberg, *Steppin' Out*, 254–59.

12. " 'Old Songs' and Jazz," *New Orleans Times-Picayune*, 24 April 1923.

13. "Piano Tuners' Head Flays Jazz Music," *New Orleans Times-Picayune*, 8 February 1927; Williamson, *Crucible of Race*, 467.

14. "Boys and Girls Learn to Know Good Music," *New Orleans Times-Picayune*, 30 January 1921; Al Kennedy, "Jazz Mentors," 57; "Annual Report, Civic Affairs Committee," 30 November 1935, NOACM; Leonard, *Jazz and the White Americans*, 42–46.

15. "Music Committee," 17 December 1923, NOACM; "Music Week Workers Set for Program Promotion," *NOACNB*, 6 November 1923; Yuhl, *Golden Haze of Memory*, 127–46, 150–53.

16. "Mayor O'Keefe Invited to Open Music Week with Address over W.S.M.B. May 2," *NOACNB*, 19 April 1927; "Music Group Names 12 Objectives for 1932," *NOACNB*, 29 March 1932; Levine, *Highbrow/Lowbrow*, 139–50, 228–30.

17. "Plan Elaborate Program for Music Week Observance," *NOACNB*, 15 April 1930; "Music Week," *NOACNB*, 8 May 1934; "Annual National Celebration of Music Week On," *NOACNB*, 3 May 1938.

18. "Radio Audience Is Promised More Folk Tunes, Less Jazz," *New Orleans Times-Picayune*, 23 February 1930; "Folk Festival to Be Part of Nat.'l Music Week Observance Here," *NOACNB*, 24 March 1936. For insight into American attitudes toward Appalachia and how those attitudes transformed the region into a tourist attraction with parallels to the cultural redefinition occurring in Louisiana, see Becker, *Selling Tradition*, 55–71, 189–222; Brundage, "Reveil de la Louisiane," 271–94; Martin, "Selling the Southern Highlands," 107–28, 146–55, 185–234; Martin, "To Keep the Spirit," 249–67.

19. Al Kennedy, "Jazz Mentors," 1–4, 7–32, 43–58. For insight into the social forces that allowed jazz to become popular with adolescents and young adults, see Leonard, *Jazz and the White Americans*, 53–55; Peretti, *Creation of Jazz*, 87–88.

20. Armstrong, *Satchmo*, 194; Pops Foster, *Pops Foster*, 128.

21. Ferd Morton to Mr. Carew, 8 June 1940, Jelly Roll Morton Correspondence, William Russell Collection, Historic New Orleans Collection, Williams Research Center; Bunk Johnson to William Russell, 17, 29 February, 17 March, 2 June 1944, 31 October 1946, Bunk Johnson Papers, Russell Collection. For insight into how the commodification of jazz reinforced traditional white values, see Leonard, *Jazz and the White Americans*, 97–106, 118–19.

22. Captain Verne Streckfus, interview by Richard Allen and Paul Crawford, 22 September 1960, Hogan Jazz Archives, TU.

23. Kolodin, "Dance Band Business," 80; Washburn, "Hawaiian Blue Room," 37; "Interesting Notes on the Pelican State," *Louisiana Tourist*, November 1938, 15, AJSPC.

24. *Sincerely Yours, New Orleans*, 48–49. For information on swing, see Leonard, *Jazz and the White Americans*, 124–31, 146; Peretti, *Creation of Jazz*, 171–72, 178–206; Stowe, *Swing Changes*, 5–8, 121–30, 132–39.

25. "Series of Jazz Concerts Closes," *Old French Quarter News*, 2 September 1949, WRPC; Roach, *Cities of the Dead*, 63–68.

26. Papa Celestin, interview by John Curran and F. Edward Hébert, 8 May 1953, Hogan Jazz Archives, TU.

27. Frances Oliver, interview, 1969, "Interviews with Musicians about Jelly Roll Morton," Russell Collection.

28. Tallant, *Voodoo in New Orleans*, 3; *Original Cookes Tour*, AJSPC.

29. Jelly Roll Morton, "A Fragment of an Autobiography," "Interviews with Musicians about Jelly Roll Morton," Russell Collection. For a comparison of racial issues in New Orleans and in other southern tourism centers, see Becker, *Selling Tradition*, 59–66; Greenspan, "Shrine to the American Faith," 45–54, 113–20, 141–48; Yuhl, *Golden Haze of Memory*, 178–87.

30. King, *Memories*, 60–61; Tregle, "Creoles and Americans," 174–85.

31. King, *New Orleans*, 333. For insight into the history of early New Orleans and the Creoles, see Hall, "Formation of Afro-Creole Culture," 66–69, 76–87; Jerah Johnson, "Colonial New Orleans," 46–57; Tregle, "Creoles and Americans," 133–41, 149–50.

32. King, *New Orleans*, 347–48.

33. King, *Creole Families of New Orleans*, vii, 7–8.

34. King, *Memories*, 327–28.

35. *Tourists' Guide to New Orleans*, 17; Saxon, *Fabulous New Orleans*, 268; West, *French Quarter Guide*; Stanonis, "'Always in Costume and Mask,'" 46–57; Kane, *Queen New Orleans*, 3–17. In just a few pages, Kane encapsulates the leading touristic images of New Orleans born during the interwar years. His piece also reveals how guide writers and defenders of local culture claimed personal contact with exotic inhabitants, such as Creoles, whom tourists might not otherwise encounter.

36. Gluck's Restaurant, *A Condensed History of Old New Orleans* (no date), 11, WRPC.

37. Secretary to the mayor to Harry Bowman, 11 May 1926, RAJO.

38. "Green Pastures Movie Script," 21 October 1935, Bradford Papers.

39. For a discussion of racial imagery and consumerism in the South, see Hale, *Making Whiteness*, 121–97.

40. "Unique New Orleans," *Louisiana Weekly*, 16 August 1930; Simon, *Boardwalk of Dreams*, 7–10; Myrdal, *American Dilemma*, 982–86.

41. "Association of Commerce and Whitney Bank Extend Welcome," *Louisiana Weekly*, 26 November 1927; "Welcoming the Convention," *Louisiana Weekly*, 14 July 1934; Charles Favrot to A. P. Touro, 25 November 1935, Alexander P. Tureaud Papers, Amistad Research Center, Tulane University.

42. "Minutes of the Regular Weekly Meeting of the Executive Committee," 19 February 1930, NOACM; "Why Call It the Municipal Auditorium?" *Louisiana Weekly*, 30 May 1936.

43. John Fletcher to "All Members on New Orleans Citizens Committee on Race Relations," 10 June 1944, YWCA Papers, Manuscripts Department, TU; statement of F. Edward Hébert, no date, Tureaud Papers.

44. Haas, *DeLesseps S. Morrison*, 250.

45. Lyle Saxon diary, 19 February 1925; "New Orleans Negro Plays Distinctive Carnival Role," *New Orleans Times-Picayune*, 21 February 1936; Mitchell, *All on a Mardi Gras Day*, 183–90.

46. *Guide Book of New Orleans*, 5; Alecia Long, *Great Southern Babylon*, 325, 336–45.

47. Hurston, *Dust Tracks on a Road*, 139–40; Hurston, *Mules and Men*, 183–246; Saxon, *Fabulous New Orleans*, 239; Daniels, *Southerner Discovers the South*, 241; Tallant, *Voodoo in New Orleans*, 3–4, 6. Hurston wrote that "New Orleans is now and has ever been the hoodoo capital of the world." She criticized whites for confusing hoodoo and voodoo, declaring that hoodoo "is not drum beating and dancing" (*Mules and Men*, 183, 185). Elsie Martinez's memoir, in contrast, highlighted whites' lingering perception that jazz stemmed from voodoo rituals: "Led by their voodoo queen, always a free woman of color, the slaves danced to rhythmic drums and chanted songs from their native Africa. Those sounds and rhythms formed a new kind of music that later evolved into an original American art form—jazz" (Martinez and LeCorgne, *Uptown/Downtown*, 6).

48. Litwack, *Trouble in Mind*, 330–31; Mitchell, *All on a Mardi Gras Day*, 162–63; Tucker, *Telling Memories among Southern Women*, 13–101.

49. "One-Man Band," 32.

50. Genthe, *Impressions of Old New Orleans*, 27; Clayre and Edith to Sarah Henderson, 26 April 1937, Arts and Crafts Club Papers.

51. King, *Memories*, 192.

52. Scott and Jones, *Gourmet's Guide*, i; Daniels, *Southerner Discovers the South*, 242.

53. Hale, *Making Whiteness*, 101; Turner, *Ceramic Uncles and Celluloid Mammies*, 43–56.

54. "Sidelights of Orleans' Day of Fun Illustrate Whimsical Rule of Rex," *New Orleans Times-Picayune*, 14 February 1923.

55. Green Orchid, *Story of the Praline*, circa 1920s, *Aunt Sally's*, circa 1947, both in AJSPC; "Bacino's," 17.

56. Turner, *Ceramic Uncles and Celluloid Mammies*, 11–20; "Souvenirs of the South," *Guide Book of New Orleans*, d; "Crumb Gifts" and "Flo Salter," *Hotel Greeters Tourist Guide*, April 1946, 26, 17, AJSPC; Stanley Arthur to Hermann Deutsch, 5 September 1942, Hermann B. Deutsch Papers, Manuscripts Department, TU.

57. "Mardi Gras Day Sees Better Race Relationship, Says Writer," *Louisiana Weekly*, 26 February 1938.

58. "Letters from Readers," *New Orleans Times-Picayune*, 21 March 1930; "Gayest of Mardi Gras Celebrations Ends after Spectacular Festival," *Louisiana Weekly*, 25 February 1939.

59. "Mardi Gras Day Sees Better Race Relationship, Says Writer," *Louisiana Weekly*, 26 February 1938.

Epilogue: Boomtown

1. Richard Dyer to editor of *New Orleans Item*, no date, "A 'Happy' Visitor" to editor of *New Orleans Item*, no date, both in Deutsch Papers. The debate occurred in July 1944.

2. Bill Broussard to editor of *New Orleans Item*, no date, Deutsch Papers. For an insightful study of the evolution of New Orleans tourism in the decades after the Second World War, see Souther, "City in Amber"; Souther, "Making 'America's Most Interesting City.'"

3. Cedric McNeil to editor of *New Orleans Item*, 15 July 1944, Deutsch Papers; Felix Aitkins to editor of *New Orleans Item*, 19 July 1944, Deutsch Papers.

4. Cohen, *Consumers' Republic*, 114–50; Weiss, "Tourism in America," 318–19.

5. Kenneth Jackson, *Crabgrass Frontier*, 172–305; May, *Homeward Bound*, 162–82.

6. Schweid, *Catfish and the Delta*, 13.

7. Mitchell, *All on a Mardi Gras Day*, 147–49. Shapiro, *Television Network Prime-Time Programming*, 103, 119; Bordelon, "Images of New Orleans," 37–39, 86–89.

8. Baker, *Second Battle of New Orleans*, 367–75, 390–91, 410–61, 472–73; Fairclough, *Race and Democracy*, 427–28, 449–53; Arthur Vernon, *New Orleans Nonsense*, circa 1970, AJSPC; Tucker, *Telling Memories among Southern Women*, 41.

9. Harrington, *Chaplain of Bourbon Street*, 31, 191, 211–13.

10. " 'Big Easy' Was Born during Dawn of Jazz," *New Orleans Times-Picayune*, 28 August 1987.

BIBLIOGRAPHY

Archival Sources

Historic New Orleans Collection, Williams Research Center
    Arts and Crafts Club Papers
    Rene A. Steigler Papers
    William Russell Collection
    William Russell Pamphlet Collection
Louisiana State Museum
    Biennial Report of the Board of Curators
Loyola University New Orleans, J. Edgar and Louise S. Monroe Library,
Special Collections and Archives
    Anthony J. Stanonis Pamphlet Collection
Mississippi State University, Mitchell Memorial Library, Special Collections,
Manuscripts Division
    Hodding and Betty Werlein Carter Papers
New Orleans Public Library, City Archives and Special Collections
    City Council City Ordinances
    Friends of the Cabildo Oral History Project
    New Orleans Police Department Arrest Records
    Official Proceedings of the Commission Council of the City of New Orleans
    Records of Mayor Andrew J. McShane
    Records of Mayor Arthur J. O'Keefe
    Records of Mayor Martin Behrman

Records of Mayor Robert S. Maestri

Records of Mayor T. Semmes Walmsley

Vieux Carré Commission Minutes

Northwestern State University of Louisiana, Watson Memorial Library,
Cammie G. Henry Research Center

Federal Writers Project Collection

Melrose Collection

Tulane University, Amistad Research Center

Alexander P. Tureaud Papers

Tulane University, Howard-Tilton Memorial Library, Special Collections
Division, Hogan Jazz Archives

Papa Celestin, interview by John Curran and F. Edward Hébert,
8 May 1953

Captain Verne Streckfus, interview by Richard Allen and Paul Crawford,
22 September 1960

Tulane University, Howard-Tilton Memorial Library, Special Collections
Division, Manuscripts Department

Roark Bradford Papers

Hermann B. Deutsch Papers

Ida Weiss Friend Papers

George Campbell Kernion Papers

Lyle Saxon Papers

YWCA Papers

University of New Orleans, Earl K. Long Library, Louisiana Collection and
Special Collections

Annual Reports of the Commissioner of the Department of Public Finance

New Orleans Association of Commerce Minutes

Telling-Grandon Collection

Periodicals

Harper's Weekly
Life
Louisiana Weekly
New Orleans Association of Commerce News Bulletin
New Orleans Item
New Orleans States

New Orleans Times-Picayune
New York Daily Times
New York Times

Published Primary Sources

Allen, Frederick Lewis. *Only Yesterday: An Informal History of the 1920s.*
New York: Harper and Row, 1931, 1964.

Anderson, Sherwood. "New Orleans: A Prose Poem in the Expressionist
Manner." *Vanity Fair* 26 (August 1926): 36, 97.

———. *Sherwood Anderson's Notebook.* New York: Boni and Liveright,
1926.

———. *A Story Teller's Story: Memoirs of Youth and Middle Age.* New
York: Viking, 1924, 1969.

Armstrong, Louis. *Satchmo: My Life in New Orleans.* New York: Da Capo,
1954, 1986.

Asbury, Herbert. *The French Quarter: An Informal History of the New
Orleans Underworld.* New York: Garden City, 1938.

"Bacino's." *Roosevelt Review* 4 (November 1941): 17.

Behrman, Martin. *Martin Behrman of New Orleans: Memoirs of a City
Boss.* Edited by Jack Kemp. Baton Rouge: Louisiana State University Press,
1977.

Borden, Mary. "A Defense of French Morals." *Harper's Magazine* 160 (April
1930): 565–71.

Brady, Patricia, ed. *George Washington's Beautiful Nelly: The Letters of
Eleanor Parke Custis Lewis to Elizabeth Bordley Gibson, 1794–1851.*
Columbia: University of South Carolina Press, 1991.

Bremer, Fredrika. *The Homes of the New World: Impressions of America.*
2 vols. Translated by Mary Howitt. New York: Harper, 1853.

Buel, J. W. *Mysteries and Miseries of America's Great Cities, Embracing New
York, Washington City, San Francisco, Salt Lake City, and New Orleans.*
St. Louis: Historical Publishing, 1883.

Cash, Wilbur. *The Mind of the South.* New York: Vintage, 1941.

Curtis, N. C. "The Creole Architecture of Old New Orleans." *Architectural
Record* 43 (May 1918): 435–46.

Daniels, Jonathan. *A Southerner Discovers the South.* New York: Macmillan,
1938.

Davis, Rebecca Harding. "Here and There in the South." *Harper's New Monthly Magazine* 75 (September 1887): 593–605.

Duffy, John, ed. *Parson Clapp of the Strangers' Church of New Orleans.* Baton Rouge: Louisiana State University Press, 1957.

Early, Eleanor. *New Orleans Holiday.* New York: Rinehart, 1947.

Edwards, David Honeyboy. *The World Don't Owe Me Nothing: The Life and Times of Delta Bluesman Honeyboy Edwards.* Chicago: Chicago Review Press, 1997.

Embury, Aymar, II. "Old New Orleans: The Picturesque Buildings of the French and Spanish Regime." *Architectural Record* 30 (July 1911): 85–98.

Faulkner, William. *Mosquitoes.* New York: Liveright, 1927, 1997.

———. *New Orleans Sketches.* New Brunswick, N.J.: Rutgers University Press, 1958.

———. *Pylon.* New York: Vintage, 1935, 1987.

Flint, Timothy. *Recollections of the Last Ten Years in the Valley of the Mississippi.* Carbondale: Southern Illinois University Press, 1826, 1968.

"Fortune Quarterly Survey: V." *Fortune* 14 (July 1936): 83–85, 148, 152–61.

"Fortune Quarterly Survey: XI." *Fortune* 17 (January 1938): 83–92.

Foster, Pops. *Pops Foster: The Autobiography of a New Orleans Jazzman as Told to Tom Stoddard.* Berkeley: University of California Press, 1973.

Genthe, Arnold. *Impressions of Old New Orleans: A Book of Pictures.* New York: Doran, 1926.

Harrington, Bob. *The Chaplain of Bourbon Street.* Garden City, N.Y.: Doubleday, 1969.

Hesse-Wartegg, Ernst von. *Travels on the Lower Mississippi, 1879–1880.* Translated by Frederic Trautmann. Columbia: University of Missouri Press, 1990.

Hoover, Herbert. *The Memoirs of Herbert Hoover: The Great Depression, 1929–1941.* New York: Macmillan, 1952.

Hurston, Zora Neale. *Dust Tracks on a Road.* New York: Harper Perennial, 1942, 1991.

———. *Mules and Men.* New York: Harper Perennial, 1935, 1990.

Iglehart, Ferdinand. *King Alcohol Dethroned.* Westerville, Ohio: American Issue, 1919.

Kane, Harnett. *Queen New Orleans: City by the River.* New York: Morrow, 1949.

Kenan, Randall. *Walking on Water: Black American Lives at the Turn of the Twenty-first Century*. New York: Knopf, 1999.

King, Grace. *Creole Families of New Orleans*. New York: Macmillan, 1921.

———. *Memories of a Southern Woman of Letters*. New York: Macmillan, 1932.

———. *New Orleans: The Place and the People*. New York: Macmillan, 1907.

Kolodin, Irving. "The Dance Band Business: A Study in Black and White." *Harper's Magazine* 183 (June 1941): 72–82.

LaFarge, Oliver. *Raw Material*. Boston: Houghton Mifflin, 1945.

Latrobe, Benjamin. *Impressions Respecting New Orleans: Diary and Sketches, 1818–1820*. Edited by Samuel Wilson Jr. New York: Columbia University Press, 1951.

Long, Huey. *Every Man a King: The Autobiography of Huey P. Long*. New Orleans: National Book, 1933.

Lynd, Robert, and Helen Lynd. *Middletown: A Study in Contemporary American Culture*. New York: Harcourt Brace, 1929.

———. *Middletown in Transition: A Study of Cultural Conflicts*. New York: Harcourt Brace, 1937.

Martinez, Elsie, and Margaret LeCorgne. *Uptown/Downtown: Growing Up in New Orleans*. Lafayette, La.: Center for Louisiana Studies, 1986.

Maunder, Elwood, ed. *James Greeley McGowin—South Alabama Lumberman: The Recollections of His Family*. Santa Cruz, Calif.: Forest History Society, 1977.

"Municipal Flags." *American City* 14 (March 1916): 244–49.

Myrdal, Gunnar. *An American Dilemma: The Negro Problem and Modern Democracy*. New York: Harper, 1944.

1950 New Orleans Population Handbook. New Orleans: Urban Life Research Institute, 1953.

Olmsted, Frederick Law. *The Cotton Kingdom: A Traveller's Observations on Cotton and Slavery in the American Slave States*. Edited by Arthur Schlesinger. New York: Knopf, 1861, 1962.

"The One-Man Band." *Roosevelt Review* 4 (January 1941): 32.

Phelps, Albert. "New Orleans and Reconstruction." *Atlantic Monthly* 88 (July 1901): 121–31.

Pitot, James. *Observations on the Colony of Louisiana from 1796 to 1802*.

Translated by Henry Pitot. Baton Rouge: Louisiana State University Press, 1979.

Priestley, J. B. "New Orleans: A First Impression." *Harper's Magazine* 176 (May 1938): 589–95.

Reilly, James Lee. "Street-Cleaning Problems in a Semi-Tropical City." *American City* 52 (November 1937): 53–56.

Saxon, Lyle. *Fabulous New Orleans*. New York: Century, 1928.

———. *Father Mississippi*. New York: Century, 1927.

Schrecker, Paul. "American Diary, Part III." *Harper's Magazine* 189 (September 1944): 379–86.

Schultz, Christian. *Travels on an Inland Voyage through the States of New-York, Pennsylvania, Virginia, Ohio, Kentucky and Tennessee, and through the Territories of Indiana, Louisiana, Mississippi and New-Orleans, Performed in the Years 1807 and 1808*. New York: Riley, 1810.

Schweid, Richard. *Catfish and the Delta: Confederate Fish Farming in the Mississippi Delta*. Berkeley: Ten Speed Press, 1992.

Scott, Natalie, and Caroline Jones, *Gourmet's Guide to New Orleans*. New Orleans: Scott and Jones, 1941.

Sinclair, Harold. *The Port of New Orleans*. Garden City, N.Y.: Doubleday, 1942.

Starr, Frederick S., ed. *Inventing New Orleans: Writings of Lafcadio Hearn*. Jackson: University Press of Mississippi, 2001.

"Summer Wonderland." *Outlook* 135 (9 April 1924): 615.

Tallant, Robert. *Mardi Gras as It Was*. Gretna, La.: Pelican, 1947, 1994.

———. *The Romantic New Orleanians*. New York: Dutton, 1950.

———. *Voodoo in New Orleans*. Gretna, La.: Pelican, 1946, 1998.

Tucker, Susan. *Telling Memories among Southern Women: Domestic Workers and Their Employers in the Segregated South*. New York: Schocken, 1988.

Twain, Mark. *Life on the Mississippi*. New York: Oxford University Press, 1883, 1996.

Walker, Joe, ed. *Research Papers, Issues Forum*. New Orleans: Tulane University Urban Studies Center, 1969.

Warner, Charles Dudley. "New Orleans." *Harper's New Monthly Magazine* 74 (January 1887): 186–206.

Washburn, Mel. "Hawaiian Blue Room." *Roosevelt Review* 2 (December 1938): 36–37, 58–59.

Williams, Tennessee. *Vieux Carré*. New York: New Directions, 1979.

Secondary Sources

Abbott, Carl. *Boosters and Businessmen: Popular Economic Thought and Urban Growth in the Antebellum Middle West*. Westport, Conn.: Greenwood, 1981.

Arneson, Eric. *Waterfront Workers of New Orleans: Race, Class, and Politics, 1862–1923*. New York: Oxford University Press, 1991.

Aron, Cindy. *Working at Play: A History of Vacations in the United States*. New York: Oxford University Press, 1999.

Bailey, Beth. *From Front Porch to Back Seat: Courtship in Twentieth-Century America*. Baltimore: Johns Hopkins University Press, 1989.

Baker, Liva. *The Second Battle of New Orleans: The Hundred-Year Struggle to Integrate the Schools*. New York: HarperCollins, 1996.

Barry, John. *Rising Tide: The Great Mississippi Flood of 1927 and How It Changed America*. New York: Simon and Schuster, 1997.

Bartlett, Thomasine Marion. "Vintage Drag: Female Impersonators Performing Resistance in Cold War New Orleans." Ph.D. diss., Tulane University, 2004.

Bauer, Ruthmary. "Sarasota: Hardship and Tourism in the 1930s." *Florida Historical Quarterly* 76 (Fall 1997): 135–51.

Bauman, John. "Disinfecting the Industrial City: The Philadelphia Housing Commission and Scientific Efficiency, 1909–1916." In *The Age of Urban Reform: New Perspectives on the Progressive Era*, edited by Michael Ebner and Eugene Tobin, 117–30. Port Washington, N.Y.: Kennikat, 1977.

Becker, Jane. *Selling Tradition: Appalachia and the Construction of an American Folk, 1930–1940*. Chapel Hill: University of North Carolina Press, 1998.

Beito, David. "The National Pay-Your-Taxes Campaign: Advertising for Political Legitimacy during the Great Depression." *Journal of Policy History* 2 (Fall 1990): 388–402.

Belasco, Warren. *Americans on the Road: From Autocamp to Motel, 1910–1945*. Cambridge: MIT Press, 1979.

Benson, Susan. *Counter Cultures: Saleswomen, Managers, and Customers in American Department Stores, 1890–1940*. Urbana: University of Illinois Press, 1988.

Berkowitz, Michael. "A 'New Deal' for Leisure: Making Mass Tourism during the Great Depression." In *Being Elsewhere: Tourism, Consumer Culture, and Identity in Modern Europe and North America*, edited by Shelley Baranowski and Ellen Furlough, 185–212. Ann Arbor: University of Michigan Press, 2001.

Blee, Kathleen. *Women of the Klan: Racism and Gender in the 1920s*. Berkeley: University of California Press, 1991.

Bordelon, Bridget. "Images of New Orleans: The Relationship between Visual Media and Tourists' Expectations of a Travel Destination." Ph.D. diss., University of New Orleans, 2003.

Botein, Barbara. "The Hennessy Case: An Episode in Anti-Italian Nativism." *Louisiana History* 20 (Summer 1979): 261–79.

Brinkley, Alan. *Voices of Protest: Huey Long, Father Coughlin, and the Great Depression*. New York: Knopf, 1982.

Brown, Laura. "New Orleans Modernism: The Arts and Crafts Club in the Vieux Carre, 1919–1939." *Louisiana History* 40 (Summer 2000): 317–43.

Brownell, Blaine. *The Urban Ethos in the South, 1920–1930*. Baton Rouge: Louisiana State University Press, 1975.

Brumberg, Joan. *The Body Project: An Intimate History of American Girls*. New York: Random House, 1997.

Brundage, W. Fitzhugh. "Le Reveil de la Louisiane: Memory and Acadian Identity, 1920–1960." In *Where These Memories Grow: History, Memory, and Southern Identity*, edited by W. Fitzhugh Brundage, 271–98. Chapel Hill: University of North Carolina Press, 2000.

Buerkle, Jack, and Danny Barker. *Bourbon Street Black: The New Orleans Black Jazzman*. New York: Oxford University Press, 1973.

Campbell, Colin. *The Romantic Ethic and the Spirit of Modern Consumerism*. Oxford: Blackwell, 1987.

Chiang, Connie. "Novel Tourism: Nature, Industry, and Literature on Monterey's Cannery Row." *Western Historical Quarterly* 35 (Autumn 2004): 309–29.

Cobb, James. *The Selling of the South: The Southern Crusade for Industrial Development, 1936–1980*. Baton Rouge: Louisiana State University Press, 1982.

Cocks, Catherine. "The Chamber of Commerce's Carnival: City Festivals and Urban Tourism in the United States, 1890–1915." In *Being Elsewhere: Tourism, Consumer Culture, and Identity in Modern Europe and North America*, edited by Shelley Baranowski and Ellen Furlough, 89–107. Ann Arbor: University of Michigan Press, 2001.

———. *Doing the Town: The Rise of Urban Tourism in the United States, 1850–1915*. Berkeley: University of California Press, 2001.

Cohen, Lizabeth. *A Consumers' Republic: The Politics of Mass Consumption in Postwar America*. New York: Knopf, 2003.

Cooney, Terry. *Balancing Acts: American Thought and Culture in the 1930s*. New York: Twayne, 1995.

Cortner, Richard. *The Kingfish and the Constitution: Huey Long, the First Amendment, and the Emergence of Modern Press Freedom in America*. Westport, Conn.: Greenwood, 1996

Cott, Nancy. *The Grounding of Modern Feminism*. New Haven: Yale University Press, 1987.

———. *Public Vows: A History of Marriage and the Nation*. Cambridge: Harvard University Press, 2000.

Daniel, Pete. *Deep'n as It Come: The 1927 Mississippi River Flood*. New York: Oxford University Press, 1977.

Davis, Jack. *Race against Time: Culture and Separation in Natchez since 1930*. Baton Rouge: Louisiana State University Press, 2001.

Davis, Mike. *Ecology of Fear: Los Angeles and the Imagination of Disaster*. New York: Metropolitan Books, 1998.

Davis, Susan. "Landscapes of Imagination: Tourism in Southern California." *Pacific Historical Review* 68 (May 1999): 173–91.

D'Emilio, John, and Estelle Freedman. *Intimate Matters: A History of Sexuality in America*. 2nd ed. Chicago: University of Chicago Press, 1997.

Dorman, Robert. *Revolt in the Provinces: The Regionalist Movement in America, 1920–1945*. Chapel Hill: University of North Carolina Press, 1993.

Doyle, Don. *New Men, New Cities, New South: Atlanta, Nashville, Charleston, Mobile, 1860–1910*. Chapel Hill: University of North Carolina Press, 1990.

Duis, Perry. *The Saloon: Public Drinking in Chicago and Boston, 1880–1920*. Urbana: University of Illinois Press, 1983.

Erenberg, Lewis. *Steppin' Out: New York Nightlife and the Transformation of American Culture, 1890–1930*. Westport, Conn.: Greenwood, 1981.

Fairclough, Adam. *Race and Democracy: The Civil Rights Struggle in Louisiana, 1915–1972*. Athens: University of Georgia Press, 1995.

Filler, Louis. *Appointment at Armageddon: Muckraking and Progressivism in the American Tradition*. Westport, Conn.: Greenwood, 1976.

Finan, Christopher. *Alfred E. Smith: The Happy Warrior*. New York: Hill and Wang, 2002.

Flink, James. *The Automobile Age*. Cambridge: MIT Press, 1988.

———. *The Car Culture*. Cambridge: MIT Press, 1975.

Fogelson, Robert. *Downtown: Its Rise and Fall, 1880–1950*. New Haven: Yale University Press, 2001.

Foster, Gaines M. *Ghosts of the Confederacy: Defeat, the Lost Cause, and the Emergence of the New South*. New York: Oxford University Press, 1987.

Frink, Sandra Margaret. "Spectacles of the Street: Performance, Power, and Public Space in Antebellum New Orleans." Ph.D. diss., University of Texas at Austin, 2004.

Fry, Earl. "Quebec's Relations with the United States." *American Review of Canadian Studies* 32 (June 2002): 323–42.

Galbraith, John Kenneth. *The Great Crash, 1929*. Boston: Houghton Mifflin, 1988.

Garraty, John. *The Great Depression*. New York: Harcourt Brace Jovanovich, 1986.

Gaston, Paul. *The New South Creed: A Study in Southern Mythmaking*. Baton Rouge: Louisiana State University Press, 1976.

Gilbert, James. *Perfect Cities: Chicago's Utopias of 1893*. Chicago: University of Chicago Press, 1991.

Gilfoyle, Timothy. *City of Eros: New York City, Prostitution, and the Commercialization of Sex, 1790–1920*. New York: Norton, 1992.

Gill, James. *Lords of Misrule: Mardi Gras and the Politics of Race in New Orleans*. Jackson: University Press of Mississippi, 1997.

Gillson, Gordon. *The Progressive Years: Louisiana State Board of Health*. Baton Rouge: Moran, 1976.

Gilmore, Glenda Elizabeth. *Gender and Jim Crow: Women and the Politics of White Supremacy in North Carolina, 1896–1920*. Chapel Hill: University of North Carolina Press, 1996.

Gordon, Lynn. *Gender and Higher Education in the Progressive Era*. New Haven: Yale University Press, 1990.

Gossett, Thomas. *Uncle Tom's Cabin and American Literature*. Dallas: Southern Methodist University Press, 1985.

Grantham, Dewey. *Southern Progressivism: The Reconciliation of Progress and Tradition*. Knoxville: University of Tennessee Press, 1983.

Greenspan, Anders. "A Shrine to the American Faith: Americanism and the Restoration of Colonial Williamsburg, 1926–1960." Ph.D. diss., Indiana University, 1992.

Grossman, James. *Land of Hope: Chicago, Black Southerners, and the Great Migration*. Chicago: University of Chicago Press, 1989.

Haag, Pamela. " 'Commerce in Souls': Vice, Virtue, and Women's Wage Work in Baltimore, 1900–1915." *Maryland Historical Magazine* 86 (Fall 1991): 292–308.

Haas, Edward. *DeLesseps S. Morrison and the Image of Reform: New Orleans Politics, 1946–1961*. Baton Rouge: Louisiana State University Press, 1986.

———. "New Orleans on the Half-Shell: The Maestri Era, 1936–1946." *Louisiana History* 13 (Summer 1972): 283–310.

Hale, Grace. *Making Whiteness: The Culture of Segregation in the South, 1890–1940*. New York: Pantheon, 1998.

Hall, Gwendolyn Midlo. "The Formation of Afro-Creole Culture." In *Creole New Orleans: Race and Americanization*, edited by Arnold Hirsch and Joseph Logsdon, 58–87. Baton Rouge: Louisiana State University Press, 1992.

Halttunen, Karen. *Confidence Men and Painted Women: A Study of Middle-Class Culture in America, 1830–1870*. New Haven: Yale University Press, 1982.

Hanchett, Thomas. *Sorting Out the New South City: Race, Class, and Urban Development in Charlotte, 1875–1975*. Chapel Hill: University of North Carolina Press, 1998.

Hardy, Arthur. *Mardi Gras Guide*. New Orleans: Hardy Enterprises, 2000.

Harris, Neil. "Urban Tourism and the Commercial City." In *Inventing Times Square: Commerce and Culture at the Crossroads of the World*, edited by William Taylor, 66–82. New York: Sage, 1991.

Harvey, David. *Consciousness and the Urban Experience: Studies in the*

History and Theory of Capitalist Urbanization. Baltimore: Johns Hopkins University Press, 1985.

———. *The Urbanization of Capital: Studies in the History and Theory of Capitalist Urbanization.* Baltimore: Johns Hopkins University Press, 1985.

Heleniak, Roman. "Local Reaction to the Great Depression in New Orleans, 1929–1993." *Louisiana History* 10 (Fall 1969): 289–306.

Hickey, Georgina. *Hope and Danger in the New South City: Working-Class Women and Urban Development in Atlanta, 1890–1940.* Athens: University of Georgia Press, 2003.

Hobson, Barbara. *Uneasy Virtue: The Politics of Prostitution and the American Reform Tradition.* New York: Basic Books, 1987.

Isenberg, Alison. *Downtown America: A History of the Place and the People Who Made It.* Chicago: University of Chicago Press, 2004.

Jackson, Joy. *New Orleans in the Gilded Age: Politics and Urban Progress, 1880–1896.* Baton Rouge: Louisiana State University Press, 1969.

———. "Prohibition in New Orleans: The Unlikeliest Crusade." *Louisiana History* 19 (Summer 1978): 261–84.

Jackson, Kenneth. *Crabgrass Frontier: The Suburbanization of the United States.* New York: Oxford University Press, 1985.

———. *The Ku Klux Klan in the City, 1915–1930.* New York: Oxford University Press, 1967.

Jakle, John. *The Tourist: Travel in Twentieth-Century North America.* Lincoln: University of Nebraska Press, 1985.

Johnson, Jerah. "Colonial New Orleans: A Fragment of the Eighteenth-Century French Ethos." In *Creole New Orleans: Race and Americanization,* edited by Arnold Hirsch and Joseph Logsdon, 12–57. Baton Rouge: Louisiana State University Press, 1992.

Johnson, Walter. *Soul by Soul: Life inside the Antebellum Slave Market.* Cambridge: Harvard University Press, 1999.

Kammen, Michael. *Mystic Chords of Memory: The Transformation of Tradition in American Culture.* New York: Knopf, 1991.

Keith, Jeanette. *Country People of the New South: Tennessee's Upper Cumberland.* Chapel Hill: University of North Carolina Press, 1995.

Kennedy, Al. "Jazz Mentors: Public School Teachers and the Musical Tradition of New Orleans." Ph.D. diss., University of New Orleans, 1996.

Kennedy, David. *Freedom from Fear: The American People in Depression and War, 1929–1945.* New York: Oxford University Press, 1999.

————. *Over Here: The First World War and American Society*. New York: Oxford University Press, 1980.

Kennedy, Roger. *Mr. Jefferson's Lost Cause: Land, Farmers, Slavery, and the Louisiana Purchase*. New York: Oxford University Press, 2003.

Kerr, Austin. *Organized for Prohibition: A New History of the Anti-Saloon League*. New Haven: Yale University Press, 1985.

Kessler-Harris, Alice. *Out to Work: A History of Wage-Earning Women in the United States*. New York: Oxford University Press, 1982.

Kimberly, Charles. "The Depression in Maryland: The Failure of Voluntaryism." *Maryland Historical Magazine* 70 (Summer 1975): 189–202.

Kirby, Jack Temple. *Rural Worlds Lost: The American South, 1920–1960*. Baton Rouge: Louisiana State University Press, 1987.

Knecht, Robert J. *The Valois: Kings of France, 1328–1589*. London: Hambledon and London, 2004.

Kusmer, Kenneth. *A Ghetto Takes Shape: Black Cleveland, 1870–1930*. Urbana: University of Illinois Press, 1978.

Lachance, Paul. "The Foreign French." In *Creole New Orleans: Race and Americanization*, edited by Arnold Hirsch and Joseph Logsdon, 101–30. Baton Rouge: Louisiana State University Press, 1992.

Lears, Jackson. *Fables of Abundance: A Cultural History of Advertising in America*. New York: Basic Books, 1994.

Leathem, Karen. " 'A Carnival According to Their Own Desires': Gender and Mardi Gras in New Orleans, 1870–1941." Ph.D. diss., University of North Carolina at Chapel Hill, 1994.

Lencek, Lena, and Gideon Bosker. *The Beach: The History of Paradise on Earth*. New York: Penguin, 1998.

Leonard, Neil. *Jazz and the White Americans: The Acceptance of a New Art Form*. Chicago: University of Chicago Press, 1962.

Leuchtenburg, William. *Franklin D. Roosevelt and the New Deal, 1932–1940*. New York: Harper Torchbooks, 1963.

Levine, Lawrence. *Highbrow/Lowbrow: The Emergence of Cultural Hierarchy in America*. Cambridge: Harvard University Press, 1988.

Lewis, Pierce. *New Orleans: The Making of an Urban Landscape*. Cambridge: Ballinger, 1976.

Litwack, Leon. *Trouble in Mind: Black Southerners in the Age of Jim Crow*. New York: Vintage, 1999.

Löfgren, Orvar. *On Holiday: A History of Vacationing*. Berkeley: University of California Press, 1999.

Long, Alecia. *The Great Southern Babylon: Sex, Race, and Respectability in New Orleans, 1865–1920*. Baton Rouge: Louisiana State University Press, 2004.

————. " 'A Notorious Attraction': Sex and Tourism in New Orleans, 1897–1917." In *Southern Journeys: Tourism, History, and Culture in the Modern South*, edited by Richard Starnes, 15–41. Tuscaloosa: University of Alabama Press, 2003.

Lubove, Roy. "The Progressives and the Prostitute." *The Historian* 24 (May 1962): 308–30.

MacCannell, Dean. *The Tourist: A New Theory of the Leisure Class*. New York: Schocken, 1976, 1989.

MacLean, Nancy. *Behind the Mask of Chivalry: The Making of the Second Ku Klux Klan*. New York: Oxford University Press, 1994.

Marone, James. *Hellfire Nation: The Politics of Sin in American History*. New Haven: Yale University Press, 2003.

Marquis, Donald. *In Search of Buddy Bolden: First Man of Jazz*. Baton Rouge: Louisiana State University Press, 1978.

Martin, C. Brenden. "Selling the Southern Highlands: Tourism and Community Development in the Mountain South." Ph.D. diss., University of Tennessee, 1997.

————. "To Keep the Spirit of Mountain Culture Alive: Tourism and Historical Memory in the Southern Highlands." In *Where These Memories Grow: History, Memory, and Southern Identity*, edited by W. Fitzhugh Brundage, 249–69. Chapel Hill: University of North Carolina Press, 2000.

Mason, Michael. *The Making of Victorian Sexuality*. New York: Oxford University Press, 1994.

May, Elaine Tyler. *Homeward Bound: American Families in the Cold War Era*. New York: Basic Books, 1988.

McDermott, M. Joan, and Sarah J. Blackstone. "White Slavery Plays of the 1910s: Fear of Victimization and the Social Control of Sexuality." *Theatre History Studies* 16 (June 1996): 141–56.

McMillan, Neil. *Dark Journey: Black Mississippians in the Age of Jim Crow*. Urbana: University of Illinois Press, 1990.

McMurry, Richard. *John Bell Hood and the War for Southern Independence*. Lexington: University Press of Kentucky, 1982.

Meyer, Robert. *Festivals U.S.A. and Canada*. New York: Ives Washburn, 1967.

Miller, Char. "Tourist Trap: Visitors and the Modern San Antonio Economy: Selling the Past to the Present in the American Southwest." In *The Culture of Tourism, the Tourism of Culture*, edited by Hal Rothman, 206–28. Albuquerque: University of New Mexico Press, 2003.

Mitchell, Reid. *All on a Mardi Gras Day: Episodes in the History of New Orleans Carnival*. Cambridge: Harvard University Press, 1995.

Mohl, Raymond. *The New City: Urban America in the Industrial Age, 1860–1920*. Arlington Heights, Ill.: Harlan Davidson, 1985.

Moore, John Robert. "The New Deal in Louisiana." In *The New Deal: The State and Local Levels*, edited by John Braeman, Robert Bremner, and David Brody, 137–65. Columbus: Ohio State University Press, 1975.

Murdock, Catherine. *Domesticating Drink: Women, Men, and Alcohol in America, 1870–1940*. Baltimore: Johns Hopkins University Press, 1998.

Nash, Roderick. *The Nervous Generation: American Thought, 1917–1930*. Chicago: Elephant, 1990.

Nye, David. *Electrifying America: Social Meanings of a New Technology*. Cambridge: MIT Press, 1990.

Odem, Mary. *Delinquent Daughters: Protecting and Policing Adolescent Female Sexuality in the United States, 1885–1920*. Chapel Hill: University of North Carolina Press, 1995.

Onuf, Peter. *Jefferson's Empire: The Language of American Nationhood*. Charlottesville: University Press of Virginia, 2000.

Ortquist, Richard. "Tax Crisis and Politics in Early Depression Michigan." *Michigan History* 59 (Spring–Summer 1975): 91–119.

Ownby, Ted. *Subduing Satan: Religion, Recreation, and Manhood in the Rural South, 1865–1920*. Chapel Hill: University of North Carolina Press, 1990.

Pagliarini, Marie. "The Pure American Woman and the Wicked Catholic Priest: An Analysis of Anti-Catholic Literature in Antebellum America." *Religion and American Culture* 9 (Winter 1999): 97–128.

Painter, Nell Irvin. *Standing at Armageddon: The United States, 1877–1919*. New York: Norton, 1987.

Peiss, Kathy. *Cheap Amusements: Working Women and Leisure in Turn-of-the-Century New York*. Philadelphia: Temple University Press, 1986.

Peretti, Burton. *The Creation of Jazz: Music, Race, and Culture in Urban America*. Urbana: University of Illinois Press, 1992.

Portes, Alejandro, and Alex Stepick. *City on the Edge: The Transformation of Miami*. Berkeley: University of California Press, 1993.

Rae, Douglas. *City: Urbanism and Its End*. New Haven: Yale University Press, 2003.

Raffray, Jeanette. "Origins of the Vieux Carre Commission, 1920–1941." *Louisiana History* 40 (Summer 1999): 283–304.

Reichert, Loren, and James Frey. "The Organization of Bell Desk Prostitution." *Sociology and Social Research* 69 (July 1985): 516–26.

Reilly, Timothy. "Heterodox New Orleans and the Protestant South, 1800–1861." *Louisiana Studies* 12 (Fall 1973): 533–51.

Rettmann, Jef. "Business, Government, and Prostitution in Spokane, Washington, 1889–1910." *Pacific Northwest Quarterly* 89 (Spring 1998): 77–83.

Reynolds, George. *Machine Politics in New Orleans, 1897–1926*. New York: Columbia University Press, 1936.

Roach, Joseph. *Cities of the Dead: Circum-Atlantic Performance*. New York: Columbia University Press, 1996.

Rose, Kenneth. "Wettest in the West: San Francisco and Prohibition in 1924." *California History* 65 (December 1986): 285–315.

Rosen, Ruth. *The Lost Sisterhood: Prostitution in America, 1900–1918*. Baltimore: Johns Hopkins University Press, 1982.

Rothman, Hal. *Devil's Bargains: Tourism in the Twentieth-Century American West*. Lawrence: University Press of Kansas, 1998.

———. *Neon Metropolis: How Las Vegas Started the Twenty-first Century*. New York: Routledge, 2002.

———. "Selling the Meaning of Place: Entrepreneurship, Tourism, and Community Transformation in the Twentieth-Century American West." *Pacific Historical Review* 65 (November 1996): 525–57.

Runyan, Glenn Martin. "Economic Trends in New Orleans, 1928–1940." Master's thesis, Tulane University, 1967.

Ryan, Mary. *Cradle of the Middle Class: The Family in Oneida County, New York, 1790–1865*. New York: Cambridge University Press, 1981.

Rydell, Robert. *All the World's a Fair: Visions of Empire at American International Expositions, 1876–1916*. Chicago: University of Chicago Press, 1984.

Rydell, Robert, John Findling, and Kimberly Pelle. *Fair America: World's Fairs in the United States*. Washington, D.C.: Smithsonian Institution Press, 2000.

Sears, John. *Sacred Places: American Tourist Attractions in the Nineteenth Century*. New York: Oxford University Press, 1989.

Seed, Patricia. *Ceremonies of Possession in Europe's Conquest of the New World, 1492–1640*. Cambridge: Cambridge University Press, 1995.

Shaffer, Marguerite. *See America First: Tourism and National Identity, 1880–1940*. Washington, D.C.: Smithsonian Institution Press, 2001.

———. "Seeing the Nature of America: The National Parks as National Assets, 1914–1929." In *Being Elsewhere: Tourism, Consumer Culture, and Identity in Modern Europe and North America*, edited by Shelley Baranowski and Ellen Furlough, 155–84. Ann Arbor: University of Michigan Press, 2001.

Shapiro, Mitchell. *Television Network Prime-Time Programming, 1948–1988*. Jefferson, N.C.: McFarland, 1989.

Sheriff, Carol. *The Artificial River: The Erie Canal and the Paradox of Progress, 1817–1862*. New York: Hill and Wang, 1996.

Simon, Bryant. *Boardwalk of Dreams: Atlantic City and the Fate of Urban America*. New York: Oxford University Press, 2004.

Simpson-Walker, Holly. "Tarpon Springs: From Health Resort to Ethnic Tourist Haven, 1880–1991." *Gulf Coast Historical Review* 9 (Fall 1993): 84–98.

Smith, Douglas. *The New Deal in the Urban South*. Baton Rouge: Louisiana State University Press, 1988.

Souther, Mark. "City in Amber: Race, Culture, and the Tourism Transformation of New Orleans, 1945–1995." Ph.D. diss., Tulane University, 2002.

———. "Making 'America's Most Interesting City': Tourism and the Construction of Cultural Image in New Orleans, 1940–1984." In *Southern Journeys: Tourism, History, and Culture in the Modern South*, edited by Richard Starnes, 114–37. Tuscaloosa: University of Alabama Press, 2003.

Spencer, Thomas. *The St. Louis Veiled Prophet Celebration: Power on Parade, 1877–1995*. Columbia: University of Missouri Press, 2000.

Srebnick, Amy. *The Mysterious Death of Mary Rogers: Sex and Culture in Nineteenth-Century New York*. New York: Oxford University Press, 1995.

Stanonis, Anthony. " 'Always in Costume and Mask': Lyle Saxon and New
Orleans Tourism." *Louisiana History* 42 (Winter 2001): 31–57.
————. " 'A Woman of Boundless Energy': Elizebeth Werlein and Her
Times." *Louisiana History* 46 (Winter 2005): 5–26.
Stowe, David. *Swing Changes: Big Band Jazz in New Deal America.*
Cambridge: Harvard University Press, 1994.
Summers, Mark. *Rum, Romanism, and Rebellion: The Making of a
President, 1884.* Chapel Hill: University of North Carolina Press, 2000.
Tager, Jack. *Boston Riots: Three Centuries of Social Violence.* Boston:
Northeastern University Press, 2001.
Tansey, Richard. "Prostitution and Politics in Antebellum New Orleans."
Southern Studies 18 (Winter 1979): 449–79.
Tate, Cassandra. *Cigarette Wars: The Triumph of the Little White Slaver.*
New York: Oxford University Press, 1999.
Tichi, Cecilia. *Exposés and Excess: Muckraking in America, 1900/2000.*
Philadelphia: University of Pennsylvania Press, 2004.
Tindall, George. *The Emergence of the New South, 1913–1945.* Baton
Rouge: Louisiana State University Press, 1970.
Tregle, Joseph. "Creoles and Americans." In *Creole New Orleans: Race and
Americanization,* edited by Arnold Hirsch and Joseph Logsden, 131–85.
Baton Rouge: Louisiana State University Press, 1992.
————. "Early New Orleans Society: A Reappraisal." *Journal of Southern
History* 18 (February 1952): 20–36.
Turner, Patricia. *Ceramic Uncles and Celluloid Mammies: Black Images and
Their Influence on Culture.* New York: Anchor, 1994.
Tyler, Pamela. *Silk Stockings and Ballot Boxes: Women and Politics in New
Orleans, 1920–1965.* Athens: University of Georgia Press, 1996.
Ullman, Sharon. *Sex Seen: The Emergence of Modern Sexuality in America.*
Berkeley: University of California Press, 1997.
Urry, John. *Consuming Places.* New York: Routledge, 1995.
Vyhnanek, Louis. *Unorganized Crime: New Orleans in the 1920s.* Lafayette:
Center for Louisiana Studies, University of Southwestern Louisiana, 1998.
Walkowitz, Judith. *City of Dreadful Delight: Narratives of Sexual Danger in
Late-Victorian London.* Chicago: University of Chicago Press, 1992.
Weiss, Thomas. "Tourism in America before World War II." *Journal of
Economic History* 64 (June 2004): 289–327.
Welch, Charles. " 'Oh, Dem Golden Slippers': The Philadelphia Mummer's

Parade." *Journal of American Folklore* 79 (October–December 1966): 523–36.

Wiebe, Robert. *Businessmen and Reform: A Study of the Progressive Movement*. Cambridge: Harvard University Press, 1962.

———. *The Search for Order, 1877–1920*. New York: Hill and Wang, 1967.

Williams, T. Harry. *Huey Long*. New York: Knopf, 1969.

Williamson, Joel. *The Crucible of Race: Black-White Relations in the South since Emancipation*. New York: Oxford University Press, 1984.

Wiltz, Christine. *The Last Madam: A Life in the New Orleans Underworld*. New York: Faber and Faber, 2000.

Withey, Lynne. *Grand Tours and Cook's Tours: A History of Leisure Travel, 1750–1915*. New York: Morrow, 1997.

Wright, Gavin. *Old South, New South: Revolutions in the Southern Economy since the Civil War*. Baton Rouge: Louisiana State University Press, 1986.

Yuhl, Stephanie. *A Golden Haze of Memory: The Making of Historic Charleston*. Chapel Hill: University of North Carolina Press, 2005.

———. "Rich and Tender Remembering: Elite White Women and an Aesthetic Sense of Place in Charleston, 1920s and 1930s." In *Where These Memories Grow: History, Memory, and Southern Identity*, edited by W. Fitzhugh Brundage, 227–48. Chapel Hill: University of North Carolina Press, 2000.

Zimmerman, Tom. "Paradise Promoted: Boosterism and the Los Angeles Chamber of Commerce." *California History* 64 (Winter 1985): 22–33.

INDEX

Abe Lyman Orchestra, 135

Acme Oyster House, 25

advertising: and First World War, 32; and Mississippi Flood of 1927, 40; and tourism development, 48, 60, 65, 68, 100, 132, 134, 190–91

Africa, 8, 15

African Americans, 229; displacement of, 152; as enslaved people, 3, 12, 16, 145, 225; and free blacks, 6, 8, 12; and image of mammy, 229–30; large population percentage of, 6, 15, 145, 150, 206, 243; and manumission, 6; and middle class, 202; and out-migration, 22, 276–77n2; and post–Civil War violence, 10; as prostitutes, 116; stereotypes of, 144, 220, 221, 233

Aitkens, Felix, 237

Alabama, 45, 56, 198, 239

Alexandria, La., 108

Allen, Frederick Lewis, 54

Allen, O. K., 79

Amer, A. S., 50, 174

American Broadcasting Company, 240

American City, 40

American Food Manufacturers Association, 47

American Institute of Architects, 154, 157

American Legion, 44, 47, 48, 178

American Revolution, 13

Anderson, Sherwood, 2, 11, 41–43, 129, 145, 146

Anti-Saloon League, 134

anti-Semitism, 11, 208

antiurbanism, 3, 14

Antoine's, 147

Arcadia Dance Hall, 119, 120

Armstrong, Louis, 200, 207, 239, 241
Aron, Cindy, 45
Arthur, Stanley, 232
Art League, 151
Arts and Crafts Club, 144, 151, 152
Asbury, Herbert, 131
Associated Ad Clubs of the World, 47
Associated Press, 25
Association of Commerce, 24, 28, 30–33, 37, 76, 86, 241; advocacy by, for road construction, 53–54; and Anderson, Sherwood, affair, 42–43; and Civic Affairs Committee, 93, 98; direct mail campaign of, 60–61; and French Opera House, 50; and French Quarter, 153, 156, 157; and Great Depression, 71; and Mardi Gras, 174, 177, 178, 183, 190; and musicians, 200–201, 204; *News Bulletin* of, 34, 35, 42, 44, 48, 54, 59, 61, 139; relationship of, with Convention and Tourism Bureau, 46–47; role of, in tourism development, 38, 39, 41, 45, 48, 57, 83, 92, 160–61, 221; and suppression of vice, 112, 139, 158; and Visitor's Route, 93; and Wilson, Harold, 115
Association of Piano Tuners, 202
Atlanta, Ga., 65, 83
Atlantic City, N.J., 37
Atlantic Monthly, 19, 68
Audubon Elementary School, 185
Audubon Park, 14

Aunt Sally's, 231, 241
automobiles, 22, 23, 24, 30, 52, 253n53; as industry, 55, 73; and prostitution, 147; and tourism, 54–56, 60, 66, 128, 155, 182, 238

Bacino's Bar and Cocktail Lounge, 231
Bailey, Beth, 130
Baltimore, Md., 16
barbers, 132–33
Baton Rouge, La., 60, 87, 89, 90
Battle of Liberty Place, 213
Battle of New Orleans, 63, 96
Bauer, Nicholas, 185
Bayhl, Rosella, 127
Bayou Classic, 241
Beauregard, P. G. T., 51, 211
Beauregard Square, 51, 211, 214
Bechet, Sidney, 197
Behre, Charles, 205
Behrman, Martin, 43–44, 47, 107–10, 122, 123; and French Quarter, 152, 154, 160
Belasco, Warren, 22
Bell, Herbert, 181
Belle of New Orleans (film), 137
Belle of the Nineties (film), 137
Benevolent and Protective Order of Elks, 98
Bienville Street, 118, 147
Biloxi (Miss.) Chamber of Commerce, 132
Birmingham, Ala., 65, 83
Black, Hugo, 86
blue laws, 46, 112, 175
blues, 198

Borean Presbyterian Church, 121
Boston, Mass., 5, 10, 52
Bourbon Street, 25, 118, 135, 143, 154, 158, 166–67, 170–71, 210
Bowman, Harry, 219
Bradford, Roark, 167, 169, 220
Brando, Marlon, 240
Brave Creoles Run, 96, 97
Bremer, Fredrika, 17
Bremer, Laville, 137, 138
Broussard, Bill, 236
Brownell, Blaine, 62
Buccaneer, The (film), 97
Buel, J. W., 7, 8
Bureau of Protective Social Measures, 112
Burgundy Street, 121, 150
Burk, Lillian, 124
bus, 56, 58
Business and Professional Women's Club, 230

Cabildo, 66, 186
Cable, George Washington, 17–18, 214–15
Cadillac Nite Club and Bar, 135
Café du Monde, 25
Café Lafitte, 167
Cajuns, 146, 218, 244
California, 2, 26, 35, 36, 52, 56, 118
Callender, Wilson, 64
Campbell, Colin, 12
Canal Street, 5, 50, 84, 145, 155, 163, 170; in Faulkner's Pylon, 192; and fireworks, 99; information booths on, 177; and "Keep New Orleans Clean" campaign, 94;

renovation of, in 1920s, 73; restrooms on, 134; and restrictions on vice, 106, 114
Capone, Al, 89
Carmelites, 150
Carnival, 20, 106, 132, 175–76, 178, 182. See also Mardi Gras; Mardi Gras parades
Carondelet Street, 99
Carrollton Business Men's Association, 94
Carter, Betty Werlein, 145
Carter, Hodding, 180–81
Caruso, M. A., 204
Casanas, B. C., 34
Cash, W. J., 114
Catholicism, 1, 8, 12, 26; and Irish, 9; Protestant suspicion of, 9, 10–11
Cave, Jesse, 84
Celestin, Papa, 210, 211
Centennial Exposition of 1876, 15
Chalmette Monument, 63
Chamber of Commerce, 32
Charleston, S.C., 2, 5, 160, 172
Chicago, Ill., 15, 18, 39, 40, 49, 65, 144
cholera, 4
City Park, 73, 88, 95
Civil War, 4, 17, 173, 229
Claiborne, Charles, 51
Clapp, Theodore, 4
Cleveland, Ohio, 52
Club My-O-My, 135
Coca Cola Bottlers Association, 47
Cocks, Catherine, 19
Cohen, Lizabeth, 238
Cold War, 237, 239

Morton, Jelly Roll, 197, 200, 208, 212, 213, 214
mosquitoes, 4
Moulin Rouge, 114
Mount Olive Baptist Church, 121
movies, 20, 81–82, 97, 99, 115, 130, 137
Muncie, Ind., 54
Municipal Auditorium, 49, 51, 73, 170, 183, 214, 222
Murdock, Catherine, 130
Music Week, 204, 205, 206
Myrdal, Gunnar, 221

Nash, Roderick, 171
Natchez, Miss., 161–62
National Baptist Sunday School Convention, 222, 223
National Education Association, 199
National Geographic, 65
National Guard, 86
New Deal, 17, 53, 71, 81, 88
New Haven, Conn., 30
New Iberia, La., 208
Newman, Harold, 108–9, 111
New Orleans: as Big Easy, 243–44; boosterism of, 35; climate of, 7, 64; French influence on, 3, 8–9, 22, 41, 165, 219, 241; historic preservation of, 27, 40, 41, 42, 71, 88, 96, 241, 256n4; industrial development of, 28–29, 33, 37, 41, 273n9; myths about, 1, 5, 18, 52, 63, 69, 100–101; postemancipation, 7; relationship of, to modern world, 1; and sexuality, 19–20, 181, 200;

Spanish influence on, 3, 6, 22, 36, 52, 150, 171, 229; and twentieth century, 25; unemployment in, 88; vice in, 6; violence in, 10; voodoo in, 7, 150, 210, 226, 280n47; white supremacy in, 7, 8, 11, 23
New Orleans Association of Commerce, 68
New Orleans Beverage Department, 80
New Orleans Citizens' Committee on Race Relations, 223
New Orleans Commission Council, 89, 222; and alcohol control, 80, 87, 122; and French Quarter, 141, 154, 157; and Great Depression, 72, 76; and prostitution control, 117; and taxation, 78
New Orleans Department of Public Welfare, 78, 82
New Orleans Federation of Clubs, 120
New Orleans Hostess Service, 209–10
New Orleans Hotel and Restaurant Association, 47
New Orleans Hotelmen's Association, 115, 158
New Orleans Jazz Club, 210
New Orleans Mid-Winter Sports Association, 95
New Orleans Progressive Union, 33
New Orleans Public Service, 63, 159
New Orleans Restaurant Men's Association, 84
New Orleans Social Hygiene Society, 112

New Orleans Times-Picayune:
coverage of fireworks controversy
by, 98–99; coverage of Prohibition
by, 113–15, 118; coverage of
women's issues by, 132–34; and
taxation, 80; and tourism, 38, 145,
148, 156, 162, 178, 202
New South, 39
newspapers, 65; *Biloxi News*, 37;
Chicago Daily News, 102, 147;
Chicago Times, 91; *Chicago
Tribune*, 40; *Detroit Times*,
51; *Jackson News*, 175; *Kansas
City Journal Post*, 91; *Louisiana
Weekly*, 201, 202, 221, 222, 227,
232; *New Orleans Item*, 31, 99,
100, 111, 116, 123, 124, 159, 235;
New York Daily Times, 6; *New
York Times*, 5, 9, 10, 40, 63; *Wall
Street Journal*, 68. See also *New
Orleans Times-Picayune*
New York, 56
New York City, 1, 12, 19, 76, 144
Niagara Falls, 12
Nixon, Louise, 144
Nott, G. William, 149–50
Nunez, A. Sidney, 96
Nut Club, 158

Ohio, 56
O'Keefe, Arthur, 60, 120, 122, 156,
219
Old French Quarter News, 210
Old Regulars, 43, 74, 76, 108;
conflict of, with Long, Huey,
71, 75, 85–86, 89, 102; and
Prohibition, 111, 112, 113, 122–

23; relationship of, with Walmsley,
Semmes, 90
Old Spanish Trail, 52
Oliver, Frances, 212
Olmstead, Frederick Law, 7, 14, 15
O'Neill, Charles, 74
Orleans Parish School Board, 203
Orleans Street, 147, 170
O'Slattery, Father, 121
Outlook, 36
Owen, Allison, 112, 178

Paris, 5, 28, 165
Parker, Arthur, 50, 112–13, 175
Parker, Walter, 66, 133
Patio Royal, 154, 160
Pat O'Brien's Bar, 138
Pennsylvania, 56, 60
Pensacola, Fla., 45
Pepper, Red, 135
Phelps, Albert, 18–19
Philadelphia, Pa., 15, 39
phonographs, 203
Piazza, Countess Willie V., 131
"Pine-to-Palm" route, 52
Pitot, James, 3
plaçage, 6
Plant, Henry, 37
Plauché, J. B., 96
Plauché, Léda, 231
Plessy v. Ferguson, 213
Pontalba Apartments, 144, 156
Pontchartrain, Lake, 37, 38, 88, 96,
97, 135
Portes, Alejandro, 36
postcards, 19
Powder Puff, 135